T0354815

# 9 SISTERS CURSED SINCE BIRTH

## A CORRUPT FAMILY DROWNING IN THEIR DEADLY SINS

### NA' VEAH ROSE

authorHOUSE®

*AuthorHouse*™
*1663 Liberty Drive*
*Bloomington, IN 47403*
*www.authorhouse.com*
*Phone: 1 (800) 839-8640*

*Published by AuthorHouse 02/28/2018*

*ISBN: 978-1-5246-5982-0 (sc)*
*ISBN: 978-1-5246-5983-7 (hc)*
*ISBN: 978-1-5246-5981-3 (e)*

*Library of Congress Control Number: 2017900582*

# ...DEDICATIONS

This book is DEDICATED to my family; most of all my supporters... Without our struggles, wouldn't be a testimony... Without our evil doings, it wouldn't be a curse... With our separation, there is no unity; therefore, our history of life has inspired me to write this book 9 Sisters Cursed since birth.

Each of us have brought our different personalities to this story, which has given us a chance to finally express our feelings, relive our past, and try to move on in the present. Despite the fact of how disturbing, humiliating, and hurtful our life experiences were, I'm willing and able to disclose our cursed story temperately.

For that reason, I devote this book to myself. I have worked hard, dedicated a lot of time, energy, and wisdom to paint the whole picture. I wrote this book to remember the wholeness we once had... Release the stress that we all needed... Revive our relationship that has been destroyed... Repair our hearts that have been broken, so we could relax our souls and have untroubling thoughts. This book is the process of reuniting our family that once prayed, strived, and cried together. Sisters that once lived, loved, and laughed with one another. Regardless of what the circumstances were, we always found a way to survive. I feel this is my personal duty to confront our status quo, lead, and transition people to see the clarity during their darkest moments. For we shouldn't NEVER give up, at NO time give in, and regardless of how hard it could be sometimes, you should NEVER STOP trying.

Another dedication goes to my sweet and understanding mother. The person that always saw the good in me, even when I was atrocious, she still consoled and prayed for me in hopes that everything would be ok. I'm blessed that she was fruitful because we wouldn't have life. If she wouldn't had made any mistakes, then she wouldn't had learned from her experiences. Most of all, it was her faith that gave us hope, and I am truly grateful.

Thanks to my lovely daughters that believed and encouraged me to have confidence in my capabilities. Their heartfelt words expressed their love and admiration. Their discrete ideas inspired me to stay committed and continue to write other books. I am truly rewarded by God to have them in my life, and I will strive to be the best mother that I have within me.

Lastly, I want to give thanks to my other half. He accepts me for who I am. He encouraged me to shift my life in the right direction, and then I found myself and my connection, which was writing, being a mentor, and a creator. He also helped me bring out the unique art, then I redesigned myself inside out, which I didn't have the courage to do on my own because I couldn't overcome fear of failure. He influenced my determination; his positive words revealed his confidence and expectations. I am pleased to have him as a best friend and husband, for our unity is our strength, and our love is our stability, which gave me the nobility to continue to do better; and I thank him for that. This is my special DEDICATION to all my SUPPORTERS…

# SYNOPSIS

The 2 words that describe the sisters' characters are WITCHES and BITCHES. Primarily because 7 sins were inherited solely through their evil relatives' spirits. Their vitalities are...

Condemned, Unfavorable, Repugnant, Spiteful, & Endlessly Demonic. Their bad blood has Satanically Intervened in a Negative way that Caused a lot of Evildoings; and their Behavior was Inauspicious as they Reacted Through Hostility, hatred, and bitterness, which had caused harm to others and themselves.

Some of the sisters' darkest paths were the history of their mother, father, and other ancestors struggling lives. But why did it have to be them? Who will they go to for guidance and simplicity? What can they do to amend their souls? When is their battles over? And, how could their curse be reversed?

There are many questions, but the answers rely on each individual. Their weaknesses overpowers their strengths, for they dwell on the past, which holds more grudges than guilt. What they fail to interpret is the difference between right and wrong, for nothing is amiss in their eyes because all they see, hear, and do is evil. They can't grasp the positive over the negative due to their luck being just that bad. And, the discrepancy amongst friends and enemies are overlooked since they resemble both, which can be amiable or cruel.

They have forgotten about the meaning of family, which is about unity instead of selfishness. They no longer know the value of love, for the reason that they dwell on hate. In reality, their power relies on the stability of their sisterhood. So, do their rivalries end to reconcile their differences? Or, does the duration of separation continues? It's difficult to see considering their pride is easier to live with but harder to let go; however, nobody determines the future but God…

They all want to be dominant and superior. For those reasons, envy, greed; indifferences, lust; rage, self-pride; and betrayal are the sins they're drowning in, but the best tools for survival are wisdom and solidarity. However, the ignorance has the sisters' blind and lost within themselves instead of expanding as a whole. They are overlooking the greatness of the word US since they feel that it's not enough progression to share. They have no leadership, nor do they understand their direction in life due to them being confused and distracted.

They need open arms, they want a loving heart, and desire phenomenal thoughts; but they must let go of their pride, their past, and enmity. Until then, they will still have that curse within.

Eventually, some of them will become exhausted and tired of receiving the same results. Therefore, the chosen one will play a huge role. She will lead, proceed, and achieve by putting all her anger to past. Then she will use her strengths, knowledge, and love towards her possibilities. She doesn't know what will be the outcome, but DIFFERENCE is what she's hoping. Regardless of her curse, she is going to fight for what she wants. She wants to give and receive love and support, to be forgiven as well as to forgive, and to be a sister instead of an enemy. Maybe it would take that one leader for everyone else to follow, or is the curse just that powerful?

# CONTENTS

# BORN INTO EVIL

---

MALACHI 1:8 *"And if ye offer the blind for sacrifice, is it not evil?"*

Shining bright from heaven, God sent his anointing to Lilith Darkmore on February 16, 1955 at Brookdale Hospital, exposing her to a world underneath that was filled with the darkness of Satan. This spiritual warfare would challenge her faith and destiny. Even though Lilith was born out of wedlock and into adultery, her future was planned well before the day of her birth. God plans are for the best, but the trials can be at its worst. Therefore, Lilith struggles overrode her peace, happiness, love, and her hope.

Lilith's life began with a disruption of evil, and with the absence of her parents, she had nothing else to hold on to but her faith. Accordingly, her faith grew stronger one hardship after another. Nevertheless, it impacted her mentally and physically as she searched for understanding regarding her personal burdens.

Lilith had faced some rough times and never had a normal childhood, given that she was less fortunate than other kids, and was forced to appreciate what she had. However, appreciation didn't get her far in her social life. School became her worst nightmare; she was getting bullied for her worn down clothes, messy hair, and the red blemishes on her face due to eczema. Ultimately, it led to her insecurities since her beauty was hiding underneath her abnormalities. That was indeed troubling, but she was more disturbed about not having any love or support from either parent.

Starting with Lilith's mother Vivian, who was an alcoholic. She never stayed sober enough to build that mental connection, and that had a huge impact on her kids' lives, especially Lilith considering Vivian always reminded her of how much she was a disgrace to her life. She despised Lilith from day one; for that reason, she treated her differently from the rest of the kids because she depraved her for the mistake that she made, which was getting pregnant with Lilith. She blamed Lilith for everything that wasn't right, but showed favor to her other children. This absence of love and affection in Lilith's life, left her full of gloom. Resultantly, Lilith had generated a great deal of hostility towards Vivian since she was tired of being treated like an outcast.

Then there was her father, who was unknown, which a couple of men could've been a possibility, for Vivian was known for her indiscriminating activities. That may have been the case, but the man in question didn't want to own up to his mistake. Unknowingly, he had a family of his own and didn't want to breakup his happy home. With no strings attached, he left Vivian alone, which caused Lilith to feel disowned by both parents. Lilith got discouraged, and no one seemed to care, which was tearing her apart. In addition to having her aching heart loss of love, and a strong desire for stability, she was headed down a path full of wrong choices.

To begin with, Lilith was the oldest out of her two sisters Martha, Elaine, and their younger brother Roy; they also had a mentally ill older brother name Ronald. That's why she had to become mature very quickly to perform her mother's responsibilities and do most of the nurturing. Under those circumstances, she had to learn how to live with ability, love with security, and laugh with affection. It was hard to do, especially when she didn't obtain any of those pleasures from anyone else. Not to mention, she was a child herself. That's what made her lost and unknowledgeable about life. In other words, my mother was born into darkness, and the burning fire had fogged her path of light and caused her to feel vulnerable. Her life had barely started, but she was ready for it to end.

Secondly, it was perceived that there was much jealously towards Lilith, for the reason that she looked different. She was light skinned, petite, gorgeous with very fine long hair, whereas her siblings looked totally the opposite with their dark-skinned and very shapely bodies. Therefore, the bitterness had caused them to team up against Lilith, which generated many arguments. For example, they consistently called her a mixed breed and teased her about the absence of her father. What was more troubling was Vivian didn't do anything to prevent the arguments; she enjoyed seeing Lilith unhappy. As Lilith cried through her painful soul, Vivian laughed her heart out.

The sad part about it was that they were telling the truth; Lilith's father was like a ghost, for Lilith never saw and knew very little about him. In fact, out of her entire life, she only met him once; and it wasn't by choice, it was by accident. One day, she and a friend were walking past a corner store, and an unknown but resembling man approached her. He asked, "Is Vivian Darkmore your mother?" She replied, "Yes!" He stared at her for a minute and told her, "I am your father!" Then he gave her 20 cents. That was the happiest day of Lilith's life as she skipped in the store and spent it all. Then she came out hoping to see him again, but he was gone with the wind; he vanished just like a ghost. That's when reality hit her, and she realized that there was not any hope for her ever having a father or mother because either direction she went deception had always taken place.

Meanwhile, she was still excited to go spread the news, but Vivian paid her no attention as she was absorbing in her usual. In fact, she started cursing Lilith out in her slurring words, "Get your frail ass out my face. You don't have a father. Didn't I tell you he doesn't want you? Hell, I don't want you either!" Then the other sisters began to laugh and tease her, which made Lilith feel like a fool.

Due to Vivian's bitterness and addiction, she couldn't control nor did she really care about what was going on in her household. Under those circumstances, Lilith was getting scuzzed up by her mother's boyfriend for years. Every night was a dream that always ended up like a nightmare on Elm Street. As she laid over the bed in complete silence and darkness, Lilith eventually dozed off. Then minutes later, her body was unable to move. Feeling trapped, vulnerable, and confused, she panicked. Her teeth were chattering, but words wouldn't come out, and her smothered screams weren't loud enough. As she helplessly laid there submerging in her tears, the crippled boogeyman started slowly whispering frightening words in her ear. She tried to tune him out, but the ethanol reeking from his breath was inflaming her nose. So, she just painfully laid there until the nightmare was over.

When Lilith reached puberty, she was no longer frightened. Instead, she was resentful from all the secrets and backed-up unhappiness. Therefrom, she wasn't afraid to fight back when the boogeyman tried to attack her in the bathroom. She started kicking, punching, and biting him until he got off her. She knew that she had to start protecting herself; no one else was going to do it for her. From that day forward, he left her alone, but she remained discreet, knowing she still had to live with the boogeyman, which caused many nightmares of his tarnished eyes, his overpowering bad breath, and his rough hands touching her. In other words, silence was haunting her, for her voice had not yet exposed him.

Three years had passed by, and she still was living a lie because she had not yet revealed the boogeyman for what he did to her. Meanwhile, Vivian was inattentive about her daughter, being that she was more distracted by her addiction. Therefore, the sadness she saw in Lilith's eyes reflected the darkness in hers, which left her uncaring. So, Lilith blamed Vivian for every misfortune she had to face.

To explain, Lilith was 14, but freely ran the streets without any rules attached. She hung out in places where teens didn't belong. In behalf of her homegirls being popular in those areas, the older crowd gave them all a pass. Then one thing led to another, and the humiliation happened fast. Unluckily, Lilith got raped again, but not by the boogeyman; that time, it was by a total stranger. What was grimy about the overall situation was that her so-called friends set it all up. Lilith was new to the group, and she was perceived as the weakest link. Thereafter, they gave Lilith a few spiked drinks that led to her blackout. When she woke up, a guy was on top of her, which caused her to have flashbacks of the boogeyman. She instantly flipped out while screaming for help. Everyone knew what was going on, but they ignored her; basically, they were used to that sexual behavior going on there.

Eventually, she managed to get away. Then she quickly ran out half naked, and staggered all the way home. Vivian did not acknowledge that something had gone wrong, and she did not have an inch of compassion for her daughter who had a look of terror on her face. A month later, Lilith began experiencing morning sickness, and she noticed she had not come on her menstruation. The fear of being pregnant forced her to tell Vivian everything that happened. Although, Vivian showed no concern, she still had the look of shame on her face.

Thereafter, Vivian made a few calls to help resolve Lilith's issue. Instead of taking her to a professional doctor, she got Lilith a bootleg pill that made her miscarry at home. The pain was excruciating; her heavy flow of blood was clotted. She spent most of her time lying in bed weak, depressed, and lackadaisical. She did not know what she was going to do, or if she was going to make it through the night. She just laid there crying and praying, hoping she would be alright. Then a couple of weeks later, the bleeding just stopped, and she was almost at peace. However, her mind was still at war, for the truth could only set her conscience free.

Due to Lilith thinking she was in the wrong, she was afraid to come forth about the boogeyman for all those years. Aware of the fact that she couldn't shake it off, she knew it was time to do something about it. Conclusively, she confided in Vivian with fear and hope that it would be the end of the boogeyman. With sadness, Lilith looked Vivian in the eyes while tears were falling and said, "That wasn't my first time being raped… because your man has been doing it for quite a while." Then Vivian said in her groggy voice, "You are a liar, you're stupid, ruined, and I don't believe you. Get out my fucking face… BITCH, you are a disgrace to me, and I hate you!" Lilith stood there dismayed. She wondered why Vivian didn't bother to confront the boogeyman before she discredited her and considered her story untrue. What really was discouraging was that her siblings didn't back her up, knowing they witnessed those ireful nights she cried out when he came in and out of the room. They also held her and asked, "If she was okay?" To her disappointment, neither of them spoke up when she needed them the most, so she had no choice but to leave home.

Lilith left with the little nothing she had along with a broken heart. The sad part about it was Vivian knew how bad the streets of New York was, and she didn't try to stop her teenage daughter from leaving, knowing Lilith didn't have anyone or anywhere to go to. Most definitely this was hurtful, thoughtless, and cruel to do to your very own child.

Lilith didn't know why her sweltering, reeking, vertical smile was drooling discolored discharge and went weeks without seeing a doctor. Also, she was homeless and underage, so she couldn't do it on her own anyway. She then confided in an older lady name Diane, who was a complete stranger. Still, the lady helped her get the treatment she needed, fed her, and then gave her a place to stay. After that, Diane started using her like a slave. She had Lilith cleaning her dirty ass apartment, running back and forth to the store, and catering to her and her company. When Lilith didn't do everything she asked, Diane made her feel like "A Nobody" in front of everybody. "I'm the one who's helping you out. You have no other place to go… if you did, then you wouldn't be here. You're nothing without me!" Diane always said, until Lilith got fed up with the disrespect and left.

Shortly after, Lilith began to follow Vivian's footsteps. She started drowning her liver with all types of thirst quenchers. She was talking to, crying with, and rubbing on the pint bottles due to her not having anyone else to confide in; also, it eased her pain. Well, that's what she thought at the time. Instead, it made her more stressed and unstable. She was moving from place to place; she carried herself inappropriately to get things she needed, and kept getting physically and mentally abused, which caused her to feel burnt out immediately. She eventually started to realize that everyone who acted like they cared really didn't. For their good deeds wasn't for her, it was to please their own personal needs.

Considering Lilith had no other options, she reached out to one of her childhood friends name Latoya for help and shelter. Latoya then introduced Lilith to her brother Damien. The first time they met their connection was full of affection. He gave her all the attention by disregarding everything that mattered. His security had so much power that it made her feel less worried or endangered. Also, his touch was very gentle, making it harder for her to resist him, which led to her getting pregnant at the age of 15. Then at 16, they got married at the justice of peace. Even with everything happening so suddenly, Lilith felt loved and wanted for the first time. He wined and dined her, and he always expressed his deepest feelings. He had the best choice of words, which kept Lilith's heart melting and made her feel like she was the special one. Moreover, he gave her hope, and sold her dreams. She thought that he would give her the stability she needed. Because Lilith never had love in her life, she was easily influenced by her perfect man in disguise, especially since he was many years older and was hiding under tailor made suits, ties, and fancy briefcases. But in due time, she would see what an evil man he could be.

Soon after, Lilith was introduced to her In-laws. They gave her the first impression of disapproval. There were no smiles, evil eyes, and limited words, which made her feel uncomfortable. They were subjective towards Lilith before they got to know her; actually, they felt that anyone who was involved with their son emotionally had to be nothing but trouble, for he exhaled adversity. Therefore, Lilith was treated like an outcast without knowing the real reason behind it.

Consequently, Lilith never got the hospitality or homely reaction when she visited, and she was unexceptionally getting brushed off. However, Lilith continued to be cordial when they were rude, for she thought that was what a wife supposed to do. So, every time Damien made his appearance, she did too.

Each visit to her In-laws became more intense, and Lilith began to feel the presence of many evil spirits. From the looks of it, her in-laws' ritual was the practice of witchcraft. Their house was enclosed by darkness but lit up from spiritual glass candles. They also had an isolated room with all types of herbal oils, special made mojo bags, and weird dolls, which made Lilith believed that voodoo was involved. Suddenly, it dawned on her that witchcraft might've been what was attacking her every time she entered her in-law's house, for she would immediately feel the heat of fire, which gave her skin a burning sensation and had her face blushed the entire visit. Also, her heart stayed racing, she had dizzy spells, and a loss of energy. After she stepped foot out their door, everything was back to normal. Lilith was frightened and felt unsafe, but she didn't have the courage to tell Damien, thinking he wouldn't believe her. Despite everything, time after time, Lilith dealt with the attacks.

There wasn't a good reason to dislike Lilith personally, but Damien's misdeeds would introduce her to many enemies. For Damien was conniving, and a deceitful liar. He secretly conspired to cause misery and unpredictably shift people's lives. He portrayed himself as this generous, devoted, and compassionate man; but he was a crooked, mendacious, evil monster. Lilith had no idea what she had gotten herself into, but it would be very challenging and have a huge impact on her life since Damien had a twisted mind from the start. Resulting from Lilith being blinded by love, she ignored all signs, even when she knew certain things weren't adding up about Damien.

As I previously stated, Lilith was always judged by her appearance instead of the goodness within her heart. Moreover, she never was the type to fit in. She kept trying so hard to get accepted, but it just made room for her to keep getting neglected. For instance, Lilith thought by her having a child would change things, and it did, but just for a little bit. For the most part, the in-laws gave them a place to stay through her pregnancy. Then 2 months after Lashaylah was born, Mrs. Oma had put them out after she found out Damien lied about paying his part of the bills, which was extremely backed up. Reality struck Lilith, and she felt furious and despaired that she didn't have a backup plan, especially when she had nowhere to go with her baby.

It never crossed Lilith's mind that Damien was irresponsible until Oma angrily disclosed, "Damien, you are a despiteful motherfucker. You con people that are easy targets, take them for everything, and then disappear. You're not going to ever amount up to shit, and Lilith won't neither." Lilith looked surprised, but she didn't show any concern or took heed, and stood strongly behind her husband.

While Oma kept babbling off at the mouth, Lilith was staring quietly in the daze, and Oma's voice started drifting further away. Until Oma pointed her finger in Lilith's face and savagely said, "I don't give a fuck about you!" Then she pointed at Damien and said, "And I don't care about you or that kid neither. Y'll going to continue to have bad luck because I cursed y'll motherfuckers until each one of y'll time expires!!!" Instead of Lilith cursing her out, she properly dressed and wrapped Shaylah up well. Then they walked out and left that place of hell. Meanwhile, God had protected them in the rain as they walked 30 minutes away to Latoya's place. For this reason, that would be the last time Lilith saw her in-laws.

Eventually, Damien and Lilith moved in together to start a whole new generation of the Daevas's. Lilith was very fertile, and kept popping babies out nearly back to back. Although her support group was limited, she did get a little help from her sisters. However, Vivian had passed away immediately after Lilith's second child Lateesah was born. Vivian had suffered from the cirrhosis of the liver. Due to her change in appearance had made her kids aware that something was wrong, but they weren't at all surprised. She was in the later stage where her nails, eyebrows, and eyes were yellow. Still, she continued drinking, and it took her life at the age of 37. Vivian and Lilith never got the chance to resolve their issues, or establish a mother and daughter bond. And though she had hoped for it, Lilith never was asked the apologetic question, "Would you forgive me my child?" But in Lilith's heart, she already had forgiving her mother, even though Vivian died with an empty soul and was drowned by booze and anger. Lilith had to let go, live, and grow with her new family.

On the other hand, Lilith didn't get any support or a congratulation for any of her upcoming kids from Damien's parents. They neglected their grandparent roles and didn't show any affection or accept any of their grandchildren. They didn't know our names, who features we had, or our personalities. All they were familiar with was that Damien had eight cursed kids. Given that Damien's family was invisible to us, we called them our dark side, but we brought the Daevas's to light with many different attributes and liveliness. The only downside about us not knowing Damien's family was the history, which had our future a little blurry because we didn't know the two different combinations of evil that adjoined.

Therefore, the viciousness on both sides had created a curse amongst the Daevas's and Darkmore family. For we inherited different types of contaminated blood that generated all different types of wickedness. What Lilith and Damien didn't know was that every time they conceived, the curse became more powerful. For the evilness within our bloodlines caused a unique creation of destruction.

In all honesty, we probably wouldn't had been conceived if Lilith and Damien would've known what they were creating. For the signs of evil continues to come out of us consistently in an egregious way. We all eventually experienced mental and emotional breakdowns about serious issues or sometimes practically nothing. I believe the uncertainty about our wicked powers had forced us to be out of control. Our actions were controversial, but no one could understand until they walked in our shoes, which wasn't easy to do unless one was born into evil.

Although this may be true, there is a saying that a curse come from sin, but at birth we couldn't do any wrong, nor were we born out of wedlock. Without a doubt, it was originated from our ancestors. I became concerned and questionable. I asked, "Can a spell come back after its broken?" I came up with the answer that it is based on the cycles of powers amongst an individual as well as having the desire and directions towards improvement. To clarify, one person can break the curse on themselves, but as a family, everyone must be willing and able for it to be effective. Meanwhile, our curse would continue to destroy and transpire through our kids and so forth. As a matter of fact, I already notice the evil that exist in some of our nieces and nephews, but it just hasn't advanced to our level of corruption yet. I pray each day for my family, and their transitions. Not only are we something special, but we are gifted and don't even know it. Instead, we use our capabilities towards our evil doings, which leaves our curse with all the power.

The darkness is our surroundings. Our eyes can't see, our ears can't hear, and our mouths can't speak about rectitude. Where do we go from here? Do we keep inviting one generation after another to continue the curse? Or, do we guide them towards righteousness? We can only allow the darkness to remain if we don't want to abstain from evil. What or who do we sacrifice? When do we make that decision? And, how do we know if we are making the best decision?

It shouldn't reflect the best decision, it's about making the right decision. However, everyone's judgment and priorities are simply based on who or what they are willing to sacrifice. Some situations maybe time consuming, so take all the time you need; but the longer the thought process, the more you can get caught up in confusion. My best solution is to follow your intuition, for the feeling comes from within, which usually is the satisfaction of RIGHT. A point to remember: A thoughtful choice comes through proposition, considerations, and expectations.

# CHRONOLOGICAL CURSE

MALACHI 2: 2-3 "if he will not hear, and if ye will not lay to heart to give glory unto my name, saith the lord of hosts, I will curse upon you, and I will curse your blessings. Behold, I will corrupt your seed..."

First thing to remember is that we are 9 sisters cursed since birth. Despite our malevolent ways, we still have a trace of geniality in our blood that is not easily circulated. Therefore, the chosen one with the strongest willpowers will discipline her bad and ordain the good into her life changes. Which sister has the capabilities within them? Is it the first child Lashaylah Daevas? Born March 21, 1970, which made her the first corrupted sister in our generation. Only time will tell, for evil cannot continue to prevail.

# ONE WICKED LIAR

Lashaylah was born with that fire in her heart. At a very young age, she was determined to stay committed to herself regardless of what she didn't have or couldn't do. For her superiority would fulfill her desires eventually. Therefore, her being less fortunate wasn't her vulnerability, it was her strength and security.

I describe Shaylah's characteristics as responsible but very much hypocritical. She is cursed by deliberate deception, especially when she pretends to have one set of feelings, but acts under the influence of another, which can be very believable if you didn't know of her. However, Shaylah is content with her deceptive ways, for she sees it as some form of entertainment.

Shaylah also takes pleasure in partying. Her weekend routine is to drink, dance, and laugh. She's an in the crowd type of person who loves to be the center of attention. At times, she's perceived as arrogant, and in her perfect little world, it's all about her. Also, she keeps that "my way is the only way" attitude. Shaylah can be extremely rude, and while she (figuratively) lives on Fantasy Island, in her eyes, not too many people are on her level, but that's just Shaylah's personality. She preys on the weak and loves to be in control. She belittle ones' character, and can be very spiteful if you double cross her. Once she feels betrayed, her anger level explodes. Her fast talk blows nothing but flames, and all types of evil spirits are generated. Shaylah would defy, disown, and disdain a betrayer without any pity. Moreover, Shaylah was one of the fierce ones, so her controversies can get physically strong; trust me, she was a beast with her hands.

It's easy for Shaylah to be unforgiving when there is consistent betrayal, but she has a forgiving heart when situations are bearable. She treats people with care and lends a helping hand anytime she's able. She is also dependable and takes care of home independently. She works hard at being the best woman, daughter, mother, and sister she could be despite her different personalities.

Shaylah also can be outspoken and bold. She says what she means, and did what she said. She hardly ever showed signs of fear, and trouble was a split image of her. Of course, New York schools can make someone tough when you're getting laughed at, chased, and jumped. Shaylah eventually turned some laughs into cries, her runs had come to a halt, and she was persistent in fighting one on one until she earned some sort of respect.

Shaylah was inattentive in school, so playing hooky was much more interesting to do. While the streets became her expertise, she lost sight of her education, and dropped out in the ninth grade. As a teenager, Shaylah was taking a lot of risk, and never really considered the aftermath, which brought about a lot of problems, but that was an ongoing adrenaline for her. Looking on the bright side, it helped her find some pieces to her puzzled life.

Back in the days, Shaylah preferred to hang around the older crowds, who were a big influence on her smoking, drinking, and clubbing. Those were the good ole days when the loud music was playing, 40oz's were passed around, and the smoke was fogging up the air. All you could hear was joyful, loud voices laughing and wisecracking while playing cards. That lifestyle could provoke anyone portentous ways including Shaylah's.

Due to Shaylah being free from restrictions, she became susceptible to sexual activities in her early teens. She wanted it every minute, tried to fulfill every moment, and strongly desired it every day. Sex was more like a hobby to Shaylah, but just with less feelings, for she never wanted to let it take control of her, and she stayed in control of it. Shaylah made it complicated for men; they didn't know if she could be taken seriously with her deceptive behavior, but her chosen ones always wore a leash around their necks.

Shaylah liked to captivate, manipulate, and derange a man's mind, which was her strongest characteristics. She was grateful that she developed them from daddy because those were her swords and shields. But what she thought was her good qualities, was some form of mistreatment from other people's point of view. For instance, if Shaylah's boyfriend cheated on her, then her cruel act of retaliation had no limitation. Consequently, his friends, enemies, and/or family members weren't forbidden. Then she would enjoy watching him reap when she threw it up in his face, and it didn't matter if he left or stayed since Shaylah always kept a backup boy toy.

When Shaylah looked in daddy's eyes, she saw nothing but evil, and that was the exact role she wanted to portray. Therefore, she trained her men to be the opposite, which was virtuous puppets. It was like she put a spell on them, and they were eating out the palm of her hands. Regardless of how badly she treated them, they continued to fall deeper in love. Shaylah wore the pants in her relationships, and at some point, she thought that she defeated men, until she came across a guy that wasn't having it. It was a little wakeup call for her, and the first time she feared a man.

That handsome guy was Jordan. He had the same charisma like daddy. Jordan was genuinely swagtastic, but the real him was hiding behind those lustful eyes, and his luscious lips, which made it harder for Shaylah to resist those butterflies she felt. So, she decided to give him a shot, but with a mindset of molding him just like the others; nevertheless, Jordan had the same intentions. After a few weeks of their puppy love, his true colors started blossoming; primarily because Shaylah was feisty and uncontrollable.

Jordan assumed he just couldn't verbally abuse Shaylah, knowing that she was somewhat insensible; thereupon, he used his dominant aggression and psychological tactics, trying to make her believe that there was no way out of their relationship but through death. Those new words were damaging to Shaylah's ears; also, a complete turn off to her. At that moment, Shaylah automatically knew that their connection would eventually be detached because any form of abuse just didn't sit right with her. However, she was too scared to break it off with him, not truly knowing if it would be a deadly outcome. Shaylah being Shaylah decided to sneak around with other guys, hoping she would come across one who could overpower Jordan's endangering capabilities.

Shaylah's actions had caused a lot of controversy between her and Jordan along with a few other guys, but things started to get a little more intense when fist fighting led to gun threats, and somehow ended up in robberies. As bad as it sounds, the odds were in Shaylah's favor now that Jordan was no longer in her life after he went to prison. Shaylah's hostile experience made her even more belligerent and combative towards men because she didn't want to give them any type of leeway or control, and every time she crossed the path with a man, it made her heart colder.

Shaylah engaged in different men for different reasons, and with pride she put labels on them. She had her sugar daddy, who was older in age, but he smelled, looked, and dressed like money. He had a luxury car, big house, and loved taking her out to extravagant places. The only way he could keep a smile on her face was by spoiling her rotten, which he had no problem doing. Still, Shaylah wasn't happy, nor was she attracted to him. But drinking massively would give her that "in the moment" chemistry. Then the next day, she would feel disgusted and embarrassed about any or nothing she thought may have happened. Because that was minor, Shaylah didn't dwell on it. In fact, she looked at him from a positive prospective, seeing he was a permanent ATM machine, and she withdrew every time she got a chance. The good thing about sugar daddies is that their quick fix isn't always about sex; they get aroused by anything. Also, her sugar daddy could never popup unexpectedly, and their relationship was confidential, which he wasn't aware of. However, he anticipated and waited on her phone calls. For many reasons, sugar daddies were effective and a factor in her life.

Next in line was her herb, who we characterized as a lame or a nerd. His appearance, communication, and style was absurd. More than likely, he was a virgin or didn't have much experience with women. So, hanging out with Shaylah made him feel like he was special. To a certain extent, he thought he was fitting in, but behind his back, he was really getting laughed at. The guy was her do boy who had no voice. He couldn't make his own decisions because Shaylah was his focal point. Her herb was the type of guy that she didn't need to have sex with, and he would still be at her beck and call.

Then there was Shaylah's gangster type who loved living the dangerous life. His communication screamed out trouble, and his attitude revealed that he didn't give a fuck! He dressed with sagging pants, fresh white Tee's, and Timbs; he was hiding under his fitted hats with cornrows hanging down his back. He always represented his squad, stayed having beef, and was well known on the streets for carrying his heat. He didn't take no shit from nobody including Shaylah. That was the rules in the gangster world, even if he was feeling his gangster girl. Still, Shaylah loved being in his presence because she was magnetized to the aggression... His thuggish style, and her being a girl gone wild definitely made them unstable soldiers, which stimulated her mind. They had no certain approach for those hardcore streets, blind by every angle, so they really didn't see the danger ahead of them.

Lastly, it was the guy who Shaylah labeled as her boyfriend. He had similar but different attributes like some of her other correspondents. Still and all, something set him apart from everyone else, for not many men were worthy of that title, especially for Shaylah. For the most part, she was sincere, kind, and her affectionate ways were very vivid. Her heartfelt words were deep and filled with emotions, so when she told him she loved him, it had to be true because it was rare for Shaylah to express her feelings. He was also the one she confided in, relied on, and respected. Although he earned his recognition, there was still a twist to that love story, and that was, he didn't have any room for fuck ups, or Shaylah would quickly find someone to pick up his slack without thinking twice about any heartbreaking. For she was definitely daddy's advocate.

Shaylah's bad deeds had followed her, and when she was put in the same situation she once had others in, she didn't realize it until it was too late. Shaylah got acquainted with this straight from Oakland, CA stud named Roni. His swag was totally different with his saggy Dickie pants and baseball caps that he wore backwards. What was really captivating was his Bay area slang, for his talk game was superb "fasho."

Shaylah was clueless about his cruelness, and he swept her young ass off her feet in no time. To her, Roni was boyfriend material, but to him, she was just another venture to uplift his ego. Little did she know that she finally met her match.

Roni's feelings got stronger for Shaylah, but he still couldn't turn from his deceptive ways and would break Shaylah's heart continuously. Shortly after they became a couple, the rumors, and then the altercations began. There were females claiming the girlfriend title, and Shaylah wasn't having that; thereupon, her combative behavior became a routine. Being petite didn't stop Shaylah from approaching BITCHES, and she was undefeated by tall, medium, and stoutly ones. Her fist pounded their faces repeatedly; her headlocks was so tight that they couldn't breathe, and her kick game was perfected like the karate kid after training. Shaylah had BITCHES intimidated to fight, but they weren't scared enough to keep their legs closed because it no longer mattered to them that they were the side chicks. Although Shaylah had earned her respect as Roni's girlfriend, she still failed to understand that the biggest problem was her man.

Shaylah was caught up, and her feelings had taken over her thoughts. She was drowned by many tears, and her heart was pounding with fear of losing him, which she wasn't trying to let him go. Roni knew he had that control. He knew that every deceitful thing he did, Shaylah would keep forgiving him for it. Therefore, he had no boundaries when it came to cheating, and Shaylah's leniency was her biggest mistake.

Shaylah's most memorable moments were the romantic candle nights Roni and her used to have. There was pure darkness, but the flames were glowing while mellow music was seductively whispering in their ears. As they laid in bed after making passionate love, feeling relieved and in peace, they cuddled while softly expressing their feelings for one another. Those were the moments she hoped would never end, but it did, which was explicitly unpleasant. For there were days that passed by, and it would be no sign of Roni. The first thing that came to Shaylah's mind was that he was with another girl, which was the cause of her raging temper. Her forceful words were speaking violently, and her feelings were hurt. As Shaylah's anger elevated, her mind was completely taking over her body. For her heart began to ache, and the gut-wrenching pain was hard to escape. She indignantly stormed out to get some fresh air, hoping that she would recover her composure. Her leisure walks turned into baby steps, and her sharp pains got a little more excruciating. Shaylah immediately thought that something wasn't right as she moaned, stooped over, while holding her stomach all the way home.

After Shaylah left the hospital, she was exasperated and cried unpretentiously. Whatever the doctor discussed with her, she had a different attitude towards being in a relationship with Roni. Still, she wanted to face him to get some closure. A couple of weeks after Roni thought the heat died down, he charmingly knocked at the door with a boutique of roses and drinks. Shaylah's blood flow instantly accelerated, and her eyes were bursting in darkness as she gave him a demonic look. Before Roni got a word out, Shaylah snatch the roses and beers, then started throwing them at him. "Wham! Wham!" was all we heard while she was wildly punching and kicking him. Indubitably, in Roni's defense, he manly held her down crying out, "I'm sorry! Forgive me for making a terrible mistake… I love you! We can work through this… I promise." Shaylah was talking and crying at the same time, which made her words hard to understand, but it really didn't matter, seeing that she forgave him again.

Everything was back to normal like nothing ever happened, for they were laughing, drinking, and partying like usual. But after a few good months, Roni thought it was time to surreptitiously cheat again. The day that Shaylah found out, she began to excessively drink. As her head started swiftly spinning, her mind was depressively thinking about every problem and solution. Then she concluded that life is worthless; proceeding on this track, her legs became lifeless as she walked to the bathroom. She frantically went in the medicine cabinet and grabbed every over-the-counter drug she could find. After she slammed the cabinet door, the mirror admired her beauty, but revealed her desperation as the tears drowned the sclera of her eyes. While she sadly stood there, her hands started to feel like it was on fire. Then they went numbed, which caused her to drop the pills on the floor, and she fell along with them.

Shaylah was lying there gazing at the ceiling when she heard voices crying and screaming out her name. As she looked in her little sisters' fearful eyes, she realized she had so much to live for, and shouldn't ever think about committing suicide anymore. That was her last day of stupidity, and she accepted that some things aren't meant to be. Therefore, she had to forever end her unhealthy relationship.

It didn't take long for Shaylah to build her confidence back. Actually, she never lost it, she just got a little sidetracked. Although Shaylah was completely done with Roni, she couldn't let go of the grudges, and it matured into bitterness, provoking her to seek vengeance. She was targeting any BITCH that interfered with her relationship, which was a motive for her implacable actions. She didn't care how they reacted, or what people said and thought about her. For that was the beginning towards her road to recovery.

One of Shaylah's most relieving and harsh acts of retaliations was towards this female name Vera. She was Roni's baby mother, previous girlfriend, and became one of his side chicks when he and Shaylah were together. So, after Vera got married to who she thought was this perfect guy, Shaylah felt that was the best opportunity to fuck with her happiness by intervening in their marriage.

Shortly after Vera's honeymoon, Shaylah alluringly made her move on the husband. He desired her anyway, which made it easier for him to commit adultery. Every morning when Vera left their beautiful home to go to work, Shaylah was the entertainment through and out the day. That was like Shaylah's second home. She cooked, took showers when needed, and comfortably lounged around naked, which was very seductive.

As they lie in bed staring at one another, Shaylah couldn't help from intensely exhaling while he was inhaling the sweet aroma from her skin. After affectionately kissing, and softly touching, Shaylah's pussy would be drenching wet. Then they pleasantly made some indescribable love making on those cozy, silky sheets.

After they both reached their peaks, they depravedly cuddled with smiles. From the looks of it, you would've thought it was smiles of passion on both ends. To Shaylah, it was smiles of revenge and no regrets, for her feelings were far from in it. She continued the affair until he fell deep in love. Then she revealed his dirty secret by leaving her panties in Vera's drawer with a hurtful letter attached, stating, "I've been fucking your husband for months. As you see, we both shared the same bed once again. How does it feel now that the shoe is on the other foot? Not a good feeling at all I'm hoping! It's my turn to sit back and laugh while you feel the hurt. I will admit that his dick was pretty good, but not good enough for me... That's why I'm giving him back; honestly, I think you should be thanking me! From your best enemy... Shaylah!"

As Vera read the note full of tears and pain, she knew that her perfect marriage had gone down the drain. She thought she had her everything, but Karma surprisingly took that away, which opened her eyes to LIFE. Although she understood why, her emotions couldn't accept it. Her animosity level was on fire, and she was ready to fight at that moment. When the time came for her to confront Shaylah, she couldn't find the courage to lift a fist. Even though she walked away unbeaten, her soul felt like she had lost the battle.

Shaylah was just getting started, and the rivals were never ending. She took pride and joy in destroying relationships, friendships, and families. She was this out of control teenager that was captivated by negative attention. The tension was so feverish that we could feel the heat standing at our front door. We heard the whispering very clearly as if they were having the conversation with us, and everywhere we went people were looking at us differently. Some made screw faces, rolled their eyes, and sucked their teeth like we all had caused the problems. That is when mommy realized she had a lot of trouble on her hands. She was unaware that people considered her daughter as this deceitful, mean, and hateful girl when Shaylah was congenial at home.

Shaylah's problematic behavior had eventually brought trouble to our home; primarily because it was hard for BITCHES to defeat her. So, their brothers, cousins, and sometimes fathers would come banging on our door using their masculine abilities to try and intimidate us. They knew it was nothing but a house full of females; still, we showed no signs of fear, especially not Shaylah. She would stand boldly in the screen door, laughing and responding back with the same aggression. Dudes would be yelling out, "Don't let me catch you on the streets 'cause Imma beat ya down like a man BITCH!" Shaylah spazzed out, "I am a bad BITCH that fucked up your BITCH, and she ran crying to your ugly ass! Why you mad? And, I hope you don't think that you're gonna get props by fighting a female… That's what I call a pussy! Why don't you go get your BITCH, so we can go for round two? And don't worry… I got some nigga's for you!" Then she would slam the door in their faces and started calling up her goons. Those were the hood niggas that did whatever to protect Shaylah and vice versa. Living life on the edge was the primary reason they loved feeding off negative energy. Many people didn't understand Shaylah unless they understood her life.

The definition of our life is misfortune because we weren't counting our blessing; we were acknowledging the consistent bad luck. Although that was Shaylah's life experiences, she always tried to camouflage it with her egotistical appearance, but beneath all of those good quality clothes, jewelry, and money, was a life full of struggles. It was hard to obtain her earthly possessions morally or intellectually, for she didn't know better. Therefore, Shaylah revealed herself to the unattractive, exposed herself to enemies, and became proficient in boosting just to make ends meet.

Shaylah was ill-behaved, but stealing wasn't a thought that crossed her mind until she started hanging around these triplets that were kleptomaniacs. Livia, Lizzy, and Lauryn were career criminals that resold stolen goods through and out the hood. Anything you wanted they had or could get it, for they made shoplifting look like it was easily done, which had Shaylah anticipating on doing the same.

To emphasize more, Shaylah and the 5-finger discount squad were out walking, bored, and broke one Friday evening. As they approached the corner store, they already had plotted to go in and steal some cool beers to drink along the way. Within minutes, they were out and had enough alcohol for all of them to get wasted. While they walked, talked, and laughed, they guzzled those 40's down like they were drinking their favorite juice. Afterwards, they started feeling a little tipsy. Then the sun became more irritating and began to roast their sweaty, brown skin. Regardless of what, they rather go anywhere but home. To kill more time as well as cool off, they made pit stops at just about every retail store they passed by.

As they walked through the automatic doors, the cool breeze was exposed to their faces. With their consoling expressions of relief, they were ready to do some browsing. Thereafter, they saw racks full of brightly colored clothes, which was alluring; the matching bra and panty sets were seductive, and the cosmetic department was full of beauty. Everything they wanted was roaring right at them, but it was only one way they could fulfill their desires, and that was to boost as much as they could.

They grabbed the largest but most fashionable handbags, then filled it up with all types of materialistic stuff. After that, the triplets headed towards the exit contentedly. On the other hand, Shaylah was walking tensely as sweat slowly dripped down her forehead, blood was circulating quickly, and her heartbeats were piercing her ears because she was terrified of getting caught. Once she made it outside, she happily exhaled and said in a reviving tone, "Wow! What a relief... I can't believe that shit was that easy. I ain't going to lie though, walking out was a little scary, but we made it out with all this shit... We definitely have to do this again!"

That was Shaylah's breaking point, and her amateurish acts of impulse became an expert in shoplifting. Until stores started using different strategies, and they caught her red-handed on video camera. After they hauled her ass to jail, she was locked up for a week before she went in front of the judge, who gave her time served. As she anxiously left the courtroom, the kleptomaniacs were waiting outside for her. Shaylah was happy to feel and breathe the fresh air; moreover, she was ready for a drink. As usual, they did what they knew best and hit up the corner store for some beers and cigarettes. It took Shaylah a few more charges, and a couple of months in the jailhouse in order to learn her lesson about stealing.

After that, Shaylah thug status was definable in her eyes because being confined was troublesome. However, she took her vulnerable experiences in jail, accepted her wrongs, and then used them to defeat obstacles. It also opened her eyes to see who her true friends were, and that's when her circle had gotten smaller. Actually, Livia was the only one she had a few things in common with, so they started hanging together solo. Two teenagers who were off track, wild, and lacking leadership was definitely a train wreck.

Shaylah and Livia were like two peas in the pod, and they caused trouble consistently. They took turns playing the roles of the instigator, and the initiator, which always ended up in some type of riot or one-on-one altercations. Most of the times, the club or party had to shut down earlier than normal due to the situations becoming uncontrollable. People running to their cars, some quickly pulling off, while others fired their guns, anticipating on killing or scaring off their enemies. Because alcohol played a huge role, nobody really cared or thought about the danger that threatened their lives. They were immaturely focused on protecting their girl and/or boyfriends, reputations, and at all times, they needed that control. Shaylah would take pleasure in walking through those rough roads, for that was her conception of surviving in life.

Instigating and initiating had eventually caused a bloody situation for Shaylah. One weekend, she and Livia decided to be party hoppers. They invited themselves to every house party and cookout without even knowing the people that were throwing it. They would mingle through the crowd, guzzling down the free alcohol, and gobbling up the soul food without a nervous bone in their bodies.

As the music was reverberating to their ears, they erotically started dancing, drawing both positive and negative attention. Of course, the men were captivated by their energy, but the females sneered and gave them the evil eyes. That didn't offend Shaylah or Livia at all, it just provoked them to stir up trouble. That day, Livia became the instigator and tried to talk over the music saying, "Shaylah... those BITCHES pointing over here popping off at the mouth. Let's stand next to them to see what they have to say!" Then they walked over there riotous and hyped. They were standing so close to the girls that any slight movement somebody was getting an elbow. Livia was the one who got the bow, more like a push. By Shaylah being the initiator, she hauled off with a strong right hook to the enemy's face. Afterwards, all hell broke loose. As people tried to intervene, Shaylah was angrily swinging and kicking with force. Bottles were broken, and blood started leaking all over the floor because Shaylah got shanked. Her adrenaline was rushing, but she felt no pain and was unaware of how much she was bleeding out. After the conflict was over, and they were thrown out the party, Shaylah then collapsed.

She woke up in the emergency room with numerous stitches on the right side of her oblique. This situation made her even more hostile, and she was ready for retaliation. Although she didn't know anything about the girls, she was good with remembering faces. She roamed the streets for weeks until she fought every girl whom she remembered that night, regardless if they did or didn't have anything to do with it. She just wanted to make examples out of them. Livia was standing bravely along Shaylah side through every battle, and that was one of the reasons Shaylah considered her as a best friend. We disagreed about their friendship, but it wasn't our decision. For Shaylah had saw something in Livia that we didn't; something that made them collaborate with understanding, and caused them to have unity. Yet, neither one of them was aware that their solidarity wasn't from the heart, it was only for those moments in time.

Some people mistakenly have misconceptions about the meaning of friends. A friend is a supporter, consoler, someone you divulge your secrets with, and a person that will stay true to the friendship, regardless of how far or long y'll are away from each other. Moreover, the love, understanding, and unity is incorruptible. If that friend lacks in any of those categories, then you should reevaluate your friend and considered them more of an associate. A best friend is hard to find, and the title must be earned, for everybody you come across isn't your friend, just remember that. Under those circumstance, Shaylah and

Livia's friendship eventually grew apart; after that, the conflicts started amongst the two, which was exactly up Shaylah's alley because she liked keeping things stirred up.

Shaylah didn't just keep things stirred up between her disputants, family wasn't excluded from all her confusion she liked to cause. If there was beef amongst any one of us, Shaylah was the sparkplug that got a kick out of keeping the feud flared up... Take a cousin for instance had an argument or fight with one of us, Shaylah more than likely would be the first to find out, and the first to make all the calls. Ring... Ring... "Hello!" Caylah answered in her hung-over voice. "Caylah... what's going on between you and Brianna? She said that you got real drunk last night. Then you tried to pop off on her, so she had to beat your ass and would do it again if she had to. She was bragging about how she gave you a black eye and all types of knots... I was in a state of shock and was just listening to Brianna talking that tough guy shit. I really couldn't believe everything she said, I know my sister, and if a BITCH claimed she beat your ass, I know you will be going back for round two!" Shaylah said hastily. Caylah had got extremely mad that she didn't realize most of the story wasn't actually what happened that night. Without much thought, she was ready to pay Brianna a visit, and it wasn't to talk. Meanwhile, Shaylah was cracking up on the other end. Before she hung up, she said, "Call me back Caylah, and let me know what happened."

Ring... Ring... "Hello!" Brianna loudly answered. Then Shaylah said, "I was calling you back to tell you about my conversation with Caylah. She's pissed off about what happened last night. I told her that you said the little scuffle wasn't that serious, but she felt like she was disrespected... Now she's on her way to your house to fight you, and she hope you're ready!" Shaylah said in a disruptive manner. In a flash, Brianna got all riled up; her mouth was running like 50 mph, and blood was rushing through her fist as they balled up. The dispute had escalated to something that really wasn't nothing in the first place, and Shaylah had accomplished her mission.

When Caylah came to confront Brianna, there was so much negative friction that others had to come in between them before things got physical. After they started exchanging the he say she say shit, it dawned on them that most of it was lies, and Shaylah was the key to all the drama. Under those circumstances, they reconciled their differences, but had a bone to pick with Shaylah. That would be the time Shaylah don't give or receive calls because she already knows what it's about. When she does finally answer, which might be days or even weeks later, she would laugh it off, and act like everything was just a joke without caring about the austerity behind it. Some of our problems became most of her schemes, which is one of the reasons she is less trustworthy.

Shaylah sentimentality can't be taken serious at times, seeing she is voluntarily a good actress. Her best roles are always performed when she is inebriated, which be the perfect times for an uncontainable urge to cry. The hilarious part about it is that she wants others to be softhearted towards a situation that to some degree may not be fully true or doesn't exist at all. We could be in high spirits, recreative, and chilling in a relaxed environment, then Shaylah would change the whole setting with her dramatic outburst, leaving everyone clueless for a split second. Her tears were like the rainfalls in the spring. Her words were repeated like a skipping CD, leaving us with only the beginning and ending of each sentence, which made it harder to interpret. In Shaylah hiccup words, she sighed, "I can't be- - eve --e's dead! They f- -nd h-r b-dy in a tub full of bl… Blood!"

"Who's dead? A bloody body where? In your tub? Calm down so we can understand you!" We all blurted out in a disturbed tone and looked with the curious eyes. Then Shaylah chest gradually started slowing down while she took deep breaths in silence. Her tears had evaporated as we stood there staring and waiting for her response. As she held her head down, she said with sadness, "They found my best friend in the tub… dead! She had cut her wrist and drowned in her pool of blood. Just knowing that she killed herself is heartbreaking, and I dread seeing her lying in a casket!"

Immediately after, she goes back to the typical Shaylah; she would be laughing and making jokes like she just didn't cry her heart out. As though her best friend's death was no longer a saddened tragedy that should've been expressed with deeper emotions. We were a little leery about the insufficient details to her story, but we modestly believed her. Then a week later, we found out that everything was untrue. She's most certainly certified as being harsh and cruel. She doesn't care what curse she puts on a person if she feels some certain type of way about them; primarily because he or she is figuratively dead to her anyway.

Shaylah is very comfortable with her character; she gotten away with her adverse behavior without having it backfire, which eventually faded. Being a compulsive liar could have some advantages, but it also has its disadvantages as well. Since Shaylah's convincing tales became questionable allegations, everything that came out of her mouth had to be confirmed by a reliable source before we could believe it. So, when something awful actually happened, and she really needed someone, nobody took her serious. Thereupon, she felt deserted, disheartened, and disrespected. The most hurtful part was that mommy, who should've been there for her, wasn't at all supportive.

This one particular incident happened on a night Shaylah was staggering home from a party and was unaware that she was being followed by a group of guys. As soon as she unlocked the door, one of the guys came from behind, covered her mouth before she could scream, and then forced her in the house as the others came in after him. The house was silent because everybody was gone for the weekend. It also was pitch dark, so the men's eyes and voices were the only identification. At first, Shaylah didn't know their intentions until they ducked taped her mouth, pinned her down to the floor, and started tearing off her clothes. Shaylah panicked, and she felt helpless as she cried in a muffled tone. Then the guys started arguing over who was going to fuck her first. After hearing belts unbuckle, Shaylah started squirming in hopes that either her arms or legs would get loose, so she could defend herself.

When one of the guys laid on top of her, the cigarette smell on his breath was so strong that it felt like she inhaled the smoke herself. While he tried to force it in her, he started grunting like a vicious animal, which sounded very creepy. Immediately after, Shaylah began to feel nauseated and violated. That's what pushed her over the edge, which caused Shaylah to become deranged and rumbustious. Everything started moving in slow motion after she kneed the guy on top of her in the balls; she tried to take another one eyes out, then she brutally started kicking and punching in every direction.

They began to pull Shaylah's hair tightly, then kicked her several times in the abdomen, and brutally punched her in the face while still trying to pin her down. Yet, they were unable to proceed their depraving behavior since Shaylah's evil powers were ferocious and wrathful, which is how she escaped. After fleeing out the front door, she snatched off the duct tape and started repeatedly screaming out, "Help! Somebody help me!" When she saw a few of the neighbors' lights come on, she ran to the closest one and was desperately banging on their door.

As the door slowly opened, Shaylah fell to her knees terribly crying and trembling with nothing but a torn shirt on. "Some guys tried to rape me... Oh my God! I can't believe I got away, it was so many of them. Can you please call the cops, Miss? My mother isn't home, and I'm so scared," Shaylah frightfully whined. The lady kindly responded, "You don't have to worry, you're safe! And I'm not going to let nothing happen to you here." Then she covered Shaylah up with a warm blanket as they waited for the cops and ambulance.

While awaiting, Shaylah kept rocking back-n-forth, and tears were slowly falling down her face as she stared angrily at the wall in disbelief. Moments after arriving at the hospital, a raped kit was performed. Since the perv wasn't able to fully get his penis in her, there was no signs of rape, but evidence of a sexual assault. They took pictures of every bruise on her face, wrist, legs, and inner thighs as evidence. Once they got the entire story on what happened, they knew the only way of finding out who all was involved was through the DNA Shaylah might have obtained during her struggle. For this reason, no further actions were taking until the results got back.

After a few weeks, the results of the skin they scraped from under Shaylah's nails, and the hair that was found on her torn shirt pointed the fingers at two former convicts named Eddie Crow and Alvin Black. They were immediately apprehended but denied all accusations. Without the suspects giving any further information, or the officers having no other leads, they were released after they posted bail a few hours later. Nevertheless, they were ordered not to go within 500 feet of Shaylah. That wasn't enough for her, knowing the other guys were unidentified and not held accountable for their actions, nor were they under any regulations, which left her exposed to more danger. Shaylah was upset and devastated, especially when mommy didn't come with her to the first appearance in court, and she had to face her nightmare all by herself. She felt abandoned and off track because no one had her back during that unexpected tragedy.

The question was... Why didn't mommy come? Was it because of the shame Shaylah had already brought on her? Or, was she worried that the story was fabricated, and wanted to protect her Christian image? Whatever the reason was, it wasn't good enough. The evidence did support Shaylah's story. So, the fact that she ignored her daughter crying out for her support and understanding was completely neglectful. It doesn't matter what Shaylah did in the past, or what anybody thought of her; as a mother, you're always supposed to love your child unconditionally.

Considering Shaylah no longer felt that devotion, she lost the energy to continue going to court to seek justice, and the charges were eventually dropped. It was disappointing for Shaylah, but it was over. However, every time she saw them, it filled her with rage. It had a long-term effect on Shaylah, whereas it was one less problem for mommy. Resultantly, their mother and daughter relationship was never the same, but the love was still there. The overall negative experiences still didn't change Shaylah's outlook on being a compulsive liar. For lying, even for something very simple, was what she enjoyed being well known for.

On the other hand, Shaylah has a humorist side. She will have you laughing until your stomach hurts, but the joke definitely doesn't be about her. If you did anything embarrassing, and she witnessed it, then all jokes would be on you when the crowd came around. Here is when things got a little more hilarious... Every time Shaylah tells the joke, it changes. It's crazy how she would put her own exaggerating details in it; even so, no one takes it offensive because everybody knows that's just Shaylah. She is a comedian, very energetic and fun to be around, for her context is generally entertaining people. If her feelings are not diminished towards you, then Shaylah would remain that easygoing, sociable person.

Shaylah and my relationship was a long process. She had that big sister ego that didn't sit well with me once I got older. Due to me being ten years younger than Shaylah, she thought that she could continue to degrade me like I was beneath her, and we had to fight it out for me to earn my respect. I was 16 when I first stood up to my big sister. That day, I wasn't trying to hear that sarcastic shit, but Shaylah kept yapping in my ear until my temper exploded. We started verbally fighting, which immediately turned to a physical one. Then destructive weapons were used, blood was shed, and our beef went on for a little over a week before she recognized our abilities were comparable. Thereafter, our bond grew closer. Our peace is what gave me a good reason to look up to Shaylah seeing that we both were mature enough to reconcile all of our differences and accepted each other's individuality.

Overall, Shaylah was and still is dependable. She will find a way to help out loved ones, and friends who are in need, for her heartbeats generosity. She's definitely outspoken and would quickly put you in your place, she is very well respected by many, and loved by most.

Presently speaking, Shaylah no longer acts or reacts until she thinks it over. She now has wisdom and relevancy for what she does. Although Shaylah's past had brought positive and negative experiences, she looks at it as exposure to real life. With that being said, she only regrets being good to the wrong people, such as mommy and a few of her siblings. She still holds grudges against them and would take that bad blood to her death bed. Of course, this is not a virtuous decision, especially while she's trying to make some changes in her life. Still and all, shaking off the curse of evil is not easy, nor is it 100% guaranteed. However, she has an advantage because the devil only has her mind, but not her soul. With that being said, her transformation can be a little more effective.

There are only a few sisters that are working on some adjustments in their lives, so they can pursue their dreams; moreover, they live with love and contentment in order to get that feeling of completeness. It may have taken some longer than others, but any change is better than none. We all could be in a better place if we stopped letting our pride hinder us from learning or teaching the lost ones, and leading them in the right direction. Because that's hard to carry out in the Daevas family, we just don't worry about who is or isn't on the same page, and we also have to remember that some people read slower than others. Therefore, our only concern is to make it through the chapters as an individual. Does this chronological curse continue to get more sightless? Or, does the experience walk the others through the way of lightness?

# VINDICTIVE TWO ALL

They say, "Two is double trouble!" Lateesah had made this statement all so true when her behavior became so cruel. At first, she was humble, delicate, and intelligent, but somewhere down the line, LIFE happened, and caused a distraction to her character. She wasn't right ever since, and that's when the evil and bitterness began.

The utmost BETRAYAL is what caused Lateesah to grieve and isolate herself from everyone else. She felt the emptiness, and her heart was full of pain, which put her in a depression stage. However, no one knew how Lateesah really felt, or what she really thought because she was walking alone talking to herself. In all reality, it was killing her inside; she didn't know how to let it all out and just cry, just talk about it, just let someone in; it wasn't her fault that she had been deceived.

If Lateesah would have released her sorrows, she could've been relieved from some of her agony. But she didn't, she wouldn't, and just because she couldn't go in that direction; she transformed into this wicked, vindictive, and offensive person that caused a lot of tension within our family. Her low tolerance is what caused her enraging quick temper. Yet, she didn't care; vengeance was encouraging to her discouragements, and violence became Lateesah's active role. Anyone within her range could feel the coldness, especially if she disliked you, and sometimes she had no reason behind it. She had her picks--which is very limited of who she was comfortable with. If we ever felt unpleasant in her presence, it was time to go, for we knew she was the type that took things too far. It's hard to imagine that a good girl can go bad, but sometimes tragedies can change someone's disposition.

Just like it did Lateesah Daevas, who was born on January 15, 1972. She was born healthy but was unblessed living that rough life in Brooklyn, New York, which really had beaten her self-esteem down. During her 4th and 5th grade moments, Teesah used to get teased about her short hair. Depressingly, she started wearing this black faded out toboggan and refused to take it off when she got to school, which resulted in her constantly getting in trouble. By mommy not having a phone, and she never received the letters that was sent home by Teesah, the teacher eventually mailed one stating, "Lateesah is not following the school code, which is no hats allowed after entering the school, but she refuses every time. If she continues to disobey the rules, she will be suspended. Can you please handle this with Lateesah, so we don't have any more problems?"

Mommy threatened Lateesah with a severe punishment if it ever happened again. Therefore, Teesah had no choice but to go to school the next day without her toboggan. Then the kids started picking and laughing at her shaggy fade. "Bald headed scallywag, Teesah don't have no hair in the back!" The kids had sung repetitiously. Full of embarrassment, Teesah set there in silence, rubbing her watery eyes while intensely crying. The fact that she couldn't do anything about it had a huge influence on her humbleness and learning abilities.

Teesah had the brains, but she dropped out of school at the age of 15. The main reason was she accidently got pregnant, and just didn't bother to go back. In all honesty, I believe she was ashamed of her actions and was disappointed that she was no longer innocent. Her sexual behaviors started when she began hanging with a sexually active crowd. Then she found herself attracted and distracted by a tall, muscular, almond color guy name Jonathan. He was walkable, but they kept their relationship on the low for a while. Then a few months later, she missed her period.

After people found out they were a couple, the truth about Jonathan began to unravel. There were rumors about his sexuality, and plenty of kinky stories from his secret gay lovers. Teesah was nauseated and devastated that she was pregnant by him. Instead of her confronting Jonathan about something she knew he would deny, she just told him a boldface lie, "I had a miscarriage last night, and my mother was mad when she found out I was pregnant... She is sending me to live with my father, and I can't see you anymore. Please don't bother to come over, it would only make matters worse. (Dial tone)" Teesah was good at fabricating stories, but she had to quickly get the courage to really tell mommy the truth, and hopefully persuade mommy into sending her with daddy.

Being that Teesah was the good one, it took mommy by surprise, but to eliminate the embarrassment, she sent Teesah along with Shaylah to live with our father in the city a week later. That didn't last for long because anything that was dealing with daddy always went wrong. Ultimately, they moved in with our cousin Tamia when Teesah was just a couple of months from giving birth to her baby. Under those circumstances, Teesah had to quickly make some money, which is the reason her and Shaylah started hustling drugs, bringing in a little over a $1000 at the end of the week. It was nothing to brag about, but it was the quickest way to make some money to provide for her child.

Around that time, Teesah was lusting over a young tenderoni named Messiah, who was very popular on the block. Since men were one of Teesah's weaknesses, she quickly got caught up in her feelings, and that left her accessible to getting hurt again. Their relationship ended as quickly as it started, seeing that they had different standpoints on commitment. Afterwards, Teesah and her nine-month-old son Kian had moved back with us in order for her to get Messiah out of her system. When Teesah arrived, she became more of a homebody due to her not wanting Jonathan to know the truth about their baby. Therefrom, Kian would never meet or get to know his biological father.

Meanwhile, Teesah met a Jamaican guy name Pierre. He wasn't her ideal man, but he was very sweet and charming. His tongue always flowed with devoted words. "Ah yah happy? Do yah waan be...? Well, mi dat man dat can fulfill your dreams if yah leh mi," Pierre said in his Jamaican dialect, with his glowing smile and infatuating eyes; still, she shot him down. After she put on her sly smile, she impolitely responded in her deep obscure voice, "I don't want nobody right now... You're not my type anyway... and I don't trust men." Pierre walked away dismayed when Teesah rolled her eyes and had this disgusted look on her face, then she immediately slammed the door. She kept breaking Pierre's heart, but his feelings were still very strong for Teesah, and she remained his priority. Instead of him giving up, he came every day with a different approach to try and win her over.

At times, He gave her flowers, expensive jewelry; all types of fragrances, or exclusive art that he drew to symbolize her; sometimes he even gave her a lot of money, but Teesah still wasn't appeased. However, she did see the opportunity to use him and was comfortable with doing it. Pierre had a good heart, and because Teesah had no intentions of being with him, she constantly criticized and abused it over and over again. Until one night, Teesah got drunk; she was vulnerable and needed some comfort, and of course, Pierre was there with open arms. That was the night he finally got to bow chica wah- wah, and he enjoyed every minute of it.

The next morning when Teesah woke up naked, lying next to a face of terror, she felt ashamed. Then she demanded Pierre to keep everything a secret. A month later, there was no menstruation. BOOM! Teesah was pregnant again. Pierre knew she didn't have love for him, but he thought it was a little hope when she decided to keep the baby. Actually, it made matters worse, for Teesah became angry, and acted extremely crazy because she was having but really didn't want his baby. Still, Pierre stood firmly by her side regardless of Teesah's verbal and physical abuse. He and his family were happy that he was having his first born, then 36 weeks later, Pierre welcomed his son Ian into the world.

From there on, his family kept trying to convince Teesah to marry Pierre and move back to Jamaica with them at their expense. She knew he could give her the life she desired, but Teesah refused, knowing she had no type of feelings for Pierre, so making that commitment would've been for all the wrong reasons.

After that, Pierre hit Teesah with another unexpected question, "Ca mi tek Ian wit mi til he starts school? Mi waan him to experience mi Jamaican culture." Everything and everyone went awkwardly silent for a minute. As I'm standing there eyeballing Teesah, waiting on her to make a decision, Teesah looked puzzled and undecided, but as she slowly responded, "Yes!" I was in a state of shock. Apparently, the family was happy, for their patwah language had gotten a little stronger and was less understood when they communicated amongst each other with smiles and hugs.

Ian was a little over two when he left, and that was the last time we saw or heard anything from him. Teesah had us convinced that after Pierre and his family moved back to Jamaica, they just vanished. Their numbers were no longer working, their addresses were incorrect, and the only helpful information was their last names. The overall situation was a bit suspicious, and the fact that Teesah didn't try hard enough or use available resources to find her son was definitely questionable. Then Teesah had gotten that call 16 years later from Ian, the call everyone was waiting for. The call that answered our unanswered question, which was, "What really happened?" All along Teesah had been lying to us. The day Ian left, Teesah knew he wasn't coming back due to her signing over her rights to Pierre.

When I approached Teesah about the situation, I saw the degradation on her face as she walked the parent of shame. Before she could tell another lie, I told her, "Save your explanation for Ian; he is going to need that disclosure more than I do." I left the conversation like that. I was disappointed in Teesah; she abandoned her son, and missed all of his special moments just because she was embarrassed and despised his father. In my opinion, that is a failing mother, and Ian resented her for that.

In the midst of his resentment, and trying to find himself, Ian contentedly started defining his beauty as a woman. Considering the ingrained Jamaican cultural beliefs, he couldn't confide in his family about his transition. Eventually, he left home, hoping to reunite with Teesah, seek acceptance, and understanding from her as well. Instead of offering him a home, Teesah sent her regards, and rejected him again, just so she could avoid criticism and embarrassment.

Without Teesah saying the words, her reactions showed that she had no love or concern for him, and that there was no hope for their relationship to flourish. Correspondingly, Ian was broken, homeless, lonely and crying inside, wondering why it had to be him. How can a mother be like that towards her own flesh and blood? Yet, Teesah was sightless to the damage and hurt she had caused. Her haughty eyes saw herself as this proud flawless woman, and Ian as this imperfect boy that she couldn't accept regardless if he was her son. That would be her downfall as she continues to drown in her deadly sins of pride. Although Ian had lost his mother mentally, he was very well loved by his father until Pierre unexpectedly died from the Malaria disease, leaving Ian grieving without a chance to say goodbye. Those were tough times for him, and the state of him being himself was irrecoverable.

Still, Teesah's life continued with ease, and that was most certainly daddy's bad blood flowing through her veins. Moreover, she had another son and relationship that she was putting more of her energy into, which left no room for anyone or anything else. That made it hard to believe Teesah when she claimed her third pregnancy was once again another accident, but how dense could she have been to keep having the same back-to-back mishaps, especially with guys she hardly knew, and she considered them as one night stands.

In all honesty, I felt that those mistakes that Teesah claimed were just another lie to cover up her insecurities. For her mistakes didn't come from the kids that she gave birth to, but rather the wrong men she chose to have them with. With that being said, Teesah's third baby father named Vince was most certainly a hazard. He ruined her body, mind, and ego, causing her to dig herself into a deeper hole and reaching the state of opacity, which made it harder for her to see the abnormalities that literally were staring her in the face.

Considering she was thrown off guard by his dominant actions, Teesah quickly lost sight of herself. Her thoughts were no longer her thoughts; her voice gradually shifted to mute as he started controlling everything she said and did, but he presented himself in public eye like he was the good guy. I wasn't fooled, and I came to my own conclusion that he was a bundle of bad news. Characteristically, His eyes were transparent like a clear glass, and I saw right through his dark heart, lies, and deceits. But Teesah ignored my voice; she was listening to her heart, obsessed over the sex, and impressed by what she thought was maturity. Actually, that was Teesah's first real relationship she admitted to; in my opinion, her worst.

For one, my best friend Kassidy and I had clashed into Vince a few years before Teesah got involved with him. We were at a friend's house party when I got a little too wasted off that "liquid Cocaine" they called Cisco. Seeing that I was physically destructive to just about everybody, Kassidy along with a few others struggled to put me in a cold shower fully clothed. Thereafter, they carried me into the back bedroom, put me on a long t-shirt, and then left out after I fell into a deep sleep. Since majority of the people at the party was intoxicated, they were unaware that someone was dirty-mindedly thinking, and depravedly watching everything.

Kassidy wasn't at all sober, but she still had that over protective mindset and continued to check on me through and out the night. During one of those checkups, she caught Vince kissing and fondling my private parts. She instinctively picked up a heavy-duty iron, then went crazy on him. When he took off running, Kassidy started yanking me with force while repetitively yelling out with anger, "Veah! Veah! Wake up, this nigga was touching you, and he's getting away… get up and come on!" Of course, I was still seeing doubles as I stumbled a little bit, but everything got on balance as we ran out to catch him. Others already had his car surrounded; they were kicking dents in his doors, cracked his front windshield, threw a brick through the driver side window, then immediately pulled him out and beat him unconscious.

We panicked, and left like shots were fired. That was the first and last time I saw Vince, until he was knocking on my sister's door. My evil eyes widened, my adrenaline was rushing, and I was ready to demolish him all over again. "Teesah… Do you know this is the motherfucker I told you that was touching me while I was drunk awhile back? I can't believe you're fucking with this nigga! He's not boyfriend material." Teesah and Vince had a dumb look on their faces for a minute, but when she saw me on the phone, pacing back-n-forth, Teesah knew I wasn't playing any games and she convinced me to let it go for that day. I respected my sister's house, but I still gave Vince the third degree the whole time he was there. It was an uncomfortable situation, but even more upsetting that I had just found out who he was after Teesah got pregnant. Therefore, my information was irrelevant because he already had Teesah where he wanted her. It was just a matter of time that all of Vince dirty laundry would eventually come out.

To begin with, I heard through the grape vine that Vince was misusing any and everything he put his hands on. Of course, Teesah was in denial about the allegations. Then she unexpectedly found paraphernalia under the driver seat while helping him clean his car. When she confronted Vince, he said with a serious look on his face, "What? Where did you find that shit? Well, it's not mine... somebody tryna set me up! Give it to me, so I can throw it away." In my opinion, that was proof of an in the closet addict; yet, Teesah stayed with him. In her fuzzy mind, she thought as long as she didn't see him do it, or he didn't admit to it, then it wasn't true, but in her heart she knew... Still, she loved him too much to let go, whereas he didn't love her enough to stop.

Truthfully, I never thought he had strong feelings for Teesah, and when he couldn't feed his habits, it really showed. He would consistently beat her; he would take her money and demanded her to stay in the house until he returned, and Teesah did everything she was told. Out of concern, I used to unexpectedly popup on her and got very angry every time I saw different marks, knots, and black eyes. When I questioned her about it, she would make up a ridiculous lie. Don't let Vince be in her presence, for I barely understood what she was saying because she was scared to talk. She barely made any movements; she was terrified to walk. Her eyes hardly blinked due to her not wanting him to think that she was giving me a sign, which was considered disobedient, and that would be the cause for another beating after I left.

Since he knew he had the upper hand, he started to depreciate Teesah even more by breaking her bones. She had a broken leg from getting shoved down a flight of stairs. Her ribs were fractured from the consistent impact of his fist, and her arm was injured after he twisted it with full force. Even though Teesah never truly clarified what happened, her eyes of fear and face of despair told everything. I then knew that Teesah was vulnerable, trapped, and unconfident;

but she didn't know how to express it to anyone, not even me, and we were very close. Without Teesah's confession, I still felt that my older sister needed me by her side, so she could feel a little safe. That's when I started hanging around her a little more than usual.

After so many years of getting beat on, nothing seemed to be severe to Teesah, not even when she got assaulted with weapons. I would never forget the day I got that call from Teesah's neighbor, screaming from the top of her lungs, "Oh my God! Its Teesah... Her boyfriend beat her up pretty badly, and she was covered in blood! From the looks of it, he might've cut her. I really don't know why it happened, or how it started; all I know is that he asked her to go to the bathroom with him, and then minutes later, he... he left in a rush, and Teesah was unconscious on the floor! Teesah told me he has beaten her before, and that's why she gave me this number awhile back in case something happened to her. The ambulance is taking her to Carolina Medical Center! She was up when they left, so I think she's going to be ok... I'm so sorry." I responded in a calm tone, but deep down I was mad as hell, "Sorry... For what? It's not your fault, but thank you. I'm glad you were around when this happened, or it could've been worse than what it is... so I thank you again. (Dial tone)"

When I arrived at the hospital, Teesah was laying there sedated. She had 10 staples along the middle of her forehead, and 5 on top of her eyelid. Her earlobe was split, and her top and bottom lip were both busted. As tears fell down the side of her face, she softly said, "Veah, he kept punching me... Then I felt some stinging; after that, I blacked out." I had a shameful look on my face when I said, "You've been lying all these years for him? That's crazy! Do you ever try to fight back?" Her response came out as a stutter, "Yeees... Iiiii... do!" I knew it wasn't the truth, but I told her that is something she shouldn't be going through. She set there quietly with no response, while I set there thinking to myself.

When the police came to question her about what happened, she no longer looked like a victim in an abusive relationship as she laid there and told a boldface lie, "I got robbed by some unknown girls that raided my neighbor's house!" I couldn't believe the words that were coming out her mouth. In a way, I felt like it wasn't my place to snitch; also, I didn't like talking to cops, so I didn't open my mouth, but I didn't understand why Teesah disregarded everything he did, and let him get away with it. Why? Because she had a blown mind.

He ruined her mind by getting into her thoughts, and made her feel insecure about herself. She was full of doubt about if she could get another man, for he consistently told her that she couldn't. He convinced Teesah that he beat her out of love, which made him full of suspicion. However, it really was to cover up his own infidelities. Eventually it came out, when Teesah caught her neighbor that acted so concerned, running half naked out the back door of her house.

Coming straight out the hospital and walking into ultimate betrayal, Teesah was hurt physical and mentally. Although she felt ran down, it was hard for her to just walk away. In the process of her confronting the neighbor, Teesah got very hostile after she found out they were fucking for almost 2 years, and she was pregnant by Vince. Unhesitatingly, Teesah punched her directly in the stomach with great force; she ragingly tried to beat the baby out of her. Somehow the neighbor got the strength to push her out the doorway, and quickly slammed it in her face. Teesah repeatedly banged on the door, but the neighbor didn't bother to open it. She then rushed home in anger to only see that Vince had packed all his belongings and left.

That day, Teesah's mind was more than blown, it became condemned. She fell to her knees ashamed and overwhelmed. As she cried her broken heart out, she thought about all her family and friends she abandoned for him. All the voices she ignored, and all the signs she overlooked because she was blind by love. Moreover, distracted by his words. Teesah had a hard decision to make, which was to either hold on, or let it go. For a while, she chose to keep running after him. Vince was all she craved, all she talked and cried about. Clearly, she was destroyed by his actions, and it left her soul interminably corrupted. The worst part about it was she never got any closure from Vince. Brokenheartedly, she shut herself out of relationships for a while in hopes that she would correct her mind, body, and soul.

A point to remember: A man that beats on a woman is a coward. A woman that accepts the abuse is weak. No relationship should ever revolve around physical or mental distress because love isn't supposed to hurt; it consoles, and finds solutions to any problem that unfolds. At times, love can get confusing or frustrating, which can result in mixed emotions that generates opposition in the relationship. That's just a temporary situation, for true love will help compromise.

Teesah, on the other hand, didn't have that choice due to losing her individuality, and became a victim of Vince's identity. Till this day, she doesn't know what true love feels like. For one, Teesah is damaged goods; she built barriers that oppose love, which causes her ego rather than her heart to take control over her feelings. Also, she doesn't know how to differentiate whether her partner wants or truly loves her. Anybody can desire a person without having a strong affection for them. That's where some people get it confused, which causes them to have repetitive failed relationships just like Teesah.

It wasn't easy for Teesah to correct her image after being in an abusive relationship, seeing that it degraded her looks and caused a mild, traumatic, brain injury. Her natural beauty was hiding beneath those dark circles around her eyes, unappealing scars and burns that was noticeable on her nude body, which caused her to be reluctant and embarrassed during exposed situations. In all honesty, her ruined appearance didn't correspond with her youthful age. Then there were those constant blows she took to the head that resulted in her slow reactions, disorientations, and sudden blackouts. It was troubling seeing Teesah under those circumstances, but it was a trial that somewhat brought her to her senses.

A few years later, Teesah began dating again. She had chosen not to be in a monogamist relationship and made time for not just one but two guys, who names were Kent and Jason. They lived in different cities, but had the same troubling background. Teesah had no problem with it; she just was living in that moment and enjoying the different attributes including sexual activities they brought to the table. Neither guy was committed to Teesah, but they both had unprotected sex with her, which resulted in another unwanted pregnancy. Teesah was furious that she didn't know which guy was the father.

When she disclosed that information to them, Jason automatically denied being the father, which was disappointing to Teesah, knowing she was more interested in him. Also, she was hoping it would've brought them closer together; instead, it pushed him further away. On the other hand, Kent was accepting that he could've been the dad of Teesah's unborn child. Surprisingly, Kent was a child himself, which Teesah eventually found out that he was only 14 years old. By her being 21, she realized that she could be charged with statutory rape, despite him lying about his age, which had her hysterical and scared. Lucky for her, Kent's mother didn't take further actions due to other distractions in her life. However, Teesah's luck would eventually run out if she continued going down her cursed route.

Meanwhile, she had 9 months of waiting and hoping that Kent wasn't the father. When December came, Teesah was full of shame after seeing that her baby girl Brooklyn bears a striking resemblance to Kent; plus, the DNA test had proven that he was 99.9% the father. Despite the negative, the positive part of the story was that Teesah always wished for a daughter, so she treasured her highly. Moreover, she was anticipating on doing that mother and daughter stuff since she never experienced that with mommy.

A few years after Brooklyn was born, she became awfully sick. When Teesah rushed her into the emergency room, she left out with some devastating news. The doctor told her that Brooklyn had a genetic disorder that was affecting her hemoglobin, which came from abnormal genes that was produced by one or both parents, and it could be very fatal without long-term treatment. Teesah looked worried, especially when they started explaining the severity of the disease. Her eyes were drowning with tears as she softly began to cry because it was too much she was taking in at that time. The doctors tried to encourage her by disclosing that, "Your child can live a normal life as long as you make sure she gets the proper care." Then he gave her pamphlets and prescribed Brooklyn medication to treat the disease and prevent ongoing crisis.

Teesah was doubtful and scared to take care of Brooklyn on her own. Unhesitatingly, she went to Kent and his family for help. None of them was as helpful as Kent's Aunt Pat Dee. She cared for Brooklyn as if she was her own and didn't expect anything in return. I don't know if not being able to conceive played a huge role in it, but Pat Dee did get emotionally attached to Brooklyn very quickly. That was a little puzzling to Teesah, so she abstained from bringing Brooklyn to her on a daily basis.

Meanwhile, Teesah was going through a transitional stage, which wasn't easy developing into an adult when she barely had a normal childhood. In consequence, her partying spirit and youthful mentality interfered with her parenting. That's when Pat Dee stepped in and played the caregiver position, even when she felt Teesah was abusing her kindness for weakness. Yet, Pat Dee wasn't letting anything that petty hinder her from keeping Brooklyn, who she felt was her gift from God.

There were times Teesah let Brooklyn stay at Pat Dee's house for days and sometimes weeks without her thinking anything of it. Until she got that call from Child Protective Services stating, "Ms. Daevas, you were put under an investigation for negligence. Therefore, Brooklyn will be temporarily placed with Pat Dee." Teesah interrupted the social worker with her argumentative responses, and then she hung up on her. Thereafter, she called me instead of Pat Dee because Teesah assumed she was the reason that case was opened in the first place. Teesah was taken by surprise, disheartened, and hurt, thinking Pat Dee had her back; but from Teesah's standpoint, Pat Dee was looking more like a backstabber, who had been plotting on taking Brooklyn the day she went to her for help. For weeks, Teesah was sleepless. The taunting thought of losing Brooklyn was slowly killing her soul, her mood was filled with anger, and her heart pumped revenge considering she had been betrayed to the utmost once again.

After Teesah lost the case and her daughter, I saw a complete difference in her. She became cold-blooded, acted extremely irascible and aberrant due to her having so many different emotions bursting out in flames, which were mainly aimed towards Pat Dee. At first, I thought Pat Dee was being mature by disregarding Teesah's actions and showing a little sympathy, but the more I observed, the more the truth was unveiling about Pat Dee. Every time Teesah visited Brooklyn, it got tenser and awkward. Every year was 365 days of persuasive lies, and molding Brooklyn into a resentful child that would sabotage their mother and daughter bond. In my opinion, I felt like Pat Dee had a lot of built up animosity towards Teesah, and when she was able to seek vengeance, she knew that Brooklyn was a perfect weapon to destroy Teesah's soul.

That was another child Teesah had lost, but it wasn't from desertion that time around; she was wrongfully separated from her daughter over false accusations. The bad part about it was that it came from people she thought were loyal and understanding. Yet, those same people were inconsiderate to the pain and suffering it had caused her, seeing that they were only devoted to their own sensibilities. As a matter of fact, the betrayal went deeper than Pat Dee's accused obsession. For the whole truth, and nothing but the truth would eventually be revealed. That ammo had blown us away, and left Teesah at another one of her weakest points, which made it easier for her to just give up. Indeed, that was one of the traits she took from mommy; the easy route seemed like the only way out when times were too much to bear. Conversely, surviving through those hard times can strengthen and guide a person to a different and good place, especially if they have a backbone and some form of encouragement, which I was that sister who consoled Teesah through it all.

The different circumstances in Teesah's life created a woman that is: isolated, reticent but dishonest. She still has a small vicinity of people she socially interacts with; primarily because she's judgmental and close-minded about realness. In my opinion, I think that anybody seen as competition, or as a threat to Teesah made her not even try to form a friendship. She wouldn't even try to be cordial with them. Instead, she would be too busy trying to pinpoint their flaws without getting to know them first. Teesah doesn't care or think anything is wrong with being detached, for its less problems she has to worry about, which actually makes sense to some degree.

Teesah, is also perceived as the sneaky and dishonest type. She proceeds with caution to avoid being seen, or getting caught doing any grimy or deceiving acts. She kept us wondering what she was up to, which was always shocking when we eventually found out... That's even IF we found out! As long as Teesah is furtive, many secrets will follow her to the grave.

Then there are two totally different sides to Teesah. When she's sauced up, she becomes perseverant, wild, and feisty. For instance, when Teesah gets a little firewater in her system and feeling a bit addled, she gets extremely loud and outspoken. One of Teesah's favorite remarks are, "Don't nobody care about me, and I don't give a fuck about them! That's why I do people dirty!" Those were the times her deep dark secrets, and feelings were expressed. She let everything out that she was holding in, since it tormented her inner emotions. Teesah would get her point across regardless of how or what anybody thought about it.

When Teesah exceeds the limit, it provokes her strongest and atrocious personalities. She starts to communicate with less words, and more with actions because her nefarious spirit loves chaos. Her persistent aggression intentionally causes opposition putting everybody in the mood to fight. There are times she could be playful, but majority of the times she's serious, and Teesah definitely doesn't know how to turn that angry mode off once she gets started. Conversely, Teesah is conservative when she's sober. She upholds amiable conversations, but doesn't like to discuss or be reminded of her embarrassments the nights she was drunk. Sobriety made her a totally different person. She would be sweet, self-disciplined, peaceful, and timid, which is more original and suitable for her personality.

Teesah inherited mommy's demure behavior and personality traits, but her substantial thirst quenching and steaming panties weren't modest at all. Even though Teesah loved the goodness in mommy, she still didn't want to continue to follow in her footsteps by being: lost, misused, and having a bunch of misled and abandoned kids. So, she gradually tried to find herself, camouflaged her emotions, and got her tubes tied, assuming more accidents were waiting to happen.

Somehow, Teesah made another wrong turn, and she didn't want anybody else attempting to get in her way. She began to lash out on any and everybody, feeling there wasn't a trustworthy soul in her presence. Her actions gave us the impression that she was screwed up mentally, for she spoke with pure ignorance. Teesah's choice of words were very offensive. In some instances, it felt like she had spoken negative situations into existence. Everything about Teesah became belligerent.

I knew Teesah's issues were getting intense when she started immaturely fighting the kids. She had her selection; and females, especially younger girls, were her preference. In fact, she disliked them in her presence. For this reason, she had many fights with all of us and majority of our kids. The hilarious thing about it was that our kids was shooting the one like they were her age or something. However, we all knew that Teesah would retaliate using her favorite weapon, which resulted in slicing or cutting whoever she felt was an enemy.

One of her victims was Lannah. That night would always be remembered just like it was yesterday. I saw vengeance in Teesah's evil eyes as she kept wildly swinging that big, sharp knife. Her reaction towards Lannah was an action of hate; a built-up emotion that she wanted to serve to someone else. Unfortunately, Lannah was just an innocent victim taking their place. As blood was gushing out the side of Lannah's neck, everybody in the house became distressed. Our little sisters were screaming because they were horrified by the unpleasant scene. Miyah was pacing back-n-forth while intensely talking to the cops on the phone. I was attending to Lannah, hoping I could stop her from losing a lot of blood by covering her gash up with a rag, and applying pressure to it. I was extremely upset and said a lot of insulting words to Teesah. Nevertheless, Teesah just stood there with blood on her hands and shirt, and emotionlessly gazed at me in silence.

When the cops came, she suddenly put on her phony cry; she repetitiously said with her head down as the cop escorted her to the car, "I'm so sorry... it was all a mistake." Her fake apology wasn't accepted, especially when she almost took her sister's life. The doctor explained, "If the cut was an inch over, it would've hit the carotid artery, and killed her almost instantly, seeing that the incision was very deep..." He then stared Lannah deeply in her eyes and said, "You are very lucky! Please refrain from troubling situations." Lannah was angry and bitter, but she was grateful at the same time. With all those mixed emotions, all she could do was cry and scream out, "My sister... How can my sister do this to me? Oh, my God, I'm going to get that BITCH!" Her tears were uncontrollably falling down her face as she held her head high and said, "Watch what I do to her! Watch!"

What I saw in Lannah's eyes was exactly what I had seen in Teesah's after that unexpected incident. I knew vengeance eventually would be taken another step further amongst the two, and Lannah definitely wasn't ashamed to express it. She had: dreamed, thought, and spoke nothing but the acts of revenge.

Lannah was even more provoked when Teesah got out on bond, which left mommy's house full of chaos on a daily basis. No one could comfortably sleep as we all were trying to prevent Lannah and Teesah from badly hurting or killing one another. Respectively, Teesah moved out and into her own place to alleviate the frustration she had caused. Everyone gradually started feeling some form of peace, but Teesah's lonely soul was wanting to continue the war.

I felt that Teesah didn't have any regrets or guilt about what she did; even though she expressed it, her heart was feeling otherwise. In fact, her evil behavior started adding more fuel to the flame. That time it wasn't with Lannah, it was our other sister Lavinniah, who was only 12 years old at the time. Yet, age didn't matter to Teesah because bullying kids made her feel she had more power.

I recall that rude awakening day; I was about six months pregnant. While Lavinniah was rubbing my stomach, Teesah kept teasing her for no apparent reason. Out of respect, Lavinniah tried to ignore her, but Teesah cruel words were too difficult to tune out, so they began bickering back and forth.

Teesah then took it to another level by jumping and pointing her finger in Lavinniah's face. Still, Lavinniah refused to fight her older sister. Until Teesah hit her with a two piece, then Lavinniah surprisingly started laying those bombs on her, which sent Teesah across the room, and into the wall. I didn't interfere at all, I just smiled and watched, for Teesah was getting exactly what she deserved.

Teesah missed practically every blow she attempted, and the shame had pushed her into the kitchen to grab a knife. That's when I stepped in from behind and put my arms around Teesah's neck with pressure. She was slowly breathing and grasping for air, but I wasn't letting her go until I knew she had calmed down. Thereafter, Lavinniah had stormed out angry, but was relieved that she finally stood up to the bully. After the fight, they stopped talking, but had a few arguments from time to time. However, they didn't clash as much because Lavinniah was also the type that isolated herself.

Teesah's multiple personalities would confront each sister with a different approach. For instance, when she had issues with Caylah, she destroyed all her valuable belongings. We all felt it was out of envy because who would do such a thing over an argument? Before Teesah and I had our first altercations, I discussed with her the qualifications and requirements to get my gun permit. Secretly, she took out an assault charge on me, knowing it would prevent me from getting one. Then, Teesah's rivalry with Shaylah had her so enraged that she busted a large lamp over Shaylah's head. Soon after, she charged at her with a knife, but mommy stood in between that tragedy. When she and Mirah fought, Teesah spit out the cursed words of: hate, death, and many other promising threats of pain and suffering that she was going to bring into her life. Sadly, the passion of hate that rolled off her tongue came from a place of sincerity. Lastly, it was her conflicts with Miyah. Teesah wanted to ruin any type of relationship or bond that Miyah had with her men, especially the ones who were valuable. Teesah would give them the scoop on how many men Miyah had, what labels she gave them, and how she really felt about him. Teesah didn't care about the complications, or anybody's feelings she hurt; she was too busy trying to rebuild her insecurities. Need to say, it's very troubling to see that "an eye for an eye" is misused amongst loved ones.

Over the years, Teesah has consistently done some immoral shit. So, the few ass kicking's she'd gotten was definitely something she deserved; nothing more, nothing less, at least for the most part of it.

There's really no justification for what she has done, but because of everything she has been through, I felt most of it was forgivable. Even though she has changed dramatically, I still remember the easy to get along with, placid, and happy person Teesah used to be. That's why her violent, depressing, and shifty attitude gets misconstrued as an undiagnosed bipolar disorder, which pushes many loved ones away. We always told Teesah, "You're grumpy for nothing, and you will grow old and be very lonely!" In a way, I feel she doesn't want it to be like that, but she's so bound up in her emotions, and unaware of the separation it's causing. On the other hand, she just may be comfortable living secluded since she doesn't have to worry about her family being subjective towards the choices she makes.

Most certainly Teesah makes a lot of childish decisions, but she's not the only one in this family that does. Still, we continue to criticize her weaknesses. Yes, I do feel like Teesah can be more of a responsible parent. Also, a devoted sister; but most of all, a compassionate aunt, especially to her nieces whom she bullies, teases, and holds a grudge against, for her own personal reasons. Yet, she wonders why they disrespects her.

As an aunt, she is supposed to put them in their place when they get out of line. Instead, she disrespects them like they are enemies on the streets, degrades them while complimenting the other nieces, and most of the time gets physically aggressive as if they were adults. For example, Lilah, who is Mirah's daughter had come to visit me the same weekend Teesah did. It had been years since Teesah had seen or communicated with her or Mirah, so I thought maturity would disregard any past issues. It didn't, and Teesah's grill face from hell, and her mumbled words had told it all when Lilah walked through my door. Lilah immediately felt the bad vibes and looked very uncomfortable, but I told her that she didn't have to worry about anything while she was in my house and to make herself feel at home.

The whole time Teesah was pacing back and forth while she was drinking excessively. Her eyes were popping out her head as she was saying her indirect remarks to whomever she was talking on the phone with. We ignored her by laughing and reminiscing about the good times, which inflamed Teesah's energy causing her devilish ways to come out.

She offensively stated, "Veah! You need to take me home… You know I don't like that BITCH!" I looked at Lilah and shook my head as I responded, "That BITCH is your niece!" In her deep angry voice, she replied, "That BITCH ain't my niece, I hate her and her mother! They fake grimy asses can die for all I care!" Everything that came out her mouth after that was, "BITCH" this, and "BITCH" that. I kept holding Teesah back, seeing that she was very hostile. At that point, I knew it was time to take her home before the situation escalated.

It's ridiculous that Teesah couldn't put her differences aside and act like an aunt for once, or at least show a little cordiality. Yet, Teesah makes them feel bound up where they can't enjoy themselves. Due to this, majority of our kids' dread being around her. Instead of Teesah acknowledging that she is at fault, she would continue to blame it on what that child had done in the past. "Hmm! Now who really is the adult here?" Disturbingly, Teesah's childish behavior answered that question, which also shattered her and Lilah's relationship into thousands of pieces.

Comparatively, Teesah treated Leah the same way as well, but as a mother, mistreating my daughter was off limits while I was around. There were times I felt the tension when Leah was in Teesah's presence. I saw the dislike in Teesah's eyes while she walked past Leah to hug my other daughter, Aaliyah. She would then go on bragging about how pretty and talented Aaliyah was. It immediately rubbed me the wrong way when I heard Leah speak, and Teesah ignored her like she was invisible. I asked Teesah, "What do you have against my daughter? If you recognized one, then you should notice all. Leah has not done nothing to you… So, what's the problem?" Teesah's response was, "Leah grown as hell. You know how I feel about kids like that!" Everyone who has been around Leah knows she's a comedian, and loves to joke around. None of my other sisters took it seriously, or had any problems out of Leah. If they did, they handled it like an adult. But Teesah always regulated things all so wrong. She mentally tormented the kids, and they will always remember how she did them through and out their youthful years.

Especially Abrianna since her and Teesah had intensely gotten physical. I was having a fish fry that day, and everything was A-OK. Until I laid down to get some rest. I remember my body was going through a lot of stress from the contractions pains I was feeling, which later resulted in a miscarriage. In the matter of minutes, the right direction had taken a left turn over Abrianna talking sly at the mouth. Teesah wasn't having it and swung off on Abrianna, then they started fist fighting.

As I'm painfully running to break it up, I see Abrianna going blow for blow, and standing toe to toe with Teesah. I couldn't believe my eyes… A pre-teen fighting her aunt, it couldn't have been me. Although they both were in the wrong, Teesah should've felt more ashamed. That is not the way any adult supposed to chastise a child. In the legal world, its child abuse; whereas, in our world, it's just life.

The environment had gotten even more hostile when Caylah came. Instead of her taking disciplinary actions, she provoked Abrianna to fight Teesah again. I understood why Caylah was extremely mad about how Teesah handled the overall situation, but influencing more drama was not the wisest solution, especially knowing what I was going through at the time. All she was worried about was what I didn't do to protect her daughter, which I thought was very inconsiderate. What did she actually want me to do… beat up Teesah? Hell no! Not even. I wasn't taking neither side considering they both were at fault. I got irritated hearing all that sly talking out the mouth, so I put everybody out my house in order to miscarry in peace.

Two wrongs didn't make it right, but nobody was apologetic, and everyone thought their defense was justifiable. In my opinion, Abrianna was very disrespectful, but because Teesah made an immature move, she got a childish response. Unfortunately, that's how it goes on in this generation. If there's no form of connection, then a child won't give obeisance. Teesah lost a lot of respect from most of her nieces, but she can gain it back if she: grows up, let go of grudges, and learn how to love again. I know the loss of her daughter made her bitter, but she must reconsider the route she's taken, before her life crumble into small pieces. Such tragedy, would make it even harder to put back together.

Another thing Teesah needs to learn is how to control her lying, which is a trait she clearly got from daddy. Even though most of her stories exaggerate the truth, we still listen, but be laughing on the inside. It's hilarious when she tries to be comparable, or more superior to us. Prevaricating for no apparent reason exposes her insecurities, gives people false impressions, and to some degree it makes her look like she has a few screws loose because of the crazy things she says. For example, most of us had kids at a younger age. So, she lied about the age she got pregnant in order to differentiate herself. Of course, she looked like an idiot when we saw that the birth certificate stated otherwise. Yet, she continued to argue with us about it. What really made her look stupid was that it was only a year difference, which still was a teenage pregnancy.

Another ridiculous lie, is Teesah swears up and down that she doesn't have bowel movements. It's even more embarrassing when she says that amongst our friends who assumes she's "full of shit," literally. In fact, going over a certain period of time without any bowel movements leaves your body polluted with toxins, which could be a serious medical issue that can result in death. What is Teesah really trying to prove here? I don't get it! Does she want to be that different? Or, does she want to get that type of attention? Well, she got it, but in a negative way since people do look at her totally different from us.

Lying is a habit that is hard to break, especially if it's not broken at a young age. Unlikely, that deceitful part of Teesah is not going to change. However, I'm the one who continues to call her bluff, which she hates because I humiliate her character. In all honesty, I do it hoping that it will put a stop to all her unnecessary lying.

Teesah's distinctive character always throws curveballs. I mean, you never really know what she is up to. Well, one day, I saw her walking with some tomboyish females, which honestly took me by surprise. Despite the oddness of it, I did not judge or question her about her sexuality; actually, it never crossed my mind that Teesah was into girls. Then week after week, I kept seeing the same females at Teesah's house. Out of curiosity, I asked her, "Are you getting a sudden taste of the rainbow?" Of course, Teesah denied any lesbian tenancies. If not anything else, that's one thing I could see is right through the eyes of a liar, but that time, I also saw elation. Me being the person I am, I went behind Teesah's back to get all the facts, and her mysterious sexual preference had come to light. Although the relationship was cut short over Teesah refusing to accept her girlfriend's bad habits, she still kept her gay spirit, which complimented her smiles.

After Teesah got over her guilt and shame, her character came walking out the closet, revealing her sexual orientation, and the reason behind her drastic change. She explained that she was tired of: getting hurt, feeling disappointed, and not being fulfilled by men who took her for granted, along with degrading her ego. Apparently, she thought the only way to revive herself was to pursue a female, for a woman knows what another woman wants. I listened and somewhat understood where she was coming from. "To each its own," I stated. I gave her much love, a big hug, and a little joke, "Make sure you don't eat the wrong fish!" We both laughed it off, but Teesah knew I was going to have jokes for life.

A few months after, Teesah had introduced me to her new girlfriend, and the bad vibes were lingering all in the air. She put me in remembrance of Vince but just in a feminine/masculine type of way. I perceived she wasn't good news as I read her body language, and scandalous was written all over her face. As I held a conversation with the lady, I realized I knew her from somewhere… Damn! It was Felicia that be at the trap houses. I don't usually bite my tongue, but because I kept my mouth shut, I also found out that she was friends and/or relatives with all of our enemies. That was definitely a no go; once again, I told Teesah she would be drowning in hot water if she continued that relationship, but it just leaked in one ear and dripped out the other.

Their relationship got off track after they started getting violent with one another. At first, I thought Teesah liked to get abused, seeing that she provoked the fights most of the times; but we were looking from the outside in and didn't know that behind closed doors her girlfriend was: controlling, disrespecting, cheating, and using Teesah as a punching bag, hoping that would pump fear into her heart. Yet, it accumulated a lot of hostility, which Teesah felt the need to retaliate every time one of us came around, knowing we wouldn't let anybody harm her. It caused a lot of chaos, and a high level of animosity between us sisters and Felicia, but Teesah didn't want to end the relationship, even when she knew it was headed towards a disaster.

Another situation that made the relationship even more unbalanced was Felicia struggles and denial of addiction; Teesah wasn't convinced, especially after experiencing the same thing in her past relationships. Still and all, she was ashamed and didn't understand why she continued to attract the same screw ups. Why? Because it's really a reflection of herself. Therefore, her relationships and her life can't be fulfilled until she improves herself inside out, but Teesah wasn't ready for that at all. Instead, she put Felicia's right shoe on her left foot, inverting the humiliation and degradation on her. She tampered with her ego and violated her every chance she got.

Teesah was unbothered about being the victimizer, for it made her feel powerful and undefeated. What I couldn't make sense of was how Teesah continued to act like the relationship was flourishing. Did she think that vengeance was her bait to bring them closer together? Or was she just blind to the fact that everything about her girlfriend was wrong from the start? The bottom line was Teesah just wanted to feel loved; she was happy to be wanted by somebody… anybody that accepted her for who she was. For those reasons, she disregarded their flaws, accepted the violence, and loved hard, hoping that was enough to keep them together.

Teesah is very open and devoted in her relationships; she also gives it many opportunities to enhance into something special. What she failed to realize is some people are not ready to change their current lifestyle just to balance out hers. In fact, they are only a distraction that keeps prolonging Teesah from being at her best. For some people's motive was to cause her distress, which exposes her vulnerability. That makes her careless and unaware of the direction she is going, or where her relationship is headed.

With that being said, Teesah and Felicia's relationship wasn't based upon love; she just was infatuated with destroying our family, and I was her main target. I always wondered how the cops knew my every move, and how much dope I was pushing. What was even stranger is that I was under an investigation for shit nobody knew I was involved in; on top of that, stickup kids suddenly knew where I lived. It was very questionable considering only a few family members knew confidential information.

They say keep your enemies close, and that was one victorious thing Felicia did. She entrapped Teesah, knowing the weakest link always spill the beans. On the other hand, Felicia's slipup was her negative talk about us on the streets, but in the drug life, I had to be prepared for everything, especially haters. Envy can be a threat if you let it, whereas confidence can be a protector forever. Luckily, that green-eyed monster wasn't effective at all.

Teesah eventually had to choose between her relationship and family, which wasn't an easy decision. Due to this, she prolonged their love-hate relationship. It seemed as if she couldn't find the strength to walk away, even when her heart was telling her so. Then when Felicia moved in with her new girlfriend, Teesah had no choice but to accept that it was definitely over, and let it go. Teesah thought that a lesbian relationship was going to be different from her straight ones, but there were many similarities. Consequently, she experienced the worst of both worlds because both sexes: lied, cheated, and hurt her the same way.

Teesah currently is facing a lot of life issues. She lost all her kids either through confinement, renunciation, abduction, or wrongful separation that ruined their mother and child relationship. Although it's never too late, it would be hard to build a close bond, repair their hearts, and amend those mistakes that caused their broken family. It might not ever be a transition, but until it does, they all will continue to be troubled, resentful, destructive, and deceiving.

Does Teesah take the entire blame? Or, does she point the finger at the ones who are also partially responsible? In my opinion, they all should be held accountable for their displeasing parts in those tragic situations. However, Teesah is the only one who's getting criticized, and being discredited for what she didn't do rather than the wrongdoings that prevented her from doing it. Of course, Teesah's guilt is eating her up inside, but what about everybody else?

When Teesah is all alone, she's drowning in tears as she cries out to God for some leniency. Her outraging acts are her way of asking us for help; yet, we ignore, misjudge, and neglect her for something she might not have any control over. Although Teesah never admitted it, I think she feels that she failed as a parent, but in her heart, she wanted to be the best mother that she never had. That is something she must live with and learn how to forgive herself in order to move on.

My heart goes out to Teesah, and one day her pain will become pleasure. She just has to take heed to existence. Remember that-- her life, mine, or yours can change in a matter of seconds, for tomorrow is not promised. So, every minute and hour of the day, we should pray about what's going on at that moment rather than dwelling on what happened in the past. Pushing forward is aiming for the future, and whatever is left behind wasn't meant to move ahead. Even though it's hard, it's good to have a clear mind, a mended heart, and a sense of direction to assist along the way. Don't rush things... just take it day-by-day.

We all need a little push and pull sometimes, but that is okay, nobody is perfect. I always would have my hands out to assist either one of my sisters, but they must get the courage to ask first. This is where the situation becomes a bit challenging because the Daevas's are full of pride, and Teesah indeed is one of them. She pretends to be self-reliant but really wants someone she can rely on, especially when she is going through rough times. Instead, she keeps it to herself, and the rage builds as her problems start to multiply, which motivates her heavy drinking. Then the water overflows our ears with frustration and insults. It's a crazy way of asking for help, but that's Teesah.

Teesah has her moments, but who doesn't. Everybody wants to feel and be independent, and I can't take that away from her. She works hard, and has her own home. She doesn't look for any handouts from a man or woman, and her bills come before fun, which some of us can't identify with. Teesah's small differences can sometimes be a good thing. It doesn't matter if she's unpredictable and acts confused; we need to let it go. We all could be in a better place, if we stay mindful of only what we do. Teesah, will eventually find her path to understanding, even though "easy" is her way, and "hard" is Teesah's life, she still can withstand. Living is reality, but surviving is an opportunity, so no one should let it pass them by.

Troubles, everybody will face them, but each individual will handle it differently. It will all be based on the severity of the predicament that might hinder or benefit them. The Daevas's are strong individuals, though they have some weaknesses. We all have been through a great deal of shit, and it's not over yet. It seems like the older we get... the more problems we have. I don't know if we're going in reverse, or if it's just our curse. I hope that eventually we can and will defeat the darkness.

# TRAGETHREE

Tragedies is what we try to avoid, but we all must face them some point in our lives. Of course, we can have some form of control over what happens, but being in the midst of the devil's circle doesn't prevent it… It provokes disasters. In our family that circle is our battlefield where all the evil spirits are released and causes misery to even the most innocent. There's no boundaries, especially when it comes to my sister Lamirah. She refuses to cleanse her soul, and her temper can't grasp onto peace. Evil mirrors her personality and character; she is very hateful, could care less about anyone else, and she loves making enemies. Her biggest obstacle was being oblivious to the fact that she was her biggest enemy. She was battling her own insecurities, but she always tried to hold everyone else responsible. It would be hard for her to right her wrongs since it's not easy to get through that diabolical mind of hers. Consequently, this would be the root of her unhealthy struggles, for the agony she caused people would eventually come back to haunt her.

Lamirah Daevas was born on April 8, 1975. She was the witch without a broom. Her condemned personalities had offset her good qualities, but she still had a little common sense, which was applied to allure people in. If Mirah feels like she's not completely in control, backstabbing becomes her major role. Mirah, also, is full of greed, which has imprisoned her life; her avarice actions have locked in her selfish ways. Due to her not wanting to overcome her mental state, she would continue to have never-ending madness, blindness, and astonishment of her heart. Therefore, she would always wrestle with vengeance, realizing it's hard for her to forgive or forget.

Mirah has a few dissimilarities. For one, she was a little slow-witted because mommy drank excessively the entire pregnancy with her. Resultantly, she was born with FASD's (Fetal alcohol spectrum disorders), which causes birth defects that involves both behavioral and developmental problems. Mommy didn't find this out until Mirah got evaluated at school and was recommended for remedial education. Hereinafter, the everlasting emotions started.

I describe Mirah as the preserving, but the hateful one. To put it differently, hateful meaning she is: shallow, spiteful, unforgiving, and can be very offensive. In addition, she has a fraudulent demeanor that reveals self-pride outgrowing any mental or physical abnormalities. She doesn't want to see herself as different in an underachieving way, so she portrays the intelligent role, which is bogus. God may have given her a gift or two, but having brains wasn't one of them.

There were four sisters close in ages, and neither one was hesitant to show who had the most authority. For this reason, Mirah and Miyah always clashed because they both wanted to be in full control. Mirah was a year older, and she wasn't trying to let that happened, so she knew eventually Miyah had to be taught a lesson. That day occurred when Mirah watched Miyah fall down a flight of stairs. Then she viciously stared at her from the top while Miyah fearfully cried in pain. Mirah wasn't thinking about going to help her, but after mommy heard Miyah screaming and quickly came to her rescue, all of a sudden, Mirah put on her dramatic act as though she was a concerned sister. As mommy carried Miyah out the door headed to the hospital, Mirah had a smug look like, "I'm nobody to fuck with!" Resultantly, Miyah's arm was broken, and she wanted revenge. She knew that her mind wasn't playing tricks on her when she felt a slight push before she went tumbling down those steps. Their animosity and conflicts amongst one another continued until they got older and separated.

Thereafter, Mirah started seeking more competitors and brought confrontation to whoever she felt was challenging. Her bright smile looked very innocent, but behind that smile was nothing but evil. She used her kindness to find a person's weakness, and then used it against them to cause hurt. Mirah strictly goes for the heart, which damaged the soul due to her doing things just that cold. In fact, most of us sisters got caught up in her destructive corruptions, especially Shaylah, Teesah, and I. We felt as though she treated us like her worst enemies, seeing that her heartless actions were not part of family values. At first, we thought that maybe she didn't understand the consequences behind her bad deeds, but that wasn't the case. For her uncontrolled anger, had fueled her viperous urge that poisoned our relationship, and caused it to be dysfunctional.

The maladjustment really didn't matter to Mirah. She wanted to separate herself from our family anyway; not only for the ongoing misconduct, but because she also thought that she was better than us. Particularly after she found a stable man, who spoiled her. He drove the newest cars, and moved her in a big house, which made her feel like she was bright as day, and we were dark as night.

Soon after, Mirah fell in love with her new lifestyle and family. She was so caught up in her new life that she started feeling shamed about her old one, and in our eyes, she was fading away. Her negative intensity became distant after she became more focused on putting her positive energy into her boyfriend Joseph and his family. I remember the time we were having a cookout at the park; we were reminiscing, dancing, drinking and enjoying our time together. Then Mirah and Joseph pulled up, but not to come and join us. Instead, they went to his family event, which surprisingly was across from ours. I wasn't bothered by that, but it was upsetting seeing our kids anxious to see Mirah. They screamed out her name; yet, Mirah gave them an evil eye and didn't care to speak back. Our kids looked puzzled and dejected seeing their aunt carried on like they were invisible.

I thought that was pretty childish of Mirah to take her anger out on our kids over us not getting along. Observing that had made my temper explode, and I couldn't hold my tongue. "Fuck you BITCH! Whatever is going on between us, it doesn't have anything to do with these kids. You are an ignorant ass BITCH! I don't give a fuck who you're trying to portray yourself as. We all know what's moving through

our contaminated bloodline. Don't act like you're better than us…
take away that so called good man of yours, and you are back to a bum
ass BITCH! Fuck you, your life, and whoever is a part of it BITCH!"
I shouted out while violently moving my hands. Then Mirah tried
to respond in her slow, illiterate, three letter word exchange, but my
boisterous voice overpowered hers, and I couldn't hear nor cared about
what she said. I wasn't trying to take it that far, especially in public
eye, knowing it gave people something to talk about, but that day was
totally exceptional.

Years had passed, and we didn't see Mirah or her kids. In fact,
things were better without her around because we felt that her presence
brought nothing but misery. Although her kids didn't have anything
to do with our situation, there was no chance of bonding with them;
Mirah's stubbornness wouldn't allow it. Yet, we were the ones who
were perceived as the betrayers, bad siblings, and the uncaring aunts.
That was the reason her kids were disrespectful to us. They used every
form of profanity to express their thoughts and feelings due to having
doubts about our love and loyalty to them.

I had to put my foot in the kids' shoes in order to see their point of
view. I thought back to the time Mirah and I were close, and her kids
were used to me being around giving them all that auntie love. Then all
of a sudden, I disappeared with no sort of communication. It was like
I abandoned them for no apparent reason, which made them feel like I
didn't care anymore. Moreover, being easily persuaded by any negative
things that was said about me. But, what they didn't know was how
much we wanted to be a part of their lives but had no control over it.

I would say that Mirah has characteristics from both mommy
and daddy. Deep inside Mirah has a good heart, and sometimes it
shows until things don't go her way. Then she would have a hissy fit,
and convert into this deranged witch. From here, daddy's personality
comes out, seeing they both carry the same traits of greed and betrayal.
Unfortunately, these characteristics only bring temporary happiness,
and lead to a lifetime of regrets. A point to remember: What might have
a chance for forgiveness doesn't mean it will be forgotten? Whatever
Mirah did can't be undone, but the doors are still open to make things

right. Nevertheless, Mirah's mentality has her blind from reality. I take into consideration that our family history led to some of Mirah's current problems. Regardless, she knows the difference between good and evil; for this reason, I can't help to think that she is just the devil in disguise and doesn't care about who she double crosses.

Mirah wasn't book smart, but she was smart enough to get what she wanted, which was the best for her and her kids since she always was fascinated over but never had the finer things. That's when the path of belonging was followed; she knew her purpose, but was unclear of what type of relationship was in her best interest.

Mirah's first boyfriend experience was with a hardcore gangster who had all the power, strength, and security like a father she never had, but getting involved with a gangster became too dangerous for her, and she couldn't handle it. Afterwards, she began pursuing a nerd who was intelligent, but boring because he was lacking a social life. Although Mirah got over on him, being a weirdo was a sign of weakness, which made the relationship a fragile situation. Then, unexpectedly, Mirah became attracted to drug dealers; she was loving that the money was fast and prosperous, but she realized it was hard for him to stay committed or free from imprisonment, which was something she wasn't financially prepared for. Considering this, she gave the laid-back kind of guy a chance. He was suppressive, cared less about what was going on in the streets, submissive, and unattractive; but by her being mindful that he was family oriented, stabled, and a token to the good life, she knew that man was worth a try.

Because Mirah was in between relationships, her unexpected pregnancy was a glitch, but she led Joseph to believe he was the father, even when she knew he wasn't. Joseph was ecstatic about having his first child that he didn't realize the dishonesty hiding behind Mirah's smile. Therefore, he asked her hand in marriage to complete their family, which was Mirah's plot to begin with.

Through in out the nine months, the biological father name Sleeze was desperately trying to stay in touch, but Mirah kept ignoring, despising, and rejecting his rights as a father. When she realized Sleeze wasn't giving up, she moved to the suburbs to keep her dirty laundry from coming clean. Since Miyah despised Mirah, her telling Sleeze any and all information he wanted to know was definitely entertaining to her. She wanted to cause trouble, and she did just that when Sleeze paid Mirah surprised visits with demands of seeing his child.

Mirah's lies began to unveil, and baby Lilah's features were revealing as Joseph looked into Sleeze's eyes and saw the truth. Joseph heart was telling him one thing, but he disregarded those feelings and continued to accept Lilah as if she was his. The beef had elevated over the years as Sleeze became bitter because Mirah continued to deny him privileges of being a part of Lilah's life. Mirah, was really being spiteful and wanted Sleeze to feel the pain that she felt when he hurt her. Being in control of his feelings and reactions, to her, was getting even. The selfish part of the story was that she secretly accepted child support from Sleeze but never gave him the acknowledgment for trying to be a good father regardless of what stood before him. It took some time, but once Lilah was older, she met and bonded with her biological father. However, Joseph was all she knew and loved… and nothing or no one could've came in between that. Out of respect, accepting, seeing, or even acknowledging Sleeze as her real father was never revealed to Joseph.

Mirah couldn't be trusted, but Joseph never really questioned her loyalty and vice versa. Every relationship goes through problems, but I must admit that Mirah and Joseph always found a solution, for their love was unconditional and strong. Due to the fact, no one or nothing could separate them.

Not even when Mirah became a hard drinker and was very controlling. During this time, she started physically and mentally abusing Joseph, but he stood there and took it like a man. In my very own words, I thought, "he was a fool for love" because Mirah's juiced up moments were the: pissy smelling, laying in your throw-up, and don't remember shit after she sobers up type of moments. She had hangovers, unwanted thoughts of her cheating, but didn't own up or even think she was at fault just because she didn't get caught type of moments. Joseph hung in there and continued to love hard.

Making wrong decisions are a part of life. Making it right is a part of transitioning, which would be complicated for Mirah, knowing she's always in denial, or feels that everything she does is justifiable. To explain, every time Mirah has any controversies with one of us, she'd attack indirectly. Day one: The argument and anger development. Day two: The sell down the river call. Day Three: Law enforcement or some type of government official knocking at your door, following up on some tips they received from an anonymous caller. Day four: We're arguing some more. Day five: Retaliation time. This is always Mirah's ammo, for she doesn't have the courage to battle it out directly. Frankly, she doesn't want us to see it coming and we don't.

It was very inconvenient for all of us, especially for Teesah. Mirah's devilish actions were achieved when Teesah had mistakenly lost her child based upon lies. Teesah was so busy putting all the blame on Pat Dee that she had no idea the informant was appearing in court on her behalf, sympathizing, and encouraging her to stay strong. From the looks of it, Mirah was supporting Teesah 100% until a copy of her slandering statement was disclosed in black and white. The day Teesah found out that information was the day I saw the biggest disappointment on her face, and a huge knot in her throat because she was choking on those hurtful emotions. Although Mirah never owned up to those accusations, the proof was signed, sealed and delivered, which Teesah hated and resented her for that.

How could a sister be so cruel but act innocent, helpful, and compassionate at the same time? It's a sister that doesn't have a cause; someone who is not content in her life until she cause depression in someone else's. Teesah, couldn't believe or never found out why Mirah took it that far. From that day on, Teesah lost all respect, and that sisterly connection couldn't get where it once was.

For the sake of Teesah not having the strength to seek vengeance, she cursed Mirah with nothing but pain, suffering, and an unhealthy life until the day she dies. She could've been speaking out of anger and hurt, but I believe Mirah is going to get every bit of what she deserves. Of course, Teesah felt it wasn't happening quick enough, but as she patiently waits, Mirah's troubling days will soon come.

Teesah wasn't the only one who held grudges against Mirah. Shaylah had a lot of animosity towards her too. The sisters' rivalries developed into adult envy. It got so bad that Mirah tried to get Shaylah's kids taking away as well. Fortunately, she wasn't successful, but Mirah showed no remorse as her and Shaylah argued over what happened. However, Mirah got offended when Shaylah started slandering her name for all the other scandalous shit she'd done, that she thought no one knew about. They were inches away from fighting, but Joseph intervened and tried to calm them down. Eventually, it worked, and they both went their separate ways.

Afterwards, Shaylah took a vacation to Virginia just to get away for a few days. Then out of the blue, her house got robbed and set on fire. This may be a fallacy, but sometimes it could be true that criminals always return to the crime scene. What a coincidence that Mirah was the first one at the scene, asking and answering questions, claiming to be a concerned sister.

Shaylah's trip was cut short to not only go home, but to report to her probation officer. Someone had informed him that she went out of the state, which was a violation. It was never proven that Mirah had anything to do with neither allegations, but Shaylah has her intuition that it was her. At first, Shaylah was thinking that it could've been a random robbery. Until she got home and saw that everything valuable was still there, except some chump change that was stashed in a jewelry box full of untouched gold. Something just wasn't adding up. Seeing that had her thinking… What type of burglar is slow enough to vandalize the house and basically took nothing, then tried to burn it down? That wasn't an act of a burglar; it was an act from someone who was bitter and jealous. For those reasons, Shaylah felt that her intuition was relevant; besides, we all knew what Mirah was capable of. The questions remain, "WHY is there so much anger and spitefulness towards your own sisters? Could this all just be a misunderstanding? Or, is envy and hate in full control of evil?" We don't have a sufficient reason why one sister can turn on the others like that.

As I will continue to state, I love all my sisters, but sometimes it's better to love them from a distance. Mirah, was definitely one of them because you always have to wonder what devious shit she's up to next. Giving a helping hand wasn't her problem, but using it as bait was the wrong solution. In other words, it wasn't coming from the heart, but who would know it's a deceitful act when you are blind by the person who is offering.

A point to remember: If you are helping someone in need, it shouldn't be brought up if there is a confrontation, or mentioned just because you need a favor in return. It should never be talked amongst others to belittle them. These are all the things Mirah does. She wants recognition when it's not due. In her eyes, some of us wouldn't be where we're at today if it wasn't for her, which definitely isn't true. We all put up a fight to try and get to a good point in our lives. Of course, there were times we needed a helping hand, but wherever we stand today is accomplished through our personal choices in life.

Mirah stands alone in this family, seeing she is very immature in a lot of ways. For instance, the fact that her daughter looks exactly like Sleeze became nauseating to her stomach, and displeasing to her eyes. We all recognized it, including Lilah herself. She looked and felt disheartened, realizing Mirah despised her for something she could not change. Still, Lilah desired love, she gave much of it, but very seldom received it back.

There were times Mirah would call Lilah's name with so much anger in her voice for no apparent reason. When she disciplined her, most of the times, it was for simple things, which always ended in a brutal beating. Mirah treated Lilah unfair, but she praised her other kids. She always compared them as the beauties and the beast; the wild and the tamed, the list goes on. The point I'm trying to make is that they all are her kids, and none of them are saints. Therefore, you can't pinpoint one child for their wrongdoings without incriminating the others. Such actions, can ruin and lower their self-esteem just like it did Lilah's. Her smiles were hidden behind her frowns. She was fearful of being unworthy and unlovable, which sometimes led to humiliation and depression. Lilah felt that all the blame is owed to Mirah because she didn't love her unconditionally like a mother should have. Through and out her childhood years, she had many wishful thoughts and hopes. One of her desires was that one day her and Mirah could have a close bond; that day, has not come yet. In my eyes, she failed as a parent. Just like our grandmothers, father, mother, and now some of our generations is facing the same results. Why? How can we make it different?

Mirah didn't make things any better since she didn't set a good example amongst the kids, and that caused them to have a love-hate relationship. Not only did Lilah feel like the Cinderella in the family, but Mirah never sided with Lilah over the other siblings when they had altercations or anything for that matter. It became too much for Lilah as she got older, so she left home in her early teens. It wasn't easy, and she struggled briefly until she met a man that filled her with joy, love, and gave her hope in life; however, she still felt that emptiness without her parents. Although neither one could get back the years they lost, it's never too late to make things right.

Mirah's corrupt character is by far the strangest, and her evil words speaks nothing but danger. So, we have no choice but to treat her like an enemy, seeing that it's nothing friendly about Mirah unless you stay on her good side. Until then, she would spread all your personal information you confided in her with. She'd tried to keep shit stirred up between the sisters, which created more division amongst our sisterhood. Most of all, she would try to get in your head if you're weak enough to let her. Mirah feeds off evil due to her not knowing how to relieve or express her inner emotions, that's why she reacts with so much hostility, but some of her actions are far from forgivable.

Speaking about forgiveness was something Mirah couldn't award mommy with because she felt that she didn't give a 100% as a parent. I, on the other hand, understood Mirah to some degree, but giving a 100% as a parent doesn't mean you must be perfect. It means giving all you can to be the best parent you can be, which I think mommy put forth some effort.

Being that Mirah couldn't make sense of it, she resented mommy and felt their bond was irreparable. Even though the distance between them traveled so far away, mommy still apperceived the hate from her. I think back to all of those obnoxious comments that were made about mommy. Mirah actually thought she was justifying the feelings she had towards her, but the outburst of words had made her sound more like she was being very selfish. "How could mommy do this when she knew I was going through that? I needed her here with me, but all she was worried about was… Blah! Blah! Blah!" I… I… I, it was only about her. As I passively listened, I was thinking, "Hey Mirah, look in the mirror… You forgot you was a grown ass woman, and living a good life with your man. Why in the hell you expect mommy to alter her decisions if you're not on your dying bed?" I just didn't get it. Mirah acted like she didn't care or even mentioned mommy was sickly. She was diagnosed with diabetes, a heart disease, and high blood pressure, which resulted in mommy needing special care and attention. Therefore, her focus was on herself to better her health. Furthermore, mommy shouldn't be the blame for none of our future decisions or outcomes.

Still, Mirah continued to bicker and curse mommy out. "You were never a mother BITCH! When I needed you, what did you do? Nothing! … I hate you! (Dial tone)" She didn't give mommy a chance to reply. As mommy slowly walked in the room, her eyes began to water, and her voice was cracking with emotions as she told us she wanted to be alone. Her cries weren't as silent as she intended it to be, for her heart was painfully hurting. I do admit that we all at some point in time put pressure on mommy, which played a major role in her depression.

It's sad to say that there were other people who helped us more than mommy. Of course, we would have preferred for our mother to hold our hands through it all, but we weren't that blessed. Yes, there are moments we revert to our past; it hurts growing up practically alone and lost. It took some of us awhile to accept it, but Mirah felt that if mommy wasn't really there as a mother when she was younger that she owes her that much to be there while she's older. If that is the case, then she owes all of us considering we all missed out. Just because a person has the title as a parent doesn't mean they are fit for the job. To put it differently, mommy was our mother, but she didn't have the proficiencies as a parent. Yes, it could've been a little better, but it wasn't. It's still no need to dwell on it because life goes on.

Part of Mirah's life was revolved around condemning both mommy and daddy for bringing her into this disorganized family. However, daddy wasn't around to feel the hatred and witness the anger she has carried over the years. The little good Mirah does have only last a minute, whereas her bad could last for a lifetime. Everyone should have a point where they want to draw that line, and change their ways, but not Mirah, seeing that her past continues to distract her present, which causes negative energy and will eventually lead to her loneliness.

Although majority of our relationships are destroyed with Mirah, there is still hope for some type of amending. If she can grow up and stop being so selfish, I'm all for it. Of course, she did me wrong, but I'm willing to forgive her and move on. I can't speak for all of us, knowing there are still some wounded hearts that have not yet been healed, or lives that are still ruined over her evilness. Sometimes I wonder has it ever crossed Mirah's mind to own up to her faults, ask for forgiveness, and lay all of her cards on the table, showing us that she's remorseful and caring. Then maybe that could lead to a new beginning for her. She should start somewhere, or she will get nowhere. Mirah is a hard person to understand, but that could change if she lived for today. This transition could result in her becoming a better mother, sister, and daughter. Maturity comes with forgiveness; forgiveness comes with understanding; understanding comes with communications, and that can create a stronger bond between all of us.

Because too much time had passed in silence between mommy and Mirah, I thought I could be a peacemaker, and at least get them to have a decent conversation. One day, Mirah and I were talking, and I thought that was the perfect time to give her mommy's number. "Mommy be asking about you. She wants to talk to you, and hope that y'all can reconcile y'all differences. When you get the time, call her… She'll be expecting it," I deceitfully said. I saw the peace in Mirah's eyes and heard the happiness in her voice. The only problem was mommy never said anything like that, she actually told me, "I don't think I'm ready to talk to her. I don't have anything against her, but she hurt me so bad… I'll pray about it, and leave it in God's hands." Mommy began to cry, then she said in a soft and sad voice, "I didn't do anything wrong. I tried to be the best mother I could be... Whatever I didn't do, I asked all of y'all for forgiveness... but all Mirah keeps doing is resenting me! Why? Why does she deny me as a mother and continues to talk down on me?" Then she got quiet and waited on me to respond, but my only explanation was, "I don't know... That's something you'll have to ask her when y'all talk. Then maybe you'll have some closure and feel more at peace."

Mommy began to pray; afterwards, I told her a boldface lie. "I gave Mirah your number, and she'll be calling you in a few!" I laughed loudly as mommy said in a worried tone, "Oh Lord!" When I got off the phone with her, as I stated earlier, I then talked to Mirah. My lies had paid off because they eventually started communicating and working on rebuilding their mother and daughter relationship.

Presently, Mirah still is battling with her past and hasn't matured in many areas. She can't differentiate things that doesn't really matter verses things that does, which is her family. Therefore, we continue to have an on and off relationship, for the reason that immaturity can become very boring and detrimental, and I don't have time for nonsense. I think Mirah can change, but her problems are adjusting to humbleness, and purifying her body from all of her corruptions. This can simply be done by letting go of her vengeful ways, which could make a big difference in her behavior, and help her see a different outlook on life.

It's troubling being a part of the Daevas's family as we are living in a negative world, surrounded by different types of negative forces, and speak all sorts of negative words. It's hard to control ourselves since we are accustomed to negativity. It seems like we can't grasp and hold onto the positive things, seeing that our lives are always challenging. It's also difficult to handle certain situation like bonding as a whole considering there is someone or something holding each of us back from it. We are easily misguided, and we never see the good in things; yet, we think we are superior. Some of us want to improve, whereas others are just stuck in their troublesome ways. Then they want someone to give them a pat on the back as though their lack of progression is okay. I try to encourage and support my sisters, which is crucial at times. Occasionally, it gives me a peace of mind, knowing I was there for them. It's tough for me to stay away from my sisters, given that our solidarity empowers us; but at the end of the day, I must build my own trust, follow my own path, and separate myself from the hostility in order to change.

I strive hard to respect, love, and treat all my sisters equally, but sometimes I question myself, "Do they feel the same? Because I always find myself trying to rekindle things." It's always so much bickering amongst us like there is no form of dignity, sisterly love, or trust. We were brought up with closeness, but our anger towards each other leaves that gap between us causing bitterness that is poisonous to our minds, bodies, and souls. "How did we let it get this far?" I don't know, and no one seems to care about the problem we have beforehand; hopefully, one day, we can hold hands and communicate as a civilized family.

# EYES FOUR-EVER LUSTFUL

On Aug. 6, 1976, Lamiyah became the fourth addition to the family. She was a beauty indeed with her: slim waist, caramel skin tone, and her very curly hair. She is serene, adventurous, but she can be devious as well. To explain, she is easygoing and friendly until someone crosses that line, which causes her to be shady in a sneaky type of way. Her hidden motives are not revealed until she causes misery upon another. She misleads consciously, and smiles with no remorse about her spiteful doings. Miyah's darkest days' refuses light since she is content with her actions and individuality. Relatively, Lamiyah, at times, appeared to be depressed, defiant, and disconcerted. For her life became troubled so soon. Her rebellious acts had caused a major distraction, but she was too naïve to realize it, which generated many mistakes, and a lot of regrets that left her emotionless. Even though her eyes looked full of joy, and her body had much energy, her heart still was defined by depravity.

It all started when Grandma Oma's cursed words came taunting Miyah the day she turned six. On this one specific night, Miyah was tossing, turning, and shivering while she balled up in her thin cover, trying to keep the cold draft out. Shortly after, she began hearing a hissing sound beneath her bed. As she slowly uncovered her head, she looked to see if Shaylah was still asleep at the bottom of the bed. In the midst, she got confronted by a huge fiery snake. Miyah was speechless and frightened as she stared into its evil eyes. Then he venomously said, "Your soul belongs to me. You will be all mine soon!" Its tongue was so close to Miyah's face that she could feel the heat, and that's when she panicked. She started screaming and racing for the door, but mommy was already reaching to turn on the lights. Miyah couldn't really get her words out, "A… Sn… Snake!" She cried out while pointing towards her bed, but it was nothing there. Only Shaylah laying there sound asleep. In a nonchalant tone, mommy said, "Go back to bed, you were just having a bad dream." But to Miyah, it felt so real and evil.

When Miyah nervously laid back down, she tightly shut her eyes, hoping it was just a bad dream. Then she heard that vicious voice again, "You actually thought she was going to believe you? Hahahaha! I'll be back." When Miyah opened her eyes, she saw a silhouette of a flying snake in the windowsill, slowly fading away. Miyah yelled, "Mommy, its right here… Look! Look!" Once again, there was nothing! Nothing but rain spattering against the window. Miyah was looking like a boldface liar, acting out for some attention, and that made mommy very angry. "Miyah, if I come in this room one more time, Imma beat you for lying. Now take your butt to sleep before you wake up your sisters!" That night Miyah convinced herself by repetitiously mumbling with her fingers in her ears, "It's not real… it's just a dream." Until she fell asleep.

The word "beat you" kept playing back in Miyah's mind through every vision and encounter with the devil. Therefore, she kept quiet about it and was remotely scared, knowing mommy wouldn't believe her preposterous stories. That was the worst part about Miyah's fight against evil because she was battling it alone. Moreover, it was happening to her that whole year. On the sixth day, a different form of evil always came to visit her in the middle of the night. Miyah knew when something out of the ordinary was going to happen; she always got that same negative energy before every experience.

Miyah's last night of being six years old wasn't quite torturing as the beginning of the year. This one particular night she saw a vision of her three older sisters shining brightly in front of the bed. They were overjoyed and hyper while they waved their hands telling her, "Come on Miyah… Don't be afraid… You're one of us… Come on, you can get everything you want, but you have to hurry up before mommy comes!" As soon as Miyah started to approach them, mommy hollered out,

"Y'all better be quiet in there, it's too late for y'all to be up. If I come in there it's going to get rough. Go to sleep, I mean it!"

Everything instantly got quiet and pitch dark, which had Miyah puzzled. What really was mind-boggling was that she never saw or heard her sisters get back in bed; yet, they were all out like a light. Miyah laid there with her eyes screwed to the ceiling, thinking that her vision had to be real if mommy heard some talking because not one word came out of her mouth. Miyah was happy the next morning; it was her birthday, but the overall taunting experiences affected her mentally, which caused her to react in a disorganized way. By Miyah being very young, she didn't understand that her weakness made it easier for the devil to interfere with her life, and he would continue until he had her soul.

Miyah's life was getting tougher by the day. She was drained from getting physically and emotionally abused from the students. They always called her bummy, poor, pulled her hair, and threw things at her during class sessions, which prevented her from learning. By the time she hit her freshman year, she dropped out of school.

One of Miyah's most embarrassing moments was the day she was walking home from school, and a group of kids that wasn't far behind started bullying her. She walked quietly with her head down in fear that she would get jumped. Instead, they continued to verbally abuse her until she passed by a group of guys chilling in front of the corner store. Then the bullies formed a circle around her and got fully aggressive. They were taking turns pushing and punching her, and they were pulling on her shirt until it got completely stretch out of place. When Miyah lost her balance, she fell and scraped her knees. Eventually, the guys that were standing in front of the store felt a little sorry, and stopped them from tormenting her.

Afterwards, one of the guys were nice enough to walk Miyah home safely. Then she explained to mommy the humiliating story; but because mommy believed in turning the other cheek, she told Miyah that she made the right decision and to continue doing that. Miyah tried her best to dip and dodge her confrontations, but the trouble had continued to follow. That's why she started skipping school and wandering the streets. In the midst of that, she bumped into that same guy that walked her home that day she got jumped, and they started hanging out. His name was Bisheem, one of the coolest and well known guys around the hood. He took Miyah under his wings and showed her the ropes for surviving the streets.

Since mommy was preoccupied with her own battles, she was unaware of Miyah's actions. Due to the lack of supervision, Miyah had unprotected sex with him and got pregnant at the age of 14. Consequently, her education walked out the door along with her ego. She didn't have the time, or the opportunity to go back to school due to the circumstances that stood before her.

Having a baby didn't actually slow Miyah down, for her courageous experience brought out her adventurous side. She was willing to undertake any negative opportunity, which made her vulnerable towards violence, alcohol, and street drugs. She always stayed under the influence, which altered her decision making. Not counting, there were many times she didn't know if she was coming or going; however, Miyah didn't care because she was living in the moment. She was a typical troubled teenager who didn't want to face her darkest past, and tried to put it all behind her by stimulating her brain with enjoyment, or by causing chaos to alleviate her anger. What Miyah failed to realize is that her past would continue to hurt her present until she reflects, accepts, and then let it go.

That was hard for Miyah; she held in so much hurt for years, and daddy contributed to a lot of it. She always thought that daddy was supposed to be the source and foundation for our family, but he wasn't. For Christmas's there was no trees, no presents, and his absence was always a disappointment. For Birthdays, there was no acknowledgment, no parties, and still no gifts. There were Easters, Valentine's Day, and Thanksgivings, but daddy wasn't there to show that he was grateful for his family because he secretly started a new one.

What was heartbreaking was the day Miyah and our three older sisters were walking with mommy to the welfare office; coincidently, they bumped into daddy, his other wife and two kids. They were looking like a picture-perfect family. That was something Miyah always dreamed of, but from that day, she knew it would never happen. The most disturbing part of that moment was daddy had a remorseless stare as he passed them like they were nobody's. Unsettlingly, mommy walked by in silence and disappointment. They all were angry that day, but Miyah was more concerned for mommy as she saw the pain in her teary eyes, and the trembling in her lips as she lifelessly walked like she no longer had a purpose.

Although this wasn't the first time daddy betrayed mommy, she was totally destroyed by the affair. Her weaken cries, and her aching heart had caused her to have many sleepless nights. Yet, daddy didn't come to console, explain or apologize. In fact, he didn't show his face for months. For many reasons, Miyah couldn't understand or forgive daddy for what he did to them, which had a negative impact on her life.

Another hindrance towards Miyah's future was that she painfully kept the tormenting secret about mommy's best friend molesting her just about every time he came over to visit, for he always found a reason to stay the night. By mommy being gullible and oblivious to her so-called friends, she was always welcoming, which exposed her kids to danger. Truthfully, mommy couldn't stay sober enough to notice that the grown man was sneaking into her kids' room late at night. Under those circumstances, Miyah's innocence was destroyed.

Miyah continues to have flashbacks about her sexual trauma. Although violent behavior didn't play a role, it still was performed with a threat of harm that made her feel daunted and helpless. As she trembled in fear, he tried to calm her down with his sweet but short fairytales. Those stories were meaningless at that time because a princess should be treated with respect, dress elegantly, have confidence, and have endless happiness; but Miyah felt she didn't have any of that. At that point in time, she didn't care. She was just hoping one of her sisters' would wake up and run for help, but that was only wishful thinking.

Before he left out, he would say in a stern tone, "This is me and your thing, so you can't tell no one. If you do, nobody won't believe it's true, and then you would be in a lot of trouble... Bye princess." Then he kissed her on the forehead. Miyah never gave any feedback; she would just lie there in shock, feeling sticky, and disgusted. She always wondered why she was a victim to such pain. "I'm only ten… How come my life is so difficult and deviating? What if I do tell mommy? Would she think that I had another bad dream and threaten to beat me again? This is too much to hold in, but I guess I really don't have a choice… Do I?" Miyah always had deep thoughts flowing through her mind, but she never revealed her darkest nights to anybody.

Meanwhile, mommy overlooked Miyah's reactions every time her best friend came around. When he held his muscular arms out to hug Miyah, she gave him a vicious look, resisted, then ran in her room and cried. When dinner time came, she barely ate and did less talking than she normally would. Miyah became quick tempered, and she started isolating herself from everybody, but mommy never took into consideration that something was seriously wrong with her child. How could she not have an intuition about anything when the signs were in her face? Did she just ignore it? Or, did she not even notice the difference in Miyah? Out of all people, mommy should've known. She experienced sexual abuse when she was younger and knew the effects it had on her behavior. However, mommy didn't express sympathy towards her dispirited child. The crime wasn't enforced, and Miyah continued being a victim until the man disappeared years later.

Because Miyah suffered physical and emotional pain from men at a young age, she despised them as she grew older. It also caused her to be promiscuous as well. Her lustful eyes and distrust in men had made it difficult for her to stay in a monogamous relationship. Therefore, she ran through men like running backs run through their offensive line. She was ecstatic when she scored touchdowns. It was a game and it amused Miyah, knowing it was her turn to play with men's emotions, and she used them for things of value. If they had nothing to offer, then she had nothing to give, and that was her means of life.

Miyah's baby father Bisheem gets a little credit for her transitional state as well. He unveiled her beauty with a complete makeover, which inspired her confidence. He materialistically spoiled Miyah making her full of greed. He stimulated her mind and body with unconditional love, and that made her feel essential. Miyah's outcast moments were officially over. Her popularity had taken place, and life seemed less complicated, even after she had her first born. For Miyah felt that her baby girl gave her a path to acclaim.

With the intentions of survival, Miyah found her gift in writing. Her expressive literary work explained her pain and peace in ways that affected people emotionally. She attended open mic, poetry clubs, bars, or any crowded place that she could entertain and potentially make money at. Her stage name was "Epic" because she always had a prodigious story to tell. Miyah would elegantly stand amongst her audience looking glamorous. She would have on her diamond rings and chains, and high waist slim fitted jeans with her long wet-n-wavy weave as she artistically stimulated the crowd with her lyricism. Epic had loyal fans and admirers that made her feel like she was on top of the world, and she never wanted to fall.

For that reason, Miyah had a mindset that men, money and popularity were the main elements of life prosperity. With that mentality, she convinced herself that she would not be a fool for love since it's the biggest distraction. She was determined not to be a reflection of mommy. She promised herself that she wouldn't go down that same path of letting one man cause her life to be a complete failure. So, Miyah loved cautiously, and never fell into deep. Even if Miyah was headed down the wrong route, she would rather enjoy life than spend her days with unwanted tribulations.

Miyah aspect of living life to the fullest was a little more spontaneous than the average, for she didn't have any boundaries. Her magnetic behavior wasn't just meant to entice her men, but her sisters' men too. Her sex cravings were licentious, which led to betrayal, for Miyah was no longer devoted to her heart because the use of her body was much more of an appeasement. That's what made her undiscerned about the impact it had on other people.

I often wondered was Miyah remorseful about the hurt she had caused, especially to some of us sisters, seeing she was emotionless and used, "I'm sorry" to a bare minimum. In fact, her withheld animosity was the justification for her seditiousness. In our family, an eye for an eye was exceptional. We all did it. However, our levels of cruelty differentiated our characters. Some of us have standards and limits of depravity, but Miyah wasn't one of them.

In retrospect, I was calmly walking through the parking lot headed to the corner store when I saw Miyah making out with our sister's boyfriend in the back seat of his car. He was tenderly fondling her, while she was slowly grinding on top of him. They were too preoccupied with each other that they didn't notice me standing there. I was disgusted, shocked, and in disbelief of their disloyalty. Instead of me intervening, I awkwardly walked away.

Although I was curious of how and why she would do that to her sister, I stayed silent about the overall situation to try and keep the peace. Still, I was leery about Miyah's unchaste capabilities. Open-mindedly, I listened and observed the anger Miyah had towards most of the sisters. Indeed, evil has full control over this family, for there are things that we all have done and can't ever take back. As sisters, we should want to resolve our family issues considering it could be a misunderstanding. Yet, our lack of communication will prevent us from that, and cause us to be confined within our feelings. In other words, holding grudges is a sign of weakness as it forces revenge, taints our souls, and continues to infect our words and actions. With that being said, the only cure for bitterness is to bear no malice. I know it's easier said than done, but seeing how we grew so far apart when we were once close should make it well worth it.

To return to the subject of Miyah, she had other troubling factors that influenced her character as well. Although Miyah wasn't the oldest, she still lacked control, seeing that she was following the older siblings who didn't have the correct guidance themselves. Therefore, she felt her obligations as a role model was limited to us younger ones. For life in the fast lane was her stepping-stone, and she did not care if we followed in her footsteps. Her best advice to us was, "You gotta do what you gotta to do in order to get what you want because you damn sure won't be getting it from home." At that point in time, it made sense, knowing we were an unfortunate family. Looking back, I wish I could've got more words of encouragement.

Secondly, Miyah was one of the sisters that insidiously tried to cause confusing and jealousy amongst some of us. She would manipulate situations, and expose negativity that caused us to quarrel. Her intentions were to never try to reunite or reconcile our differences. She wanted us to have that disconnection simply because she had no sense of togetherness. Nebulously, it intrigued her by causing adversity between us. For the most part, I was too young to realize her devious actions, but as I had gotten older, it became clear to me. My judgment has changed about Miyah, and I no longer see her beauty that I once admired, in view of her attraction being altered by her evil deceptions.

I don't resent Miyah; no one is perfect, and to some degree, we all have done some deceitful things to one another. Different circumstances have come in between me and Miyah's relationship, and we are not as close as we used to be. I feel on a serious note, I can continue to go to her for advice, but can't confide in her on certain situations because she doesn't know how to keep secrets at all, which is my pet peeve. If I tell something confidential, then it supposed to be between her and me. Instead, the news spread like a plague. The crazy part is that 95% of the story is untrue. She would add her lies into it, which would portray the situation worse than what it really was. Miyah doesn't see anything wrong with gossiping or lying. In fact, she's so used to doing it, that she can't control herself.

Despite Miyah's indiscretions, she was genuine also, especially towards her kids. Her good parenting was something she learned through her own experiences. She was a single mother, but still managed to focus on receiving, leading, and believing that she had the capabilities of being a responsible mother and supporter. She also ameliorated on being their friend regardless of what obstacles stood before them. The love and stability Miyah shared with her kids had showed them the importance of family, which made their bonds unbreakable.

Through and out Miyah's parenting, she had to work a little harder, and push her three youngest boys with a little more aggression in hopes that they would grow into independent men. She didn't have help from their fathers by reason of them being either unknown or unsupportive. During Miyah's wild life phase, she was sexually involved with multiple guys, which left her with a few unwanted pregnancies; yet, Miyah wasn't worried. She felt if the guys were out of sight, they were out of mind, and she never had a problem moving on. Her lustful eyes only had visions of who and what could satisfy her needs, and that was a characteristic that definitely correlates with our daddy's.

She also inherited her unsympathetic attitude like him as well. For example, a few weeks after Miyah had her son Jabari, her body was back to normal, and she was ready to get her groove on. Precipitately, she invited her new friend Rico over. Before the night ended, they were between the sheets. Let me rewind back, Miyah decided to come clean with Ruben, who was a previous one night stand that Jabari was his son. Ruben was eager to see him, so he asked Miyah if he could come to visit. Miyah agreed, but then she unconsciously invited Rico over. While they were making passionate love ignoring everything else, Ruben was sternly knocking on the door. Because I was unaware of what was going on, I opened it. In an irritated tone, Ruben asked, "Is Miyah here?" Before I responded, he was trotting his big muscular ass towards the back room. When he opened the door, he observed his son peacefully laying in his crib wide awake while Miyah was mounted butt naked on top of Rico. Ruben instantly got enraged, he shoved Miyah on the floor, and then began power punching Rico until he was knocked unconscious. Meantime, Miyah stood there speechless, calm, and apathetic like seeing Rico unresponsive and covered in blood wasn't something serious. I, on the other hand, was hollering out, "Stop it please before you kill him!" I don't know if reality hit Ruben after hearing those words, but he stopped, ran, and then speedily drove away.

Moments later, Rico gained conscious, then started mumbling words that we couldn't understand. Afterwards, he slowly got out of the bed and was painfully holding his stomach while he put his clothes on. Miyah was sitting in the living room too embarrassed to say or do anything for Rico. Out of consideration, I gave him a rag to clean himself up, and asked, "Do you need me to call the ambulance?" Even though both of his eyes were damn near shut closed, his forehead was knotted up, and some of his teeth were gone, he still didn't want help. So, we did not get the police involved. As

Rico limped out the door, Miyah unsympathetically said, "Talk to you later. Get home safe." Rico responded lightly, "OK! I'll call you when I get home." He had such a disappointing look on his face, and that day his self-esteem had descended; for those reasons, he and Miyah stopped seeing each other.

Miyah had a few inappropriate rumors floating around town about her that she wasn't proud of, nor was she not ashamed. If all or any of the hearsay was true, then it was her life and learning experiences. As a matter of fact, the gossip didn't even tarnish her reputation, for the men continued to be magnets. They spoiled her, adored her, and didn't mind going to war for her in hopes that they could eventually build a passionate relationship. Of course, Miyah led men on, but her appetite was too big, so settling for one was like settling for less.

Sex was Miyah's encouragement, but it also became her rude awakening when she came across the wrong guy who was spreading HIV through and out the triad. News travels quickly in the south, and Miyah found out before they had gotten serious. If that wasn't the case, she would've been another one of his victims. Just the thought of being exposed to a deadly disease had scared the shit out of Miyah, which changed her perspective towards sleeping around with different men. She pumped her brakes a little, and got her mind right. Then, she married a French guy name Raphael. At first, I thought she finally found the love of her life, but after observing, I noticed that they didn't have chemistry as newlyweds. Although that was a little suspicious, I was happy for her new beginning.

Miyah's family was complete; she had a father for her kids, a nice home, and her security was locked in. However, marriage is not a walk in the park. Therefore, Miyah and Raphael would face a few hurdles that led to their divorce. For the most part, Miyah continued to live her life to the fullest, but at some point in time, everyone should want a change. Unequivocally, the beauty of life comes with the opportunity to take a step in a positive direction.

Miyah feels unsuccessful and wished she had a better chance at life while she was younger, but her obstacles defeated her, and she stopped believing in herself. Despite her failures, she finally realizes that it's more to it in life than just sex, alcohol, and fun. Although she will always love and continue to enjoy herself, her mature age has kicked in. Now she must embrace womanhood to the fullest to be a positive role model for her children and grandchildren.

Miyah is a very fun person to be around, for we all had enjoyable experiences with her at one point in time. She got us drunk, showed us her way of partying, and exposed us to potential valuable men. Miyah was always straight up when it came to situations like that because she loved having a blast, and those are the copacetic things about her.

One of the disturbing perceptions I had about Miyah was that she maturely handled things when it was prosperous to her, but acted childish when it came to small problems amongst the sisters that could've been easily resolved. I guess some of us just lost track of family values. Adding to that, years had passed in silence. Neither one wanted to talk, nor no one was apologetic as our pride remained concrete, which played a huge role in the separation amongst our sisterhood.

Sometimes I wonder what is wrong with this picture. At the same time, how can separation grow further apart each day and each year? For every season is a different season that rotates in a cycle, which goes up and down from sister to sister. Consequently, it causes us to react on a level that puts people in harm's way. We don't care who is around, or who we hurt considering we put our feelings first. Surely, that's immature, but we have no form of control. Primarily because it takes a strong mind to lead a strong follower. Therefore, a weakened soul must retain potentials of being responsible, loyal, and productive to gain power in life.

We all feel like we have something to prove, something to lose, something to love, and something to give. Nevertheless, our lack of respect, our burst of pride and vengeance will walk along our miles of separation, which causes repulsive frustration between us all. Then I am left with this question, "Why does family have to come first when they are the first to cause hurt? Just because family shares the same blood doesn't mean they can't cause more pain than a stranger." With that being said, family is a word that defines love, and it's not limited by a bloodline, but extends to those that are dearest to your heart. Sometimes your true family does the most damage, and you can find peace in the arms of a friend.

# DIRTY MINDS... VICIOUS SOULS... LEADS TO BROKEN HEARTS...

---

Malachi 2:17 "You have wearied the lord with your words. How have we wearied him?" You asked. By saying, "All who do evil are good in the eyes of the lord, and he is pleased with them" or where is the God of justice?"

Mommy came to a halt after giving birth to her first four. It was in her best interest, but since daddy was devoting more of his time sleeping with his mistresses and conducting other shystie businesses, she really didn't have a choice. Daddy could be gone for weeks, months, and years if he desired. Deep down inside, he knew that mommy would still be waiting on him. She was just his naive wife that gave birth to his kids, but for any other position she was useless, and like the worthless man he was, he had taken total advantage of her. Now, mommy knew that, but she didn't have the courage to walk away, and she lacked the confidence to get another man. Therefore, she waited… and waited… until he knocked at the door.

When he did find the time to come, she tried to play hard to get, but it was a little game she liked to play, knowing he would forcefully take it. Those special little moments she was appreciative of because that passion of love never existed until she met him. For that reason, it had made it an unbreakable bond. Then after a week or so, he would be back to his normal routine. He was gone with the wind, but left his sperm behind. It was four years later, but only took one time for mommy to get pregnant with child number five.

# FLAMING FIVE

I didn't ask to be here, but God created me for a purpose. I, Na 'Veah Daevas, was born on June 16, 1980 at Kings County Hospital in Brooklyn, New York. While mommy laid on the hospital bed, her legs were wide open, and the doctors and nurses were shouting out, "Push! Push! You're almost there!" It was beyond mommy's imagination as she was struggling to get my head out. "My vagina is on fire, oh my God, she need to come out now," Mommy screamed with devastation, and was determined to deliver me as quickly as possible. With pain, she tightly gripped onto the bed rails, held her breath like she was constipated, and kept pushing, yelling, and squeezing as the doctors and nurses were cheering her on. It worked, and I came out fiercely crying while mommy laid there peacefully in relief.

I weighed eight pounds and nine ounces, which was mommy's biggest baby thus far. As she held me, she felt that I was something special, and she knew I would develop into something different. Primarily because the day mommy found out she was pregnant with me, she also gave her life to God. So, she felt it was some sort of connection. I am the fifth oldest, and sometimes I feel blessed, while other times I feel cursed.

It all started out when daddy denied me but was having unprotected sex with mommy anytime he felt like it. Therefore, it was a huge possibility that I was his, but he didn't have the decency to be by her side during or after my birth. In my eyes, he was thoughtless and inconsiderate. On top of that, he stopped supporting her financially, which really wasn't a lot, but anything was helpful. His only justification was, "How do I know what you were doing while I was gone? ... Besides, she doesn't look like me." It was an ignorant statement to make, for I barely had all my features. It wasn't my mother's fault that he chose to run in and out of her life. In all reality, he didn't want to take care of his responsibilities. He had a selfish mentality that wasn't suitable for a good husband or father. Instead, he invested his time worrying about what was in his best interest, but mommy continued to accept his abuse, and he continued breaking her down piece by piece.

Mommy tried to stay strong in our presence, but there were plenty of nights we heard and saw her rocking back and forth while crying herself to sleep, for the entire burden was wearing her down; it was also discouraging for us to hear. Mommy was aware that her broken family was at the beginning of their struggles, and still had more obstacles to overcome. Therefrom, she prayed more frequently, but the troubles were coming so quickly that it overpowered her hope. Slowly, she began to give up, but it never failed that our donor always was in the right place at the right time.

It seemed like he enjoyed having full control over my mother's: voice, vision, thoughts, and emotions. He knew that he could sell her another dream, and she'd fall right back in bed with him. Then, Mother Nature didn't come the next month, and neither did he. Now she was on child number six, and I was only three months old, but life had to move on without him, as we unwillingly tasted every bit of poverty.

In some ways, I blamed mommy for allowing him to constantly humiliate her. She let him strong arm her weak spots, and abuse his position without caring about the effect it had on his kids. In fact, it made us feel bitter every time we saw mommy cry. She spilled out her lonely heart with tears of pain, as she hoped that God would come and save us all. What was even more saddening, was knowing there was nothing much that we could do to make her happy. However, she was never alone in her struggles for survival because we experienced them as well. Those daunting moments of our lives will never be forgotten.

Memories last forever, it doesn't matter if they are good or bad; they will stick with you. Some memories will even alter your decisions in life.

At the innocent age of four, I was so confused; I didn't understand why my father molested me. I wasn't old enough to interpret the meaning of his wrongdoings, but I was smart enough to know that it was discerning to my soul. I couldn't recall how long it was going on, for he was never a constant figure in my life. What I do remember is the horrifying day he attempted to. Then later that night while everyone was asleep, he came and finished what he started. I never made a sound or spoke a word, I just laid there and stared in the eyes of the devil. During his salacious acts, daddy never commiserated for stealing the very virtue a child is blessed with, my innocence. Instead, he made it seem like a prevalent moment shared amongst father and daughter. Though I was young, I could feel my purity escaping, and it was a scary feeling. I was aware of the exposure to evil would change my life, perpetually. Then I started dodging him every time I heard his masculine voice call my name, or when he held out his arms for a hug or some form of engagement. I didn't want to be near such a lewd man. I wanted to be invisible and drift away, after discovering that my father was the monster in my closet.

Every time my father came around I was reminded of the undesirable moments we shared. Instantly, my entire demeanor would change, which concerned mommy because I was normally energetic and happy when I saw him. Mommy began questioning me, "What's wrong baby? You haven't been yourself lately. You know you can tell me anything if that makes you feel better." When I looked in my mother's bothered eyes, I saw sincerity and felt safe to confide in her. I asked in a stuttered but frightening voice, "Why Daddy keep touching me down there? I don't like that, and it hurts a lot." While I slightly touched my irritated vagina, mommy told me to lie down on the bed so that she could look at it. When I opened my legs, all she saw was redness, which confirmed my story. Mommy started hyperventilating. She was angry and devastated that her husband, who was my father, was molesting me. All the duplicitous things he had done was hurtful, but this by far, was the most troubling. As she impatiently waited for him to come back, she was comforting me, and she told me that it wasn't my fault.

When daddy finally arrived, assuming that his little secret was safe with me, mommy confronted him with bitterness and anger. Of course, he denied my accusations with a straight face. Although mommy didn't believe him, her love for him still stood strong. While her hurtful tears kept falling, she got weak in the knees, and her heart started to skip beats. The rage had took over, and she immediately went off. In her painful voice, she asked, "Why? How? She is your child! What were you thinking about?" Instead of him responding, he simply left, unapologetically. He was more upset that he got caught, rather than the pain he had caused me. As always, he walked away without any repercussions.

As of today, I'm puzzled about why mommy didn't take further actions to put my father away. If I had gotten raped instead of a simple assault, would it have been a different outcome? What was the debate? Was it because she loved him too much, or she didn't truly believe what I told her? As I was getting older, it became even more complicated. I just couldn't understand why she had more kids by him. Who was she really trying to protect her heart or us?

Mommy's reason for not getting the cops involved was primarily because she was protecting us from getting taken away by "BCW", which is social service. She explained that BCW was already investigating her about negligence. Under the circumstances, the secret had to be concealed for the sake of her not wanting to lose all of her children. That excuse didn't alleviate none of my pain, but rather caused disappointment. In my eyes, I believe that the truth would've exposed his black ass, and they would have taken him to prison. In that case, he would have been the only one who would've been taking away. After that, she was supposed to have held her head high, and kept her faith in God to keep us together as a family. Well, that's how I wished she would have handled it. Honestly, I don't know if I am more hurt by the sacrifices that mommy didn't make for me, or that my father never viewed me as his beautiful, innocent baby girl and abused me. I speculated why my parents did not want to shield me? Secondly, was my mother not selfless enough to protect her child despite the cost?

Looking back, I can answer a few of those questions. I feel like mommy wanted him to stay free, so he could keep running back to her; moreover, she didn't feel complete without him. She was hoping to build something that was never anything from the beginning. Despite the assaults, infidelities, hurt, and all the lies, she became accustomed to that life.

# OPEN EYES! SHUT MOUTH!

Molestation was always happening in our family. On numerous accounts, it was never exposed because the: eyes that saw, the ears that heard, and the victims who experienced it, would never open their mouths. For this reason, others weren't aware of the traumatic situation, which made it tolerable. Why didn't they speak up? It was either because the victim was scared, embarrassed, or felt guilty about the overall situation. As a choice, the bystander was more than likely protecting the victimizer. I was a victim, and my memories can't ever be obliterated. I would always remember the night that one of my favorite cousins made me look at him totally different. It all started out when I was seven years old. I didn't know that hugging, kissing on the cheeks, and getting so much attention from my big cousin was headed towards the unthinkable. However, those overnight stays at Unk's house had made it possible for the nightfall to be exposed to daylight.

My cousin Floyd was like a ghost. His corrupted mind, and his deviant behavior was invisible to everybody since he was very loving, caring, and giving. I rarely saw him get mad, but there had to be something destructive going on in his head if he tried to rape me.

It was a few years between my father assaults; therefore, feeling offensive was in the back of my mind when my cousin attempted to violate me in such a passionate way. He used a different approach, which threw me off on what he was doing. First, the kiss started on the cheek, but ended up on the lips at night when we went to bed. I was young, and thought he was showing me love. With all of that intensity coming from a male's eyes, I felt important, so I looked at him and smiled like everything was alright.

Despite the starvation, and all of the degrading conversations I overheard about my mother, I still wanted to go stay the night over Unk's house; I really enjoyed hanging out with my cousins. Most of all, I was eager to see Floyd. I still was unaware, or maybe I just didn't care that he was wrongfully embracing me because he didn't cause me any harm, and that's why our bond continued to stay strong.

I was delighted when he held my hand while we walked to the corner store, and he bought me anything I wanted. I kept a smile on my face, and lectures I always held; if no one else wanted to listen, Floyd showed interest in my conversations. He would smile back, and showed genuine concerns about my issues that I had in my life. All those times I got picked on, had arguments, or any altercations, he would always come to my defense. I looked at him as my superman; he guarded me when my own father didn't. Lacking that father figure in my life, made me crave that love and affection from another man. I was looking for that masculine love and understanding, which was my biggest mistake. At that moment in my life, I felt joyful that I finally had my hero. I felt as though my search for love had ended, but it left me open to attack.

Through that entire year, he used my vulnerability against me. In all reality, he thought by me being half his age had made it easier for him to take advantage. He was slick by playing it safe because he didn't want to expose his desperate impulsions, until he knew my mouth would stay shut. Instead, we would play kiddie games in a sophisticated way. We had a ball playing "Hide-N-Go Get IT!" I thought he used to cheat when he consistently found my hiding spots, then I had to do whatever he wanted. "Red Light, Green Light, STOP!" Was another fun game, but he just implemented differently. Our body parts was the traffic control, and he used to avoid getting pulled over in the wrong areas. We always played together, and there was constant laughter, for he made inexcusable things seem so funny. We had a close connection, not only as cousins, but as my brother and friend. But it's sad to say that he used our bond to fulfill his desires when he wanted to play house and be the husband instead of the father. Thereon, it took a turn for the worse.

I remember that night like it was yesterday. We were packed like sardines all through Unk's place. Floyd and I always made sure we slept next to each other. As we hugged up to go to sleep, I thought I would be having sweet dreams. Instead, it was one of my worst nightmares. One of the most depressing and heartbreaking memories a seven-year-old couldn't imagine would happen to her.

As the night was ending, lights were shut off, and the room became pitch dark. Everything and everyone suddenly got quiet because they fell asleep, except for Floyd. He couldn't fight temptation anymore, so he felt it was perfect timing for him to take it to another level. When he kissed me on my cheek, once again, I thought it was a goodnight kiss as I tiredly laid there with no reaction like I normally would. That's when he became overly aggressive. Then all of a sudden, this cold feeling had come over my body, and my heart was pumping rapidly as I was having flashbacks of what my father did. I froze up and didn't say anything because I was afraid. In my mind, I kept saying, "I know this is not happening again. I thought he really loved me!" But then I realized I was just another victim of seduction and abuse.

I got angry and tried to push him away, but he quickly reacted as he stood firmly over me. It was like I was in a boxing ring, trying to fight my way out of the corner. Yet, he kept controlling me with those powerful jabs. Figuratively speaking, there wasn't a referee to decide whether I was capable to continue, or disqualify him for violating the rules. I was feeling defeated, but then I remembered what mommy told me, "If anyone, I don't care who they are… tries to hurt you in any way… don't let them because they are bad people. Do whatever you can to let it be known." I remembered that since it was one of the most valuable advice mommy ever told me about a man. Ensuingly, I kept trying to scream, but it came out like a low mumble, which might've sounded like one of us were having a bad dream.

All of us kids, big and small were all in the same room; some were even lying next to us, but not once did they checked to see was I okay when I cried for quite some time. Deep down in my heart I felt like at least one of them saw and heard what was going on, but no one did anything to stop it. "Why?" How come my Unk didn't hear anything when his room was directly next to ours? Was it because he was comatose from all of the brown bottles he drank that night? I felt trapped and all alone, even when I was surrounded by family. How could a seven-year-old get out of such a difficult dilemma without any help?

My heart was beating like it was going to explode through my chest. My tears dropped, exposing my frightened emotions. Finally, the foam from my saliva drenched his hand, and he slowly removed it from my mouth, which made my words clearer, and my voice louder. I don't know if he panicked or got impatient. Whatever the case may have been, I was grateful that I didn't actually have sex with my cousin.

As his tight grip, had slowly released my immature body, he whispered in my ear softly, "Shhh! I'm so sorry, please forgive me... I won't do it again." I quickly got up, ran to the corner of the room, bald up on that cold wooden floor, and then I prayed. I don't recall going to sleep that night. All I remember is the vision of torture, the thoughts of abuse, and the silent words of hatred.

The next morning, I woke up due to the boisterous sounds from the other kids. I removed my head from the cold, decrepit floor, and quickly jumped up in fear. To my surprise, Floyd was standing right there in front of me, speechless. He didn't know what to expect, and I didn't know how I was going to react. It was an awkward moment for me when we stared at each other in complete silence. My eyes revealed my feelings of confusion and resentment. That moment, Floyd realized I would never look at him the same. Then I slowly started stepping back to keep my distance and hurtfully walked away.

I never mentioned what happened that night to anyone, but every time I had to stay over Unk's house I felt uncomfortable. I was cautious, and worried that Floyd would try it again, but he didn't. Every time we walked past each other, I gave him a disgusted look as I rolled my eyes. What I hated the most was when an adult told me to relay messages to him. All of those built-up emotions wanted me to only say how angry I was, and how much pain he put me through, but I didn't have the courage to let it all out.

In a way, Floyd showed some guilt and regrets for what he did. I didn't only see it on his face, but I heard it in his voice when he spoke to me; also, he was being extremely nice just like a big cousin is supposed to be. I was no longer impressed because that dark secret had stood in between my feelings, and our best moments. With that being said, we never had gotten to build our bond back.

May Floyd rest in peace… He is gone, but will never be forgotten. Even though he took all secrets to his grave, he still suffered a great deal of punishments for his evildoings. I always knew that it would eventually catch up with him, but death wasn't what I expected or wanted.

Floyd was diagnosed with cancer after getting admitted into the hospital for a fatal injury he had gotten from an altercation. He didn't fight the battle too long because the cancer had spread quickly and took his life. I was mournful of his death, but it was a coincidence that he died seven years later, which was the same age I was when he tried to molest me. Yes, my resentment and anger remain since I didn't get any closure. I never understood why my favorite cousin would demean me in such a harsh way. How could his warm heart be so cold, and no one saw the signs. Or did they see it, and just kept their mouths shut? Did people misinterpret him due to seeing this courageous, affectionate, and generous, young fellow through and out the day but didn't recognize the devious, sex craved victimizer at night?

My intentions are not to degrade my cousin or lose any family members over it, but looking back and thinking ahead, Floyd had deceived me. Sadly, there are numerous victims who suffers from some sort of molestation each day. However, it should never be kept a secret, nor should it go unpunished. It's too late for me, but could be on time for someone else. From this perspective, never try to protect a loved one, and always speak to be heard because it's better to let it out than to hold it in. Undisclosed information gives the victimizer leeway to do it repeatedly.

Those incidents with my father and cousin changed my perspective on men and my life. For one, I kept a close bond and communicated with my girls about practically everything, especially about their body parts. I informed them on how to avoid being a victim of sexual assault, and on preserving their innocence. I wanted them to know the difference between respect and disrespect, and to make me aware if someone made them feel uncomfortable in any way. For the sake of me being worried about my kids going through that same torture or even worse, I was overprotective of them. I barely let my kids stay over people's houses, but if they did, I constantly called to check up on them. Certainly, I always questioned them when they got home. Maybe if mommy interacted with us a little more, was a little cautious, and more observant of our surroundings, it could've prevented the abuse some of us experienced.

A parent that is inexperience and careless can still grow, and become a better parent. Mommy never got to that level. I feel like she tried but only to a bare minimum. She never really wanted to face the facts considering she was in denial about practically everything that went wrong, such as the sexual abuse. Deep down in my heart, I felt like mommy knew about most of our assaults, but she was that bystander that had those open eyes but shut mouth. As victims, where did that leave us? It left us lost and enrage! It caused us to have mixed emotions, not only towards the victimizers, but mommy as well. She was more to blame for letting it continue on without doing nothing, when she knew in her heart something was wrong.

It's been decades, but my memories would torment me forever. I still try to come to a conclusion on who was mostly wrong. Was it what my father or what my cousin did? In all reality, there is no comparison because molestation shouldn't play a role in any child's life. Still and all, my father should have never looked at me as a sex toy, and just cared for me. My eyes are now open, but I always had a shut mouth about my family secrets for so long. Presently speaking, I'm relieved that it's finally out.

As I previously stated, BCW constantly supervised my mother's house. They made sure we had food, shelter, and that our living situation was safe. Mommy never reported my abuse, but BCW became concerned about child molestation after they received reports from anonymous callers, who stated that we were being sexually abused by our father. Of course, the accusation was exaggerated, but we all had to continue getting checkups. They found no evidence, but it was an ongoing investigation.

Every visit was awkward because we had to go in a cold room, and take off all of our clothes while they inspected every inch of our bodies. Then they talked to us separately and privately asking us all types of personal but scary questions. Mommy already prepared us, so we knew how to answer some questions, but the unexpected ones, we answered them the best way possible. We were kids and thought we were doing right by covering up things and was hoping that we didn't get separated.

Meanwhile, they randomly popped up at our house for inspections. Sometimes we had to stack the can foods on top of each other, then move them all to the front of the cabinet to make it seem like we had a lot of food, but we really didn't. The refrigerator had just enough food in it to pass the inspections. We had to be dressed decent with greasy faces and pretty smiles to make it seem like we had no problems at all; nevertheless, the real truth tormented our hearts and thoughts.

I hate to remember, but it's hard to forget all the times we ate peanut butter and jelly sandwiches for breakfast, lunch and dinner. There were also times we mixed flour, water, and sugar to make what we called homemade pancakes; not to mention, oodles of noodles were the main source of food we kept in our cabinets. The worst times was the end of the month when we had to share plates because it wasn't enough food to go around. When it got to that point, mommy went to this place called the pantry to get that free welfare cheese, milk, and can foods that lasted us till her food stamps came.

We never really had a place that we could call home, or a father who we called dad, but we had each other through all of our struggles, which made it very depressing just hearing mommy cry to God and wondering how she was going to get through it all. She always hoped that tomorrow would be a better day and wished that daddy would come back into her life to help her improve as a woman and mother. What mommy didn't realize was that she didn't need daddy for progression, she just needed to change her mindset. But the love she had for him had overpowered her soul, consuming all the virtues for self-improvement.

Love is a compelling emotion. Even if we tried, we still cannot demand, control, or make it vanish. For it's much bigger than us, and when you carry it deep within your heart, you cannot dictate: what, when, or how your love will express itself. You cannot sale, buy, or trade love. Therefore, you cannot make a person love you, or prevent who you fall in love with. Although love is supposed to bring forth happiness, choices that people make can alter the meaning of such a pleasurable word. Unfortunately, it can be a hindrance in one's development and confidence. When you love someone like my mother loved my father, you can be taken advantage of, and also be too forgiving. She always had an excuse for why daddy did or didn't do something like she was the only one to blame.

I don't recall daddy ever buying us gifts, clothes, or just giving us that daddy time; however, if mommy had no one else to turn to, she didn't hesitate to reach out to him for help. He never voluntarily offered his assistance to us, but he did agree to help pay the rent or buy food at times. My mother was always grateful for whatever he did. In her eyes he was trying, but from what we saw, it really wasn't enough.

It shouldn't take a struggle for a father to help his family. A father should maintain a home, protect, and provide for his children regardless if he is in the mother's life or not. What type of man can lay peacefully at night in his big nice home with no worries, while his seven kids lived in a worn-down apartment with their welfare recipient mother, who had no other income? A worthless one.

During this time, we were living in an apartment on Ocean Avenue in Manhattan, New York. We were there for a little over two years, which was the longest we ever stayed in a place without the welfare paying for it. Mommy was still battling the hard knock life with seven kids, and another on the way. Every time she gave birth to one more child, it had open the door for one more problem.

The problems mommy faced each day were problems she could've prevented by not having any more kids. For some strange reason, mommy thought bearing kids was her destiny, whereas the more kids she had was more of a misfortune to us. For as long as I could remember, we hardly ever went shopping for material things; mommy couldn't afford it. However, people gave us their hand me downs, and we treasured them like they were brand new. We also were really thankful when we received contributions from churches. We got all types of new stuff including toys. It didn't matter that they were cheap, blessings were always priceless.

I remember those times mommy would walk through the door with countless bags. We used to shout with joy and dance around as though it was Christmas. Then we'd race and ramble through the bags, playing tug of war over the clothes or shoes we wanted. What one couldn't fit, the other sister could; if more than one of us were able to wear it, then we shared it. We always wished that those donations could've happened more often, but it didn't. Regardless of what, mommy tried her best to keep us decent with the resources she had available. It wasn't much, but anything was better than nothing. Still, we always dreamed and desired to be under better circumstances.

Like having both parents in the house, striving together to make ends meet. It would've been delectable to have dinner at the table while talking and laughing amongst one another. I would've enjoyed having family vacations, or family nights out just to get a break from our boring house. We should've had memorable moments of us sitting around a Christmas tree, while opening up presents, or having birthday parties, blowing out candles and making best wishes. I can go on and on about what we desired, but the fact is, none of these occasions paid us a visit. The good life didn't bother to stop by the Daevas's place, but it did manage to appear in our dreams that never came true.

A different family could've been great, but our destiny was cursed. We were born into evil that had blindfolded our lives from virtuous behavior. We had two parents with different lifestyles, and they were on different levels; even so, both sides played a huge role in corrupting their seeds. Their decisions were based only upon their needs and gains, but they were overlooking the fact that their plague progressed when they created eight balls of fire.

My father was the worst because he would rebuild remotely, so he could destroy. On the other hand, my mother was wrongfully remodeled into a haunted foundation. She couldn't defeat the ghost that was hiding in her closet. For mommy was simple minded, feeble, and forgiving, which caused her ongoing ignorance, and endless pain.

Daddy was a huge part of mommy's vulnerability. He knew all her broken angles; he figured out each individual sharp curve. He even managed to displace STOP signs as he violated all rules, but enforced all betrayal. For many reasons, mommy had planted her soul deep into darkness since she couldn't repair herself from all the damage. Mommy always stumbled in her own pity due to her falling for every trap, trick, or treat because she sees no evil, even when they are in eye view. Also, the volume in her voice was lowered. Her soft-spoken words remained unheard, and her broken heart continued to get crushed.

Without any guilt or shame, daddy continued to use mommy's fragility as leverage, seeing that she would do anything to make him happy. Just like the day he sent his cousin Bella over to our place when she needed somewhere to stay. With very little information, Bella was officially living with us within minutes. There was no if's, and's, or but's about it, daddy knew that mommy would've taking her in without any interrogation. Mommy was always willing to help, especially when she became a Christian. She faithfully spread her arms to those who were in need. She knew it wasn't accommodating to her family, but felt she was doing her work for God. At the end of the day, we suffered because what little we did have, was not enough to share. It was like more people, and less food; little room turned into having no room. In fact, it made another opportunity for neglect.

Within a matter of weeks, mommy and Bella were the best of friends, and her short stay seemed like it was never coming to an end. Mommy was so friendly and generous to Bella, not suspecting she was a mistress in disguise. From the time Bella walked through our door, her intentions were wrong; but when she realized mommy's heart was in the right place, Bella started feeling guilty. Her conscience was eating at her, knowing mommy didn't deserve what stood before her. Bella was clueless on how and when she was going to confess, assuming that her eyes would eventually reveal her deception.

It took Bella a few nights to reach her deepest thoughts. When she finally came to a conclusion, she resolved it cowardly. She was too ashamed to look mommy in her eyes, and tell her she was daddy's woman on the side. She didn't want to admit to mommy the love she had for her husband; moreover, she didn't want to expose her future relationship with daddy. Being that Lashaylah was the oldest, Bella assumed she would understand the affair better, so she confided in her. Bella sadly expressed how sorry she was for hurting mommy, and she hoped the information would put a stop to mommy's pain. It was really an add-on to her aching heart since mommy bruises never healed from all of the other deceptions she'd encountered.

Two women, sleeping under the same roof, in love with the same man, and accepting his deceiving ways was a straight up Mack daddy move for my father. The dumbest part about the overall situation was neither one wanted to lose him, but the reality was, they already did. Daddy was always pulling BITCHES out of his pockets, which made it complicated to refuse infidelities.

Mommy walked around lifeless and speechless for weeks, but Bella was still living with us like she wasn't part of the problem. Mommy cried out to Bella in a distressed way, "This man has hurt me to the core, and I continue to accept it because I love him, but… what am I doing wrong? Why…? Why doesn't he love me the same? What have I done to deserve this?" Then she held her head down as tears were fallen on her lap. Her body had got numbed, and her head was throbbing as the hurtful thoughts kept pounding on it. Bella couldn't give her an answer, knowing the right answer wasn't going to make it any better. She just kept quiet and comforted mommy for the hurt she'd caused her. Without a doubt, mommy forgave her. When Lashaylah notice mommy was a little too vulnerable, she got extremely mad and decided to take matters in her own hands. So, she got Lateesah involved, and they figured out a game plan, which was to disassociate mommy from any inconvenience.

After their collaboration, Shaylah and Teesah started screw facing Bella. Then they took turns aggressively shoulder checking her, which was an early warning for Bella to get the hell out of dodge. Bella felt the tension all that day; still, she ignored it. She knew nothing was going to happen while mommy was there. But the moment mommy walked out the door headed for church, Shaylah and Teesah put on their boxing gloves, and they beat the shit out of Bella until she took off. More than likely, she went back on the streets where she resided, and we never saw or heard from her again.

On the other hand, my father didn't show his face for a few months. When he did, he wasn't remorseful. He didn't even give mommy an explanation. He felt like his actions were acceptable because he was paying the bills at that time. Well, at least that's what mommy thought until another surprise visit came banging at our door early in the morning.

We were barely awake. Some of us were yarning, and some of us were wiping cold from our eyes. When mommy finally got the energy to open the door, it was the U.S. Marshals holding up an eviction notice. He said in a rude voice, "Ma'am, your rent is three months past due, so we are here to make sure you vacate the premises, and you have less than thirty minutes to remove all of your belongings." The humiliation on mommy's face was a look we would never forget. Mommy knew it was impossible to get everything out in that time frame; therefore, we only grabbed what we could take by hand. All of our furniture, and the rest of our things were thrown out on the side of the street, leaving us with nothing. We were hurt, but most of all, embarrassed that all the neighbors were standing outside looking, talking, and laughing at us.

While we were in dispossession, my little sister Lalannah was hiding in between the box spring and mattress that was leaning against the wall. We started calling and looking for her, then suddenly the mattress slowly began to fall. It firmly hit the floor along with Lalannah, which resulted in her broken leg. Just thinking that the situation couldn't get any worse was only wishful thinking because it most certainly did.

Later on that day, we walked to the train station. As we took that ride to Aunt Martha's confined apartment, we began to cry. We knew that we were on our way to even more hard times. Mommy didn't want to, but she had no choice. The shelters only had four beds left, so she took the oldest three with her while Miyah, Lannah, Daishah and I had to go to our Aunt's disorganized house. On the other hand, Caylah had the best opportunity to stay at Aunt Ava's house getting all the true love and affection, while we were getting neglected.

We were ages eight, four, three, and two; but had the responsibilities as an adult while we were there. We had to feed, bathe, and dress ourselves; thanks to Miyah, she was a big help. We were the mistreated kids versus our other cousins, who were also staying there, which made it hard for us to become comfortable, especially when it was over 13 people living under one roof.

Our living arrangements were heinous. We used to sleep on the hard wooden floors with sheets instead of blankets and no pillows; oppositely, our cousins were laying cozy on the beds and couches. To us, they were getting pampered as usual. We were the first kids that starved, and the last ones to get fed, which plenty of nights our stomachs were growling because we didn't get enough to eat. There were also many nights we were woken from all the loud talking, and people staggering all through the house. Out of curiosity, we did what most kids would do, and we started peeping at what the adults were up to. Our eyes were open to curiosity when we saw lighters flicking, glass pipes inhaled like they were cigarettes, and clouds of strong smoke floating in the air. After the air cleared up, all we could see were: glossy eyes, paranoid looks, and twitching mouths. We heard nothing but slurring words as they wildly interacted with each other. That was a late-night routine, which seemed like it wasn't going to ever end.

When the company finally left, Aunt Martha and her boyfriend started getting it in. Dick out, ass up, noise making, and the bed squeaking was far from music to our ears. From the looks of it, they showed no consideration for us kids. I guess by them being on cloud nine had made them react so openly, or they were just immune to living alone. Regardless of what it was, we weren't used to seeing none of that, but living under someone else's roof, it's all about their rules.

After everything was said and done, the brighten sun would be coming up. Due to the lack of sleep, we would be too tired to get up at times. However, we were never really anxious to see another day because we weren't happy. We weren't having fun like normal kids. Instead, we worked like slaves, we were always called to get this, or we had to clean up that. It was something we coped with for months, which was very depressing.

The times mommy came to visit, we were so happy to only become sad when she had to leave us again. We cried for our freedom, but we didn't have the courage to speak up. We knew that if we told the truth about anything that went on, then the situation would've gotten even worse once mommy left. Therefore, we patiently waited until she came and got us, which was about three months later, and that was the happiest day out of those 12 weeks. We were jumping up and screaming, "Yay! We're going with mommy today!" We were even more excited when mommy gave us coloring books with crayons. It was time to get the hell up out of there! Immediately, we rushed to get ready, impolitely said goodbye, and off we went walking to the train station.

While riding on the train, we colored in our books the whole way there. We were just smiling from ear to ear because that was a very special moment for us. Even though we didn't have much with mommy, she offered that love that nobody else could ever show or give us. The comfort we felt was unconditional and encouraging. If that took being in the shelters with her, then we disregarded everything else and were grateful that our family was all together. These unfavorable experiences made us focus on what was important; for this reason, it was hard for us to unshackle ourselves from that bond we shared going to that awful, but convenient place.

Once we arrived, they gave us a whole wall with eight cots lined up side by side. The beds were confined and uncomfortable. It felt like we were laying on just the bed springs, for the metal was torturing our bodies. We had slight and slow movements when we tossed and turned. At the same time, any sudden move would've resulted in a sudden fall onto those rocklike floors. In other words, the place was a danger zone. Then there were the thieves that slept about five feet away from us, which overwhelmed our minds. So, anything we thought was valuable, we had to hide it.

Mommy would stash her book of food stamps and cash underneath her large breast considering she got robbed blind by those thieving ass bums plenty of times before. When the lights went out, most people fell asleep. That's when the prowlers started lurking around. Before you know it, everything of value was stolen, and it's nothing you could do about it. There were many times those sneaktheives left us penniless, and we had to eat what food the shelter was offering, until the first of the month came back around.

The thoughts of eating those distasteful meals makes me quiver. Having watered down greens with a bland taste had made it hard for us to get our good source of many vitamins and minerals. The unseasoned and rare looking meat didn't give us much nutrients and proteins because we barely ate it. Furthermore, their starchy foods were mushy since it was overcooked, but if we didn't eat, then we starved.

After messing over that slop, our stomachs started bubbling with pain as we ran back and forth to the bathroom. Our asses barely touched the toilets, but our loose bowels were already coming down. Then we became nauseated and overpowered by sickness that caused severe and persistent vomiting. Our cries were weak. Our faces were pale. Our bodies were blazing hot, and our faces were dripping sweat from the high fevers; right then, mommy knew it was food poisoning. We'd be laying on the cots lifeless for hours, hoping the sickness would just go away. Mommy didn't show much affection, but she did pray, "In the blood of Jesus, I bind that devil up, and remove that sickness in Jesus name... Amen... Amen." Afterwards, she started speaking in tongues, which was never understood, but at that age, it seemed like it worked.

Before we got the desire to eat more of their food, we used to wait until our stomachs were roaring starvation. When we eventually stood in line for a plate, there were always some ghetto ass kids trying to start a fight. We'd be standing there rolling our eyes, snapping our fingers, bobbing our heads, and bickering at one another, trying to get our points across. Still, we always winded up being the victims; mommy always told us she felt that humbleness was our defense. Backing down eventually became annoying, which set off those ticking bombs, tick... tick... BOOM!

Another unpleasant thing about living in the shelters were every morning after breakfast we had to leave out, and we couldn't report back until six that evening. Since majority of our family stayed in Brooklyn, and with Manhattan being almost an hour away, it wasn't convenient to travel back and forth with seven kids every day. So, we just wandered around. There were times it was too hot, and we damn near froze to death when it was too cold. We had nowhere to go but walked for hours, leaving our legs restless. Mommy barely had money to spend, so there was no form of entertainment, which was very boring, and it made the time seem a lot slower. We had got to a point where we each brought out our own sense of humor to keep us occupied in order to distract our sadness. On the other hand, we were thrilled when we did make it to Brooklyn because we were around people we knew. Moreover, we missed our neck of the hoods, and we couldn't wait to move back there.

In between our unstable ordeal, Shaylah decided that she didn't want to stay at the shelter anymore. Subsequently, she moved in with one of her guy friends. The little bit of freedom and happiness she'd got there, was better than the tremendous amount of suffering we went through at the shelter. Not to mention, Shaylah was determined not to come back with us until mommy moved into her own place, which didn't seem fair that at the age of 14, she had a choice. None of us wanted to go through it, but we went through our struggles together. Instead of mommy enforcing, she did what was easier for her, but would be harder for Shaylah in the long run. Me, looking back, I couldn't understand how mommy was so content with her decisions. Even though she knew that she was making the wrong ones, she still never tried to correct them. How come?

In the meantime, living in the shelter along with other distressing problems were a burden on mommy's body, which caused an early and extremely heavy menstruation. If she sat, walked, or even stood there, the overflow of blood still came through her garments. In disbelief, she quickly walked to the bathroom to avoid the public embarrassment.

As she undresses, red tears were moving rapidly down her legs. Before she knew it, her feet were standing in a pool of blood. She panicked and got very emotional while scrubbing her panties in the sink. It really became a concern when she had to change her drenching pad every hour on the hour, which went on for almost two weeks. Instead of her going to the hospital, she kept praying, and eventually it helped alleviate some of her ongoing depression.

We fought the battles of the shelter for almost six months. Then the welfare placed us into what we called the Slaughter Hotel. Nothing but destruction happened in that hood. In spite of us moving into a one-bedroom box, our spirits were uplifted a little bit, feeling we had some privacy and freedom. A few weeks later, they accommodated us with an extra hotel room down the hall, which was a blessing; also, gave us more breathing space.

Soon after, BCW had reopened our case. They felt that once again mommy couldn't support us, which was very well true; regardless of what circumstances stood before her, she was determined to keep us sisters together. She refused for us to receive anybody else's love, in the sense that she wanted us to have only her love. It was hard for her to genuinely show it considering she didn't know how; therefore, her love wasn't enough to console us for very long. Still, we all held each other hands through those trials and tribulations in light of the fact that only the strong could survive.

Thereafter, mommy moved Lateesah, Lamirah, and Lamiyah down the hall. They took advantage of their unsupervised time, whereas us younger ones were trying to enjoy the moments with the very few toys we had. Of course, we lost interest really quick, until we started interacting amongst each other more. We loved playing, "Ring around the Rosie." We would hold hands while singing the lyrics and going around in circles, until we screamed out, "We all fall down!" Whoever set down last was out!

We also liked to play "Duck, Duck Goose". It was the dizziest, most heart racing, but fun game we played with constant laughter. Then the mice would bravely come wobbling out their hiding spots, and eating the crumbs off the floor. They always spoiled our fun because they came out anytime of the day, which had us screaming, racing for the bed, and we were too scared to get back up; most of the time, we just fell asleep.

Not only was it infested, it was one of the most deprived rooms as well. For one, we had to use the tub for everything, such as washing dishes, clothes, and ourselves. Secondly, the jammed windows were a hazard for both rooms when we didn't have any other options in case of an emergency. There was only one way in, and one way out. The rooms also stayed humid; we were inhaling heat, and exhaling flames, which caused constant grogginess and irritation. The Slaughter Hotel wasn't even close to a place like home, but anything was better than being in the shelters. In fact, it was one step closer to getting a permanent place to live, although it seemed like it was a long process. Living there was a horrible experience for any child to go through, and even more devastating for any family to realize they're living in poverty.

It never failed that our misfortune was always someone else's blessing. We were poor, but mommy always felt she was doing God's will by helping people who she thought was needier than us. That's why she had no problem with welcoming three runaway teens into our cramped up hotel rooms. One of them was our cousin, Sophia along with Amber and Iesha. Since they were around the older sisters' age group, they wanted to stay in their room.

Mommy was always complacent with trying to please others, but what she overlooked was how much she wasn't pleasing us. For every person she helped, left us with an even bigger disadvantage. Whether it was food that we needed, space that we barely had, and love that we really couldn't feel. It affected us in every little way because we were the ones who needed the most. While mommy was thinking she was counting her blessings for being a blessing to others, her kids were highly disappointed.

# WITCHCRAFT INTERVENTION

Our disappointment had quickly turned into fear when our older sisters' room became surrounded by demons. It was Teesah, Sophia, Amber, and Iesha playing around with a séance that a guy from Haiti had taught them. They were oblivious about it backfiring if it wasn't taking seriously, or if it was done wrong, which in their case it probably was both.

First things first, they lit six candles, and turned off all the lights. After that, they randomly chose a page out the bible, which was the book of Psalms chapter 23, verses one through four. Then they started reading the words backwards, but they could barely pronounce them. While they read each word slowly, they were laughing like it was a joke, but none of them knew that those diabolical words were provoking the demons.

The room was silent. The wind was blowing so heavy that you could hear the whistling in the air. Then the jammed windows flew open for the first time, which was eye-popping, and assured them that witchcraft was real. Frighteningly, they stopped saying the verses, then they dropped the bible with regrets, but it was too late, seeing that they already invited the demons in.

The room started rumbling, everything started shaking, and things began falling and breaking. The six candles strongly stood in place but was barely lit. However, the wax was quickly melting. Teesah, Sophia, Amber, and Iesha were fearfully looking at each other. They were at a loss for words, but their minds were thinking the same. All at once, they quickly tried to make a run for the door. While they were running, a negative force lifted Sophia from the floor, then slammed her aggressively against the wall. Her legs and arms were widely spread, and her eyes rolled to the back of her head. Suddenly, she began to speak strange words in an evil tone of voice.

Closer to the door was Teesah, who tried to turn the knob, but the door wouldn't open. The knob consistently turned, and Teesah's hand was stuck to it like glue. Resultantly, her arm kept twisting until it was broken. She was terrified, in pain, and crying out for help, but it was pointless because nobody in that room could do anything about it.

In the middle of the floor was Amber and Iesha, who were at a standstill like mannequins. They could see everything that was going on, which was terrifying and very disturbing watching Teesah and Sophia suffer. They were forced to hear their dramatic cries. As Amber and Iesha tears dropped, they thought that was the end of life since it was no way out.

While the devil's tragedy was going on in the room, the power of God was in the elevator. It was mommy, and us younger ones coming from church. Mommy was the type of Christian who would feel the anointing after church service, and praised God all the way home. That night she was crying, praying, and speaking in tongues; at that time, she said God was dealing with her.

God's energy was dynamic! But when the elevator doors opened on the fifth floor, everything seemed so cold and dark. The negative energy was the reason mommy had a gut feeling that something wasn't right and decided to check on the older kids. As she approached the door, she heard crying and screaming. She quickly turned the knob, and the door slowly opened. Everybody looked puzzled when Sophia fell to the floor and laid there struggling for her breathe. Her heart was pounding with fearful beats; her body was sluggish as if the demon jumped out of her, and walked his weaken soul somewhere else.

Leaning against the wall on her knees was Lateesah. She was holding her broken arm and was hysterically crying out, "Call the ambulance! I need... I have to get out of this room. Oh my God! He still in here... I can feel him! I'm so scared mommy... Please don't let him hurt me again, please!" At the same time, Amber and Iesha were shaking and screaming from the top of their lungs, trying to explain to mommy about what happened. Mommy didn't have to witness anything, but she knew they were telling the truth. Therefore, she opened her bible, and in her glorifying voice, she read all the verses in Psalms 23. Everything and everyone became calm and collective.

After Lateesah came from the hospital, they all discussed what happened. The creepiest part about their stories were each of them saw it from a different vantage point; however, they could agree on the part about the demonic force controlling that room. After that night, the room never felt the same. They thought the demons were still amongst them just waiting on the right time to come back. They became paranoid and distracted by anything out of the ordinary, but hoping that it was just all in their minds.

Meanwhile, life had to continue. Slowly but surely their thoughts started fading away, but that night would never be forgotten. Just like some of the other disasters that settled in our minds, such as getting picked on about our mice infested rooms. We knew we weren't the only ones who had them in that hotel, but it was just embarrassing that people actually seen our mice. This specific summerish day, everybody was outside. Kids were running and playing up and down the block, while grownups drank their 40's. Everyone was just enjoying the moment. In the middle of us actively playing, Caylah began to feel something funny in her spacious shoe, so she started jumping up on one leg trying to take it off, and a dead mouse came flying out. We had an awkward look on our faces, but what was even more humiliating was that the other kids saw it, and put us on the spot.

They were laughing real hard while pointing at the ground. That was a derogative moment for us. All we could hear as we walked away, with our heads down was, "The mouse was living in her shoe… Ugh their house is dirty, and their clothes look old! Y'all need to leave and go crawl back in that hole with the mice!" Then they laughed even harder. Our feelings were hurt because they were speaking the truth. Our impoverished conditions were exposed through our appearances. The soles on our shoes were worn down. Our clothes were either too big or too small. We had thin and cheap looking coats, stretched out toboggans, and we were never in style. As we got older, it became even more discouraging, and increased our desire for a more lavish lifestyle.

To our surprise, the gossip spread like a wildfire, which made it worse for us at school, given that we stayed in the limelight of humiliation. At lunch time, I remember sitting alone or with the unpopular group because I didn't have any friends. On several occasions, some of the disrespectful kids would come from behind and pull our hair or throw things at us. We would just ignore it like nothing never happened, which made us look like cowards. So at recess, they would taunt or attack us, knowing that we weren't going to do anything about it. It got so bad that we stopped playing outside since running into trouble wasn't fun at all.

A few days later, Lateesah had an altercation with some girl who lived downstairs from us. After Teesah beat her ass, she took her Walkman, and then ran. Within a matter of minutes, a group of guys and girls of all ages were banging on mommy's room door. When mommy unlocked it, they came bum rushing in, looking for Teesah. They were rowdy, and began making threats, demanding mommy to buy a brand-new Walkman or else... Mommy didn't know the full story, but in her honest voice, she explained, "I don't know what went on, but my daughter is not here. If she took the Walkman, then I'll pay for it. Until then, y'all need to leave, and we'll settle this when Teesah gets back!" They left with a lot of hostility, and we were shocked, but happy they were gone. The entire time, Teesah was watching everything from the other room, then came creeping through the door after she saw them leave. She tried to justify what happened, but the bottom line was she took the Walkman.

Mommy had to go to the corner store and trade some food stamps in for cash in order to buy the Walkman. It wasn't really beneficial to us because selling any amount of food stamps put a dent in our refrigerator, especially when we had extra mouths to feed. Not only that, but also the war was ongoing with Teesah and the people downstairs. Fights after fights in connection with vengeance being a motherfucker. The fact is, they didn't care about getting a new Walkman. They were more bothered about Teesah whooping the girl's ass, and then taking it, which was a form of disrespect on their territory. Unfortunately, we all had to suffer for that, and believe me that experience was extremely dangerous. It was so destructive that the welfare people had put us at the top of the list, so we could move out of there as soon as possible.

During the intervening time, Lashaylah came running back to mommy eight months pregnant. She eventually told mommy that she was too embarrassed to tell her about the slipup, and that was the real reason she left. I don't think it really mattered when mommy found out, seeing she showed no signs of anger in spite of her 15-year-old daughter standing there with a popped belly.

Simultaneously, mommy had read in the newspaper that daddy was in jail for embezzling over $100,000 from the government. He wasn't incarcerated for long, which I believe it was out of respect of him having connections with the mafia. It really didn't make any difference to us, but it did have an impact on mommy. Even though she was getting a break from all of daddy's duplicitous acts, she still mourned for his presence. It just wasn't easy for mommy to get past her feelings for daddy. Consequently, there were times she laid in bed all day rocking herself to sleep, and she even went days without eating, drinking, or bathing. Her love for him had weakened her mind, which tried to take control of her body. Her faith in God was the primary reason why she didn't commit suicide.

The few months that daddy was locked up, mommy had got acquainted with a truck driver name Gerald. In behalf of her vulnerability, she didn't take into consideration that Gerald was invited into our family a little too soon. He treated us good and all, but the fact that we didn't have a father played a major role in us welcoming him, except for Lateesah. She couldn't see any good in Gerald at all; primarily because he wasn't daddy, the man she thought would eventually be in our lives, which was nothing but hopes and dreams.

After Gerald moved in, we moved into the other room with the oldest ones. It was definitely overcrowded, but we didn't care. It was all about seeing mommy happy and smiling again. The only thing that bothered mommy was as a Christian, fornicating was considered backsliding, and mommy definitely didn't want to feel like she turned her back on God. For that cause, she put some thought into it, but temptation took over, and forced her into an adulterous relationship. Following behind that was three miscarriages, but God knew she didn't need anymore.

Finally, the welfare people had found us somewhere to stay, and we were moving out of that awful place. We were blessed to leave the worst at the most appropriate time. We had a new father, a happy mother, and soon we would have a complete home. We were breathing again. We were moving away from some of our worst enemies; most importantly, we were headed back to Brooklyn with our family. It was so exciting to start a new beginning, and we were praising God for making it all happened.

# THE WEAK, WILD, AND THE WICKED

---

Malachi 3:15 "And now we call the proud happy;
yea, they that work wickedness are set up; yea,
they that tempt God are even delivered."

When Gerald arrived to pick us up, we all were packed and ready to go. We were anxious about riding in a car for our very first time. Then we lapped up in twos, and headed back to Brooklyn. Everything looked different from a car's point of view. The clouds seemed so bright, and were moving in the same direction that we were. However, the roads were cluttered with cars and impatient people. We continuously heard beeping horns, as people intensely sped past us. Despite that, I can't forget the influential music that sent a message to our ears, and exhilarated our spirits. That remarkable moment made us clap our happy asses all the way to our new home, and created an everlasting impression of satisfaction.

We arrived at St. Marks Place unaware of our surroundings, but our positive persona had made it easier for some of the people to welcome us into their hood. It felt awkward that all of our neighbors were outside watching while we were moving into that condemned two-story house, which was modified into two apartments. It really didn't matter as long as we had our own again.

A few days later, the social service accommodated us with some furniture. In the living room, which we turned into a room, had a pullout couch. In our room was only two full-size beds closely against opposite walls. A door over was mommy's room; she had a full-size bed, and one simple woodish designed dresser. Our entire apartment was simple, and it was a little complicated being grouped up in threes to each bed. Taking into consideration that we had been through worse, had made it much easier to adapt to our current circumstances.

Every night we rotated beds, so everyone could get a chance to sleep next to their favorites; most of all, sleep without getting pissed on. For those reasons, everybody hated when it was their turn to sleep next to Mirah or Daishah, not wanting to smell like pea the next morning. It was a little excusable for Daishah, she was only three, but Mirah was ten years old, which was considered more of a problem. Still, Mirah never wanted to walk the hall of shame, and somehow she always found a way to put the blame on Daishah, but we all knew the truth.

To change the topic, our restricted life always ran into a brick wall. It may have started off with something small, but the outcome had a bigger effect. Our customary lifestyle was repetitiously troubling and depriving. Grievously, sharing was basically our routine. For one, we only had very few wash rags and towels, so we either shared rags or washed up with our panties. There were also times we had to wait to dry off if someone else was using the towel. Just imagine standing there uncontrollably shivering while waiting on your turn to dry off. Then when you finally get the towel, it be completely damp, which didn't feel refreshing, nor warmed you up. Brrr! I can still feel the breeze. For two, sheets and covers were a necessity that never gave us the full effect. We didn't know about matching bed sets because we never even had anything to match. Our new sheets and covers were somebody else's old stuff. Therefore, the wear and tear from previous years of usage was apparent.

First off, the dinginess was a permanent stain in the sheets. Secondly, the covers were so washed out that the fluffiness was no longer there. Thirdly, the lint balls wouldn't come off, despite the tremendous effort. Then we had those wool like covers that irritated our skin, and made us itch like we had some type of disease. But to keep warm and to stay clean, we had to ignore all negativity, and continue to adapt to the same sleeping and washing up habits. Yes, those were just the small things, but in the back of our minds, we were tired of those minor burdens. We were exhausted by living the SAME life and getting the SAME results. We always had an "I had a dream" of living a DIFFERENT life with DIFFERENT parents' speech. But we had to come to an understanding that life couldn't get any better. For every half of a step we took, there was a whole step backwards we fell. No matter what, our accursed troubles always seemed to follow us.

We were living a hard life, and it was killing us softly to pretend that we weren't. Although it was a process, we learned how to disregard our situations for that moment and blend in with the neighborhood. It took a couple of weeks, but we eventually started hanging out with the kids who lived in the next building. We thought our family was big, but it was over 12 of them, and they had a lot of brothers. It was discouraging seeing that their family was much bigger than ours, but had a more suitable and satisfying home. They dressed fresh to death, had all types of toys, and many electronics. They also looked happier than us, but I understood why. The bottom line was that we were happy to just get accepted by the cool kids.

Our biggest question was, "Why us?" Especially when we saw other kids with stuff that we knew we could never get. The expressions on our faces were saddening. Our hands were reaching out because we wanted it, but we knew if we asked that we would get rejected. Just by us knowing that there was no possibility of having anything a kid dreamed of, made it even more painful. But living daily through these struggles had caused us to build a bulletproof vest to protect ourselves from the new wounds that were going to be aimed at us. Desperately, we just kept a fulfilling imagination and hoped that one day it would come true.

Like we were hoping that one day Santa would bring us presents for Christmas. We were good and respectful kids; why wouldn't he reward us? Year after year we saw no signs of Santa, and that's when we stopped believing in him. Then, one Christmas Eve, we thought that if we had a Christmas tree, Santa would bring us lots of presents. So, Lannah, Daishah, and I decided to design our own. We went to the park, and cut down a small tree. It had very little leaves on it, and the branches were almost rotten, but it was good enough for us. We then had to lean the tree against the wall because we couldn't find anything for it to stand on its own. Afterwards, we put different colors of mommy's yarn for the decorations. Our ornaments were made out of paper and rubber bands, which had the tree looking beautiful in our eyes. We were happy for that spare of the moment, but we were even happier when the social service brought us a couple of present a piece on Christmas day.

Every holiday and birthdays, mommy had a shameful look in her eyes. She was embarrassed as a mother, but she kept crying and praying for a better day. Her constant prayers had led her to Saint Luke's Tabernacle Church, which she eventually joined. In all honesty, I think mommy was allured by Pastor Payne's caring heart, welcoming soul, and captivating smile, for that's all she talked about day in and day out.

Mommy started lusting over this man, claiming that he was her chosen husband. Looking back, I think that mommy's statement was totally inappropriate. The Pastor already had a wife with kids, so did she actually believed that God was going to take him from his family, and place him with ours? Her desires were an act of selfishness, which was caused by her wishful thinking of living her dream life. Somehow someone else's husband was a part of it.

Mommy, mentally disregarded both of their vows considering she never really got the true feelings of the words that were expressed on her supposedly, special day. Therefrom, her mind was easily influence with just a little touch of affection, and any form of encouraging words. With that being said, her lust for the Pastor had her opened, but closed-minded about his true love for his wife.

Moreover, she didn't look at it as an act or a thought of sin; she felt it was going to be an act from God. Although she knew that vows weren't meant to be broken, "Till death do us part," means exactly what it says. The only two ways out of the old, and in with the new was either God take life from his wife, or adultery would play a huge role. Either way would be the wrong direction, but immorality does exist, just like the thoughts in my mother's head. What made her even think that God should take away happiness from Pastor Payne's family, for her to sit in the luxury chair up on the pulpit as the pastor's wife? It's a possibility, but in all reality, mommy was delusional. She was so messed up in her head and heart that it caused her to mysteriously walk on the misleading roads with her kids' following behind her.

Eight kids and counting at that moment in time, and mommy had no doubt in her mind that Pastor Payne wouldn't take on her burdens. There may be some, but not many men who would actually settle down with a woman that had countless rug rats with no income. I just couldn't see it, but due to mommy trust in God, she believed anything was possible, and nobody couldn't change her mind if it was pertaining her faith.

Mommy's faith in God was so strong that it caused a distraction in her relationship with Gerald. Christianity didn't actually create the problems; it was the lack of respect for lusting over another man, who was the pastor of the church she was going to. Mommy never missed bible study, prayer meetings, or choir practice just so she could see, or get the attention from him. She was so deep in, that it began to seem like an affair was going on between the two. Gerald had then realized it was out of his hands, but before he could call it off, mommy had found out she was pregnant. Mommy knew that fornication was a sin, and she felt ashamed about it. However, she couldn't change the situation, and nine months later Lavinniah was born.

Given birth to Lavinniah was one of the most dangerous situations mommy was in because she nearly lost her life. Days before her due date, she began bleeding, which was the beginning stage of her hemorrhaging. Her face became pale, and her blood pressure was extremely low due to her losing too much blood. The doctors became very concerned and thought it was best to perform an emergency C-section. It was the right decision, and it was a blessing that mommy made it through that delivery; plus, Gerald was by her side every step of the way.

A few months after Lavinniah was born, we began to see a difference in Gerald. His attitude changed, and his attention was no longer focused on us. From here on, we realized he wasn't the man we thought he was. Then again, we didn't see the bigger picture, since mommy was more to blame for pushing him away. She continued lusting over Pastor Payne during and after Lavinniah was born, which became a complete turn off to Gerald. It also was his justifications for his infidelities. Any excuse was better than none, but the way Gerald executed his betrayal was an indication that he lost all respect for mommy. His affair was too close to home, and mommy was too nonchalant to see that Gerald was unfaithful.

There is always a time, even if it's the wrong time, the truth will eventually be exposed. That time was the day Shaylah was hanging out in the next building with some friends. Then Toya, who had something against us from day one, decided to spoil their fun. As soon as she walked up, she bluntly said with a smile, "I'm having sex with your mother's man… not only because I want to, but because I can." It was amusing that she had something to rub in Shaylah's face, which was definitely shocking and insulting, but Shaylah didn't show it. Instead, she boldly replied, "I don't give a fuck! You won't be the first or his last. I don't understand, why would you do my mother like that? She stays to herself and is friendly to everyone. You even speak to her every chance you get; yet, you sleeping with her man. I'm not getting it! Besides, he is too old for you anyway!" While Shaylah was talking, her veins were popping out her temple as she got very angry, not just at the girl but Gerald too, especially when she was the one who had to tell mommy that hurtful news.

Shaylah held her composure while Toya went on about how Gerald used to tell mommy he was working, but he was really sneaking over to her house. She also bragged about how he consistently gave her money. What was really fucked up, was that their affair was going on before mommy got pregnant. Basically, they both lost sight of their relationship beforehand, but neither one had the courage to walk away.

Shaylah dreaded telling mommy, but she was obligated as her child to do so. As the words slowly came out her mouth, mommy looked disappointed but didn't show how much she was hurting, even though we all knew she was. For the reason that Mommy was never the confrontational type, she did absolutely nothing. She continued her relationship with Gerald, and she continued speaking to her neighbors as well. Mommy went on as though nothing never happened. Primarily because she was in love with another man. Then again, mommy always felt less than a woman because of the way daddy treated her, which made her feel like she had to always settle for less.

Despite all the negativity, mommy never held grudges against anyone. She never showed not an inch of anger, even when most of the people deserved it. Mommy always said, "It's in God hands." I understood that a little, but there is a point when shit shouldn't be tolerated. Mommy needed to stand up for herself, and stopped people from taking advantage of her, especially men, but that continued to be her biggest downfall.

During that moment in time, Mirah was getting seduced by an older guy named Jacob. So, home was far from her mind while she was distracted by: Jacob, the streets, and her bad habits. Plus, the excitement from getting excessive money, and having lots of fun was keeping her occupied. Being a teenager becomes mentally difficult, for you're at a transitional state. Mirah's hormones were raging, her body was changing, and she thought that she was in love, which caused her to be rebellious towards mommy. In all reality, she was just falling in her older sisters' footsteps. She saw it wasn't a problem with them hitting the streets at an early age. Therefore, she knew she could do it too, which was the truth, seeing that mommy didn't enforce, or barely disciplined her.

While Mirah was busy on the streets, we were at home fighting for peace after Toya's scandalous news. Actually, Toya had her own motive for her actions, which was to continue ruining our lives. For whatever reason, she kept adding fuel to the flames whenever and however she wanted. Just like the day Shaylah and Tyesha were chilling on the stoop, laughing and talking amongst each other. Toya wasn't feeling the positive vibes, so she came outside just to test her abilities. With lots of aggression, and in a deep demanding tone, she said, "Yo, go to the store for me!" When Shaylah realized she was talking to her instead of her sister Tyesha, she then replied with a serious look, "No, you go yourself!" As their eyes connected, they both knew that shit just got real. Toya was a known bully, and she didn't like taking no for an answer. Conflictingly, a tough girl like Shaylah, didn't like to take orders. There stood two strong individuals with a heart full of pride. They were determined not to be perceived as weak, and that's what ultimately caused them to clash. Then more of Toya sisters came outside, and Shaylah felt outnumbered. Subsequently, she fearlessly but cautiously walked away.

Moments after, Toya and the Brady bunch came knocking at the door, wanting to fight Shaylah. When mommy looked out the peephole, she was shocked to see a crowd of boys and girls outside waiting on her daughter. Of course, mommy wasn't down with the dispute, and all of us were too young to do anything about it. Trying to keep the peace, we ignored the knocking and didn't bother to open the door, which gave the enemies more confidence and control. Conversely, Shaylah felt defenseless, and she knew eventually she had to face them in order to earn her respect.

When the intruders returned the next day, Shaylah's baby father Raheem was over there, and he couldn't put up with all the inconvenience they were trying to cause. As her protector, he went outside, stood in front of those loud mouth trouble makers, and then peacefully asked, "Why do y'll have a problem with my girl?" All he heard was, "That BITCH this… and that BITCH that!" But they didn't give no reasonable explanation. Raheem knew the only way to resolve that issue was for Shaylah to fight one on one with whomever. Shaylah was definitely down with that, but they all refused and eventually left.

The tables had turned when Shaylah became confident and in control. As they walked away, Shaylah knew that they had fear in their hearts. They weren't used to anybody standing up to them as a whole and weren't courageous enough to fight on their own. They were afraid to lose, knowing it would mess up their reputations. For that reason, it made them angry. The beef was blazing, and the plotting was perpetual, which left the block unsociable and violent. Under the circumstances, Tyesha and Shaylah's friendship was disjoined, not because they wanted to, but because they had to.

The confrontation went on for weeks. Each day, was a different reason for them to come knocking at our door. This one particular day was with a very intense approach. It was about ten guys, and some of them were her brothers. Amongst them were also 12 girls, a partial amount of them were her sisters. That night had just begun when they surrounded our front and back door; there was aggressive banging coming from both angles, and we were scared while mommy kept looking out the peephole. She was terrified when she saw: sticks, bats, knives, and guns patrolling them. All we could hear was, "That BITCH fucked my man! Come the fuck out hoe, so I can do you dirty!" Of course, it was false accusations, but Toya had it out for Shaylah. It was either out of jealousy, or because Shaylah made her feel powerless. Whatever the case may have been, I know that night, they were in full control, and none of us were safe.

While we waited quietly and patiently, hoping they would go away, Shaylah and Raheem held each other tightly. They felt if they were going to die, why not go in each other arms. The clock was ticking, hours were slowly passing, and they were still rowdy in front of our doors. We all were nervous, which prevented us from sleeping and eating. Then us younger ones started to cry, and mommy felt it was time to pray in hopes that they would peacefully walk away.

When they realized Shaylah wasn't coming out, they left. It was finally some peace and quiet. Then a few minutes later, we heard voices. It almost sounded like they were speaking in tongues, for we couldn't understand the weird words they were saying. Out of curiosity, Shaylah and Raheem peeked out the window. They saw Toya and her crew gathered around our building performing black magic. It was so powerful that you could hear dogs from out of nowhere howling, and then suddenly our lights and heat went out. It was dark, very scary, and got so cold. Our teeth were chattering, and we were shivering uncontrollably, which was that one time we didn't mind piling up in the same beds to keep each other warm. That night was a lot of praying going on, especially since we couldn't call the cops for protection without a phone. That was one frightening and sleepless night.

The next day, mommy walked to the pay phone and called the landlord to complain about the electricity problem. When he came to resolve the issue, he was totally shocked about what he saw, given that he'd never seen anything like it. His eyes looked puzzled as he explained to mommy that only one wire was burnt, which was impossible with all them being closely attached that the others didn't catch on fire as well. When mommy saw her own visual of the tampered wires, she knew it was far from a coincidence, but she was happy that the problem could be fixed.

Later on that day, a little before bedtime, the lights went off again as they did the night before. Everything mimicked yesterday's terrifying encounters, including the time. The dogs sent us our warning with their loud howling. Then, immediately after, the lights and heat shut off. This consistently happened on and off for about a month. We coped with it because we dread going back to the shelters, and the landlord dealt with it since that was his duty.

During that month, it became clear to us about what was going on as we began: seeing, hearing, speaking, and doing evil things. That was nothing but a sign of black magic that caused evil spirits to form against us, and Shaylah was the first to witness it. While Shaylah was chillaxing in the living room on the pullout couch, she became hypnotized by an old, crinkled up, black lady with paint on her face. Her inflamed eyes looked very wicked. Her dog shaped teeth were chopping quickly as she stood in front of Shaylah, laughing in a witch-like voice. Shaylah became unresponsive, but she heard her heart beating fast, and felt her body getting weaker. That's when she got frustrated because she realized she didn't have the strength to get up and run. She also didn't have the power in her voice to scream. Therefore, she laid there until the witch disappeared, leaving nothing but dusty air.

Without any hesitation, Shaylah got up and fearfully ran straight to mommy, holding her chest. During her panic attack, she tried to catch her breath, so she could clearly tell mommy about her gruesome experience. Mommy repeatedly hollered out, "In the blood of Jesus! I rebuked you Satan!" Shaylah was still terrified and didn't feel comfortable staying there, so she anxiously walked to Raheem's place. While she was walking, it felt like someone was following her. As she dreadfully looked at the brick wall, she saw a shadow behind her, but when she turned around, there was no sight of anyone. So, she quickly picked up her pace.

Shaylah felt a little peaceful once she arrived at Raheem's spot, but when she tried to get some sleep, she couldn't. On the other hand, Raheem was knocked out. While she was laying there, she started feeling something slowly crawling up the bed. When she nervously looked down, a long neck witch jumped up and was staring at her while she wickedly whispered, "Help me wipe the blood off." Shaylah quickly closed her eyes. As her adrenaline rushed, she determinedly replied, "No!" When Shaylah opened her eyes, the witch was nowhere in sight. Shaylah began shaking Raheem, but he wouldn't budge; it was like he was in a trance, and Shaylah didn't want to take any chances, knowing he wasn't able to protect her. Unhesitatingly, she got up and ran all the way home. Shaylah was devastated, and her tears were everlasting, for she wanted the witches to leave her alone. That night, her and mommy got on their knees and continued to pray, in hopes to break the curse.

The next day, evil attacked Teesah, and she started having asthma attacks. Normally, she knows what triggers it, but during that time, it was happening unexpectedly for no apparent reason. Her coughing and wheezing were frantic, and she was short of breath. Then her chest was tightening up with intense pressure, and her itchy throat was inflamed. She barely could talk, which made her panic even more. She felt like she was near death because she was lightheaded from the lack of oxygen to her brain. That was Teesah's first severe attack. She tried breathing in bags, and walking around the block taking slow breaths of fresh air, but nothing worked. Right then, mommy knew it was time to take her to the hospital. In a sluggish voice, Teesah said, "No mommy... didn't you pray for me? I have faith that God is going to heal me, just wait and see." While Teesah tried to catch her breath, mommy saw how pale her face was, and knew Teesah needed medical attention. Even though they had to walk ten blocks away, it was well worth it.

At the hospital, the doctor had disturbingly explained to mommy, "Your daughter lungs were an inch from closing. If you wouldn't had brought her here in time, she would've died." Mommy was speechless, but grateful that she made the right decision. The doctors then prescribed Teesah some medicine to prevent her from coughing and wheezing. They also gave her an inhaler, which wasn't effective as it should have been. For weeks, Teesah wasn't talking, and she was inactive due to her lack of energy. All she felt like doing was sleeping since laying in the bed was the only thing comforting to her.

Then Mirah came home, and her weakened soul had opened the doors for the witch to leave Teesah's body, and jump into hers when she came in close contact with Teesah. Subsequently, Teesah was instantly: healthy, energetic, and out of the bed like nothing ever happened. On the other hand, Mirah's high spirits had spontaneously turned into an evil one. She was no longer thrilled to see our other sister, Miyah. It was like her hatred went from 50 to 100 so suddenly. We knew that she and

Miyah always had controversies, but this time, it was a little different and more consistent. It wasn't a second that went by without them arguing. There were always punches being thrown, and hair pulling. They were quick to throw objects at one another, which resulted in cuts or knots. The craziest part about it was Mirah always initiated it, and she had no reason for her actions; she just had the urge to do cruel things to Miyah.

She did sneaky shit like spit in her food, or hide one of her shoes, which was something you wouldn't expect from an older sister. Mirah's vicious ways were like an incurable disease that was spreading, and causing a catastrophe in our home. Our home didn't feel at all sacred, seeing that it was corrupted by evil. Every day was a different vision from a different sister. The curse was terrifying, especially at night when the demons came to haunt us. We had many insomniac moments and several pissy incidents because we were afraid.

While we were petrified of what was going to happen next, Mirah was joking around, mimicking the demons that were coming to visit us. Before they came out, we felt their presence, but we didn't know their purpose for being there. We held each other tightly at night; we were scared to open our eyes when we heard weird noises and soft but raging whispers, saying, "Open your eyes and look at me, or you will be sorry you didn't." That was the night I couldn't resist; I opened my eyes and saw something I would never forget.

I looked up at the broken door that was leaning against our bedroom entrance. There she was, an illusory lady in a white, long dress slowly walking through the little space to enter our room. Then she stared at me with such an evil look. Her eyes were bloodshot red, her nose was cuspidated, and her lips looked like it had crow's feet. She never took her evil eyes off me until she faded away in our bathroom. I was dazed, my mouth was opened, but I couldn't say anything. I had goose-bumps, and as soon as my fearful tears had dropped, the wicked lady came back out. She looked me directly in the eyes while she put her wrinkled fingers to her lips. In other words, she was telling me to be quiet. Then she walked back into that small space and disappeared. I was weak in the knees, but I was able to run and scream. "Mommy! Mommy!" I hysterically cried. She replied in an unease voice, "What happened? What's wrong?" As I stuttered, I was pointing towards our room, "A witch… some bad lady went through that hole! She's going to take me next time, I'm scared!" Mommy told me that God wasn't going to let her. Then she continued reading her bible aloud, but something seemed strange. My heart was skipping beats, feeling that something else was bound to happen. I believed it was out of God's hands, for the evil spirits were too powerful. It was so strong that night time wasn't their only option anymore. Then the next morning, I saw something else.

After that long scary night, I thought the daytime was safe. As I was creeping in the living room, trying not to wake up Mirah and Sophia, the floor squeaked, and I froze up. When I looked at them to see if they were awake, I saw a colorful horse leaning over their bodies. Its long fiery tongue was blazing towards their faces. I roughly rubbed my eyes to make sure they weren't playing tricks on me. They weren't, so I screamed loudly, waking up everybody. Yet, Mirah and Sophia laid there comatose. Everybody else came running to see what was going on. I was pointing and asking in a panicky voice, "Do y'll see the rainbow looking horse? It's right there… looking right at me!" But nobody saw what I saw, or felt how I felt, which made me furious and frustrated. Not to mention, I was intimidated when I saw the colorful horse smirking at me and blowing fire towards my direction. I felt defenseless because I wasn't hallucinating, for the devil was clearly after me. I cried my heart out while asking, "What the devil want from me? What did I do? I'm not bad, mommy. Why does he want me?"

My mother didn't have an answer, so she made all of us get in a circle, hold hands, and repeat a scripture verse out the bible. "Therefore, submit to God, resist the devil, and he will flee from you." (James 4:7). Everybody said it, except Mirah. She refused to surrender to God. Hereinafter, it was hard for her to oppose and challenge the devil, and any other evil spirits within or around her. On the other hand, the rest of us were compliant considering we were soul believers. At that moment, we felt peace like the demons had departed from us; well, at least some of them.

A few weeks passed before the BCW had paid us another visit. The neighbors realized that the voodoo didn't defeat us. With bad intentions, they reported to our case worker that we were living in a condemned building with no lights or heat. That was confidential information. The only people who would've known about that was: our household, and the people who were responsible for doing it.

When BCW came out to inspect, they were absolutely shocked that we were living there, seeing that the apartment wasn't suitable for anyone to live in. Each room gave them a negative attitude about our wellbeing. There were mice that were running on top of the stove, water bugs crawling under our beds, and behind the refrigerator; moreover, we had lead poison that could've caused us serious health problems. The worst part of the house was that there wasn't a ceiling in the bathroom. It was just an open space with visible rusty pipes that wasn't secure at all. The place had spoken for itself, and it was indeed hazardous, so they gave us a week to leave, or we would be placed in foster care.

Mommy was lucky… they could've taken us away on the spot. Even though mommy wasn't mentally or physically unfit, she had absolutely nothing to offer us but love. Respectively, the case worker showed some empathy and took into consideration that it might be in our best interest to stay with her. If we would've went into the system, then we eventually would've gotten separated.

Separation wasn't our destiny because through all the trials and tribulations, mommy managed to keep us together. It was our journey to cross the paths of: struggles, hardships, and heartaches as a family. Even if it wasn't by choice, we still had no other options. As we continued to walked the roads of darkness, we all were gloomy inside, but we just hoped at the end of that journey was a brighter day.

Back to the TL2 we went. It was like we were starting all over again. Our own row of cots, and surrounded by strangers and thieves was what we became accustomed to. Living in the shelters were never a sweet dream, but our nightmares only lasted for about a month that time. Then they placed us in another dump of a Hotel.

Going through the halls were like walking through a junkyard. It was trash everywhere. There were beer bottles, cigarette butts, used toilet paper, etc.; you name it, we saw it. OMG! The nauseating pea smell was so strong that our eyes watered up, and the scent settled in our nose. It was like we were inhaling contamination. Although we were eager to leave the shelters, walking in that hotel had us wondering did matters get worse. Most of all, we were nervous about what we would see behind our room door.

The room didn't look like the hallways, but it wasn't a place that we wanted to stay permanently, seeing we were definitely living in another danger zone. There were gang bangers who weren't afraid: to rob if they had to, body a nigga if they wanted to, or curse out old people just for the hell of it. This neighborhood was loud and terrifying. We were scared to go outside because we were afraid of what type of crime we'd see. Most of the time, it was just smelly and dirty bums laying outside the building, which we were always hesitant to pass by them. We also saw dope addicts shooting up in the hallways. Then they would be leaning in one position for hours, but they would never fall. The drunks would be staggering up and down the halls, loudly cursing, but slurring their words. They would angrily break bottles as though they were mad that it was empty. That wasn't a good image or environment a child should be brought up in. That's why mommy kept us in like prisoners.

Staying isolated in our room opposed to being outside was much more preserved, but we were constantly jumping out of our sleep every night due to the: guns going off, fights breaking out, bottles splattering, people screaming and banging on doors, walls, or whatever else they could bang on. That hotel wasn't for families; it was for gang bangers, bums, and drug addicts. So, we couldn't understand why the social worker would take us out the hood, and move us into the ghetto.

Mommy never had a plan B, but she had to think of something really quick. Even quicker when we walked into a war zone. It was bullets coming from every direction; dead bodies lying on the ground, others were badly wounded, and some were hiding or running for their lives, including us. For bullets can't see the target, even though its intentions are to aim at the enemy, but the innocent bystanders somehow lose their lives. Mommy didn't want any of us to be that next victim on the news. In a New York minute, she did the unthinkable…

Without the welfare people assisting us, mommy packed our bags and prepared to move down South. Her first welfare check she sent: Shaylah, Teesah, and Miyah to North Carolina. Mirah decided to stay with her boyfriend Jacob. How unfit was mommy to let another teenage daughter make her own decisions? Meanwhile, us younger ones stayed isolated in the hotel room until mommy got her other welfare check.

While awaiting, our seclusion was more of our bonding time. We put all of our difficulties to the side, and enjoyed our last days there. We laughed, even though shit wasn't funny. We played, even when we had nothing really to play with, but most of all we cried because we had something to be emotional about. We even had our own little prayer sessions, hoping things would work out for the best when we left the city. Somehow being at our worst had caused us to consolidate our differences, which made the time go by quickly and smoothly without any commotion. We were in an ugly situation, but the beautification was us being together.

"Together" was mommy hope, whereas "Separation" was her despair. Her incomplex mind had caused our life to be complicated. She was more focused on what was right instead of concentrating on getting right. Her intentions were out of love, but she didn't have an outlook on the facts of life. All she was experienced in was bearing children. Mommy kept high expectations, but she wasn't driven enough to get any job done; she believed God was going to do it all. "God helps those who help themselves!" Hezekiah 6:1. You can't be lackadaisical and expect blessings to come knocking at your door every time, which was mommy's perception of how God worked.

I describe mommy as naïve, but she was also content, seeing she was complacent with her situation. She truly believed that our destruction was the beginning of our construction. Her attentive and amiable ways had giving us a good feeling that everything would soon be okay, even when we knew it wasn't. She had an invigorating heart, but was a lost soul because it was hard for her to find herself. She had just enough competence to pass her by, and the only form of guidance was coming from her personal ordeals. For many reasons, mommy was gullible and oblivious, but she overlooked that fact since her mirror didn't show that reflection.

My father, on the other hand, was a very intelligent person; also, a con artist, which means he scammed his: family, friends, and enemies by deception. That "Mr. nice guy" who he was perceived to be, was truly, "Mr. Ugly" underneath. Everything he touched was pleasure for him. Every word he spoke was fraudulent, and every movement he made was nothing but betrayal. He deceived many and achieved most, for he used his intelligence, swag, and attraction to scheme on people to prosper. Nobody knew his deepest thoughts, and couldn't see through the darkness in his eyes. For his charming imposter was used differently for each individual. I despise him for that, but the fact that his blood is flowing through our bodies has given us some of the fire that is blazing through our veins, which is nothing but immoral. To some degree, we are just like him.

# PSYCHOTIC SIX

Lalannah Daevas is a split image of daddy with a little touch of emotions from mommy. Lalannah was also an 80's baby who was born on October 6. She was one of the dark-skinned sisters, with a repulsive heart that pumped atrocious blood, since the day of her nativity. Growing up she always thought she was incommensurable because she felt her features weren't appealing enough. Therefore, her actions were more coerced than ours. She felt it was her position to be our protector and supporter. If she wasn't going to be recognized for her beauty, then she was going to be acknowledge as the beast.

Being in the spotlight was her intentions at first, until she started craving for more. Her greed grew as she reached puberty. Her devotion became emotionless, which caused her tainted behavior. She was one of the mendacious ones, and it had gotten so bad that her presence started coming off as phony, and we couldn't believe anything she said. Even though we shared the same blood, her good deeds were no longer in our favor as the envy led to Lalannah's spiteful ways.

She became ferociously chaotic when she gave up on herself. Moreover, on her sisters, for her insecurities had shifted her hostility towards us. She hated our dissimilarities because our reflections were the features she wanted to see when she looked in the mirror. Our popularity was also something she desired. In other words, the love we received was something she didn't feel or get enough of. As a deduction, her mind became thoughtless, and her words became cursed.

Lalannah consistently talked negative and delivered it as well. There were times we despised her being in our presence because at the end of the day, the outcome was some sort of dispute. Her dominant ways became too audacious, for she thought that she was untouchable and victorious. The look in her eyes showed: rage, hurt, and evil during her belligerencies. Her brain began to oppose reality. She became distant from the real Lalannah we knew, and La- La land was the world she was living in, which had us believing that she was a little psychotic.

Contrastingly, the doctors thought that a manic-depressive illness was a big issue. They felt it was a need to monitor Lalannah with proper treatment. There were times they had to take precautions and quickly restrained, sedated, and admitted her into the hospital. It was weeks, sometimes months that she would be staring at the white walls hazy and feeling paralyzed, but that only controlled Lalannah momentarily.

Lalannah had that fight in her; she didn't take shit from anyone, not even mommy. I remember the first time she disrespected mommy, and it wasn't the last. We all were in the room arguing back and forth, we were damn near fighting. Then mommy woke up, and quickly put an end to all that nonsense. Lalannah, on the other hand, was mouthing back as though she was an adult defending herself. Mommy told her in an aggressive voice, "Shut up before I shut you up!" She was shocked as her eyes widened when Lalannah responded with anger, "You don't tell me what to do cuz I don't have to be here!" Mommy immediately started swinging on her, and Lalannah didn't hesitate to swing back. It was like she changed into someone else for a split second. When she came back to reality, she stopped, cried and yelled out, "Nobody cares about me!" Then she walked out and slammed the door. Mommy hollered, "You better get back in here, or imma beat you some more!" Lalannah ignored her demands and continued stomping down the steps. She didn't come back for hours. Then she walked in silently and calm as though nothing never happened. Instead of mommy tearing that ass up, she just put her on a punishment, which would make any child feel like they have the juice.

After that, Lalannah started getting in trouble at school for lashing on, or cursing out teachers and students when she didn't get her way. Her raging acts were harmful. She threw chairs, books, and pencils at whomever. She even walked out of class whenever she felt like it. She wasn't there to learn; she was there to get all the negative attention. Her consistent suspension from school had led her to be a teenage dropout. She never got the feel of high school because her anger took over her mind, and she was also ready for boys to explore her body.

Her outraging acts towards guys were a little more dangerous. She had less pity on them, and they showed no mercy on her. Lalannah was like a bobcat going to a pit-bull fight; she was dominant but got dominated. Still, that didn't stop her aggressive actions, it just made her more competitive.

I remember Lalannah telling me about how she caused a grown man to stoop to a 15-year-old level. It was one springish evening, when crowds of people were chilling in front of our building with their music playing. People were talking amongst their own little circles. Then out of nowhere, Lalannah felt the need to be disrespectful by intentionally interrupting the grownups' conversation. One of the guys advised her to stay in a child's place and out of grown men's faces. Lalannah felt insulted, so her curse words started flowing, "Fuck you! Pussy ass nigga. You don't run me BITCH... I'll spit in your face!" He replied calmly, "When you do, I'm going to send your young ass home crying." Lalannah hated threats, for that was a green light to attack. That's when she spit on him, and his quick response was a blow to her face. Then the fight escalated from there. Her punches were with full force, but his was with more aggression; however, Lalannah toughed it out. While he wrapped his hands tightly around her neck, her mouth began to widen as she was grasping for air. Everybody was watching, but no one was stopping it, even when they knew it was wrong. When he finally let her go, she felt a little discombobulated and embarrassed. Therefore, she picked up bottles after bottles and started throwing them. All you could hear was splattering glass, and all you could see was people moving out of harm's way.

The bad part about it was the moment Lalannah violated him, was the time everybody felt that she had gotten what she deserved. Of course, she was in the wrong, but what made him right to literally fight a child, a young girl at that; and not a family or friend did anything, but talked about it. Deep down some of them niggas wanted to say or do something, but they were afraid of what the outcome was going to be. For that nigga Knots was well-known and respected, that's exactly why things happened the way it did.

Lalannah still remained untamed. She even brought all the adversity into her relationships. Once again, the cycle trickled down, and she became sexually active in her early teens. She was eager for some attention and yearning for a lot of love; when she found it, she didn't know how to utilize it. In fact, she didn't know what love was. She took men feelings for granted, and used their bodies for punching bags. That was the way she showed her affection, and if the guy had a bad reaction, then she felt he had proving his love for her.

Lalannah was very bossy in her relationships, which was not attractive to most men. Still, she managed to find a few suckers for love, or fools that wanted some good pussy. Lalannah was the one who enforced the rules, and he either followed or got left. She most certainly was another one of daddy's clones. Everybody meets their match eventually, and Dwight was hers. He didn't mind going across her head and forcing her to listen, which kept her viciously smiling because any negative attention was a turn on to her.

Lalannah temporarily tamed acts were just an act. She wanted him to feel powerful, so she could turn around and make him feel powerless. She always tried to get her five minutes of fame, even if it caused a lifetime of misfortunes. Just like the day Lalannah and Dwight came to visit me, which was perfect timing for her to prove a point. It was like everything Dwight said or did, Lalannah came off blunt and very disrespectful. If he asked, "Who?" She would say, "None of your damn business!" If he walked funny, she'll say, "Damn nigga, you walk like you got fucked in your ass. Is you a faggot or something?" She was trying to cause problems, and the heat was definitely warming up the room. Dwight face was looking stern and concerned about how he was about to react in front of me considering that was the first time we'd met. I do agree that confronting a straight man about his sexuality is a No-No, but Lalannah didn't care, and Dwight didn't neither.

They were standing so closely and angrily in each other faces while exchanging spit as they argued. After Lalannah hauled off and punched him in his nose, they started fighting. Blood was leaking everywhere as they tussled all over the place. They forgot all about being in somebody else's house. It was a disaster. I mean, picture frames broken over heads, lamps thrown, any visible and harmful object was flying in the air. Lalannah blew that whole thing out of proportion, so we had to control her in order to stop the fight.

Trouble! Trouble! Trouble! Was the first impression my boyfriend Charles and a few of his family members thought. I couldn't blame them, especially when Lalannah started swinging on everybody who tried to hold her back. In a brutishly crying tone, she hollered out, "Get the fuck off me you pussies! Y'all don't fucking know me... Y'all on this nigga side? Ooow, all y'll nigga's going to die!" Then she looked at Dwight and said in a crude tone, "Nigga I hate you, and that's why I fucked around. You ain't shit nigga. You nothing to me!" While holding Lalannah, I calmly was talking to her, hoping I could get through her reckless mind. Eventually, I did, but she still was mad enough to no longer want Dwight in her presence. In a riotous manner, she advised him to go back home because she didn't want him anymore. We felt that Lalannah was speaking out of anger; therefore, Charles took Dwight with them until the air cleared.

Lalannah, of course, didn't know that part of her tantrum was triggered from her hormones changing in connection with her being pregnant. Although she was young, having a baby made her mother instincts kick in immediately. She became submissive and looked very happy that she had someone to love, hold, and could learn to know while he grew. More importantly, she had someone that would cherish her, and be devoted to her unconditionally. A person that would look past her flaws, comfort, and protect her from harm. Their bond would continue to grow stronger each day, and they would have that special way of communicating. Can you imagine that certain look in their eyes when they are away from each other, and both of them are feeling that same emptiness, or just hearing that pitiful cry when the child wants his mother? Well, That was the connection they had as a mother and son.

Certainly, the baby had made Lalannah and Dwight's relationship closer, but very much unstable since they couldn't live as a couple in someone else's place. So, they were moving from place to place with limited funds. Given that they had more than enough help from Dwight's mother, they managed to survive as parents, but they couldn't sustain their relationship longer than a couple of years. After that, they went their separate ways.

Lalannah and Dwight's love/hate friendship remained because of their child they shared together, but their breakup had brought out Lalannah's sexually promiscuous ways. Although she performed like an exotic dancer, her role was much more like a pimp. She appeared to be enjoying what she was doing, but in her heart she really wanted to find true love; however, it never worked out like that. Her mindset was too immature for a grown man. For this reason, Lalannah got the pleasure out of sleeping with everybody else's men, and hoping she could veer them in her direction.

She either danced herself into a man's pants, or forced herself on him. Then manipulated him into giving her what she wanted. Lalannah spent money unwisely, but she indulged in every dollar. She had the pleasure of making them cum and was pleased when they came back for more.

They kept a crazy conversation going while the reggae music was playing. They guzzled down drinks until they got all the way turnt up, and that's what brought out the kinkiness. Tic! Tic! Tic! The vibrating flow of Lalannah's derriere. As she wined slowly, she provokingly took off her pants, and left nothing but seduction lingering in the air. After gently hitting the floor, her edible chocolate body started grinding while she popped her ass with ambition. Then she would complement herself by massaging her physique from top to bottom. Her legs coordinated with the music, while she fondled with her pussy. It was all in the guy's eyes that he was fascinated. As his dick rose, he started masturbating, but not for long.

Lalannah would interrupt him with a little touch, "Aaaah!" He would softly moan while his eyes were closed. As she rubbed his head, she would climb on top of him just so he could get a little feel of that wet-wet. Then she gradually grinded down on his dick, giving him a taste of it. "Mmm... Ooow shhhit!" He felt so good that he entrancingly started sucking her tits, and firmly gripped her voluptuous ass. Afterwards, they began to fuck. Moments later, they'd be erotically tongue kissing until they both reached their peaks. Before the night was over, she would make him leave, but that was Lalannah's scheme. She fulfilled men needs, but she never revealed any type of feelings, which had them craving for more. Her only downfall was being too wild and aggressive, which eventually chased them away.

Lalannah didn't care. She believed only the tough guys survived, which was the type of man she was looking for, but felt she never came across one. That's why she was so used to treating guys like they were weak. Most of the men she preyed on were guys that didn't have a significant other or confidence in themselves, but they knew how to treat a woman. On the other hand, she cherished the so-called confident men, who were also players that had wifey's at home, and looked at Lalannah as their side chick. It was hard for her to find an honest man because she was going about it the wrong way.

Headed in the wrong direction had led Lalannah into a married man's bed and an unexpected pregnancy. Due to the guy being married, Lalannah thought it was best not to tell him about the baby and take on the burdens herself. Times eventually got extremely hard, so she decided to go to the guy for help, but he was already doing 15 to 20 years in prison. Lannah knew she was in a bond, but she felt it was only temporary; finding a sucker came easy to her. The bama was Carlton. He was a mama's boy that was infatuated with Lalannah. He did everything in his power to make her happy, while she did every disrespectful thing in his face. It was disgraceful to see.

With every good there was bad. For instance, when Carlton moved Lannah into a home, men that she was fucking were there too. When he got them a new car, it was transportation for her men as well. In fact, Carlton knew what was going on, but didn't care because he: was blinded by her love, whipped by her sex, and lost within her game. He was so ruined that he lost his job for pissing hot; not because he did drugs, but from all the smoke he inhaled by the people who were neighboring him. Thereafter, his car got totaled when Lannah's other boyfriend wrecked it. Carlton's life collapsed in a matter of months.

He made lots of enemies resulting from Lannah's consistent public outbursts; plus, some of his family cut him off over her.

Carlton's mother was one of them. She was flustered by his crazy and deranged girlfriend; moreover, the change in his behavior and environment. Her main concern was Carlton's safety. She knew he wasn't accustomed to the hood life; in fact, he never really experienced being misused considering he was a homebody. However, his momma couldn't help him that time around; Lannah was controlling his every move. She kept him on a tight leash until his value depreciated. After he lost everything, Lannah then vanished.

Lannah left home with one child, and arrived back with two, which left her even hungrier. Therefore, she continued her mission on a different set, but sort of the same environment. The stage was her means of support. As she got intimate with the dance pole, her bare skinned flowed smoothly around it. Her prodigious booty muscles were vibrating to the beat, and her body was winding in heat. There were a lot of heads entertainingly shaking, their eyes were fulfilled, and their pockets were charitable. They wanted to eat that "Sexy Chocolate" as they repetitively screamed her name, and fantasized about buying the new eye candy that was put on the market.

It was unbelievable that Lannah was a novice to the stage as she stole the spotlight. Especially when she utilized her movements amongst another female, which was breathtaking and memorable. Most certainly, her two-piece sparkling pink suit accommodated her curves as she elegantly walked away.

Lannah enjoyed making that cash, but in the midst, she found another sucker for love, and he didn't leave any time for her to kick up those heels. Herbert was a close friend to damn near everybody's family because he was just that friendly. His weak spot was females and money. He was the type of guy that observed girls while they were younger and couldn't wait until they got old enough, so he could contribute to their needs. Lannah was one of them, but he was unaware that she was ahead of her game, and he was behind on his. Herbert had high expectations for their assumed relationship, but Lannah already knew that they didn't have any form of connection without his money.

Herbert also didn't know the true meaning of love, so when Lannah started verbally and physically abusing him, his love became stronger considering it fulfilled the attention he was yearning for. With this mentality, it was easier to prolong their relationship, seeing that they both had something in common. They were wanting to defeat their insecurities, and succeed their popularity, in order to accept themselves for who they were.

Meanwhile, Lannah continued being a BITCH, and she treated Herbert like the shit she flushed down the toilet. She didn't care about his feelings since he wasn't the man she really wanted. He was just someone she needed at that time. Lannah was imperceptive like daddy, and the fact that he treated mommy like nothing was the primary reason she wanted to return the favor, and treat men like they were trash.

Matters deteriorated for Lannah when she mistakenly got pregnant by Herbert. She hysterically cried to me, "Veah, I can't have no child by this inflated, unsightly motherfucker... Oh, hell no, this nigga must put a hole in the condom because pregnancy was not even close to my plans!" That moment, she knew that their unflattering relationship had to end and immediately left town to terminate the pregnancy.

A few months after, Lannah had bumped into an African dude name Akeem. He was chocolate just like she liked them, he had money just like she needed, and he was sweet and charming, which was exactly what she wanted. In fact, he was single. They hit it off smooth, and it gradually progressed into a serious relationship, and both feelings were mutual.

I could see the glow on Lannah's face, and I saw a change in her behavior because she felt complete. Akeem made her feel beautiful, wanted, and most importantly loved. Everything she was longing for was staring her in the face, and she wanted to enjoy and make the best of it.

She eventually had two kids with Akeem, but their crammed apartment was too small for a family of six, and they needed something bigger. Subsequently, Lannah took the initiative and went through the shelters to get her own place. She handled things maturely when it came to following the rules there, although the shelters were totally different from when we were growing up. They were newly built apartment buildings, and you had your own personally space. There wasn't a set time to leave, but you had a certain time to sign in. Moreover, you could have visitors, but they couldn't stay overnight. It was much easier to adapt to, and cozier to stay in, which Lannah did for a little over a year. Soon after, she got her vouchers to get her own place.

Everything was going just fine for Lannah, the kids, and her relationship. Yet, the excessive tiger milk, and the fulfillment of Mary Jane had caused her actions to have a negative twist. That's when Akeem and Lannah started having public disagreements. It was tormenting, not only for their relationship, but for the kids as well since they were mostly in the middle of it all. The kids became voiceless; they were too scared to speak. So, they cried out of fear, hoping that would put a stop to all the anger and the fighting. At times, Akeem was man enough to walk away, but there were times it was rage all through the mad house.

The constant bangs against the walls accompanied by loud arguing, had the kids jumping out their sleep plenty of nights. They would be peeping out their doors, and afraid of what they were going to see, but most of the time, they sadly saw their mother crying. Lannah tears were tears of hurt; tears of disappointment within herself, for she wasn't just failing in her relationship, but as a parent as well.

Lannah kept drowning her sorrows in that full to empty bottle, and clogging her lungs up with that Maui wowie, which provoked her to be a little more aggressive than normal towards the kids. The severity of their discipline was not delivered properly because she was taking all her anger out on them. They have been called every curse word in the book. Her clenched fist didn't hesitate giving them a two piece to the face if they said anything out of the ordinary. Furthermore, she used any type of object with full force to beat them.

Since my kids weren't used to seeing or getting that type of discipline, their summer visits had left them with some disturbing memories. One of those thoughts that kept lingering in their minds were the horrible beating their cousin Kiarah got. It was so brutal, Kiarah reported it to the social service, but denied all accusations when Lannah confronted her about it. It was all in Lannah's eyes, and embedded in her deep voice that she was really pissed, but she didn't violently act until she reached her trigger point.

Lannah started mushing Kiarah in her face with one finger. Her evil inflamed eyes stared Kiarah down as she slurred at her words and said, "BITCH, how the fuck you going to tell them I'm mistreating you? Imma show you what mistreatment really is when I fuck you up, then you can run back and tell them that, and maybe they'll find you a new home!"

For hours Kiarah took the verbal abuse while she set in silence. Her saddened eyes were full of tears that would not fall. Her heart was pumping pain and fear over all of the nonsense Lannah was screaming in her ear. As much as it was horrifying to Kiarah, it was intimidating to the other kids as well. It was a hurtful sight to see Kiarah getting out the shower with water dripping from her body, and as she approached her room, out of nowhere, Lannah came striking her with an ironing cord consistently and ferociously.

Kiarah's screams had made the kids infuriated. It sounded so intense, and from her body movements, you could tell that it was a fiery feeling. The torture went on for longer than 5 minutes; it may sound short in time, but the seconds went by very slowly. After the brutality, Kiarah had long and deep bruises all over her body, but Lannah still didn't show any remorse, and continued to curse her out afterwards.

The kids tried to comfort Kiarah in a disquieted way because that was the only thing they could do, but when they saw all those black and blue marks on Kiarah's back, they were in disbelief, and my kids were ready to come home. I heard the fear in my kids' voices as they cautiously tried to explain what happened but felt at ease when I told them I would be there in a jiffy. As my kids were leaving, they expressed how they felt sorry for Kiarah, knowing that wouldn't be the last time she would experience that kind of outrage, since Lannah's problems continued to escalate, and her sanity started to deteriorate.

Every day it was something deranged going on with Lannah. Whether it was with Akeem, the kids, sisters, or someone off the streets. Lannah's name spoke bad news, and all of that negative energy was inexcusable, which pushed many people away, including Akeem. They would depart in their relationship, seeing the damages couldn't be fixed. They realized that two mentally challenged people didn't mix well together with kids involved.

Afterwards, Lannah had hit ground zero, and her depression stage took place. She woke up in tears, and cried herself to sleep at night. Not to mention, the monkey on her back was hard to resist. There were times I received phone calls from Lannah about five in the morning crying out for help, and sometimes wishing she was dead. There were even times she would just scream out my name, "Veah!" She said repeatedly. I heard the pain and emptiness in her voice, but I knew there was nothing I could do when I lived about 600 miles away. Therefore, I tried to give her words of encouragement. I told her in a sleepy voice, "I can be there for you the best way I could, but only you can make a difference in your life... You should want what's best for not only you, but your kids. I know it seems hard, but nothing comes easy. So, you can cry, but let that be temporary. Get your strength up, and get your life together for real." Of course, she sounded a little alleviated as she responded, "Ok... I love you!" But because she was contaminated by intemperance, she did not remember anything we talked about the next day.

Lannah's depression became a little more disturbing when she gradually started losing her appetite and weight. She isolated herself from everyone, but her kids. They watched her breakdown and didn't know what to do about it. They tried everything in their power to make her happy, but she never smiled. They gave her their sweet conversations, but she didn't respond. Moreover, they tried to cater to her needs, but she no longer had any desires. Three weeks had passed by, and Lannah had no food or fluids in her body. The only water flow was her tears she was drowning in. The lack of nutrition wasn't the only thing that made her weak; she lost her strength through all her discouragements as well.

As Lannah looked in her kids' distressed eyes, she knew they were grieving because of her. There was no doubt in her mind that something had to change. Without delay, she took the first step by going to the emergency room for help. She wanted her vitality back, and getting admitted into the hospital was her only hope.

Lannah didn't eat for three weeks, which gave the doctors a reason to believe she was suicidal, and thought the kids could be at risk. Unfortunately, they called the welfare without informing Lannah about their actions. As the social worker stood beside her bed and explained, "Lannah, I'm from the Department of social service... My name is Mrs. Loretta, and I will be handling your children's case while they are being placed in the system. I was told that you are incapable of providing a safe environment for your children. Therefore..." Before Mrs. Loretta could get another word out, Lannah angrily said, "No! No! Oh, hell No! How they going to fucking play me... Y'all trying to take my kids away from me because I can't eat. That have nothing to do with them... I love them... I need them... they all I have! I won't do anything to hurt them, y'all can't fucking do this!" Mrs. Loretta responded, "It's out of my hands, but I do have in my possession your past cases that have been closed. It states that you've been admitted plenty of times into the crazy house. However, this is only temporary until we finish investigating, but you must get yourself together if you want your kids back home... Until then, is there any family members that is willing to take them?"

Lannah laid quietly and weakly in her bed with an IV in her arm, which prevented her from expressing the anger that aroused through her body. Still, she cried and fluently used curse words like it was another language. Then she told Mrs. Loretta to get out. With unanswered questions, Mrs. Loretta waited outside the door while Lannah talked to her kids.

Lannah reluctantly explained, "Mommy is not well, so y'all going to live with someone else until I get better. Ok?" As tears quickly fell down her face, the kids just stared with pain and agony. Although the two youngest ones were too young to understand, the two oldest had an idea of what really was going on. That's when her son Demetrius intensely blurted out, "Why? For how long? Why I can't take care of you until you get better?" Lannah hesitantly responded, "Because you can't do what the doctors can do, but I promise I'm coming back to get y'all... I love y'all. Now give me a hug and kiss, and go with that stupid BITCH!"

As the kids walked out, Lannah stared at the bright ceiling, praying to God that things would get better, but it didn't. It was torture being without her kids, for she felt so lonely. Particularly, when they put her in between the four white walls of craziness again. Then restrained and sedated her for 30 days. When she finally got released back to reality, her mind was even more delusional from all the poison they injected her with, which supposed to help, instead it hindered her from the norm.

As Lannah calmly walked home, she realized she no longer had one because she got evicted. What made matters even worse was finding out that she lost custody of her kids as well. Even though the kids were placed with family members, they still were separated. Demetrius went with his grandma, Kiarah went to Aunt Martha's house, and the two youngest went with their father Akeem. Lannah was hysterical, for her life had collapsed within a month. She stood there lifeless, and was clueless about her next move. Suddenly, everything started spinning; her heart was racing, and she began hyperventilating as she was losing it.

She then closed her eyes and started talking to herself. In a serene tone, she said, "I can't go crazy... I have to be strong... Think Lannah! What should I do? How can I do this when I have no one to turn to? Calm down Lannah... Think about your kids. They need you. Wake up Lannah... there is no time to sleep!" When she opened her eyes, everything was bright and so real. It wasn't a dream, it was her living nightmare, and it was time for her to overcome her fears. She was afraid of making mistakes, and being recognized as a failure to her kids and family. She feared being deserted. Moreover, she was discouraged about being different. When she took heed to her life and realized that fear is agony, she started thinking clearly.

Lannah didn't have too many places to go. She ran out her welcome almost everywhere, but one person she knew that she could turn to was, Miyah, which she did. Miyah put on her big sister shoes, and took the initiative to help her out. First, she contacted the social worker for updates on Lannah's case. Then she got her mail forwarded to her address; most importantly, she gave her a place to stay, and a shoulder to lean on like a concerned sister would do.

Lannah eventually took matters in her own hands and maturely started communicating with Mrs. Loretta herself. Then they set up weekly visits, so she could see her kids altogether as a family again. It was special and happy moments for all of them, but when it was time to depart, it had gotten very emotional because being separated was too complicated. It was even harder for Lannah knowing the long process she had to go through to get them back.

When she appeared in court, they required her to take parenting classes. It was also enforced that she must undergo a Prime for Life program, and pass all drug tests. Considering Lannah was diagnosed with a bipolar disorder and other mental issues, it was mandatory that she continued counseling and treatments. Furthermore, it was imperative that she appeared at every court date and visit. If missed without good reasoning, she would have to start the whole process over again. Lastly, the judge recommended her to stay out of trouble, and find a stable home. Lannah had some challenging responsibilities ahead of her, but this helped determine what was important in her life.

The challenges were quickly defeating Lannah. She wasn't used to rules and regulations; therefore, she continued to drink and smoke, which led to failed drug tests. Ultimately, she stopped attending the Prime for Life program because she felt it was pointless. Overall, it was difficult for her to stay out of trouble; she consistently had fights, and most of the time the cops got involved, which resulted in her going back to the crazy house. Even though this was an excuse for why she would miss a court date or visit, she never needed one, being that those two and parenting classes were the easiest to stay devoted to.

In fact, her devotion towards Miyah had lessened since both of them have that dominant reputation, and they eventually started bumping heads. First, Miyah became leery and cautious after some money and jewelry were stolen. She didn't believe her kids would take from her, so she assumed it was Lannah. Thereafter, Lannah tried to take control over everything that was moving in Miyah's house, and that caused a feud between Miyah, her man Calvin, and Lannah. Not to mention,

Lannah threw shade on Calvin's loyalty. Although he was one of the most unlikable men, we all knew how Lannah got down. We considered her as one of the flirtatious sisters. She would try to seduce your man just to see if she could get what you have. If she didn't get the type of attention or affection she wanted from him, then the animosity kicked in. Adding to that, the accusations, arguments, or fights started over her wanting to stay in control of the situation.

Lannah's lack of respect for our men were over them not giving into temptation. However, there were some that did, which was more of an eye opener for us. In a way, it was a good thing but bad because it was coming from a loved one. Lannah had deceived a lot of us over her imperfections and insecurities, but I don't think she saw it like that, since her dirty dealings were meaningless to her. How do you cope with a sister that is always provoking someone else's man just to feel wanted? We may be self-content with ourselves, but how much confidence do we have in our men? For an easy slip, can lead to a hard fall, and Lannah would be thrilled to assist.

Without any remorse, Lannah is blind to the fact of how much hurt she could cause a person because it's nothing but a game to her. Still and all, its betrayal coming from both parties, and both should be held equally accountable. Although there is no love lost towards my sister, I still have lack of respect for her and all the men she defeated.

I describe Lannah as a charming person, but she can be a victimizer as well. Meaning-- she has the potential of intriguing and enticing people with her amiable charisma. She has that special touch, and those captivating words to get what she desires. She also has the drive to influence people, and the energy to entertain them. On the other hand, Lannah will betray you when it's least expected. She would trap someone by making them believe she is fully honest and generous, then reveal her corrupt and destructive ways. In fact, she has certain preferences on who she wants to victimize. It's cruel in most people's eyes, but Lannah doesn't care or have any regrets. She will lie, cheat, or steal to get what she wants; smile, cry, or mislead to receive what she needs. In all reality, who is the fool? It's not her; it's you!

Presently, Lannah is focusing on her transitioning, so she can make a significant change. At first, it was challenging because she was afraid that humbleness would make her feel less superior. She was frustrated about losing her expressive voice and defined character, which caused uncertainty about letting go of all that anger she had locked inside. But if you truly want something to come to an end, you must have some form of acceptance. When Lannah lost her kids, she gained knowledge of what she values in life. She stopped resisting, started controlling her feelings, and is currently learning how to limit, but hopefully put an end to all her madness.

A few years later, the judge granted Lannah custody of her kids, except for Demetrius since he was already of age. He also was facing similar problems like Lannah, and being rebellious was the number one issue. I guess because he had a lot of anger built up inside. He felt that neither parent played a huge role in his life, which could create a problem child. Lannah still doesn't tolerate his behavior, but she has the ambition, and is discovering new ways to become a better parent to all her kids.

Lannah is a strong individual, but at one point, she let her weakness overpower her strengths. Although her tears have not yet dried, she's no longer letting her fragility interfere. She is still self-conscious about herself, but it doesn't influence her decisions in life anymore. Despite that, she still seeks attention and affection from someone she can call her own. Thumbs up to Lannah for putting forth the effort towards trying to make a difference.

A point to remember: Most people must strive to get at a good place in life. Even if it's not where you want to be, it's still progression. Just know that life isn't easy, and there will always be challenges, so you must prepare yourself for obstructions and sometimes failure. Problems are like a ghost, you can't see it until it sneaks up on you. Instead of running from it, try to handle it accordingly by contemplating through your issues that stand before you.

Bad situations can come big or small, but the first step is learning to understand, and be receptive to the substantial problem. Try to communicate with supportive people who can give you some viable advice. Emotions need to be eradicated, for decisions can be altered when you have the wrong mindset, which can lead to poor judgments. Most definitely take your time when thinking things over; some situations you can't control. You must also take steps in moving forward, and your focal point should be on the solution and not the problem. If you can, try to be decisive on what may be best for you, without any regrets. It's best to always think positive. The negative talking and thoughts will only make matters worse and tenser toward your issues. I know it's easier said than done, seeing my sisters and I have been, and are still going through problems. In fact, at times, we still making wrong decisions. After all, we were giving the opportunity to confront our problems, implement change, and aim for a new beginning.

# SOUTHERN TECHNICALITIES

---

## *A new beginning, and another atrocious ending*

MALACHI 2:10 "HAVE WE NOT ALL ONE FATHER?
HATH NOT ONE GOD CREATED US? WHY DO WE DEAL
TREACHEROUSLY EVERY MAN AGAINST HIS BROTHER,
BY PROFANING THE COVENANT OF OUR FATHERS?"

Mommy was off to a fresh start, which was the beginning of a clean slate. She didn't know what to expect. So, she took baby steps just to be a little cautious until she felt complacent about her movement. Down south was a major transformation, but mommy's instincts, and the word of mouth had her believing she was making the right decision. She knew we would be safer; to some degree, we would have more stability, and a better opportunity for advancement. With mommy wanting a positive outcome for all of us, she was delighted to leave the city.

Although New York was our home, it devalued our lives, and influenced many decisions that were made. Regardless of what, majority of us were immune to it. That's all we knew and didn't care to move, but we didn't have a choice since most of us were underage and needed security. In the midst of moving, we showed mommy some resentment and anger resulting from us not only being consistently unstable, but we were moving to a state that we didn't know anything about.

Our understanding was that we were starting completely over in a different environment. We were still trying to grasp onto the fact that: people would be speaking in different dialects, and we would be surrounded by folks living a tamed, and rather boring lifestyle. Because we had been through so much in our own city, we were also concerned about being an outcast, and not being accepted in a place that wasn't our home. We were seeking a new beginning, but if the relocation did not provide a transition in our lifestyle, then it was meaningless. We were oblivious to what North Carolina had to offer, other than it being a state where affluent and retired people resided. On the contrary, we were used to a city that never slept, living life at a faster pace, and amongst most people who were impoverished. At that time, we didn't know about retirees; we mainly saw people working on the block. Both states were intimidating to us in their own way, but we had to depart from our past to arrive to our future.

Down South we went, Midway, North Carolina we headed to strive together as a family. There was no turning back, couldn't stop in the middle, we just had to steadily put one foot in front of the other and keep going. We had to continue to express our distinctive personalities, and utilize our minds considering we would eventually diverge in our own paths that would lead us to different futures. Still, we shared: the same blood, same struggles, and the same prayers, in hopes of an improved outcome. Although damaging words were coming out of our mouths, optimistic thoughts were wondering in our heads, while we road across the Brooklyn Bridge.

It took us over nine hours to get to North Carolina, which was very long and uninteresting. All we could do was stare at trees, picked out luxury cars we wanted, and dodged deer's when we got closer to the south. We noticed the difference as soon as we arrived in the country. The roads looked deserted, they had less lights, and everything was completely silent after dark. They didn't have buildings because people mostly lived in houses. Out of curiosity, us younger ones started blabbering out questions, "Where are all the people at? Do they play loud reggae music? Why do they have so many bugs and unfamiliar animals?" Mommy was laughing at us. Then she responded with a smile, "This is the south girls." We surprisingly looked at each other, assuming it was going to be a long process to adapt to, but we were also looking forward to meeting new people, and making the best of our changeover.

Our first place wasn't our own because we had moved in with Aunt Ada Mae, Uncle Henry, and their three kids: Hunter, Harriet, and Sally. We had our inside giggles, for it was unbelievable that their names were even country. In fact, they lived and ate like country folks too. They were well organized, and each had their own beds and bedrooms. Although we overcrowded their house, they had a spacious home, their own yard, and a porch. It was undeniably convenient that we didn't have to walk up many flights of pissy steps to get into our apartment. Plus, we no longer had to use our fire escape for a porch, and we had a huge yard to play in. That difference was the good part of it.

What we disliked about the country was the difference in their food. Our food took you on an adventure of cultures, and ethnic groups. In fact, we are well-known for our franks, sausages, pizzas, and we loved the hero's, Chinese, and Jamaican food. We cooked to make our food flavorful, which we enjoyed the sweet and spicy taste. On the other hand, southern meals reminded us of the slavery days; everything was grown, freshly picked, and cooked mostly homemade. Yet, their meals involved a lot of fatty foods. They are well-known for eating the whole pig, they love fruity pies, and gravy over everything. Surprisingly, they even ate animals that came out of their backyard. Their food also had a different aroma, and looked better than it tasted. Their food was bland, like they were afraid to use seasoning, but heavy-handed on the barbeque sauce or gravy they smothered over their meats.

We had a loss of appetite for meats when we discovered that Uncle Henry was killing squirrels and possums. He chopped off their heads, shaved off their skin, cut them into bite size pieces, slowly cooked them, and then served it for dinner. As we looked with disgust, they ate with pleasure. They had the greedy chew; they licked and sucked their fingers, and the worst part of it all was the after burps, eww! What a complete turn off! It was most certainly ringing southern bells.

The first week we felt welcomed; we actually bonded like a family, but as time passed by we started seeing their true colors. We began feeling like strangers instead of relatives because they treated us like we were completely destitute. The first sign of resentment revealed itself, when a conversation completely stopped once we came in the room. Awkwardness filled the air, as the stupid looks on their faces exposed that we were the topic of discussion. Then came the complaints, which was something different every day. If we used the bathroom, flushing the toilet ran up their water bill. Coming from New York we didn't have a water bill, so it was difficult trying not to use the bathroom as much. What really took the cake was when the dinner plates got skimpier meal after meal. It was funny since we wasted their nasty food anyway, but observed their actions as they did a 360 on us really quick. Eventually, the constant mistreatment became a burden.

Another burden was creepy Uncle Henry. Although we never could put our fingers on it, there was always an uneasy feeling that something wasn't right about him. While we played outside, he used to sit on the front porch rocking slowly and silently in his old wooden rocking chair. With his suspicious eyes, he gave us these weird looks while he puffed on a stinking cigar. The look could've been perceived as an indecent look, or I'm ready for them to get the fuck out of my house look; either way, it most certainly made us uncomfortable.

The thought of us walking on pins and needles had constrained us to be less in their presence as much as possible. Therefore, we stayed outside or in the room until it was time to eat or close to our bedtime. This was our mechanism to keep the peace. The warmth in the house without a doubt turned cold, which indicated that we overstayed our welcome.

It's understandable that they weren't used to an overcrowded house, but Aunt Ida Mae knew our situation beforehand, and she still offered to help. In my opinion, I felt she really just wanted another story to gossip about, but shamming as though she was the savable aunt. Instead of her trying to help my mother figure out a quicker or better solution, she stubbornly acted harsh and rude, hoping mommy would get the picture and just leave. Alternately, it caused us to have animosity against them, which resulted in our negative disposition towards that side of the family.

Things got more hectic when our cousins expressed their condescending, slick words to us. Then they began to act arrogantly, as though they were better than us. Conflictingly, our older sister's ghetto feedback would be hurtful but real, especially since the country cousins didn't have enough money to reconstruct their facial looks or bodies. Certainly, beauty wasn't their forte, and their plumped shapes didn't complement their appearances either. When measuring attractiveness, they were no match for us. Indeed, the feud was ablaze! So, mommy and Aunt Ida Mae had to put an end to the ongoing enrage. It was no other choice, but for us to go our separate ways.

We lived with Aunt Ida Mae a little over a month until mommy received her welfare check. Mommy was so eager to move into her own place that she desperately signed a lease to an old greenhouse on Creepwood Drive, which was just a few blocks away from Aunt Ida Mae's place. It couldn't happened quick enough, for they were so happy to see us leave, and we were eager to go. It didn't matter if we were going to be without electricity for a couple of weeks. We just wanted our own space and the opportunity to feel comfortable. Living at Aunt

Ida Mae's house didn't provide the harmony that we hoped for on the road to our new beginning, but it did make us embrace our own home.

Like usual, we were overjoyed about moving into a new place. We were jumping, dancing, and running all through our spacious house. It had 4 big bedrooms, "WOW! No longer packed like sardines." A huge kitchen and living room, "OMG! We have enough space to pray and eat together; we could laugh and watch T.V. as a family… we're so happy! Aaaah!" The bathroom wasn't so big, but we were grateful we had one, and we could flush the toilet as much as we wanted.

That house was a prime example of, "You can't judge a book by its cover." The outside of the house looked very old, but the inside told a different story. My only aversion towards the house was this unappealing, outdated gas heater that was mounted to our living room floor. It was a big, rusty, dark brown tank with a wide pipe connected from the heater through the ceiling. It was pointless to have, and most certainly looked unsafe. "Hazard control," I said. But that's one of the disadvantages of staying in an old place. Overall, everything else was looking great for our first, new, country home.

Our house didn't have any electricity, but we always stayed in survival mode. During the day, it was open blinds so that the sun could shine brightly through our windows. Then at night, we had candles lit to alter some of the darkness. It didn't bother the older ones, but it was a little taunting for us younger ones. In a way, the house seemed somewhat haunted. We heard but didn't see what or who was taking them creaky footsteps, or making squeaky noises outside the window. The scariest part was the thumping coming from the roof. By us going through worse had made it a little easier to get through the night, especially when we cuddled up with our eyes tightly shut in hopes that the morning time came quickly.

The most exhausting part about not having electricity was the need of cooking; everybody gotta eat. Therefore, mommy and Shaylah had took turns cooking at Aunt Ida Mae's house. It was indeed challenging, especially dealing with the phoniest. For example, one evening Shaylah went up there expecting to cook our food quickly because we were starving, but she had to wait a few hours since Aunt Ida Mae was preparing her meal. Then she purposely left everything out of place. It was dishes piled up, stains on the counters, and the floor wasn't swept; in other words, she expected Shaylah to clean it up before she started cooking. Shaylah was mad, but she swallowed her pride, and put her attitude aside considering she had little sisters to feed.

Despite Shaylah being cordial that day, she was extremely fired up from Aunt Ida Mae's unacceptable actions. Aunt Ida Mae is one of them country folks that you will eventually have to curse out. She befriended people with her smile, then discouraged them with her compulsive gossiping. It's difficult for her to have a decent conversation about what's going on in her life when she was always meddling in everyone else's. Primarily because her life was a bit boring; yet, she had her sneaky and vindictive ways that she didn't want anybody to know about. Aunt Ida Mae is one of those aunts that you practically have nothing good to say about. From my perspective, she hasn't earned the respect or title as an aunt.

A flashback moment: It was a sizzling summer day when I was slumped over and so drained just thinking about the long walk I had ahead of me. The drips of sweat was burning my eyes as they raced down my face, then splattered and soaked through my shirt. It was damn near 100 degrees, and I was anticipating on catching a ride. Suddenly, I heard a loud horn; I exhaustingly turned my head, thinking the lord has answered my prayers, but it was the devil rubbing the heat all in my face. For I saw Aunt Ida Mae and her daughter Sally driving past me with an unsympathetic wave, and their big enigmatic smiles. She didn't even bother to ask me did I need a ride, especially when she knew where I was going, and she was headed in the same direction. Moreover, she knew the temperature was overwhelmingly high, and my exhaustion was apparent. From that day forward, I considered her a cruel person, and felt she envied us, seeing we had the potentials that her kids were missing.

Speaking of her kids, their characters were identical to hers. They also resented us for being who we are. Similarly, we disapproved of who they were portraying to be. Unfortunately, as a family, we DO NOT stand strong; also, in public view, we are all invisible. Although we're related through blood, there's no acknowledgement by sight.

Getting back to the point about our electricity... It eventually got turned on, and we were finally settling in, so our house stayed lit up. "Star light... Star bright... there's no more darkness... Hooray! We have lights... We have lights!" The hardship was finally over! No more Aunt Ida Mae because we threw her nonsense in the trash; her kids, guess what? Trash! All of their phoniness stayed at their house because we didn't need it or wanted to deal with them. Yet, mommy being mommy still chose to communicate with her family considering it was in her nature to try and keep the peace, regardless of the circumstances that was interfering with us bonding.

While mommy was accompanying herself around the negativity, we were maintaining the positive things at home, such as: putting up curtains, hanging up paintings, and rearranging furniture. Although we couldn't afford brand new household goods, our hand me downs worked just fine, and turned our house into a decent home.

After everything was established, it was time for the older sisters to seek, find, and mingle in the area. Meanwhile, us younger ones played amongst each other in our big yard, entertaining ourselves by climbing trees, and walking through the woods, hunting for treasures. In a flash, our sisters got familiarized with different areas in the city, and they were popular with the boys. That's when their fun kicked in, and their partying began. North Carolina wasn't as bad as they thought. Although New York would always be in their hearts, at that point in time, it was just a brief thought in their minds.

Meanwhile, we were getting acquainted, and mommy was searching for a church to join, which she always had poor judgments in choosing. After she attended a few churches around the neighborhood, she decided to make Divine Baptist her home. When mommy was a part of any sanctuary, she stayed devoted. She attended every service, and paid her tithes and offerings faithfully.

Mommy's problem wasn't about her loving God so much, it was getting deeply and emotionally involved with the wrong Christians, which was her downfall. "Quote... Unquote..." For that reason alone, we hated going to church with mommy. Thank God, we only had to go on Sunday's, but it didn't seem fair that she only made us younger ones attend, while the oldest stayed home and played house with boys. Surprisingly, this sort of treatment was common; life was never fair to us anyhow.

Anyway, we were happy to hear that our little sister Lacaylah was finally moving back with us after eight years. Primarily because cancer started attacking Aunt Ava's body, and she couldn't properly care for Caylah anymore. Then a few months later, Aunt Ava was no longer suffering, for God had called her home. We all were heartbroken when we heard the news, in respect of her being like a second mother to all of us, and also one of those favorite aunts that you never want to lose, but God had gained one of the best angels. R.I.H. Aunt Ava, I know you're still watching over us.

Right after we welcomed Lacaylah home, our cousin Sophia came back to live with us as well. Even though mommy was drowning in generosity, it was more to it with Sophia. She had a special place in mommy's heart, seeing she treated Sophia like she was her very own. Regardless of the huge responsibility she took on, mommy always looked at things in a good way, even when she had the question "How?" in her head. Mommy knew she barely could take care of us, let alone somebody else's child, but her faith was believing in all the positive things she did instead of the negative things she saw.

## #1 FACT: FAMILY + HARDSHIP – WEALTH = NOTHING BUT LOVE

After all, problems were always an interference in our life. It was a hindrance to our progression, destroyed our happiness, and humiliated us every chance it had. Just like that fall day. We had been settled in for a few months, but weren't in North Carolina any longer than six months, and we had already made the front page in the local newspaper.

To begin with, it was late in the evening, mommy had left for church, and Miyah was the only one there to babysit us that day. Although Miyah always took very good care of us, that particular day she was less observant. On the other hand, I wasn't because it was just one of those days I felt a little leery, especially when I passed by that old gas heater in the living room. My first instincts always told me to look up in the ceiling where the gap was, and I always did. This time, instead of seeing just darkness, the pipe was surrounded by fire. Without any hesitation, I started hollering, "Miyah! Miyah!" As I ran quickly to the back room damn near out of breath, I said in a concerned voice, "Come! There is a fire in the ceiling!"

Miyah didn't check, and she didn't seem at all worried about it. She just took an uneducated guess and said, "It's a gas heater, so it supposed to do that." Then continued doing what she was doing. I was younger than her, but I had a gut feeling something was wrong. Instead of me joining in with my little sisters to play, I kept looking up to check on the ceiling, and each time it looked like the fire was spreading.

Before I could run and tell Miyah again, one of our neighbors were knocking aggressively on the door and blurting out, "Y'all roof is on fire!" Without hesitation, but in fear, we quickly ran out the house half-dressed. Some of us just had on under clothes or a long t-shirt, but none of us had on shoes. That was the least of our worries, for we were lucky that we made it out unharmed.

While we stood across the street in the neighbor's yard, we shockingly and sadly watched our house burn down. Shortly after, we heard the disquieting whining of the fire trucks sirens as they were approaching our location. "Nee Naw! Nee Naw!" Then we started hearing the intense braying of the ambulance and police sirens. The whole north end of Creepwood Drive was covered in Red, blue, and yellow lights, but the fire wasn't put out in time to save any of our stuff. We lost everything in the blink of an eye… Aaaah damn, here we go again!

It was very embarrassing when tons of people were coming from different parts of the neighborhoods being nosey. In fact, the news reporters were too. They were snapping pictures, and asking us all sorts of questions. Clogging up our ears with, "Who? What? Where? How? And Why?" It was too much for us to handle, and mommy came just in time.

Mommy left from hearing the good word, and ran straight into hearing bad news about the worst fire of the year destroying her home. Her tears drenched her shirt as they fell like heavy raindrops. Some were tears of joy because she was happy to see her kids' safe, and some were tears of sorrow since she lost everything and had to start all over again. We were just at the beginning of our journey, and a tragedy ended it for all of us. That was the first sign from Satan that the curse would continue to follow. He revealed to us in so many ways that misery is our happiness, and that we would fail more than we progressed. It was said by our late grandma Daevas that we would never have a good and easy life, and so far, it was true. The evil would continue to prevail, and mommy continued to believe that God's power couldn't be defeated.

We were the talk of the town and had the picture of the month in the newspaper, but we weren't at all presentable for the front page of anything. Our hair was shaggy, we had a bleak and dark look on our faces, and our under clothes didn't complement us either. In other words, we were looking a hot mess, and became someone's charity case because we were homeless again.

# THE LIFE WE WERE GIVEN

Being fairly new in town, and being recognized as the New York family whose house got burned down was most certainly humiliating and depressing. However, it quickly became helpful towards us. Because we were considered an emergency case, we were priority, and in a matter of days, they moved us into the Colony projects. People were donating clothes, furniture, and household goods. They also gave mommy a check; regardless what the amount was, anything was helpful, and we were blessed that people gave us that much support.

We were never unappreciative about where we had to live, but when we heard the word "PROJECTS," we associated it with the word "GHETTO!" When we lived in New York, we stayed in the "HOOD!" A place where the unfortunate families live in apartment buildings or houses. Contrastingly, the GHETTO was definitely the projects, but lucky for us, we never lived in them up north. Of course, we hated those shitty ass hotels, but that was only temporary. As for the shelters? Well, I would never wish that experience on anybody. Long story short, the PROJECTS are the slums, and we didn't want to live like that, but didn't have any other options. Miserably, off to the ghetto we went.

We were shocked when we arrived at the Colony's. In our eyes, we saw luxury. "Are these the projects?" We asked. It was, but it didn't look like them at all. They looked like brick homes in a black community. It was clean, spacious, had playgrounds, and a personal driveway. It was nothing like we expected, and we were loving it. It also was a stress reliever for mommy when she found out that her rent was under $100. "WOW!" Now that was truly a come up for us.

While we were moving into our apartment, the attention was encircling us. There were people coming on their porches watching, a few of them waving, and a lot of those dragging "Hey's." We also saw some whispering and giggling. It became very clear to us that country folks were nosy, and news were like a deadly disease to them because it spreads quickly. For one, if people come from the other side of the projects just to see who moved in are, "Nosy!" A person that asks a million and one questions and barely knows you is most certainly, "Nosy!" It was weird, especially when people stared and didn't speak, which is something Northerners hate; it's a form of disrespect, or expresses that you're looking for trouble. I assumed in the south it wasn't a big deal.

Southerners were easy to pick up on, and somewhat easy to adjust to, seeing they were very friendly and jubilant. On the other hand, northerners are reserved, very serious, and uneasy. For instance, we don't think that we must associate with a person just because they're our neighbors, it doesn't always work out like that. Furthermore, we like to mind our own business and stay out of everyone else's. Although most people do it, gossiping can sometimes be misinterpreted, and when shit gets misconstrued, it can cause conflicts that could've been avoided. That was one of the country folk's issues. Especially, the older ones considering they couldn't keep their mouths shut.

Flashback moment: While we were taking things in our place, one of the older ladies that was standing next to her friend was talking under her voice, "Girrrl, I heard it was about 15 of dem, and dey came from Neeew Yark. Mae Lee from up the road said dey ain't nuthin but trouble!" The friend's eyes had widened, and her head started rolling when she said, "Dey bet not brang dat shit down hea! But girrrl Janie had told me dey were some po folks dat got burnt out dey house... ain't dats something? She also said dat dey ole mammy is a fake Christian. Dat's why that shit happened to her cuz God don't like ugly... uh-huh!" They were so deep into their conversation that they didn't realize how loud they were talking. That was the least of our worries, for our main concern was getting settled in.

We didn't have many boxes to unpack, so we got established in no time. Afterwards, us younger ones anxiously walked the neighborhood to see what the project kids were all about. With the tough experiences we had in New York, we already had made up our minds that we weren't going to relive that life again. So, when the first set of kids came an approached us, we reacted very aggressively. We heard them discussing the derogatory comments beforehand. Then they degradingly said, "Why yaw on our side? Ain't yaw the new po kids from up the road?" Before my sisters got anything out, I angrily responded, "This poor kid will beat your ass BITCH! And yea we are the new kids on the block... Do y'll want to fight or what?" My sisters were fiercely standing beside me with the screw faces, and their hands up yelling, "We ready! Come on, we can have a one on one!" They started whispering while we sternly stood there waiting. Then the nappy headed, bony, dark-skinned girl nicely said, "My name is Kimberly... Do y'all want to be friends and play?" We agreed, being that they were the ones who backed down. After that day, we started hanging out daily.

We became the popular four in those projects. The kids loved how we talked, danced, and they were feeling our swag. We finally got some positive attention, and it was prominent. Getting teased was tossed out the window. Even getting beat up, or jumped for no apparent reason had stopped knocking at our door because scary didn't live there anymore!" Finally, we had overcome being an outcast. We always wanted to be in the spotlight, and now that it was beaming on us, we wanted to make the best of it.

Of course, the fame enticed the haters when their reputations were no longer relevant after we came on the scene. That wasn't our fault, we were just trying to meet, not compete against anybody. Yet, the competition was rising as days went by. Still, we had the projects on lock, and they were enjoying the new kids on the block.

It was a matter of time controversy was going to intrude, but who would've thought it would come a few weeks after moving in. I was the first one to get into a fight. It was with this black as midnight, beanstalk looking boy named Jack. He was trying to put on a show in front of the hater squad, and I wasn't having it. There were laughing and chuckling when he said, "Yaw think yaw all dat because yaw from New Yark... Yaw ain't nobody!" Once I got riled up, I put his words on mute when I crushed his sole in front of his audience. In a cool but fierce voice, I blurted out, "Who the hell is your ugly ass? ... Looking corny and dusty ova there. Yeah, we are from New York! We wild, rough, and pretty... lame ass country boy. You need to wipe that black off your face, and that butter off your teeth with your long ass feet!" "Ooow! Ha-ha, hee- hee, heh," was all I heard, and that definitely turned Jack's smile upside down. That's when he balled his fist up and was ready to fight.

At first, I was a little intimidated, seeing he was tall as fuck, but I didn't show any signs of fear. That day, I was willing to do what I had to do to earn my respect. So, when he set it off on me, I reacted instantly. We were standing toe to toe, throwing blow for blow. "Don't let no girl hang in there with you, beat her up!" I heard over there. "Yeah, you getting him... keep punching!" I heard over here.

On round two, Shaylah came running outside and hollered out, "You better beat his ass, or I'm going to beat yours!" That was a psychological thing for me to gain leverage, which was helpful, but it wasn't that easy fighting a boy. However, he looked more like the wimp after we fought two rounds, and both times it was a tie. He had a knot on the left side of his forehead, and I had one on the right of mine. Considering I was a girl, he thought it was an automatic win, but LOSER wasn't something I wanted to hear or be anymore. With this in mind, I brought my heart of stone, and my soul of destruction to that field, which the average girl wouldn't had tempted to fight him like I did. My respect was definitely giving, and my confidence increased tremendously.

Indubitably, the altercations didn't stop there. With destruction, I had to continue showing off my hand skills until the kids were too intimidated to fight. Adversely, the older ones were not liked by females at all. It was clear that a lot of girls really envied them because they desired what they had. It wasn't about the material things; we was in need of that. It was more about my sisters' confidence they built along the way that made them more competitive. The uniqueness they were born with showed the radiance on their faces; also, having a mindset of their own had separated them from others. In other words, most country girls had no type of control over their thoughts, sensibilities, and passions. In fact, they didn't know their worth; they were too damn spoiled, and didn't know what it was like to struggle for everything. Therefore, they took life for granted. That's why my sisters had a lot of enemies because they were ravenous, and they showed determination to get to their desired place. Since the country girls didn't try or understood them, they became angry and bitter. Indeed, the beef was cooking, but my sisters weren't at all surprised, and they didn't care as long as they were getting all the good vibes from the guys.

We just took things day by day, hoping for more positive outcomes. Each day was a new day and brought new experiences. When kids knocked at our door, they wanted to hangout. It was amazing how the kids were idolizing us, and loved to be in our presence, which was a big difference from New York. Majority of the kids didn't reject us, being that we all were going through our different struggles.

Struggles were the only thing we had in common, but we were diverse in so many ways. Some people enjoyed the difference, but a lot of them hated it, which always brought conflicts knocking at our door, mainly to fight one of the oldest. After they fought and proved that they were very proficient with their hands, those BITCHES thought twice before they knocked at our door again.

Overall, the south wasn't too bad. Trouble comes and goes in any city, state, or country. So, always try to make the best of it. If anything drops or gets lost, just pick up what's left and keep going. That's coming from me, and I am a leader. I was born to lead, but I didn't take control of my own destiny until I was 12 years old. I thought dancing was my purpose in life. I loved it, enjoyed entertaining, and danced like everyone was looking. With this idea, I decided to put together a dance group, hoping that eventually we would become famous kids performing on national television… In the interest of Janet Jackson being my idol, and that I loved TLC's style, I chose to have a mixture of both trends.

Everybody is not fit to dance, but some people has the potential to get taught, and believe me, teaching them country girls weren't easy.

They had no rhythm, no character, or confidence. Moreover, they were very stiff, but Daishah, Lannah, and I gave out dance lessons for weeks. Then we had a dance off to narrow down our options. Resultantly, we picked Lila, Luna, Olivia, and a few other kids as backup dancers. The group was called "Sky is DA limit" because that's what we were aiming for.

We met daily after lunch in our driveway, dressed appropriately, and we were ready to sweat. Lila's mother, Grace gave us a nice black boom box that had our music thundering through the clouds, which made it impossible to not move to the beat. She also bought me the Janet Jackson and TLC tapes to show her support for our group. Every day we danced to "Rhythm Nation" and "Ain't 2 proud 2 beg," for those were our theme songs.

There were times the simplest dance moves got messed up by one person. Ultimately, the whole group was punished; we had to start over, repeatedly when these mistakes did happen. At times, we were overworked, "Practice makes perfect," and it eventually paid off once we got the dances down pact, and we memorized all the words to both songs. I was proud of myself and the group for our hard work and dedication. We were finally prepared to perform in auditions for talent shows in hopes that we could get enough fame to be a part of Janet J's or TLC's dance group, hell, anybody's group. It was just a dream when we realized that fame cost money that none of us had. Unsuccessfully, after a year, we departed as a dance group, but remained friends.

My younger sisters and I still had love for dancing, but we were back focused on just being kids. It got bored for me quick because I wasn't feeling that kid stuff anymore. I wanted to be more than the new kid on the block, playing in the hot ass sun with the other kids. I wanted to be me, and loved all over the world, but I had to figure it out. While my little sisters were out being kids, I was in the house thinking about my next move.

One day, I was in the house cleaning our room, and minding my own business while Miyah and her friend Kassidy were having their "Whatever, Whatever" conversation. Then the whispering began, and shortly after, the broom was touching my leg. When I turned around, I saw them giggling like the shit was funny. It was agitating to me, that's why I gave that BITCH a warning, "Do it again, and it's going to be trouble!" Then I gave her an impish look. Yet, the fat BITCH took me as a joke, and she did it again. I turned around so fast, snatched that broom, and started beating her with it. Miyah hollered out, "Stop it! Stop it, Veah! It was my fault. I told her to do that!" I'm staring at Miyah and Kassidy with anger, while holding the broom in the air, waiting to swing again. Kassidy sincerely said, "I'm sorry... I was in the wrong." Still, Miyah the trouble maker was laughing because that was entertainment for her. Anyway, that was the day Kassidy and I became friends.

Kassidy Parker was her name, and she was 12 yrs. old just like me, but she didn't look like it. She was over six feet tall, about 400 pounds wide, but still had the potentials of being just as beautiful as I was. We kept an interesting conversation, and enjoyed hanging out together; above all, we both had adventurous souls, curious minds, and the determination to find an outlet for many different reasons.

Every day we were hanging out. We were walking up and down town, living those pleasant moments, in a different environment each day since Kassidy knew just about everybody. In a matter of months, we became the best of friends. Then shortly after, I started hearing terrible rumors about Kassidy, which was hard to believe until she set me down and confided in me. Her deep dark secrets were strictly on a best friend bases, but it seemed like everyone knew. Oh! I forgot in the south everyone assumes.

Kassidy told me that she was sexually active at nine years old with her brother's friend, Craig. He would come around the family to eat, laugh, and talk as a cover up. Then when everybody went to sleep, Kassidy would sneak up the street to meet with Craig. She was in love with him, but he was just fucking her, and it took Kassidy a long time to realize he didn't care. After him, she just went buck wild.

She said a guy could say, "Hey baby," and that was enough attention for her to indulge in him. Afterwards, her self- esteem was lower than before considering they didn't want anything to do with her anymore. When I was hearing her stories, I felt sorry for her, and I didn't judge her. As a best friend, I was willing to help her out. My words of advice were, "You have to build up your confidence. It's going to take patience and determination. At some point, you may even think it's too difficult because it was for me as well. Still, I did it... and you can too."

First things first, I asked, "What made you doubt yourself?" I had a pretty good idea, but I wanted her to let it out, let it go, and move on. With her chunky sad face, she replied, "All my life I was called fat Kassidy. At home, on the streets, and in school, I was physically and mentally abused... but I never fought back because I didn't know how. When kids threw things at me, I sat there and did nothing. When girls smacked me, I did not only turn the other cheek, I turned my whole body and walked away. Getting criticized for being me had made me look at myself differently. Being that I couldn't or didn't confide in anybody was the reason my wounds never healed. That's when I became vulnerable... towards men especially." Then Kassidy held down her head with shame.

It was too late to feel ashamed, for what she did was already done. The only thing that mattered was to what degree she wanted to correct herself. What really shocked me was how a young girl was persuaded by men so often, but had a lot of brothers, and her father in her life. I never asked her that, but I didn't have to after hearing her self-explanatory conversations. Kassidy always talked about how close her family was, but how distant they acted.

Her brothers were more focused on their girls that they didn't take the time to try and understand her. She depressingly explained how much she loved her father, and their communication would be great if he remembered what they talked about the next day. Then there was her holy mother who would look at her differently due to all the unholy things she had done. For those reasons, she didn't feel comfortable discussing any of her business to anyone, until she met me. She felt in her heart that I was trustworthy, and I was. From that day on, we were more than friends because she became my sister.

Every morning Kassidy was knocking at our door, hoping that our mentality would rub off on her. She wanted to think, talk, dress, and fight like us. With pleasure, my older sisters and I had made it happen.

Her confidence was growing every day, but the hardest problem was her weight, seeing it was slowly melting away. Yet, fat Kassidy still was walking with a new attitude as she felt and saw a difference in the mirror.

Instead of Kassidy spending her monthly check on snacks, and her grandma style clothing, she wanted us to go with her shopping for fashionable clothes that had a little touch of our New York swag. Then we worked on her hair, but since she barely had any, we had to add some extensions, and it really brought out her features. Kassidy was loving it, loving herself, and her smiles turned permanent.

Although everybody has a mind of their own, I still gave her suggestions on how to handle men if she was going to continue having sex. Facts: "The easiest is the sleaziest!" Keep that in mind, and you'll play hard to get every time. Lastly, we taught her how to defend herself, but she had to overcome her biggest fear. Our question was, "Which girl you're mostly scared of?" With an embarrassing look, she replied, "This girl name Sasha! She's older and teases me the most… I hate her!" When we told Kassidy to show us who the girl was, we couldn't believe our eyes. She was literally a little over 5ft. tall and petite… approximately my size.

The first thing Miyah said was, "Kassidy go punch her in the face, keep swinging, and you bet not stop!" Kassidy did exactly that, but as soon as Sasha started swinging back, Kassidy had turned around and walked away. Sasha continued punching her all in the back while Kassidy had her eyes closed. "You better fight back! You can't win like that! You want to be a loser all your life?" Miyah shouted out. It had to trigger her subconscious sense of ability because Kassidy turned, started swinging with full force, and throwing Sasha all around. Kassidy walked away with her first win. She was proud and recognized her capabilities.

Kassidy most certainly felt like one of us, and her mother Mrs. Parker didn't like that at all. She blamed me for every horrible thing Kassidy did, but in all reality Kassidy was bad off before I became her friend. All I was guilty of was making her feel courageous, confident, and happy. Conversely, her mother wanted her to stay delicate, doubtful, and hopeless. Therefore, Mrs. Parker thought it was best to send Kassidy off to a fat farm that didn't work, seeing she gained more weight. She tried keeping Kassidy on punishment, which was pointless because she kept sneaking out.

Mrs. Parker tried everything in her power to keep Kassidy away from me. However, I was the one that was helping her find beauty within herself. Her mother didn't see the positives things or the improvements. She saw only the negative in me, but she was blind to the fact that the corruption in her daughter came from the men Kassidy associated herself with. That was something me or Mrs. Parker couldn't control; she was already strung out on them, and their heavy petting. Instead of Mrs. Parker communicating with her child, hoping to find a solution that was suitable for Kassidy, she just reviled her with words that made matters worse.

The times Kassidy couldn't hang out with me, I started bonding with Lila and her mother Grace, who stayed three apartments down from us. They were inviting me to eat dinner with them, and go on trips. For the first time, I played with the real Barbie and Ken. I really enjoyed being with them. I got all the attention I wanted, and all the love I needed, which made me feel emotionally attached.

I started spending the night, but then the nights turned into weeks. I was getting the feel of how a home really was supposed to be, and I didn't want to leave. I had my own bed, new clothes with shoes to match, and my hair stayed done. I also liked that I didn't have to wash out my panties and hang them up in the bathroom to wear the next day since Grace bought me so many. She even bought me all kinds of toys, a nice purple and pink bike, and she taught me how to ride it. Furthermore, we took a lot of pictures everywhere we went, and I was accepted and treated the same at all family events. It couldn't get any better than that.

One day, I had told her in a shy voice, "I wish you was my mother." She smiled and said, "Well, I'm not, but I can still be your God mother and treat you like my child." That was good enough for me. A mother figure was what I really needed. When it was time for me to go home again, I cried. I just didn't want to go back to that life. Contentedly,

Grace and I went to ask mommy could I live with them. She said, "Yes." But from the look on her face, I could see that her feelings were hurt. Still, she let me go for the sake of my happiness; also, it was somewhat beneficial to her.

I visited mommy daily. I kept that pretty smile and shiny face; Grace put enough grease on me that could've lasted for days. It was discouraging that my sisters thought I was acting funny, but I really wasn't. I just wanted to experience those special moments with my God family, for God sent them to me at a perfect time. Facts: "A child should always have that feeling in her heart. The warmth of love and security." At that point in time, that was me, and I never wanted it to end; but I also didn't want to lose my FAM who was making me feel uneasy when I came around. I had thought jealousy somewhat played a role, seeing they kept trying to convince mommy to make me come back home, but why would they want to take my happiness away?

Meanwhile, Shaylah was moving out and into her own apartment, while Aunt Martha was on her way down south to move in with mommy, due to her being concerned about her safety. Aunt Martha's life in the city was similar to making the wrong turn into some strange woods, and then getting trapped by wild animals. Although it was a difficult and dangerous situation, she survived by hanging out on a limb until the day she fell. Aunt Martha managed to get away with a little wear and tear, but she never thought twice about going back in that same direction.

When Aunt Martha arrived, she had the power to influence mommy. Anything auntie didn't like, she brought it to mommy's attention by criticizing the way she was handling her business. Aunt Martha really didn't like that I was living with Grace. In all honesty, I didn't think she liked anything about her at all, and that didn't sit well with me.

The day I went to mommy's house, was the day I realized Aunt Martha's presence was an interference, for she said some offensive words that made a light bulb go off in mommy's head. In Auntie's instigating voice, she expressed, "Lilith, why you let that lady put a perm in this girl head? You just let her take over your child. That couldn't be me... And why she's living down the street? I mean, what that lady doing that you can't do? Soon she's going to be calling her mommy. That child need to be home with you, and she could go visit them... You doing things backwards!" Mommy had this ridiculous look on her face saying, "That's where she wants to be, and nobody is taking over my child! Grace consults with me before she does anything... The devil is a liar!" I left because I didn't want to hear or come in between that mess.

While I was walking back to Grace's house, I had the worst pain in my heart. I was actually scared that mommy was going to tell me I had to come back home. The next day, she did, and I was angry at the world. I cried my heart out, I barely ate, didn't get much sleep, and I wasn't talking to anybody. I couldn't understand why everybody was so focused on intervening with my happiness, and wanted me to come back to that disastrous life.

# TECHNICALITIES TO OVERCOME

During this time, Kassidy had just got out of training school, and we didn't see each other for numerous months. She was informed not to go far from the house, and of course, she couldn't hang around me. Therefore, she had to sneak to do everything. We both were depressed and didn't want to be at home. Despondently, we took a long walk to talk and relieve some stress. During our collaboration, we had come up with a plan... We were going to run away.

Kassidy anxiously said, "I have a homeboy that we can go chill with for a few days, but I don't know if you would have a problem with it being his sister's house... She doesn't care; plus, she be at work all the time, but it's up to you. What do you think?" My response was, "I'm with it... let's get it!" We didn't have any clothes, money, or food. Honestly, we weren't for sure if we had shelter, but it beat going home.

During our walk, we made pit stops at a few people's houses. Nobody was aware that we were runaways because it wasn't out of the ordinary that Kassidy came to visit. We would sit around long enough for them to offer us something to eat, and we ate as much as we could, not knowing the next time there would be a good meal offered to us. We then realized that not having money was going to be a big problem; still, we didn't think about what we were going to do about it. In fact, we really didn't have a strategic plan about anything, but we were going to survive the best way we could.

It was getting dark when we headed to Kassidy's homeboy's house. He wasn't there when we first arrived, so we broke into an abandon house nearby. While we were waiting patiently in that dark, oppressive house, we sat on that uncomfortable wooden floor, and sung our hearts out. Xscape 90's album was definitely "Kickin' it," and Kassidy's soprano voice was echoing through that empty house, which sounded extremely beautiful. When we got tired of singing, our voices never were lost for words as we talked… and talked… but we started feeling drained from the heat. After we dozed off sitting up against the wall, we heard a car door close. As the cop approached the front, we ran out the back door and didn't stop until we got to her guy friend's house. Thank God he was there…

Although we slept on his floor, we still were a little cozy sleeping on those cushy covers and pillows. After we woke up, we splashed water on our faces, then continued our journey. Our first stop was the grocery store, for we were starving. We were walking through the store eating easy opened food and drinking sodas. On our way out, Kassidy had put packs of hot dogs under her huge breast. I, on the other hand, grabbed a few candy bars, and slipped them in my pants pocket. We figured that would last us until we thought about our next scheme. We assumed we were doing great team work. So, right after, we walked into an apparel store because we were tired of looking like yesterday. We stole clothes, panties, and some flip flops to match. Nearby was another one of Kassidy friends' house where we took showers and changed clothes. We were fresh, dressed, and headed towards nowhere; but just anywhere that wasn't home.

We were lollygagging through the back roads to stay out of sight, but Kassidy's brothers were thinking the same way we were. Surprisingly, they caught us off guard when they pulled up next to us, and they forced us in the car. We weren't scared about what our parents were going to do, we were just mad that we got caught. When we arrived in the projects, everybody was standing outside strangely looking at us. As soon as the car came to a halt, I quickly jumped out and started running through the path straight out the projects. Mirah's boyfriend chased me down, which was unbelievable considering he had a bad leg. When he caught me, I aggressively started kicking and swinging at him. Vigorously, he picked me up, and then carried me all the way home. I was cursing him out and screaming aloud, "Let me go! I don't want to go back… I hate all of y'll, and if I go back, I'm going to kill myself." He ignored me… He didn't say not one word… like what I said went into one ear and out the other.

When I got home, mommy and Aunt Martha were all in my ear. "Blah! Blah! Blah!" I didn't care. With rage, I stomped to the bathroom and locked myself in. As I looked in the mirror, the reflection of sadness appeared as my sorrowful tears fell. A voice in my ear said, "It's time for you to disappear forever; look in the medicine cabinet, and there you would find your answer." Although I still heard mommy's voice, everything just seemed quiet to me. When I opened the medicine cabinet, Advil's was the first thing I saw. I then started ramming them in my mouth, but once I started gagging due to the awful taste, I spit them all out.

Mommy started banging on the door, and I destructively opened it, screaming at the top of my lungs. "I rather die than be here!" When my mother saw the opened pill bottle, she didn't hesitate to call the ambulance, and I didn't try to stop her. When the ambulance arrived, they asked, "How many pills did you take?" I bluntly responded, "I don't know." They rushed me to the hospital, and that's when shit got real. I got extremely scared when they started pulling out all types of crazy tubes, preparing to pump my stomach. I didn't know that's how they treated overdoses, so I quickly changed my story. "I lied about taking those pills… I just thought if my mother saw me unhappy… she would send me back to Grace's house because I don't want to live at home."

Instead of them pumping my stomach, they brought in a psychologist, who asked many questions about the problems I had at home, or any other issues I encountered. After the assessment, she believed I was still capable of hurting myself. She recommended that I be under further observation, along with medical treatment. I didn't think they were talking about the crazy house until they shipped my ass off to a mental institution. Then my senses instantly kicked in when I entered that building. I'll never forget the: white walls, crazy screams, and imbecilic talking. I knew I didn't belong there, and I felt as empty as the cold, white room that surrounded me.

Prior to admittance, they wanted me to take some big white pills that would help me be more relaxed, which I refused. I was calm enough, so how relaxed did they wanted me to be? They then hit me with, "Your refusal will give you a longer stay." I candidly replied, "I don't care!" I really did, but I didn't reveal my concerns. Then I had to strip down, get searched, and wear an all-white uniform. My room had a cot between those four bright walls with not much room to do anything. Depression struck me hard when they trapped me behind that heavy, metallic, secured door. Loneliness visited me, and left me with only my: thoughts, body, and soul. I was unrelaxed on that thin mattress, as I stared at the luminous ceiling, and pondered the events that led me to this moment of solitary. I just got myself in some deep shit. With full of regrets, I started praying, and I cried myself to sleep. Undoubtedly, the situation went further than I thought.

In the mornings, they let certain people out for breakfast. I and a few others were the first to eat. While eating that disgusting food, I started a conversation with a few girls, just to get some information about the hospital. Katie, who was suicidal, was in there longer than she should have been, and she blamed it on those big white pills she was taking. Therefore, she advised me to keep refusing it if I wanted to make it back home, and I did exactly that. Another rule that was enforced to get a ticket up out of there, was eating. The food wasn't at all edible, but I only had to finish a proportion of it for approval. Remarkably, I stayed on top of that.

I was there for about two weeks, and trouble suddenly intervened. As a group, we all were quietly watching TV, when this certified girl named Stephanie had swung off on me. I quickly got in defense mode, shoved her on top of some girls that were sitting on the couch, and then started punching her all in the face. The staff came rushing in with a needle and handcuffs to restrain Stephanie. Being mentally ill like she was, the hospital policy was to keep handcuffs on her at all times. Rules were broken, and lawsuits for negligence could've been pursued if anyone was harmed.

Approximately, a month after that incident, I was standing in front of a judge. Instead of a courtroom, they had us in something that looked more like a conference room. The judge was sitting on one side with two sheriffs on the left and right. On the opposite side sat: Aunt Martha, her sister in Christ, and me. Like usual, my mother wasn't there, although she knew that family technicalities were important. The only place she always seemed to make it to--was the church. Her reason for not coming is still unknown. However, her absence in my moment of need, created a feeling of sorrow and disappointment.

As I sat there anxiously excited, tasting freedom that was only doors away, I was also furious that mommy wasn't there to support me. While the judge was discussing my behavior over the weeks, I stared at her with a blank look. Everything was good, but two things went against me, which was the refusal of the medication, and my bad attitude. Consequently, the judge had sentenced me to 60 days in a madhouse for bad kids. I was pissed! My body felt tensed when I jumped up and tried to jump over the table to get at the judge, but the two Sheriffs had grabbed my arms to restrain me. Then that evil judge had immediately given them orders to detain me. While I was being carried out, I shouted in anger, "You old white BITCH, I would've fucked you up if you wasn't on the other side of the table... I hate you! You're trying to ruin my life... ughh!" I cried the whole time sitting in the back seat of the Sheriff's car, while listening to him give me some good advice, "In all honesty, if you learn how to control your anger, and don't let the anger control you, then you would get more positive outcomes... Think about that, and try it sometimes... you'll see."

I thought about it for a second, but my mind couldn't stay focused on that while I was thinking about where I was headed. I knew we were getting close when we started riding up those steep hills and saw nothing but mountains. Moments later, we arrived at the institution, which was secluded just like the crazy house, but dissimilar on the inside. It was vibrant, the patients were robust, and the staff was cool. They introduced me to everyone, showed me my room, and then explained the guidelines. It was straightforward, you abide by the rules, and then you earned points and privileges. If you refuse not to... then you lose your freedom.

Of course, I was thinking, well damn! I'm not getting out any time soon, knowing how my temper was. Even though I had to put a few people in their place, I still earned my points in about a month, but I thought I couldn't leave until my 60 days was up. So, I wasn't pressed. Then one day, I surprisingly got a visit, but they weren't there to come see me because it was time for them to take me home. Although I disliked Aunt Martha at that time, I was very happy to see her. I ran and packed so fast to get up out of there. I gazed out the car window as we sped away. The building slowly faded behind the trees and hills, along with my negative experiences. I smiled as I reminisced over all I had overcome in a matter of months. Then I pleasantly greeted my freedom with appreciation as I closed my eyes, and inhaled the fresh smell of nature. Though I wasn't fully on track, I was a little more focused.

# UNDERSTANDING REAL IN REALITY

When we arrived home, all of my little sisters ran and hugged me yelling out, "We missed you so much... We glad you're home, don't leave us like that anymore." It made me feel special, and I realized what matters the most. Even though I was still resentful, I was always respectful, and my family I truly loved unconditionally. Grace and Lila were also my family too, and I loved them the same; therefore, I made sure every day I visited.

I no longer felt that I couldn't live without staying with Grace. Spending time in the looney bin had made me see a different perspective in life, and realism changed my mentality, but it also created my stony-heart. Primarily because my happiness was put on hold just to please everyone else's. I couldn't change what happened, that's why I didn't dwell on it; however, I acted on it from time to time.

During my transitional stage, my father popped up at mommy's house. I really didn't understand why, or cared to see him. But something wasn't right, I could feel it in the pit of my stomach, especially when he suddenly tried to act like a father, but none of us wasn't buying it. To us, he was like a dead man walking. Our conversations were short, we never had a bond, and it was too late to build one.

As expected, Damien had something else on his agenda. He perspicaciously started getting acquainted with too many people in the south including Grace. They seemed too close but were trying to cover it up in front of me. Still and all, she didn't know what he was capable of. He was using her, and everybody else he encountered. Once again, he played that role as if he was trying to do the right thing.

He had people believing they were buying houses for cheap in another state, expensive cars for the low, and lowering their phone bills if they used a different plan. It was all a scheme, and it became apparent when he ran Grace's bill up to $5000. Then another neighbor was complaining about her new car that she never received, and a fictitious home she had put a down payment on. All of the bogus contracts and promises suddenly revealed the indecent man that my father really was. Unfortunately, for them, it was too late.

The last memories I had of daddy was his blue sweat suit that he wore the whole time he stayed down south, which was over two weeks. That was unusual, knowing he was a suit and tie type of guy with a briefcase, and he never wore the same outfit twice. Besides, it was strange that he came empty handed but had a portfolio full of papers.

He also was trying to be a man of discipline, which wasn't going to work on me. I despised him, and I couldn't wait to expose my wrath. The day finally arrived when he tried to tell me what to do. I blatantly replied, "Who the fuck is you? You haven't been in my life, so don't try to be a daddy now because it's too late... I don't need one." Then I angrily walked away, headed towards Grace's house, and he followed behind me. As soon as I got in, I slammed the door directly in his face, and I watched him fiercely knock. I didn't feel like he deserved my respect, just like he didn't feel like my mother or his kids deserved his.

He thought mommy would side with him but she didn't. She told him, "Why now you want to be a father, a husband, and a supporter? They're older and have a mind of their own... I'm not going to convinced them, and get their hopes up high! You are the devil, and he is a lie!" Damien was speechless... He knew she was right, and he was also surprised that mommy finally stood up to him. It was really nothing he could do but fall back.

The end of 1992 was the last time I saw my father. I believed he knew that he wasn't going to see us again. For he had this different look in his eyes like he was trying, but he didn't know the proper way to say goodbye. He was running from his punishment that was bound to catch up with him. His guilt started eating at his conscious due to him being a deadbeat father. Forgiveness is what he wanted, but with his blood flowing through our bodies, he knew that he wasn't going to get through to us. Therefrom, he left to go back to New York with a sad and remorseful goodbye. Then A few weeks after, they found his body in an apartment building unresponsive. There were all types of rumors about his death, but the truth is still in question. Ironically, none of the family members actually identified the body before he was cremated.

With him having dealings with the mafia, we assumed they were affiliated with his death. Reason 1: A deal had gone downhill, and Damien's name was written all over it. OR… Reason 2: He was in debt, and didn't pay it back before the deadline. If that was the case, then that sealed the deal on why he came down south, and scammed all those people out of their money. Once his time ran out, and he didn't have the full amount, he started planning his getaway. Desperately, he used Grace for her phone to make calls out the country in order for him to get ghost. However, scheming had become his enemy and defeated him. This is my theory, but whatever the case may have been, he took it all with him.

Mommy was never informed on if Daddy's death was accidental or a homicide. In all probability, someone got paid some "hush-hush" money. I'm insinuating this because when mommy got the call that Damien died, the man specifically said, "Mrs. Daevas… your husband Damien Daevas was found in an abandoned building dead… He was tied up to a chair, stabbed over 15 times, and could've been like that anywhere between five to seven days. I'm sorry ma'am, but it looks like he was tortured." He didn't disclose his name, or who he worked for. We don't even know how he got the number to reach mommy.

About a week or two later, mommy had finally got in touch with my father's sister, Rosetta. She bluntly said, "The police told me that they found him in a hotel room naked with an empty liquor bottle next to him… They ruled it as accidental, saying he died from alcohol poison… My brother wasn't a drinker, but they're trying to tell me he was an alcoholic… I still don't have closure. The bad part about it, I didn't even get the chance to see my brother's body before they cremated him… I don't believe anything they said… I mean, something just not sitting right with me. I feel like my brother was either murdered, or he faked his death; who knows... I don't really know if these are his ashes. I have very little information, but I'm in need for more answers." And she left it just like that. So, Damien's death was, and still is a mystery.

Our father's death wasn't at all sad. Shaylah was the only one that shed some tears. We couldn't cry about anything; he was never around. We couldn't talk about what we missed because he did nothing but bad things. Still and all, a little part of me felt unhappy that I would never get the chance to bond with my daddy, and he would never get the chance to try and be a father. Although life goes on, not having a father had a huge effect on my behavior.

To me, daddy's death wasn't a good or bad thing, but I hope he rest in disharmony for all of the evil he's done to people. He left his kids, wife, and victims behind with nothing but bitterness. Moreover, he set mommy up for failure. For the adversaries he gained when he came down south was now mommy's enemies. They blamed her for daddy's duplicitous actions, but it wasn't her fault. Everybody should be held accountable for their own actions, and mommy wasn't a part of his schemes. She certainly didn't get anything out the deal. That man was lethal. He caused mommy hurt while he was alive, and it continued after his death. Daddy was someone she will always remember, but can presently leave him in the past. What they had is literally dead and gone.

Meanwhile, mommy was focused on getting us some support. It was a little difficult at first because daddy was a bigamist leaving behind another wife, and her two kids. Providing that he and mommy never divorced, the other marriage was voided, which made us entitled to his money. Finally, we received some type of support from this man, but it was so sad it took death for us to get it.

Everything was falling in place. During this time, Aunt Martha the chatterbox had moved into her own apartment, and boy was mommy's house something peaceful. Everyone was stabled and more focused on their own lives, at least for the time being until Aunt Martha felt like meddling in someone else's business.

As soon as things were calm and collective, Boom! Teesah, Miyah, and Sophia got in a confrontation with a well-known family named the Thompsons. It all started at a party; there was alcohol served to a lot of underage kids, which played a huge role in everybody's reactions. As time passed, heads started spinning, and people's grim looks of rejection gave off bad vibes. Once a staggered walk turned into a bump, the fighting had begun. It was too many people for my sisters to defeat; resultantly, Teesah pulled out a knife and gave one of the girls a buck-fifty. Then all three of them took off running scared; not of the people, but of going to jail. Our block was on fire with the war going on between us two families. It made mommy furious and worried for her kids' safety, hearing the rumors about the Thompsons were out to get whoever was involved.

Teesah played it safe by not showing her face around. Oppositely, Miyah and Sophia didn't give a fuck. The next night, they were out walking and anticipating on having some fun. Then suddenly, a dark colored car was slowly driving behind them. Before they realized it was the enemy, the car started driving full speed, and ran them over. They both were rushed to the hospital, but Sophia suffered the worst. She had a broken arm, leg, bruised ribs, deep cuts, and scrapes on her face. Conversely, Miyah suffered minor injuries. That was a wakeup call for them, and they had realized the beef was far from over. To some extent, they wanted to fully blame Teesah because of her bloodthirsty act. For they felt that they could've fought it out like usual, even with them being outnumbered, whereas Teesah felt she was protecting herself by any means necessary. Teesah was eventually charged. Considering it was her first offense, she got off with probation. Yet, the battles continued with both families.

My mother continued hearing bad news about her kids, and she knew something eventually had to give. Especially when there was constant banging at her door... Boom! Boom! Boom! While looking out the window, seeing her porch full of people with knives, sticks, and bats, she asked, "Who y'all looking for?" They replied, "Those Daevas's!" Because there was always someone trying to harm us, mommy eventually became fearless. Therefore, she opened and stood in front of the door as our protector, and the only way they were getting in was if they totally disrespected her. Mommy wasn't the confrontational type, but she wasn't going to see her kids get hurt. If they were going to be Billy bad asses, then they had to go through her first. God was truly on mommy's side that day, seeing it was a lot of angry people. Besides all the profanity they used, they refused to violate her, so they left.

Mommy was fed up, and she was screaming at the top of her lungs, "Something has to change. Y'all keep bringing trouble to my house… Do y'all even care about y'all younger sisters? What's really going on with y'all? I tell you what, it's time for y'all to go back to New York until everything dies down. I'm not waiting till later… I'm sending y'all right now! Pack up." They were happy to hear that and was ready to go, but regardless how long they stayed away, the Daevas's will always be hated by the Thompsons.

A year later, they arrived back, and Teesah was more of a homebody because her son needed most of her attention. Conversely, Miyah was worse off than before. She was "dangerously in love" with the streets. She was determined to survive independently, and she kept a combatant rush. Trouble was her name, and money was her game. Yes, Miyah was certainly wild, curious and aggressive. Her coming back down south was just delivering a message that she was back. Of course, everybody heard the word; she was extremely loud, and when people talked about us, nothing good came out of their mouths. They didn't care how old or which one we were; we all were bad seeds in their eyes. Miyah didn't care what they thought while she had vengeance in her heart, but she did want to keep the trouble away from mommy's house, and started hanging down at Shaylah's place where the partying began.

Meantime, mommy was having problems at church. In behalf of her kids, they started looking at her differently. The constant rumors that floated through town had gave the congregation something to gossip about. It was a great deal of animosity, and she no longer felt welcome. Under those circumstances, she knew she had to leave. People felt we were an image of mommy, but they were wrong; we were totally the opposite. Mommy didn't raise us to be that way, but her failures in parenting led to our rebellious and chaotic nature.

When mommy departed from the church, she also was preparing to move to another city. Without much thought, Kannapolis was her first choice. While she was traveling back and forth to get settled, we were split up amongst Shaylah and Aunt Martha's house. Staying with Shaylah at the age of 12, made me feel like I was raising myself. I was free to do what I desired. I made my own rules, and I didn't have a curfew. Ultimately, the streets raised me, and being that everyone else was focusing on their personal lives, no one ever sat me down to try and show me the ropes of life. I had to learn on my own through all the pleasures and pain. Furthermore, opportunities presented themselves frequently, and that became a dilemma once I reached puberty.

My stay at Shaylah's house was not only self-reliant, but it felt haunted as well. I used to hear strange voices, whispering vicious words in my ear while I was asleep, "Without me, your soul is lost... come to me, and I'll give you everything." I never responded, I just kept my eyes closed, pretending I was still sleep. Thereafter, a powerful force roughly pushed me. I was going through those same attacks off and on. At times, I felt like I was dreaming until Shaylah talked about her own confrontations with the devil.

She told me about the horrifying day when she was chillaxing on her leather sofa, reading the newspaper. Then, out the blue, she heard a creepy voice say, "Turn around!" She was scared as hell; she froze up and couldn't find the courage to look back. Then her body started feeling weird and numbed, while her head was forcibly turning. She tried to close her eyes but was unable to. Suddenly, she saw a vision of a man in black; his face was shining so brightly through her head that he could've read her thoughts. Instantly, her eyes started rolling in the back of her mind like she was getting hypnotized. "Wham!" He just disappeared, and everything went back to normal. Shaylah was scared and skeptical about her place ever since. Her horror story had me intense, and I was confused in whether we were possessed, or if her place was haunted. Whatever the case may have been, I was afraid to stay there.

It wasn't a long stay; mommy had quickly moved into some apartments called the Gardens. The place was incredibly boring, but we tried to make the best of it. I got adapted instantly due to me learning a little street mentality and started navigating around the city. I became well known over there, seeing I was bold, beautiful, and brilliant, which brought me some compelling attention. For I lured in the boys, and I offended the girls.

Flashback moment: Walking in that middle school, on the 8th grade hall, all eyes were on me. However, I held my head up high, turned my nose up at the girls, but put my innocent smile on for the guys. It was obvious everybody was talking about me as they were finger pointing, and some were barely whispering. Right then and there I knew it was going to be a long year.

In most schools, you will always run into a bully. Mine just happened to be in my homeroom class. Her name was Stephanie, and she also had her suck up crew tagging along. Being the new girl, I needed to stay humbled, and far away from trouble. Therefore, my interactions with the students were limited, which made the bullies dislike me even more because I paid no attention to them. By me being the new target, they began to follow and fuck with me. "Hey new girl, I'm going to see you after school, so be ready to get your ass kicked!" Then the suck ups would laugh while walking away. I killed them with the look on my face like I had no worries.

After school, they followed me to my bus and kept running off at the mouth. I started thinking back to my New York incidents. Without fear, I did a complete stop, I turned around with my evil, bloodshot, red eyes and said, "Stop talking and pop off then... I will beat your ass, and then one by one I'll fight your pussy ass friends... I tried to be nice, but now y'all got me in a bad mood... Watch out because I know voodoo. Y'all started, now I'm going to finish, and for all of you who don't know... I am truly wicked!" They were speechless as I walked away. When I got on the bus, people were giving me dap, in respect to me standing up for myself.

The tables had turned, and day after day, I was out to get them instead of them being out to get me. They eventually told the teachers. Then the teachers sent home a letter informing mommy about the matter. With my innocent look, I explained everything. Then convinced her to send me back to Midway to keep me from getting in trouble.

Mommy loved less stress and more peace. That's why she agreed, but I had to stay with Mirah, who was considered the responsible one.

Mommy had less responsibilities and plenty of space; she only had Teesah, and the four youngest ones living with her. During this time, Teesah was on her second child. It was definitely time for her to be on her own, but it seemed like Teesah was afraid to be alone, and wanted to stay with mommy as long as possible, which mommy didn't mind because at that time, Teesah hardly ever got in trouble.

What was going on in Kannapolis didn't mean too much to me; I was enjoying my stay with Mirah. What more could a young teen ask for? Mirah always had a few people over. They would be sipping on their bottles, dancing to their old timing music, and of course, there were some lustful men around. That was the time I met my first love; his name was Black. He was average height, had that dark smooth skin, and dressed fresh to death, but was ugly as fuck. After all, his looks weren't what I was attracted to; his money was much more appealing.

I had to get ahead of the game since I was behind all my life. With this mentality, I started thinking outside the box, "What if I do this... would that make things better? Or, how would I do that just to make things right?" I didn't have time to think adolescent thoughts, knowing I needed to independently take care of myself. From here, I started dating Black, and he began coming around a little more than usual. Mirah's boyfriend Joseph didn't like what was going on because I was young, but it wasn't his call, it was my sisters. Mirah, on the other hand, understood my purpose considering our life was rough, and she knew as a teen, I needed a lot of stuff. With this consideration in mind, she gave me some advice on how to juice a nigga without opening my legs, but I was already trying to figure that out myself.

Black was far more advanced than me, but I still controlled my own mind and destiny. He couldn't influence me to drink, that wasn't my cup of tea. He couldn't convince me to smoke because it irritates your throat, and it's also a toxin that would've been unhealthy to my body. I also looked at sex as a threat to my body as well as my mind and soul too. Under those circumstances, abstinence was the best choice I made. Of course, I wasn't a saint, and I was curious about a lot of things, but I wasn't going to let anyone interfere with me finishing school and becoming a lawyer. Instead of leading Black into the middle of nowhere, I put everything on the table, which he stood by my decisions; plus, agreed to wait until I was ready.

In the middle of my puppy love, Mirah was trying to end her love triangle between Joseph and Sleeze. To some degree, it was too late, especially when a baby was involved, and both men trying to express their fatherly love. Yet, Mirah thought Joseph was the only one entitled to that responsibility, and purposely took it all away from Sleeze. Taking someone's child from them can cause a great deal of pain. So, every time Sleeze felt hurt, he took his anger out on Joseph. We could be at a grocery store shopping, then Sleeze unexpectedly showed up, and Joseph started running. There were times it was aggressive knocking at the front and back door; it would be Sleeze and his goons coming to rough Joseph up. Sleeze showed up at parks, movies, and restaurants. Basically, he showed his face anytime, and any place he wanted to because he liked having the opportunity to cause chaos. Thanks to Miyah for having that vendetta against Mirah and wanting to retaliate. She deviously watched every chaotic moment from the back seat of Sleeze's car, and she did not feel an inch of remorse.

Flashback moment: It was Kassidy, Black, and me at Mirah's house by ourselves. We had no car, it was too hot to walk, and we were bored as fuck. Then we started meandering through Mirah's movies, and there we found some porn. "They are some freaks!" I expressed. It was actually my first time seeing something like that, but not Kassidy and Black. They were definitely anxious to watch it.

When it first came on, we were quiet, and our eyes were glued to the television. We were mesmerized by the moaning and fucking they were doing. The sounds were like, "Bap slap, smack… Bap! Bap! Bap! Ooow! Yeah, fuck me harder… Slap! Slap! Slap! Mmm." Suddenly, we heard banging at the door. We shockingly looked at each other thinking, "Ain't Mirah out of town." Slowly, I tipped toed to the window, peeked out the blinds, and saw Sleeze and his crew. They all had the ill grill looks, and the words that were coming out their mouths were distasteful. They weren't out there to just pay a visit; they were coming to demolish things like usual, and Black was going to be in the middle of it all.

While they continued to bang, we were trying to find Black a good hiding spot. He crawled in the closet, and we threw a lot of clothes on top of him. Meanwhile, Sleeze was blurting out, "Mirah! Joseph! I know y'all in there, and I'm not leaving… Open the door. If I kick it in, it's gonna make matters worse." I eventually opened the door, and they bum-rushed in like policemen. They searched the house, looking for Mirah and Joseph. Instead, they found Black in the corner of the closet shaking. Sleeze immediately yanked him up, gave him a few blows to the stomach, and then started asking questions. "Who the fuck is you? Why the fuck is you here? Are you Joseph peoples?" The questions were coming so fast that Black was stuttering and unable to complete his sentences. However, Kassidy and I were there to defend him. We were blurting out all types of shit like, "He barely know Joseph… He is not from here! No, he's not for me… That's Kassidy's friend!" Before they left, Sleeze delivered a message, "Tell Joseph I'll be back for him… And tell Mirah she can't never get rid of me. I know she sees me every day in my baby… Oh! Give Lilah a kiss for me, and here are a few things for her." They were bringing in a basket net, swing set, a carriage, all sorts of clothes, and other miscellaneous things a baby might need. Then he walked out like he did nothing wrong.

Kassidy and I looked at Black and asked, "Are you alright?" His response was, "Yeah!" But the expression on his face was straight embarrassment. Days later, the newlywed couple came back from their vacation to only become daunted by Sleeze threats; well, at least Joseph was. The most degrading part about the whole situation was that they took everything Sleeze bought back to the store, and got a refund. Then spent the money on things that she wanted, which didn't have nothing to do with Lilah.

I wasn't there to judge anybody, even though I felt she did wrong. All in all, I had liked staying at Mirah's house. I was comfortable, and she was far from strict. As long as I went to school every day, did my homework and chores, I was free to go as I pleased; it was mainly to the projects to hang out with Kassidy. Each day of the week, Kassidy and I always had something up our sleeves. Eventually, we added Black to our team, and he started coming to Midway more often just so he could be around me.

This was the first time I got familiarize with drug dealers since I had one for a boyfriend, and I was enjoying every bit of it. I never saw the drugs, but I saw all of the money because he didn't mind giving or buying me things. I stayed fly and kept fresh sneakers for school. I had plenty of gold rings and chains considering he'd like seeing me in the finer things. Oh! And I loved when he dropped me off at school in his fly cars, seeing I got all of the attention and props. It was a good but also a bad thing, knowing girls wanted what I had. Yet, the only competitive thing against me was that they were having sex.

A year has passed, and I was still a virgin. Some people were surprised, but they weren't convinced, in view of all the things he was buying me, on top of him still coming around. Then there was Kassidy and Miyah, who stayed in my head about how Black was going to leave me for somebody else if I wasn't having sex with him. To me, I felt like it was a jinx because right after, I started seeing a difference in him.

# VIRGINITY WAS MY ENEMY

I started to have doubts about my relationship, for the love was still there, but his quality time was slowly vanishing. Then the rumors began about him and this BITCH named Angelina Jones, who also was my classmate. Angelina and I were both a class prize. She had good looks like me, but the swag... ughh! I don't think so, and the intelligence... Oh, hell no, it wasn't much comparison. I was pissed, and knew I had to handle this shit. Without much thought, I knew who would be the best candidate for drama. (Drum roll) Of course it was Miyah.

As we were walking towards Angelina and her boyfriend Tyrone, I saw the guilt in her eyes. I did no talking, I just confronted her with a punch to the face. After that, I blanked. When we landed on the ground, I was on top of her, and continued punching her redundantly. Tyrone was unaware of the reason why we were fighting, and he tried to aggressively stop me. Indubitably, Miyah did intervene, so we could continue fighting. It was over quick, and the win was too easy. Angelina's mother called the cops and tried to press charges against me and Miyah, which was eventually dismissed because they didn't come to court. I guess those threatening messages paid off.

From that day on, Angelina and I were enemies. Every time I saw her, I taunted her without words, but just my looks. For my visage was a split image of the devil, and I wanted my message to circulate that I wasn't nobody to fuck with. Disrespect is what I hated, and trust is what I lost. Thereupon, my attitude had progressed to another level.

Afterwards, I confronted Black, and he quickly hit me with a bold face lie. "What? Come on man... I don't even know who you're talking about! Whoever told you that, needs to get their facts straight. Honestly, it wasn't me! You the only girl I want." He had a dumb ass look on his face, but he said it with sincerity. Still, my gut feeling was telling me something different. Then he tried to butter me up with a 24-karat, elegant, Alexandrite ring, with my birth stone. As I pleasantly stared at my redressed finger, I forgot about all the other nonsense just for that moment.

I had forgiven him that easy, but I surely didn't forget. With vicious intents, I had to think of a way to pay him back. Savagely, Kassidy and I deliberated on how to make him suffer surreptitiously. "Hmmm, I want to hit 'em where it hurts... and that would be getting deep in his pockets, let's set his ass up!" I said determinedly. Although I was unfamiliar with that type of vicious act, I was actually feeling good about it.

We had got Loco, Blaze, and Slick to handle my dirty deed. They were the stickup kids from the projects that was down for whatever. Without hesitation, they were down with it. I was the one who planned it all out. I would give them the destination and time; when they robbed that nigga, I would get my cut, simple as that. The deal was sealed and would never be disclosed, as long as they paid me.

Black always came to see me around the same time, so they were in the cut waiting around. When Black pulled up and shut off the car, Loco and his crew quickly had all of them surrounded. After they Click! Clack! Their guns... Blaze yelled out, "We got your black ass now... Yeah, all y'all give it up! Chains, money, anything in this motherfucker that's valuable! I don't want to hear no talking, don't want to see any sudden moves, or somebody is getting one of these bullets!" Their faces weren't covered, and their looks expressed nothing but seriousness. Immediately, Black and his boys started taking off their shit. I knew everything was going down, so I was peeking out the window, watching everything with a grimy smirk on my face. I was a little sympathetic that his friends got caught in the middle of my fiasco, but fuck it! More money for me.

Afterwards, Black came running in the house and was looking all stressed out. "What's wrong? Are you okay?" I asked. He responded,

"Me and my boys just got robbed, and they got us for everything!" In my fake concerned voice, I replied, "When? Where? Everything? How much?" I really was asking just to find out how much my cut was. He angrily explained, "These little niggas were in the front waiting... They got about $800 from each of us. My chain, bracelet, and ring is gone... They took Ti diamond earrings, and Montae watch... Damn we got caught the fuck up." While he's going on and on whining like a little BITCH, I was calculating in my head. "4X800=2400, that leaves us $800 a-piece; pawn all the jewelry, and then split that... Damn! We're all coming off with at least a stack." That was good enough for me, and I was definitely ready for Black to leave. He gave me a sweet kiss goodbye... I'll see you later, and I gave him a big hug filled with happiness. Immediately after, I walked and met Loco and them. Because Blaze was 18, he went and pawned the jewelry. Ching! Ching! They gave him $850 for everything. Everybody walked away with a smile on their faces, and nobody spoke about it after that day.

Black came by to see me a few days later, and he quickly got back on his feet. I didn't feel any different; therefore, I continued acting the same. He asked me if I heard anything, or if I knew the guys' names, and that was my time to tell my bold face lie. "Nah!" I said. Then I changed the subject. Not one time did it cross his mind that I had something to do with it. He thought I was too innocent, and of course, I played the role; I needed him around. Even though I would never fully trust him, I didn't want to leave him considering he was my security. With this in mind, I continued to plan ahead by keeping him close to me, and away from them hoes. It was only one thing left to do... give up my virginity!

I was inexperienced in relationships, which brought a lot of peer pressure, and not much of good advice. Ultimately, I gave in, and was thoughtless about the mistake I was soon to make, but I had no one to blame but myself. By me being uneducated about sexual activities, I confided in Kassidy, which she replied with many answers and tips. In spite of me knowing I wasn't ready, I was still willing to go through with it. Truthfully, I didn't want to give up what I thought was the best thing that happened to me. I knew my time was going to eventually run out, but the closer it got for Black to come, I got scared. I really couldn't see myself being sexual active, but I had no one to tell me to do the right thing due to them wanting me to be categorized the same as them.

I was blind to the fact that my purity allowed me to stand out from the crowd, and emphasized my morals and values. I was cherished by many, and considered a trophy because no one had taken my treasure. However, I got lost in the world of materialistic things, and I forgot about everything else. As a 13-year-old, I didn't understand the science behind sex, love, and boys until I experienced it for myself. I was one of those teens that had to learn the hard way.

Flashback moment: The next day, Black came over, and that particular conversation was definitely on another level. He was shocked when I said, "I'm ready to have sex." A year of teasing and no pleasing, without a doubt, his horny ass was down. On the way out the door, I got nervous and wanted Kassidy to come along with me. She had no problem doing that, and as long as Black was getting what he wanted, everything was okay with him as well. So, we left to get a room. I remember vividly, pulling up at the Motel 6. A hotel where most drug dealers went to make money. It would be considered as a low budget hotel today, but was modish back then. I was hysterical while we waited in the car until he got the room. For everything seemed to be moving too fast, and the room seemed to close, knowing once I left from there, I wouldn't be a virgin anymore.

As I slowly entered the room, my heart was skipping and beating fast, in light of me knowing what I was about to do was for all the wrong reasons. My mouth wouldn't open up to say, "No I can't do it" because I was a coward; moreover, I didn't want to ruin the moment. Under the circumstances, I tried to make myself comfortable until the time came. While we were all watching TV, we talked a lot and laughed a little, which made my body feel more relaxed. Then we asked Kassidy to excuse us for a moment. When she went to the bathroom, he began to kiss me, but it didn't feel right. Although he had a gentle touch, it just seemed rough to me. He unromantically took off my clothes and got straight to the point. In my head, I was thinking, "OMG! It's happening... He's touching my stuff with his thing... Oh no, it hurts!"

My position was motionless, and my mouth was screaming pain. I then started feeling disgusted and displeased, so I couldn't wait for it to be over. It seemed like it took forever, but three to five minutes was a short time. I couldn't go back and change anything, for what's done was done.

As we got up, we saw blood on the sheets, which made my soul really full of shame and remorse, whereas Black was flattered and happy. Although I got what I wanted, which was shackles around his ankles, I no longer needed that. In point of fact, that day, my bond was broken. I no longer felt like the same, "Lil Veah" because I wasn't, and I saw everything very differently as reality kicked in. Meanwhile, Kassidy came out smiling, and she looked happier than I was. Her exact words were, "You did it BITCH! How was it? I know it was painful because I heard you, but it won't be the same next time." I didn't respond to anything she asked or said, I just sat there quietly and patiently waiting for the next morning, so I could go home.

When I left that hotel, I cried since I was frustrated with myself. The only vision that kept popping in my head was Black's ugly ass on top of me. When I made it home, I went in the room and secluded myself. I didn't want to be bothered with family, friends, or my boyfriend. I wanted to think in peace and clear my mind, and hopefully fill it with happy thoughts. Then I heard the bad news, "Veah! Kassidy told me that you are having sex. Mmm... when mommy find out that, she's going to be mad!" Big mouth Miyah said. I just ignored her but wasn't surprised; yet, I was angry that the news was broadcast very quickly. Thanks to my so called best friend Kassidy, and trouble making Miyah; they were the main two that convinced me to do it. But I had to suck it up; I realized I fucked up, and would eventually have to face the family.

The first person I saw was Aunt Martha, and with the look on her face, I knew she had something to say. "Now Veah! I don't want to believe what I'm hearing about you, but if it's true, I will be very disappointed." My response was, "I'm disappointed in myself, but I can't change nothing I did." Aunt Martha eyes had widened, uh oh! Here comes some lecturing. She started off with asking me, "Do you remember telling me that you would never have sex until you finished school because you don't want anything stopping you from becoming a lawyer?" That was true, but I came back with, "That's why you never say never."

Then she went on about pregnancy, protection, diseases, and cheating. I stood there and listened, but sometimes I get to that point where I don't give a fuck, and that was one of them points. Ring! Ring! "Hello! Hey Lilith… Veah's here, I know you wanted to talk to her… Okay, here she goes." When I got on the phone, she was hollering out some of the same shit Aunt Martha said. I gave the silent treatment until she was finish talking, then I left with an attitude. I don't know if I was angrier about mommy letting me get off too easy, or that everybody was looking down on me. It could've been a little of both. I just needed somebody, more like my mother to show a little more concern, ask more questions, so she could understand why or what drove me to that point. I was confused and miserable while I was walking, and my thoughts were all over the place.

During my breakdown, Black was brownnosing me just about every day. If for a second he thought he was getting some more of my cookies, he was setting himself up for a rude awakening; I was completely turned off. However, I already gave up the goods, so I had to keep him around for a little longer.

# TREACHEROUS ACT #1

A few months later, I still refused to have sex with Black. Then, out the blue, an interesting rumor started floating in the air. Wow! Miyah and Black had fucked, really? Even though they both denied it, I felt it was some sort of truth to the story. The guilt was written all over Miyah's face, but she didn't have the heart to tell me. I guess she was embarrassed, and didn't want to be perceived as a backstabbing big sister. Yet, I ignored it and continued acting like the naive teenager, which I really wasn't. I just didn't care, and with my new mentality, nothing sweet was going to come out of it. Vindictively, I cursed Black with nothing but danger.

During this time, I started staying back at Shaylah's house with her evil spirits. Acknowledging that I wanted to give into evil had made me fearless. So, when the man of darkness came to see me that night, I looked him straight in the eyes. In a creepy voice, he said, "You're ready to start your new life I see." Then he touched my head and started chanting. My eyes were closed, and my body was stiff, but I felt warm and villainous. Even with the kids there, the room felt empty. Then a few minutes after, he was gone, the wind stopped blowing, and the kids were running around like they didn't see anything that happened. My body was dripping sweat, and my heart was pumping fast because I knew it wasn't a dream, although it was the next morning.

That would be the last time I had any engagements with Black. I didn't care what he had to offer, I just wanted to end it. Roguishly, I had my special goodbye planned for him, which was going to be a special treat for me. I was going to get the pleasure out of disbanding that trifling motherfucker. That night, Miyah had a get together at Shaylah's house, so Black and I went in the back room to get out the spotlight. He tried to make moves very quickly. Oh really! This nigga actually thought he had it like that, OMG! He truly was whack. But I let him have his last moments... While he was caressing my body, his hands started fondling down my pants. I led him to believe he was getting some pussy. I started whining on him slowly, softly kissing on his neck, and nibbling on his ears. Then we both erotically started taking off our clothes. As he gently laid on top of me with no protection, thinking he was going to stick it in, I charmingly whispered in his ear, "You have to eat my food before you get the dessert." Of course, he slobbered all over it, and when I reached my climax, it was all around his mouth. But distinguishing between now and then, his head game was weak. Regardless, nothing else happened after that; I fell asleep.

When I woke up, Black was knocked out. Then I saw somebody tip toeing through the door, it was Miyah. She was trying to get my attention by pointing down to the floor and whispered, "Veah, Look! Look at his dirty drawers!" Eew! Black's underwear was full of shit stains... For an 18-year-old boy that was a damn shame. His drawers looked like a toddler getting potty trained. I was totally disgusted; but in my eyes, I no longer saw him as my boyfriend. Therefore, it wasn't any debating on what we were going to do next. We both looked at each other, shook our heads, and smiled because two evil minds think alike.

First, Miyah advertised it to the company she had over, and all the guys were laughing and talking amongst each other saying, "Oh shit that nigga nasty... He's a shitty butt! What the fuck... Is that filthy boy up?" They couldn't wait to clown Black. Meanwhile, Miyah slowly walked back to the room with his drawers hanging on the broom. Then she placed it on the door knob so that could be the first thing he saw when he woke up to get dressed. We left the room door wide opened, turned up the music, and everyone was talking louder than normal on purpose. "Aaawaaawh!" Black started stretching and yawning when he sat up. After he noticed I wasn't lying next to him, he quickly headed straight for the light switch. There was those doodle stained drawers, dangling on the door knob, and the light was shining brightly on them.

He had the most embarrassing look on his face while he was getting dressed, and he didn't have the audacity to come out the room.

Everybody hollering out, "Come out the room muddy butt! It doesn't make no damn sense that someone your age doesn't know how to wipe his ass, and this nigga trying to get some pussy... Hahahaha! You need to get your dirty ass out of here before we run you up outta here... You done my nigga; aye, for future reference, niggas use tissue after taking a shit, you can buy a roll for only 50 cents!" All jokes were on Black, but he was a little too quiet in the back room, so I went to go check on him... Wow! This nigga had jumped out the window.

I didn't see or hear from him in a week. Then his homeboy Montae came over, and rowdily said, "Yo Black got locked up for manslaughter... After we got robbed out here... that nigga been carrying his 45 ever since. So, when some old cat tried to run in his pockets, he shot and killed that nigga! It's crazy, but that shit is real. Oh! He's constantly asking about you, and want you to come see him." I crudely responded with the grill face, "What? Oh hell no! Black know I'm done with his ugly ass... Tell that lame if he keeps the doodle stains in his drawers, he doesn't have to worry about any inmates taking his ass, but if they do... Please tell him to use some tissue because his ass is going to be extra muddy and bloody. Besides, what he could do for me incarcerated?" Montae was standing there shocked and said, "No comments." I came back with, "My point exactly."

Eventually, Black took 7 years' as a plea bargain. After he found out how much I didn't give a fuck about him, he started writing letters to his boys, bragging about how he slept with Miyah and me, and was appreciative of the double pleasure. Literally, he was only meaning a few minutes, well at least for me. I was really glad that he finally admitted it. Truth be told, I wasn't even mad. I just was surprised that Miyah embraced him in the shower, at the same hotel, and probably in the same room that I lost my virginity at. I was somewhat loss of words, but I saw it as an opportunity for improvement.

Moving right along was too easy. For yesterday didn't hold me back from the current day, and I was more focused on my future rather than my past. I was an inquisitive 13-year-old that operated like an adult.

My walk, talk, and capabilities had changed. My mind maturely moved to the next level, and my body looked fully developed. I was ready for whatever. I did what I wanted, when I wanted, and how I wanted because I had no type of enforcement. Mommy was in another city, my father was dead, and my sisters didn't care what I did, if they were enjoying their lives.

It was one summertime when the old projects were booming. Every day after dark, it was like a block party. People from all over the triad were posted up chilling in all different types of fancy cars, and playing different types of loud music. Although it was an adult environment, there were plenty of us underage girls, but it didn't matter to those perverted men. All they saw were booty shorts, asses popping, and big tits bobbing around. The crowd conversed openly, as people from all over flaunted the streets. Overall, it was all about having fun, which Kassidy and I always found ourselves doing.

The parties didn't end until three or four in the morning, but sometimes Mrs. Parker would stop Kassidy from hanging out. She would holler out the screen door, "Kassidy! Kassidy! It's time fa you to come 'on in… It's too late fa you to be out thea now!" Kassidy looked embarrassed, feeling that it kind of revealed her age, so she responded with anger, "Darn momma! I'm coming, shoot!" When Mrs. Parker finally accepted that Kassidy and I were friends to the end, she started letting me stay over, and that night was one of those times.

Even though we had to go in early, our night didn't stop there. We started communicating with the guys through Kassidy's room window. When one guy left, another one was coming. It was an all-night rotation with a few interesting conversations. What really caught us by surprise was when Livia's boyfriend Drew had popped up at the window, trying to holla at me. Although I didn't look at him that way, we talked for a minute, but when he started discussing sex, I ended it. I always thought he was a cool guy until that night… I should've seen it in his eyes that something wasn't right.

When everything died down, our bodies were feeling restless. As soon as our heads touched the pillows… we heard soft tapping at the window, and it was Drew again. "Can I chill with y'all for a little bit?

My cousin not home yet, and I lost my keys," Drew said suspiciously.
I was already thinking it was too late for company, but Kassidy said
it was okay, and he quietly climbed through the window. Without any
reluctance, he coercively started touching me, and I immediately sissy
slapped him. As I struggled trying to push and kick him off of me, I
looked over at Kassidy, and she wasn't at all taking it seriously. Instead
of her trying to help me fight him off, she had this mystifying look in
her eyes, and a fulfilling smile on her face.

She watched and didn't budge while he forced himself in me. I
began to scream out, "STOP it! STOP! Get off of me!" As he tried
to cover my mouth, I firmly bit down on his fingers and didn't let go
of them. His painful words were, "Ouch! Ouch! Ouch! Let go... Oh
shit let go!" He didn't realize how loud he was until Mr. Parker came
busting through the door. Quickly after, Drew jumped out the window
with his pants halfway down, and Mr. Parker angrily hollered out, "I
bet not catch you near my damn house no more, or imma kill ya dead!"
Then he staggered to the head of the bed, and in his slurring words,
he said, "Y'all hoes need to keep them legs closed, I should whoop yo
ass Kassidy, and send Veah home... shit like this not gonna happen
hea. I should put your fat ass on a punishment. I tell ya what... After
tonight, no more company, and no more sleepova's!" Aware that Mr.
Parker was three sheets to the wind, and he already assumed we were
having consensual sex, we didn't tell him anything. Not only because
he wouldn't believe us, but he wouldn't remember shit the next day
anyway.

I felt nasty, violated, and was ready to walk to my sister Shaylah's
house. Quick as a wink, I snuck out and ran home in tears. After
scrubbing off all the filth in the shower, I broke down to Miyah. "That
nigga Drew raped me... He stuck it in with no condom, and Kassidy
didn't even think about helping me... I'm so mad Miyah! He gotta get
it." Her enraged remarks were, "For real Veah! That grown ass man...
I gotta tell Livia this shit! Don't worry Veah, we going to get his ass
fucked up." Of course, I didn't bother to tell mommy. To me, it was
pointless if she wasn't going to do anything about it.

The very next day, Miyah had confronted Drew. She boldly stood in his hatchet-face, looked him directly in his depraved eyes and said, "What's popping? You violated my little sister you dirty motherfucker!" His big buggy eyes stared at Miyah for a few seconds without no feedback. Then he cowardly punched her in the face and ran. Miyah didn't sweat that sissy hit, knowing he was going to get the bad end of the stick pretty soon. About an hour later, she had Tank, Rob, and Skeet waiting near Drew's cousins house. When he finally came out, oblivious to everything, a monster punch had instantly forced him to the ground. He didn't attempt to swing back, he just balled up like a baby fetus, making all types of painful sounds.

They lumped his ass up for a minute, and no one came out to help him. Consequently, his nose and ribs were broken, he had two black eyes, a few knots, and was walking with a limp. That brief moment of lust and betrayal, had cost him a disfigured face for a few weeks. I was pleased, seeing he got what he deserved to a certain degree, but it still wasn't sufficient for his crime. I wanted the worst to happen to him. In fact, castration would have been even more satisfying. However, something was better than nothing. Furthermore, if I would had taken mommy's route, he probably would've walked away, effortlessly.

Meanwhile, I distance myself from Kassidy for a little bit because I had that big question mark stuck in my head. I couldn't figure out why she did absolutely nothing. Was she enjoying it in the interest of getting aroused, or was she enjoying it because she wanted me ruined just like her? Part of me was feeling she had a jealous spirit, but the other half was sympathetic about her wanting to feel just as important. Yet, her low self-respect and esteem, continuously held her back. Even though she was struggling with her insecurities, she should have protected me; I would have done the same for her. With this in mind, it was time to figure out if she really was my true friend or not.

The space between Kassidy and I had given me an opportunity to bond with my big sister Shaylah. At that time, Shaylah was always hanging out with her home girl Tara, who lived down the street from her. One night, Shaylah convinced me to go over there with her. I wasn't too keen on meeting new people, but I went anyway. Since I didn't know what to expect, I put on my gangsta look when I walked in there. Oh, wow! When I walked in the living room, there was this 5'6, pure chocolate, nicely built, handsome guy melting on the couch. We both were mesmerized when we caught eye contact. The chemistry was all in the air, that it took our breaths away, and we both were speechless. With a smile, Shaylah was delighted to say, "Levi, this is my little sister, Veah... Ain't she so pretty? Veah, this is Tara's brother Levi... He's sexy right? Y'all make a cute couple." It didn't matter that he was a few years older than me, I still wanted to hangout, and we clicked instantly.

After a few weeks of dating, we had become a couple, and it caused his simple past to have hostility amongst his perfect present. All of his ex BITCHES were mad that I was going with the popular football player. We weren't even having sex yet, and I was already hearing indirect threats. In Midway, rumors got around quickly, and the word on the streets were—Levi's ex-girlfriend Bambi wanted to fight me. "OMG! Really... Why she mad that a Diva took her place? I'm not worried about it until she says it to my face!" I aggressively said to Levi.

Because Bambi was Miyah's age, as soon as she heard the news, Miyah came and got me. We walked straight up the block towards Bambi's house. Wow! What a coincident, she was chilling outside with a crowd. Miyah calmly but loudly said, "Yo Bambi, come here for a second... I need to ask you a question!" Bambi looked intimidated as she was approaching us. Miyah came straight out and asked, "Do you want to fight my sister? If you do, then we need to settle this shit right now! I know my sister can fight her own battles, but you're my age, so me and you going to get busy." Bambi answered in a timid voice, "I don't wanna fight yo sister... especially not ova Levi... I don't want him no moe! People always tryna keep shit going because I never said dat... I don't even know or have a problem with yo sister." Miyah response was, "That's all I needed to know." Then we slowly walked away with our ears opened, ready to hear if the nosey crowd had something to say. After that, everything was cool, calm and collective.

# TREACHEROUS ACT #2

After a few months, Levi and I took our relationship to another level. He worked hard enough for me to stop the teasing and start doing more pleasing. Therefore, I gave him the goods, and it was definitely pleasurable. The difference between Black and Levi was... Black had more money, but Levi had better sex and was more affectionate. His plumped lips gave me pleasant kisses day after day. His soft hands rubbed smoothly down my body, and his tongue eulogized my vagina, which kept it dripping wet, but he wouldn't be for long, knowing a fine young guy like him couldn't stay faithful.

Because Miyah and Livia ran the streets, they always were the first to hear and spread the news. It was shocking and disappointing to hear that Shaylah and Levi had slept together. Oh, no... Not again! Another one of my sisters deceived me. What's really going on with this picture? Is this how sisters supposed to be? The deepest thoughts in my head was... what am I doing wrong? I realized the problem wasn't me... it was them, and I had to get to the bottom of it.

Before I received the bad news, I was at Tara's house the night before having a delightful time with Levi. Then mommy surprisingly popped up at Shaylah's place. She was wondering where I was at 1 o'clock in the morning. Instead of Shaylah lying for me like she always did, she spitefully told mommy where I was at. In an angry tone, mommy told Shaylah, "Go get her right now! She has no business at no boy's house period."

When Shaylah came to relay the message, she never told me that she was the one who blew up my spot. She just said in a sly tone, "Yeah, I don't know how mommy found out, but she knows that you're down here, and sent me to come get you... She is rrrreal mad."

As soon as I walked through the door, mommy started beating me with her cheap belt. It was hard enough to make me pissed off because it stung a little, but I didn't cry; I took it like a 'G'. Then she said, "You on a punishment, and you can't see that boy anymore... You hear me?" If she wasn't taking me with her, I knew she eventually had to leave, then her rules would no longer apply to me. Yes, indeed I heard her, but it went into one ear and out the other.

The next day was when everything came out about the unfaithful act that happened behind my back. For that reason, Mirah was pissed off at Shaylah, assuming she snitched on me intentionally. With a serious look on her face, Mirah asked me, "You didn't hear that Shaylah and Levi had sex? Miyah haven't told you yet? That is the rumor going around! Why do you think Shaylah told on you? She feels some type of way about you and Levi's relationship. That's real fucked up! She should be ashamed of herself." I had this confused look on my face, for the reason that Shaylah was the one who introduced me to him. I needed answers immediately, but directly from the sources.

Shaylah was the first one I confronted. With a straight face, I calmly asked her, "Is it true that you and Levi fucked?" She dishonestly responded, "No!" I stared at her shameful looking face for a minute, but she couldn't look me in the eyes, knowing she just told me a boldface lie. I then said, "I at least deserve the truth. If y'all did fuck, then why would you want your little sister to be with a guy like that?" I never would forget how she was smiling, sitting on her bed, looking remorseless when she said, "Yeah, it happened, but it was before your time. I was drunk, and we fucked only once with no strings attached. Then when he met you, I saw how much y'all liked each other, so I decided not to say anything." Regardless of her telling me they had sex, I still had a gut feeling that she wasn't telling me everything, and I was going to find out. I then asked her, "What does liking someone have to do with you hooking me up with somebody you slept with? You should've let me make that decision instead of making it for me... You sure it didn't happen while we were together?" She was looking guilty as hell while shaking her head saying, "No! No! No!" I knew she was going to stick with her story, but there's always two sides. That's when I knew who I had to talk to next.

I furiously walked down to Tara's house to confront Levi. She was having a house party, so I hid my anger behind my pretty smile until we got in the room by ourselves. He hugged me tightly because he was happy to see me, but I pushed him away. I wanted to look him straight in his face while we talked. Without prevarication, I asked, "Is it true that you cheated on me with my sister?" He held his head down for a few seconds, and then tears started rolling down rapidly as he shamefully said, "Yes!" He was unaware that I just ran reverse psychology on him, and that's why I knew he was telling the truth.

My boisterous response was, "Why? When? How could you?" He sadly said, "Last week, we had a little too much to drink; one thing led to another, and next thing you know... we woke up next to each other. I'm so sorry, and I truly regret what happened. Would you forgive me?" My slanted evil eyes gave him a stare he would never forget. As I was taking deep breaths, my supersonic heart was thrashing through my chest when I pimped smacked his ass twice, then replied, "Forgiving you, will be the last thing I do... You are a shady ass nigga, and I deserve better... It's over!" I slammed the door behind me and unsociably left out. It was less than six months, and our relationship was already over. It really came to reality when I was walking home, and the song "End of the road" was loudly playing in somebody's car that drove past me.

Men come a dime a dozen, so I wasn't going to let one man alter my life. As quick as they come... could be as quick as they go, and Levi was one of them. I didn't shed a tear, I didn't lose any sleep, and my heart wasn't broken because I didn't love him. On the other hand, I was hurt that my sister betrayed me. That was another rude awakening. For I acknowledged how dirty and heartless a man could be, and how devious a sister can get, but it still was hard to understand why. On a serious note, if I can't trust my sisters, then who can I trust? So far it was nobody, but myself. For my reliance on: honesty, competency, surety, and stability is only within me.

Although I forgave Shaylah, I would never forget what she did. All at once, I became well aware that adulthood means getting exposed to the real world. That is to say, it wasn't my first, and it wouldn't be my last time getting bamboozled by a man. I would experience the good, the bad, and the in between through and out my relationships. The question was and still is, "Am I prepared?" Hell no! I don't know what my future holds, and I will continue walking the path of darkness, until I see many days of light. I can't give up, knowing I will be considered a failure. Mistakes may break you, but knowledge is what makes you. Accordingly, I will use my wisdom, and enhance my courage to stand strong.

Everything that happened through and out the year of 1993' has all been put behind me. It was a new year, and I had a different outlook, although I became very hostile. I thought it had something to do with my ongoing experiences with the man of darkness. For I started having unpleasant spells on a regular. There were times I felt all-powerful; I saw nothing but destruction, thought evil, heard all types of wicked voices, and spoke hateful words to whomever, and did it whenever. I really didn't know what was happening to me, and at times, I thought I was going crazy. With faith, I started praying to God, and during that moment things felt better.

Despite me being a scorned child in a cold place, I still had a few positive things going on. I was leading my own path of life, of love, and of hope. I was still in school, thinking very intelligently, and moving swiftly. My goals were to stay determined and become successful. My uniqueness I brought out was definitely an attraction to people, mostly men, and I used that against them. I put on my talk game, and was working their brains to get what I wanted without sexual favors.

Facts: To females of all ages that are thinking about, or are currently sexually active: DO NOT have sex for the wrong reasons because the fulfillment would only be short-term. The long-term satisfaction is making YOURSELF the main factor. Sex is not the only way to make your man commit. You can inspire a man to commit by your inner and outer beauty, your intelligence, security, determination, independence, and confidence; the list goes on. However, it's up to the individuals to find those special something's to win your man over. Just DON'T downgrade yourself in the middle of searching for it. Of course, there is room for mistakes because they can be corrected, but if you don't learn from it... then what's the purpose? I slipped and fell hard, but every time I fall it would be different and hurt less as I utilized the wisdom from my past experiences. Take heed to the false hopes a man gives or shows you; nine times out ten, it's only to get in your panties. When you find "Mr. Right," you will feel it. Not only sexually, but mentally and emotionally as well.

# LECHEROUS LIVING

*Lust, Lies, and Greed*

MALACHI 1:14 "BUT CURSED BY THE DECIEVER, WHICH
HAVE IN HIS FLOCK A MALE, AND VOWETH, AND
SACRIFICICETH, UNTO THE LORD A CORRUPT THING.

Moving here... moving there... my mother was everywhere, and somehow, but I don't know why she manage to move back to Midway. She couldn't have thought it was going to be a fresh start due to it being horrible the first-time. In fact, we moved to a bigger battlefield while she was gone. Yet, she was determined to go through it all over again, and moved into one of the biggest houses on Wildwood Lane. It had four enormous bedrooms, and a finished basement. It was enough for all seven of us.

Miyah speculated that all the fun was going to happen in the basement, and it did. Mommy was a little suspicious, but she wasn't sure what was really going on down there. Primarily because it was happening when she wasn't at home. When mommy left to go to church, there would be a gang of niggas pulling up right after. This time around, Miyah was hanging out with some dope dealers from tre-fo. Some of them looked strictly like killers, but Miyah loved that type of crazy environment; she was insane herself. I suddenly wanted to be a part of that life, and of course, Miyah didn't mind me following her reprehensible footsteps.

# LUST OF THE FLESH

Miyah introduced me to this guy name Tyrell, "Young T" for short. Damn! This nigga had enough swag to catch any girl's attention, and I was one of them. He had a lot of money, a serious talk game, felt very warm, and compassionate. That's why I melted right in his arms. Young T had made caramel nigga's relevant to me. He treated me like a queen. Everything I said, he agreed. Anything I wanted, I received, and every word he said had touched my spot. I needed that encouragement, and loved how he admired me, which was one of my weaknesses. He slowly lured me in, and four months later, he hit the jackpot.

We fell deep in love in no time. There wasn't a moment Tyrell didn't want to go without seeing or talking to me. Therefore, he took the initiative to bring me lunch to school, or waited to pick me up afterwards. He was surprisingly popping up everywhere I hung out at, but I didn't see anything wrong with it at the time. I was just happy to have him in my presence. My smiles lit up the room, and Miyah was delighted to change it. She waited for the right time to reveal her secret that she'd been holding in for quite a while. With a delusive look, and her permanent smile, she said, "Yeah... Kassidy used to mess with Tyrell, and she is in love with him... She's going to be real hurt when she finds out this. Are you going to tell her when she comes home from training school?"

I was shocked, but I believed her because at that time, Kassidy and I weren't on good terms. So, she and Miyah were hanging tight. I bluntly asked Miyah, "Why would you hook me up with him in the first place if Kassidy had him?" With that stupid ass smile on her face, she responded, "He doesn't want Kassidy... It was just a fucking thing, and she got caught up in her feelings. Anyway, y'all weren't friends for a while, so I thought it didn't matter!" She couldn't stop laughing, but that shit wasn't funny to me at all. In an irritating tone, I said, "It doesn't matter that we were mad at each other... Friends have them type of problems. It matters to me that Kassidy is going to be hurt that her best friend is going with someone she's in love with... and it's all your fault. This is really fucked up... I don't even know how to tell her. Damn, you be doing some spiteful shit, Miyah!" Miyah shrugged her shoulders and unsympathetically walked away laughing.

Miyah devious ass was counting down the 30 days when Kassidy was coming home, for she was itching for trouble. As soon as Kassidy got out, she came over. That was the first time we talked after that incident with Drew. We quickly rekindled our friendship, but I knew that eventually I had to tell her the bad news. Before I could mention anything to her, Miyah had blurted out, "You know Veah go with Tyrell, and they're in love." The room got silent. Kassidy eyes looked sadden because she was hurt. I was speechless for a minute, but was eventually able to say, "Let's talk privately, so I can tell you everything." Even though I didn't let Miyah devilish ways get to me, it still was an awkward moment.

We took a long walk, and conversed for a while, just like the old times. But this was a conversation I never thought we would be having, and from Kassidy's body language, I knew she was uncomfortable with it. I genuinely explained, "I met Tyrell through Miyah, which neither one of them told me about any dealings he had with you until Tyrell and I made it official. Then Miyah grimy ass came out with everything. It doesn't matter how mad I was at you, I would never do nothing spiteful like this; I'm your friend. I'm sorry if you're hurting, but I can't change that we are in love with the same man. If it will make you happy, I'll breakup with him."

I really didn't have any intentions on leaving him, I just wanted to hear what she was going to say, and also make her feel that she had the upper-hand. I truly believed she wanted me to leave him, but she softly said, "Although I'm really in love with him, I wouldn't want you to do that. Hell, he didn't want my big ass anyway. If y'all have feelings for each other like that… Then go for it. It's not your fault that you didn't know about us." Then we hugged and headed back to the house.

Speaking of Tyrell, he was there when we got back. I didn't sense any chemistry between them two, but it still was weird that we all were in the same vicinity. Yet, we continued having fun like usual. Tyrell still adored me like normal, and Kassidy played it off like she was okay with the whole situation. At the same time, Miyah made lots of jokes, "Damn Tyrell! You got it going on… both of your girls here! Who's going to be in the back, and who got the front?" Of course, she didn't get a response. We just brushed it off. I knew Miyah was trying to intervene in me and Kassidy's friendship, but it was unbreakable.

Kassidy and I started back hanging out, and I wasn't home that much, seeing the streets were our entertainment. We always found something to do, and something new to get into, which left little time for Tyrell and I. It didn't matter to me; I was getting bored doing the same routine. That is when I saw a change in Tyrell's attitude like he was losing trust in me. He started asking questions like, "Where were you? Who was you around? And why do you have on those tight ass pants and that revealing shirt?" I had a skeptical look when I answered, "My best friend, and because I been wearing it… What's up with all these questions?" I didn't want to be too rude, but I really wanted to say, "It was none of your damn business!" He truly began to act overly possessive, and I sensed the aggression in his tone.

That is when I had a problem with him popping up everywhere I was; only a stalker could find where Kassidy and I were hanging out at. Considering I was young, I confused his controlling acts for love. Sign #1 Persuasion: "Baby, I thought you loved me! It seems like you love Kassidy more than you do me… She's not your friend; she's trying to keep you away because she really wants to be close to me. Can't you see she's coming in between us? Get in the car… You coming with me, and all of that hanging out shit is going to stop! You my girl, and it is time for you to start acting like it!" That was the first time I felt belittled and very intimidated, but I was gratified that he wanted me all to himself. Little did I know, he was breaking me down in order to rebuild me.

As time passed by, things were getting worse, but I already was in too deep. Sign #2 Emotional abuse: When I got dressed up, or got my hair done, and looking all gorgeous, his response was, "You not going anywhere! Who the fuck you're trying to impress? That don't look right on you anyway, so take that shit off now! Do you actually think somebody would look at you like that? I'm the only one who would ever want or love you! You hear me?" I knew the real answer to that, but the look in his eyes made the lie come out timidly, "Yeah, you right." I started thinking to myself, and wondering, "Who is this new guy? He is definitely not charming anymore." Yet, I continued being with him, thinking that I loved him, but the bottom line was I started feeling confined and humiliated, which was weakening my identity, nobility, and confidence. Then I started questioning was it worth it or not. At times, I felt like it was worth it when he acted like Mr. Wonderful, but those times got shorter and shorter.

Sign #3 Sexual abuse: His change in behavior was such a turn off that I didn't want to have sex with him, and that provoked him to take it. While he was forcing himself on top of me, he whispered in my ear, "This my pussy... Nobody else would never get this... You my property now!" Afterwards, he started roughly having sex with me, but I just laid there in disbelief while dissolving in tears. When he was done, I wanted to get in the shower to wash the filth off of me, but he wouldn't let me. He angrily said, "Lay your ass down, and you bet not get up, or I'm going to fuck you up!" He kept taking me by surprise, and I couldn't sleep that night. I just stared at the ceiling thinking... hoping that all this would just go away, but he made it seem like it wasn't up to me. He controlled everything. He controlled where I went, who I hung out with; what clothes I could wear, when I was able to take a bath; and if I could speak or not. If for any reason I got out of line, he threatened to beat me.

As the relationship continued, I no longer had a voice. Therefore, he left me no choice but to defend myself the best way I knew how. Sign #4 Physical abuse: All the things he told me not to do, I did it. I made myself look pretty, I went and hung out with Kassidy, and I spoke up for myself when he found me. In front of Kassidy, he seemed okay with it, but as soon as we got out of her sight, he had back hand slapped some sense into me.

After wiping the blood from my nose, I hauled off and sucker punched him in the eye. Then he blindly pulled over on a secluded road. I jumped out and ran, but he caught me, dragged me back to the car, and started beating my body up. The punches were coming fast that I didn't get a chance to fight back due to me trying to protect my face. Once house lights started coming on, Tyrell quickly pulled off and headed straight to mommy's house. "If you tell anybody, then you're dead!" He sincerely said. Me being naïve, I believed him, so I kept my mouth shut. Any bruises I had, I kept covered up. I was glad mommy was home because Tyrell wasn't able to spend the night. Still, he slept in his car to watch my every move. Mommy, of course, didn't pay close attention to us, so she had no idea what was going on with me.

The beatings continued, and sometimes he didn't have a reason why; he just did it because he could. He felt dominant when he manipulated me, and I felt like this powerless girl who lost all rights to herself. It was like I was all alone fighting a battle that I couldn't win. I had cries that no one could hear, and words I could no longer speak. I needed someone, but the only person I felt I could confide in was Kassidy.

One day, she had come over, and instead of me dodging her like usual, I cried on her shoulder. "He's beating me Kassidy... It's like everything I do is wrong unless it's what he wants. I can't do anything! I'm so scared of him, and I don't know what to do... I'm tired of not being able to be myself. I need to put an end to this, for I can't take it anymore!" Kassidy was very mad when she asked, "How long have this been going on? Why you haven't told anybody?" I whispered while I was peeking out the window, "He said he would kill me... He's watching everything I do. He's probably listening to us right now. This shit been going on a little over three months, and he's real crazy." Kassidy responded loudly, "Well, I don't care where that nigga at, we going to have to jump his little troll looking ass!"

Kassidy spoke to soon; Tyrell's dictatorial ass came over right after our talk. Him and the crew went straight to the basement and started getting it in. Being restricted from hanging around guys, I had to stay upstairs. Kassidy accompanied me with a little pep talk, "You too pretty to take this abuse... Come on now, Veah. You and your sisters taught me how to defend myself, and now you letting someone bully you. That nigga doesn't love you if he's hitting on you. Wake up now... because you deserve better than him!" She was right, and suddenly I felt like I drunk some courage juice as I bravely got up, and I went downstairs with everybody else. The shocking look on Tyrell's face wasn't at all unexpected. His whole demeanor changed, and I kept rubbing it in with my beautiful smile and interesting conversation. He tried to talk with his evil eyes, but I ignored him. He then came over to me smiling, and charmingly put his arms around me, but with a firm grip, hoping I'd get scared and go back upstairs. Although I was really scared, and my heart was pounding, I still didn't leave, knowing he was going to beat me anyway. So, why suffer the consequences sooner instead of later. I just calmly moved away from him, and continued enjoying the moment.

Eventually, we all went upstairs after the guys left, but Tyrell stayed. As soon as I went to use the bathroom, Tyrell sneakily came right behind me. He locked the door, punched me directly in my mouth, and silently walked out like he did nothing. I ran out crying, and blood was gushing from my mouth because my tooth went through my lip. Miyah, Teesah, and Kassidy were furious and mad. That's when the fighting began. Teesah jumped on his back punching him all in his head, Kassidy big ass was trying to get him down, while Miyah and I was punching him any place of contact. This little guy was burly, and he was handling all of us. Once he flipped Miyah on the floor, he then ran out the house.

While I'm looking in the mirror, tears were falling as I'm cleaning my deep cut underneath my lip. At the same time, I see Miyah laughing while asking, "Why did he lash out on you like that?" I didn't really feel like explaining myself to her, but every time it's a serious matter concerning someone else, Miyah took it as a joke. I didn't think any part of it was funny, and I had to do something about it if I wanted to put an end to it. With Tyrell's mentality, the only way out of that relationship was getting the cops involved.

Considering none of us had a phone, somebody had to walk with me to the pay phone. The only person that was willing to go was Kassidy. While we were cautiously walking, we tried to find something solid for protection, knowing he was still out there somewhere. Before we even got a chance to find anything, the bushes started wiggling, and then Tyrell jumped out of them. Without any hesitation, Kassidy and I frightfully ran back. I started banging on the window while I was fearfully looking behind me hollering out, "Open the door! Hurry, hurry up!" When Miyah opened up, she started picking and laughing at us. "Damn! That short guy has y'all scared like that? Hell, Kassidy can handle his little ass by herself! Let me find out y'all pussy like that." What Miyah was unaware of was how long I was getting abused and didn't understand the fear Tyrell had built up in me. I sarcastically responded, "BITCH! Why don't you walk with us then? And, why you didn't do nothing when he flipped your boney ass over? … Yeah, my point exactly!" To make a long story short, I never got the chance to call the cops; in all reality, nobody was brave enough to walk with me.

A week had passed by, and I didn't call Tyrell, or see him. Although I missed him a little, I was pleased that my life was back to normal again. Until the day I saw him standing in front of my school waiting, but it was too late to turn away because he already was walking towards me. My eyes widened, and my face expressed nothing but fear, not knowing what to expect. He walked up to me cool, calm, and collective. Then said, "I'm sorry for what I did… I miss you, can't live without you… I'll do anything to get you back." Most certainly I fell for those whack ass lines, so I responded, "I need some clothes, shoes, and money!" He granted me my wishes, and I forgot everything that happened. At the time, I thought that relationships were based on fighting, breaking up, then making up, seeing that my sisters were going through the same thing with their men. Still, there are levels to fighting, and getting abused shouldn't be tolerated at all. I was young, dumb, and had so much to learn, which that experience alone taught me a lesson.

Those fun moments reminded me of the first time we met. It was nothing but laughter, love, and bonding. Only this time it was around his family instead of mine. They were some invigorating country folks that loved to drink, eat, play cards, and be loud, which I enjoyed. His sister Haylie, his mother Thelma and I were getting very close during my summer break, and Tyrell didn't like it at all. He was the jealous type; if somebody put more smiles on my face then he did, or if I showed more attention to someone else, he would get jealous. His jealousy had elicited his anger, which caused him to abuse again. His sister and mother watched him pound me in my face, punished my ribs, and stomped me while I was on the floor because they were too scared to defend me. In fact, if they said anything, he would beat on them too. He tried to regulate everything; by me not having none of my family around, he knew that he could do anything to me, and he did just that.

Flashback moment: I remember those torturing nights Tyrell would get drunk, made me take off my clothes and twirled around while he just stared at me. If I looked a little bit like I didn't want to do it, then he would keep slapping me until I did it right. That was hard to do with tears falling down my face, while my lips shaking in the process of me trying to hold in my cry, but put on a fake smile at the same time. I felt way out of my character, and I no longer reflected Na 'Veah Daevas due to me being an image of Tyrell's life.

Even when he wasn't in my presence, he tried to control me. When he went to hang out with his boys, I hung out with his sister. If he didn't know about it, or I wasn't back before he came home, then he would have his belt ready to beat my ass like a runaway slave. While he whipped me with all his might, he would violently blurt out, "Every time you disobey me... you get whooped. I tell you what to think, and if you don't like it... you get a beat down. You bet not ever leave this house again unless I say so! You like to hang out huh? What? You trying to leave me for somebody else?" The pain was like fire burning my skin. I couldn't do nothing else but scream and cry out, "No! Ouch! You hurting me... Why is you doing this? Ouououch! I haven't done anything, please stop!" He stopped, but it was when he wanted to. Afterwards, he would have the audacity to grease up my bruises.

I also despised the times he would handcuff me to the chair, so I wouldn't go anywhere. I would be in his room for hours without a TV or food, but Haylie did all what she could do. When I had to pea, she brought me a pale. If I was hungry or thirsty, she would cook me food and bring me drinks. Furthermore, she kept me company, and gave me a big sister talk because she was concerned. "Veah, now I know that Tyrell is my brother, but he is doing you wrong; you don't deserve that... Look at you... You too pretty to be taking his shit, and too young to be living a life like this. Think about your education first, for these no good men will always be around. Girrrl, you better get out while you have a chance. No woman deserves to be a man's punching bag, and Tyrell has a history of beating on females. He was always and still is a troubled child, and momma couldn't never control him. If he beat his own mother and me, then what makes you think he is going to stop hitting you? Think about what I'm telling you Veah, and watch his every move. The boy is crazy!" It was sad that a non-related person cared for me more than my family, and she took the time out to give me some good advice. I took heed to everything she was saying, and she had me deeply thinking. Even though I believed every word she said, I knew it wasn't going to be that easy to walk away.

Love is a powerful word, but it shouldn't be used to hurt or abuse someone. Love is carried in the heart, and nourishes your soul. It's the precious feeling you get when you feel like butterflies are flying in your stomach. At times, love can be mistaken, as the lustful eyes only see what they want for that moment in time. For everything that looks, feels, and seems right, can sometimes be wrong, especially when the bad outweighs the good. If you're mistreated in any kind of way that makes you feel less than yourself, or if it has a negative impact on your life, then it's time to reevaluate the person that you're with. Never mistake pain, disrespect, or lies for love because you will look like a fool every time. I know it's not that easy to do in every instance, but try. In fact, it takes a strong person, and a tenacious mind to walk away. Only you can build your strength and confidence. Just remember that you must feel important for your life to become relevant so that you won't settle for less.

It's true that <u>love</u> is blind, but <u>lust</u> is only a distraction like Tyrell was to me. Our relationship was complicated, corrupted, and confined. Urgently, I had to figure a way out of that crisis, safely. I didn't want to ever have an oppressing summer like that again. Therefrom, I planned my getaway accordingly. It took me a week to convince him not to handcuff me every time he left, and that was the day I took all of his money out the drawer, which was a little over $500. Then carefully walked out and never looked back.

Instead of me taking the main streets, I ran through the woods, and walked through some paths not knowing where I would end up at. Unexpectedly, I winded up at a gate with a convenient store right on the outside of it. I was looking for a way out before I climbed over the gate, but there was no exit, so I had no other choice. While I'm coming down the gate, a ravishing voice asked, "Do you need any help? Are you okay?" He held out his soft hands to help me down, then smiled gracefully when I looked him in his eyes. With a stressful stare, I told him, "I'm stranded, scared, and lost. I have nowhere to go, but I have to leave quickly because this guy is after me." I started crying and nervously looking around in fear. Then he compassionately said, "Don't cry baby… I'll help you get home. Where are you trying to get to? Who are you running from? Don't worry, nobody is not going to mess with you while you with me. I'm well known in the Tre. By the way, my name is Sebastian, but everybody calls me Loco." As my tears were slowly falling, I looked up and softly responded, "Midway, and thank you so much." I didn't want to give him any more information, but I did feel a little protected with him. While we walked and talked, he was whistling and waiving down cars until he found me a ride home.

I was very happy to see my family, but a little discouraged that mommy was more concerned about moving back to New York than my whereabouts. Come on now, I was only fourteen. I had no business with a boyfriend or staying gone for weeks at a time without permission. She didn't even discipline me for doing it. If I didn't have any regulations, then who or what should I follow? I was the only answer to this riddle, but I knew it was going to be difficult solving it alone.

For the reason that it seemed like mommy didn't care about my issues beforehand, I didn't confide in her about what was going on when I was missing. Still, I had fear in my heart, and was scared for my life, knowing Tyrell would soon come after me. Every time I heard any type of noise, I jumped in fear. Before I left out the door, I peeked. Anytime a car passed me while I was walking, my heart skipped beats. I felt like I was on the run because I always found myself hiding out; I was afraid that I'd be captured, contused, and in another catastrophe, all over again. I was walking on eggshells, and my life was even more complicated than before. What was really heartbreaking is that I knew if something bad was to happen to me, none of my family would show any concern until the cops came knocking at the door, telling them that I was murdered. Considering this, my best bet was to always have somebody with me until we moved back to New York.

I was glad that we were moving from Wildwood Lane, assuming that it would be harder for Tyrell to find me. Then his boys came over for Miyah, and they found out we were moving back to the city. OMG! Tyrell was really going to be angry. A half an hour later, Tyrell appeared. He started begging me to come talk to him, promising me all the usual, and kept asking for forgiveness. I refused to give in, and made sure I stayed visible, just in case he tried to do something slick. Before he left, he passed me a letter saying, "Veah, why is you treating me like this? I love you, and I can't live without you. Please don't move to New York, I will be no good. I'm sorry for everything I did, and I'm working on my ways. I promise I will change. Yeah, I know I tell you this all the time, but just give me another chance. If you don't, you will never live peacefully because I'm going to make your life a living hell. You can run, but you can't hide! You better watch your back. I can find you wherever you're at… It's your choice if you want to live or die. Hope you make the right decision, and just know that I love you with all my heart." Now, this was two different personalities trapped in the same body, and he meant every sentence he had written.

I was intimidated a little but wasn't worried as much, thinking we were leaving shortly. Then I got some disturbing news from mommy, telling us, "Y'all not coming with me yet, Imma send for y'all on my next check. Y'all going to stay with Martha until I get situated." My eyes got big, and my heart sunk in my chest. I was lost for words as I was petrified and mad at the same damn time. For I knew it would be hard to dodge Tyrell for three weeks, but I didn't say nothing. I just set back, listened, and had the screw face the whole time. A few days later, I still was silent. Moreover, I detached myself from the family; I no longer felt like I had one. For mommy slowly was dissociating herself from being that vigilant mother, and some of my sisters were betrayers. Nothing was balancing out, and I was getting fed up with everything and everybody. I had so much fire burning inside me, and eventually I was going to explode.

The day mommy left... there were no hugs or goodbyes from me. I still couldn't believe she was leaving us, especially with Aunt Martha, who we felt mistreated us growing up. Anyway, I was older, and I definitely wasn't going to take any of her shit. Meanwhile, I began seeing an unknown blue Toyota Camry parked outside of Aunt Martha's house. I couldn't see who was in it because of the tinted windows, but I had a feeling it was my stalker, Tyrell, and I wasn't trying to step foot out that house. After hours had passed, the car eventually left; and on the porch was a gift with my name written all over it. Then day after day, I kept receiving something.

Sometimes it would be money, flowers, chocolates, etc.... Anything he thought would put a smile on my face, which it didn't at all. Yes, I accepted his gifts, but I didn't want to make that same mistake in accepting him back considering I didn't want to be trapped again. I loved my freedom, my beauty, and my unique character that I didn't reveal to the world. Solely because I was getting abused by this delirious and deranged guy. With that being said, our relationship was dead, I was done, ta-ta... It was most certainly over. Poor boy was lost of course; basically, it was hard for him to accept rejection. For this reason, he didn't give up trying. We talked a little, my smile was something slight, and letting him touch me was very slim. Although I kept refusing to go against my decision, he still kept coming by Aunt Martha's house every day for three weeks straight.

The day I was leaving was the day I felt comfortable to walk through the projects and say my goodbyes to some of my friends. As soon as I got off Aunt Martha's block... OMG! A white Lexus pulled beside me, and it was Tyrell. I froze up, but my fearful eyes were still observing my surroundings, and hoping I could run to safety. That day, the projects seemed deserted, so I did a U-turn and started fast walking back to Auntie's house. Tyrell jumped out the car with his charming smile, and he passed me some roses with a card attached saying, "I'll miss you, and you will always be in my heart. Love you 4ever. Make sure you don't forget about me when you go back to the Big Apple." Then he amiably said, "I have a going away present for you in the car… Holdup before you say anything! You don't have to get in the car to get it… I was just hoping you say yes." I flat out said, "Yes to what?" Then he gave me a gift bag with a beautiful lavender dress, a pocketbook to match with a phone inside of it; primarily so we could keep in touch with each other. That was too cute and thoughtful, so I sincerely smiled for the first time, in a long time. Then he politely asked, "Can you have dinner with me? No strings attached, I just want to spend these few hours with you before you go. I promise I won't try anything. Pretty please! Just do this one thing for me." I hesitated, but I eventually said yes and willingly got in that nice luxury Lex.

When we pulled off, I suddenly got a gut feeling again, but it was already too late because we were out the projects. When I looked over at Tyrell, his expression was no longer a pleasant look. Right then, I knew I was trapped again, and I had to quickly think of a way out of it. I was thinking so hard that my head started hurting. We both were silent, and the car was full of tension; yet, I didn't' show any fear until we passed all the restaurants, and he turned onto the highway headed towards Winston. I calmly asked, "Where are you going? You know I can't go far because my bus leaves in a couple of hours." He looked at me all angry, and then tried to back hand slap me; I saw it coming and blocked myself. In a heinous tone, he yelled out, "Did you actually think you were going to leave me? Didn't I tell you it's your choice if you wanted to live or die? Well, I guess you made your choice huh? You said it's over right? When we get to Winston, I got something for yo ass!" I was terrified. My legs were shaking, tears were uncontrollably falling, and I barely could get my words out when I pleaded, "I… I… I thought you loved me. You said you wasn't going to do nothing to me… Please just let me go!" Of course, he didn't release me, or respond to anything I said.

When we arrived, it was kind of strange that he parked the car two blocks from his mother's house. Once we started walking, he held my hand tightly all the way there. When Thelma saw the tears, and the frightening look on my face, she said in her slurring words, "Why are you treating that gal like that Tyrell? You need to let her go if you're not going to do right by her damn!" In an Irate tone, Tyrell shouted, "Shut the fuck up, and stay out of my business... Don't tell me what to do with mine! Yo, I have to handle something real quick, so don't let her leave, or I'm gonna fuck you up... Real talk!" Thelma had a boozy look when she replied, "Fuck you! You ain't going to do shit... I brought you in this world, and I'll take you out nigga! You just like yo no good daddy." Tyrell wasn't paying her any attention. In fact, he looked paranoid as he left out the back door in a hurry.

Right after, Thelma said in an uptight tone, "You better leave before he gets back and hurt you. I know my son, and he's up to no good! It's not worth it baby... I wish you the best, but just not with Tyrell." With no response, I quickly took off walking until I got to the Citgo gas station where I approached an older man coming out the store for directions to Midway. He asked, "Are you walking baby because Midway is a great distance on foot? I'll give you a ride if you need one; I'm headed in that direction anyway." I cried out, "I have no money, so I can't pay you, but I'm in danger and need to get home!" He meekly said, "Calm down... I don't need any money from you. I don't know what's going on, but let's leave, and get you home... By the way, my name is Mike."

I most certainly didn't trust him, but I was much more defenseless with Tyrell; he had that power over me. I looked at this older man as feeble and incapable of harming anyone, which made me feel a little more comfortable with him. While we were riding down the highway, he asked me, "Are you hungry?" I was happy he asked that question because I was starving. He stopped at a Chinese restaurant along the way, which was also a block away from his house. He convincingly said, "I have to stop by my house to drop off a few things if you don't mind." Me being naïve and thoughtless, I didn't think I was jumping out of one bad situation into another, so it wasn't a problem, just like it wasn't an issue on him giving me a ride.

I waited in the car while he unloaded his things. Afterwards, he hit me with, "Do you want to come in and eat while I get out these uncomfortable work clothes?" I was a little skeptical, but what the hell, I went in anyway. I was chopping down those chicken wings when old ass Mike came in the living room butterball naked. I immediately stopped eating, jumped up, but couldn't make a run for it, seeing I was backed into a corner. He then ran and tackled me down, football style. The only thing that was running through my mind was, "I can't let this motherfucker rape me!" Everything started moving in slow motion. I began to get hot, and things started looking blurry as I was enraged. My body got numbed, and that's when I saw the man of darkness jump into me. I immediately became vicious and started fighting him off. I was going crazy. I cracked a lamp over his head, which caused him to stumble to the floor. Then I picked up a vase and repeatedly beat the shit out of his dick and balls. After I spit in his face, I gave him the evil eyes while I fiercely walked out.

I began to transition back to myself moments after I was walking. My body was weakening, and my emotions started kicking in. Then came the crying and the frustration, especially when I felt overheated, tired, and dehydrated from walking on that lonely highway for a little over 30 minutes. Before I passed out, a black Cadillac slowly pulled beside me. I exhaustedly looked up and saw Sebastian. I was most certainly happy to see his face again, and he had no problem giving me a safe ride home.

When I got to Aunt Martha's house, I was miserable when I found out Miyah, Lannah, and Lavinniah had already left. With a little influence from Aunt Martha, Daishah and Caylah wanted to stay with her. They were afraid to move back to New York after Aunt Martha had told them all sorts of horror stories about kids getting murdered, being on drugs, and the astronomical amount of needy families in the city. It sealed the deal when she told them about how the rats were the same size as cats, which was true to some extent. I understood that she believed they would have a better life in the south, but just not with her. Aunt Martha didn't plan on giving them a better life considering she had her own selfish motive that would only benefit her in the end. My sisters were too young to recognize real, but it wasn't their fault, it was our mother's. She gradually was giving up her obligations to us, so she could have less responsibilities, and that enabled our vulnerability to just about anyone and anything.

In the middle of me taking all of this information in, I cried to Aunt Martha explaining everything that happened to me. In an unconcerned tone, she said, "Lilith and I thought you ran away again." I was shocked that they labeled me as a runaway, but not once did she say anything about them reporting it to the cops. After everything I told her, not once did she ask me was I alright, did I need to go to the hospital, or did I want to take out charges on Tyrell. I know I was out of control, but I still was young.

What is the outlook on real parenting? Do you chastise when wrong and eulogize when right? What do parents do when times get hard? Do they abandon their child? Or do they withstand their situation? Of course, parenting is complicated, and kids make it even more difficult at times; still, taking the easy way out can be one of the biggest mistakes to make. In mommy's case, it was, and it ruined us. We always needed a lot of love, but we only got a limited amount of it. We wanted but got very little attention. We had a lifetime of desires, but none of them was fulfilled. So, you can imagine how that altered the way we felt, perceived things, and acted. Furthermore, we conspicuously delivered evil with our Enraged, Vicious, Immoral, and Loathsome behaviors.

Previously, I stated that is was suspicious for Tyrell to park the car two blocks from his mother's house; well, it was because the car was stolen. It gave me chill bumps when I saw the same car Tyrell came and picked me up in on the local news broadcasting how a lady was beaten, kidnapped, and carjacked. Unflinchingly, I stood there; I wanted to hear every detail to the story.

The fiend was hysterical while she explained what happened. "Yesterday Young T called and asked me for a ride, which I had no problem doing. In the middle of me running him around, he asked me can he borrow my car for a few hours. When I told him not right now, he instantly got violent. First, He... he swiftly backhand slapped me, and it left me in a daze. That's when I came to a complete stop. Then he came around to the driver's seat and constantly started punching me in my face until he knocked me out. I don't know how long I was out for, but when I woke up, I was in the trunk handcuffed. I couldn't see anything, but I heard young T and a female arguing about him taking her back home. Poor girl was crying the whole time, and he still continued to beat on her. I was afraid to scream or anything of that matter because I didn't want him to hurt me again. With pain, I laid silently in fear and tears. After hours of the car not moving, and me not hearing any talking, I had a feeling he was gone. From there on, I started screaming and kicking the trunk, hoping someone would hear me. I thank God for sending that young couple pass my car. If it wasn't for them, I would've died in there... I was dehydrated from the heat, and I didn't have no water or food for a little over a day. I just kept praying, and that's why I'm here today willing and able to put a stop to Young T's brutality."

I couldn't believe the whole time I was in that car an old lady was in the trunk. Then I thought back like damn, that's the reason he didn't handcuff me because he used them on her. I was too scared, especially about him still on the loose, and the cops had no leads of where Tyrell was at.

Instead of me staying at Aunt Martha's house, I walked straight to Shaylah's place. Shaylah had just moved on the other side of town, and he didn't know where she stayed at. Therefore, I felt somewhat safer there until mommy sent for me. Without any questions asked, my sister always welcomed me into her home, and I always felt like it was my own. Shaylah was unaware of what was going on, but she kind of figured out that something was wrong, seeing I was too fidgety and paranoid. Assumptions is a motherfucker, and considering I lost all my trust in Shaylah, I just let her keep on assuming, but that was a mistake on my end. If she would've known my situation, then maybe she would've been a little observant and mindful of my whereabouts.

After watching the news for a week, I knew Tyrell wasn't apprehended. Due to him being on the run, my dumbass assumed the coast was clear. Cautiously, I began to mingle through the neighborhood. On my way back to my sister's house, a grey compact car started driving closely behind, I thought it was going to hit me. When I looked back… I damn near had a heart attack when I saw Tyrrell driving it. I immediately took off running, hoping I get to Shaylah's house before he caught me, but the car was a little faster than my track running legs.

When he jumped out and tackled me to the ground, I said to myself, "Damn! I was about ten steps to safety. OMG! It's over for me." Before I could fully scream, he covered my mouth and dragged me behind some huge trucks across the street from Shaylah's house. He had such a long and tight grip on my neck that everything began to look cloudy. His voice seemed so far away when he said, "You see what you're making me do? Why did you leave me…? Why?" With my mouth still covered, and my body embedded in the rocks, he used only one hand to punch me in every sensitive part of my body. It was like a nightmare, and I felt helpless as I laid there crying and unable to do anything.

He couldn't force me into his car because Shaylah was talking on her porch to Sebastian's brother Phil at the time. Pervertibly, he decided to pull my skirt up, ram his finger in me, and pleasured himself with a quickie. While he was violating my body, he whispered in a strange tone, "Once I get finish with you… you're dead… I hate it had to come to this point, but If I can't have you, then no one else will. I told you this over and over again, now imma show you better than I can tell you. Oh! And I'm going to dispose your body where nobody won't be able to find it. Piece by piece, every part of you will be gone." While I'm grasping for air as his hand was getting tighter around my mouth, I was thinking of a way out. I knew that my confined screams would go unheard, so why even try?

While I'm in my deep thoughts, I was staring at my sister and devastated that she couldn't see or didn't know I was in danger, but she was only a few feet away. That instant, the game clicked. If I can convince him that I loved him enough to stay down south and move with my sister so that we could be together, then maybe he would think twice about hurting me. Then I started mumbling my apologies.

Afterwards, he loosened up his hand from my mouth, and I dishonestly cried out, "You didn't give me a chance to tell you that I'm not moving back to New York anymore. I asked Shaylah could I stay with her in order to be with you. I even asked her could you stay with us too... and she said yes. I tried to call and tell you, but your phone off. Isn't it? If you don't believe me... you can ask her right now." Of course, the lie came out perfectly, but I was hoping it was enough to convince him to go ask Shaylah, and I would be good. He hesitated for a minute, but he eventually gave in and intensely said, "You bet not mention one word about this to anybody, and if you're lying, imma getcha!"

When we started walking, I felt relieved. I knew once I got in front of my sister, she would protect me. As we approached her, she surprisingly said, "I've been waiting on you for a minute. Where were you at? And why are you coming from that way?" In an unsuspicious tone, I replied calmly, "Tyrell and I was just walking and talking... Can you come here? I need to talk to you for a second." While Shaylah and I was in the room, Tyrell and Phil were in the kitchen talking. I had this troubling look as my tears started falling, and then I whispered, "He's been beating on me Shaylah, and he said that he would kill me if I don't want to be with him, but I want it to be over. I'm scared to tell him that because he is real crazy. We weren't really walking and talking... He was torturing me behind those trucks across the street. I told him all sorts of lies, and he let me go. Look what he did to me..." Then I lifted up my shirt, and her eyes widened when she saw all of those bruises on my body. "Oh no Veah!" Before she said anything else, I asked, "Can you be in front of me when I breakup with him? Then he won't be able to hit me." Of course, she wasn't going to let him do anything, but I was just making sure we were on the same page.

Shaylah had fiercely called Phil in the room to let him know what was about to go down, while I told Tyrell to go get the car, and park it in my sister's driveway. When he got back, Shaylah and Phil was standing in front of me. Then I bravely yelled out, "It's over Tyrell, and I don't want you anymore. You too abusive, and I don't need you, your fist, your money, nor that fake ass love you've been giving me... Goodbye you insecure ass nigga!" His eyes got real big, he clenched his hands, and then he charged directly in my direction and tried to jump over Shaylah and Phil. They started roughing him up really bad, but he eventually got away and ran out the house.

I then used Phil's phone to call the cops. I gave them all of his personal information, described the car he was driving, and told them he was wanted for the: carjacking, kidnapping, and assault on that woman from Winston. When they eventually caught up with him on the highway, it was a high speed chase through Midway and Winston. Ultimately, he got caught, and got the taste of his own medicine. He was confined, controlled, and humiliated, but couldn't do a damn thing about it. Although I wanted to, I didn't bother to press charges because I was leaving anyway. I just was glad that I woke up from my worst nightmare and could start back having sweet dreams, now that I had my life back.

That relationship was on a level of its own, and it taught me something totally different than the last two. I've learned that a man can also envy his girlfriend due to his own self-doubts. He builds his confidence through empowering and controlling others by weakening their souls. In other words, he does not accept himself, and he will persuade you in doing the same. Your self-esteem is everything, for it's created through knowledge and accomplishments, which helps strengthen your belief in oneself. Once that starts to fade away, then you lose your dignity and no longer see the reflection of you. At that time, that's who I had transitioned to, for my audacious actions were the cause of me learning the hard way. I had to experience the worst in order to learn what was best for me. Tyrell taught me not to show fear; it's a sign of weakness, which can be used against you to gain control. Even if you do have fear in your heart, always have the courage to fight back. Always remember that abuse is an act out of anger and jealousy, which is a misdeed that misleads, so don't confuse it with love. At times, it could be a disillusionment, but look at it this way, "Sometimes you have to lose nothing in order to gain something!" With that being said, I will be strong where I stand, I will talk with confidence, fight with my knowledge, and live life to the fullest.

I had the lustful eyes for that moment, but it wasn't time for me to find love; it was meant for me to continue exploring. I was young, full of fun, covered in beauty, and I had a load of knowledge. Still, I didn't know the full meaning of life. I eventually gained that wisdom because my brain absorbed information quick and easy as I was ready to experience something new. I was seeking a man who had: a strong mentality, a suitable lifestyle, and a courteous personality. A strong-willed man could hopefully lead me in the right direction towards my destiny. Until then, I was just a ravenous teenager who needed to eat; basically, I was out there hunting for wild animals.

Meanwhile, I was headed back to New York. I was less of "Lil Na 'Veah," and more of "Miss Veah," for I had higher expectations and wasn't going to take shit from nobody. All eyes were on me when I walked down Broadway Street, but I ignored the attention. I was just ready to see my family. The first thing I saw when I entered the apartment… was the whole apartment; it was literally that small. Yes, we were definitely living that Brooklyn lifestyle again.

I gave hugs, kisses, and made small talk with everyone. Then Miyah and I left out to have some teenage fun. The first stop was the corner store where we bought one of the cheapest beers on the market. We got three 40 ounces of Midnight Dragon for only $3.00, and we didn't even need any ID… We couldn't go wrong with that. Thereafter, we walked behind the Broadway Junction station headed to the Park. That's where all of the young teens went to either play ball or get drunk. That day, I got fucked up real quick considering it was my first time drinking. My body felt relaxed, warm, but totally disconnected from the norm. My head started spinning, and I was seeing doubles. Miyah barely understood my vociferously, slurred words. Then I got this nauseating feeling passing through my stomach and forming quickly in my throat. I also got this congested sensation in both of my watery eyes before I threw up everything I ate that day and started crying at the same time. This is when Miyah panicked, knowing that she couldn't take me home like that. With this in mind, she tried to keep me out late as possible, hoping I would sober up. We tried to walk around, but I barely could stand. She tried to feed me, but nothing wouldn't stay down. Therefore, she had no choice but to take me home, anticipating on mommy being in her room like usual.

She held me up while I staggered all the way home. As soon as we got in, Miyah took me straight to the bathroom. Before she could put me in a cold shower, I had to take a shit. In the process of me using the bathroom, I had to throw up again. Well, everybody know that you can't do both at the same time without a pale literally in front of you. The end results were absolutely disgusting and embarrassing. My excuse for that mishap was, "I was drunk, and I barely remember anything." Although I was sticking to my story, Miyah had a hilarious one of her own, which she had no shame in broadcasting it. During that shameful moment, Mommy never came out her room, but she did holler out, "Y'all keep that noise down… I'm trying to sleep!" My God! Everything goes unnoticed with her.

The next day, I had a terrible hang-over, and stayed in the bed almost all day. My head was repetitively throbbing, and my stomach was upset from all the poison I poured into my body. In spite of the bad experience my first time drinking, I still enjoyed myself, and we continued doing the same routine almost every night. It got to a point when school started, I was occasionally playing hooky just to go to Canarsie with Miyah. I wanted to drink, have fun, and hang around boys. During that time, Miyah was already an abortive student. So, I sensed she didn't give one fuck about me going to school; if she did, I wouldn't have been with her in the first place.

Of course, mommy never found out about it; actually, it didn't seem like she was interested in our school life either. She didn't even realize the days missed, or my grades going up and down on my report card since her mind was more focused on God, like usual. In the meantime, at Thomas Jefferson High School, the teachers didn't seem to care, and the students didn't either. Students were constantly disrespectful to the teachers, fights always broke out, and repetitive interruptions in class was the reason we barely learned anything. The teachers still got paid to teach, but instead of them educating us, they just watched us act out, which provoked us to lose interest in our education and attendance. I was one of those individuals as boys became more of my learning tools.

Indeed, New York was the right place to find one. Every day the streets were filled with people of different cultures, which gave me an advantage to explore even more. I didn't have a preference and was checking out everybody. For a second, I thought my eyes were playing tricks on me, but when I did a double take, I saw this smooth skin, golden brown, medium tall, handsome guy standing against the building talking to my cousin, Rahkeem. While I was sizing his fine ass up, he was pleasantly doing the same. Undeniably, I wanted him, and knew he was going to be my man.

His googly eyes expressed words that were unspoken. Our lips seemed like they were already touching. His arms looked like they were ready to hold me, and our hearts were preparing to connect, for it was love at first sight. Wait… Hold up! All of those feelings, and I didn't even know his name, but before I could even ask, my cousin Rah was already coming to give me all of that information. Micah Knight was his name. He was single, and wanted to know if I was available as well. He was digging my style, digging my smile, and captivated by my beauty. I most certainly was pleased with his admiration. Then after a few long and intimate conversations, we were in a relationship. All the young adults on the block adored our devotion and passion for one another. Negatively, the she-devils my age were maliciously hating on me. They were mad that I accomplished what they were unable to get after all those years of trying, which was Micah.

With Micah living a couple of blocks over on Marcy Avenue had made it easier for us to be together every day. We walked with affection, talked with respect, and we played around like big kids. The only thing that wasn't emotionally involved was sex due to me not being ready yet. For almost a year straight, I was okay with him just sucking on my tits. He was inexperienced in all levels of foreplay, but I coached him by showing him how I wanted my tits to be: caressed, massaged, and licked. Finally, to reach my peak, I told him to softly graze my nipples.

Time had eventually showed that I wasn't sexually attracted to Micah; it was more of his looks and personality that was appealing to me. Yet, that could only hold a part of our relationship together, and the other half would be explored with someone else. Because Micah didn't have the capabilities to step his game up, his friend Tyson did. I anticipated on someone much better looking, but his talk game was right, and his swagger was tight. Thereafter, I gave sexy chocolate a chance. What the hell, you only live once. So, why not get laid bursting in pleasure. Then, regret it later.

Resultantly, Tyson and I started secretly hanging out at his mother's house, which was in the same building I lived in. Just by hanging around him for those few weeks, I knew it wasn't going to be nothing but a fuck. The only chemistry I had was him making my pussy wet. For he was good at embracing it, licking it, and that made me want to give him a little bit. A month in, I decided that I was ready, which was the quickest I ever gave it up.

While Tyson was seducing me with his tongue, I had a vision of Micah and Rahkeem standing in the hallway talking. I thought that was the guilt getting to me, but I still let him continue. When he put his big load of chocolate in my cakes, another vision popped in my head of Micah catching me walk out of Tyson's apartment, and he looked heartbroken. Then he immediately got enraged. With much guilt, I said to Tyson, "I can't do this... Stop! Get up! This is not right." He looked disappointed when he charmingly replied, "Did I do something wrong... or you just feel bad that you have a man? No problem if you do, I understand, but can we still be friends?" Hell no! But I didn't tell him that. Then he walked me out.

I got goose bumps all over me when Tyson slowly opened the door. There they were, Micah and Rah standing there just like they were in my vision. Right then and there I knew what was going to happen next. I slowly started walking with my head down as guilt was written all over my face, while Tyson was smiling going down the stairs. When Micah angrily came and asked, "What the fuck was you doing with him?" I dishonestly replied, "We were just chilling... It was nothing like that. Who the fuck you think I am?" That's when we started fighting, but Rah broke it up. Then Micah shouted out, "It's over!" After he destructively walked out, he confronted Tyson outside, but Tyson gangsta ass bluntly said, "Don't come approaching me like that... Didn't you already ask your girl? That shit is between y'all... I don't have nothing to do with that son." Then he walked away. A thug ass New York nigga would've knocked Tyson the fuck out over his response, but Micah was more of the pretty boy type; moreover, he knew Tyson was nobody to fuck with.

That whole week apart from Micah left me sick and lonely. For I knew beforehand that I made a mistake, but I was starting to realized how much he meant to me. In spite of me wanting him back, I didn't make much effort; I really didn't think I had to. On the other hand, a young lady named Mikki had made it her business to reconcile our discrepancies. Every time she saw me, she would always say, "When the time is right, I need to talk to you and Micah." I would smile and continue walking because I knew what she was up to.

A few days later, she finally got us together and honestly expressed, "I can't believe the cutest couple has broken up. Now both of y'all need to stop it! What ever happened… get over it! It couldn't be that bad if y'all smiling at each other like that. I watched y'all these past few days, and the both of you looked miserable without each other. I hope y'all thinking about getting back together." We did… and everything was back to normal, but there was still no sex involved. Suddenly, I began to feel like that life wasn't for me. I wanted more, but neither mommy nor Micah could've gave it to me because it was too much. Right then, I knew it was easier to get it down south. With very little persuading, mommy had sent me on my way.

# LUST OF THE EYES

Arriving to Midway with an open mind, I knew eventually I had to get on my grind. Intellectually, I began doing some critical thinking about the "What if's". If I get this money popping, then my problems would be solved... Right? What if I go the wrong way, and get lost trying to find my way back? What will happen to me then? What if I can't do it? Will my life be ruined? I really didn't know. I had quite a few questions in my head with very little answers. Then I started thinking about the "Why's?" Why do I have to stress about my independency when I'm still someone's dependent? It just didn't make much sense to me. Why mommy wasn't supportive like a mother should be? Why? Even though my age read adolescent, I didn't really have a choice but to have a mature mind. Hereinafter, I had to take immediate action. STEP 1: Find somebody you can learn to trust. STEP 2: They MUST have heart, but vulnerable for you. STEP 3: They have to visualize what you see, and that was getting money! The first person that came to my mind was Sebastian. He had a desirous mind, and a heart made of steel. He also had the hots for me, which made it even better for him to be a part of my team. Of course, he was a nice looking guy, but that wasn't my interest; my attraction to him was his passion to make money.

When I finally ran into Sebastian, he was already hustling in the Tre, but was nickel-and-diming it. Since he was willing to take it to the next level, he decided to come to small town Midway, knowing it was a goldmine. Crack was the main drug popping off at that time, but they barely had a good source of supply. So, we had plans to lock the town down, but getting the right amount of cash was a big issue. It's a true saying that, "You have to spend money in order to make it." Therefore, we both knew what we had to do. Because we had little to no money, we needed to find an outlet to speed up the hustling process. Here's where STEP 4 comes in at: You have an option to get the money the foul way, which was corruptly take it, or the legitimate way, which is to add a more established person into the circle. That person MUST meet all qualities of STEPS 1-3 including a quality and some quantities of their own.

This is when Sebastian introduced me to Charles. He was a singled parent working at Fabian's restaurant just to make ends meet. Having said that, he was looking forward to making that extra money. We all were in need of hard cash, so our motive was to gain profit. STEP 5 only pertains to me: Do whatever I had to do without getting my hands dirty, but still be making enough money to my satisfaction.

Sebastian and Charles weekend routine was coming to Shaylah's house to drop off, hit the block, and count the cash. Then the following weekend, they'd do it all over again. Sebastian was going the hardest because he had that street mentality. Conversely, Charles was more of the investor, observer, and collector. He was the nerd who had the car and the money that Sebastian most definitely was eating off. Then there was me on the sideline; primarily, I provided the safe house for the drop-off's and pickups, which I got paid a good amount without being the face of anything. In fact, I didn't have to get my hands dirty at all since I had two men that adored me and wanted to keep me around. Not only that, they enjoyed my company. They even started competing to win me over. Indeed, it was gratifying, but I chose money to be my boyfriend. For the record, Sebastian was more of my type, but Charles was the breadwinner... I know you get the picture and the plot. Especially, coming from a girl that had lust of the eyes. For my appetite was big, meaning my thoughts were filled with greed. While I had those two victims of passion, why not get the full satisfaction of: attention, money, and luxury?

After all, I didn't have any bills to pay or mouths to feed. I wasn't even clubbing at the time. Therefore, I was content with just taking care of me. I blew most of my money on jewelry, clothes, shoes, and booze. That was the time Shaylah and I used to get twisted. Then when Sebastian and Charles came over, she would become extremely flirtatious, wanting all the attention on her. I didn't care; for one, neither one of them was my man. It was strictly business. Secondly, Charles and Shaylah were in the same age bracket, so he was more suitable for her than me. Thirdly, while she was doing all that extra, both niggas were still clocking me. To me, all of it was petty shit. I was focused on a major come up, and dick wasn't going to make that happen.

Charles started coming over Shaylah's house every night after work, and Sebastian was on the block getting it popping. He wanted to get his pockets right as quickly as possible. He figured Charles would eventually get his street mentality tight and catch on to his schemes. In light of this, Sebastian's eyes saw nothing but green, while Charles eyes were visualizing pussy, which was a distraction. As long as Sebastian was bringing back his money with interest, he didn't know or care what Sebastian was getting out of it. He was focusing more on trying to get acquainted with me. At that time, he thought I was 16, but at that age, I was still too young for him. That was my first time ever considering dating a guy that old, but he was really a gentleman and loved to spoil me. Cha Ching! Got' em! I had his ass wrapped around my finger in no time, with no problems or pussy. What made it even better was that I really didn't like him, which made it easier to play the game and still have money coming in both ways.

Every day I was digging in Charles pockets for any and everything I wanted, knowing that I was something he craved for. Why not take advantage of the old man, especially when he thought he could take advantage of me because I was younger. I think not! Little did he know, I was the mastermind of it all, and having control had given me the power. If I wanted more, he would have less. In fact, I was planning to eventually take over his shit.

In behalf of his pampering actions, I knew sooner or later he would want some satisfaction, and I needed leverage in order to prolong it for a bit. I wanted to make him feel wanted, and give him hope that he was waiting on something special. Consensually, for 8 months straight, Charles paid me $100 to cater to my tits with his wet tongue, and

$250 to devour my magic bean. Wow! Indeed, I consistently reached my climax, and I enjoyed every fluctuation of his tongue. Getting my pussy ate wasn't exactly new to me, but the way he did it was totally different than my past situationships. I guess because he had much more experience. I knew that freak shit wasn't going to last forever, but I was going to run that race until I reached the finish line. If my strategy didn't go accordingly, then I would have to go to plan B.

Sebastian was my alternative, and surely he got the same treatment as Charles. I know I wasn't supposed to mix business with pleasure, but I was looking at it like it was business to business. I was the manufacturer selling pleasure for a compensation without offering the demanding goods; also, I was keeping a long term relationship with both partners, and operating both ways, which was legal and illegally. Resultantly, the two were on my heels.

My next deed was to have them both feeling like they were competing against each other, hoping it would fuck up their friendship. Strictly for that cause, Sebastian and I hung out during the day time, while Charles and I hung out at night. When they finally got together, they both would brag about the good times they had with me.

Meanwhile, Sebastian and Charles's money started rolling in more quickly. PHASE 1: Sebastian began to splurge more, flaunted a whole lot, and got a little bigheaded, but not big enough for me. He had jewelry galore, clothes for days, and a captivating personality to go with it. PHASE 2: At this point of his life, he thought he had enough money to win me over; respectively, he asked me for his hand in marriage. Aaaah! That was so sweet. Even though I said yes, I knew I wasn't ready; still, I played that role. I looked at dresses and rings, but jumping the broom just wasn't my thing. I had to be content with myself to share it with someone else. Moreover, I wasn't finished with Charles yet.

On the other hand, Charles was indeed smart with his shit. His nerdy ass wasn't doing any flaunting. He was just stacking that cash and splurging on me. I respected him for giving me that stability. His well-balanced life had influenced me to focus harder on mine. His romantic ways had me questioning everybody else's, but his curious questions were unanswered because I didn't know what or who I wanted.

Flashback moment: Charles had taken me to an exotic restaurant and filled up my stomach with value. Then he got me a nice hotel room to make me feel relaxed. Afterwards, he started making it rain on my pudenda. I was pleased until he threw an extra $500 on it along with a condom. I instantly got offended since it made me feel like I was a prostitute. After that, I turned him down and was ready for him to take me home.

Although I wasn't feeling him at all, he still came around, but it was strictly about business. However, my thoughts were overwhelmed with desires of wanting more. While I'm contemplating on what direction I'm headed, Shaylah and Charles were getting it in. Well, not exactly; he was really trying to be spiteful, and she was just being the lady of pleasure, like usual. Therefore, neither one was truly fulfilled emotionally.

After months of procrastinating and oblivious to Charles mishap with my sister, I decided to submit to the nerd and have sex with him. I tell you one thing, he took pride in what he did. He had no problem with tasting every inch of my body. When he smothered his plumped lips over my twinkling toes, I thought my clitoris was about to explode. Thereafter, he massaged warm baby oil smoothly on my skin, and he took his precious time while we were getting it in. Although the sex was impressive, it was meaningless; I did it for the love of money. While I was thinking business propositions, he was thinking of a relationship development. My wet-wet had his mind sliding all over the place, but I thought it was too soon to make things official. I carefully thought it over, and a few months later, I said yes. I felt like he was the best opportunity for security and advancement. Therefrom, I didn't care how much Sebastian was heartbroken and mad. I had to do what was best for me, not him. Sebastian was just a minimum provider, and I needed it to max out. When he knew he couldn't compete, he had no choice but to get over me.

Taking our relationship to another level was very interesting, knowing we were the total opposite. The only two things we had in common were accumulating money and intelligence. Not to mention, most of his family wasn't a feast to one's eyes. At first, I thought I was walking through a dense forest untouched by humans, but everyone is entitled to their own opinion. I really got turned all the way off when I saw clothes, shoes, food, or whatever filth you can think of greeting me at the door. It was extremely dirty that I didn't want to maneuver from one end of the apartment to the other; therefore, I stood in the cleanest spot, which was their porch. As soon as Charles came out, I had to get it off my chest, "Is this how you live? If so… I can't sleep here. Hell, I can't sleep with you, seeing that you are flat-out nasty! You have to take me home." He looked embarrassed when he responded, "I'm staying with my sister until I get on my feet, but I'll have my nephew clean up the back room and bathroom just for you… Is that okay? I really want you to stay." I gave him the "What you talkin bout Willis" look as I responded, "Different strokes is for different folks… So, the only way I'll stay here is if the whole house is cleaned and sheets washed to my expectations. If not, when you get off, I want to go home."

While I was awaiting, his nephew Austin was trying to get his flirt on. "You too young and pretty for Charles. You need to leave him and be with me. Will you be my queen?" He jokingly said. All I could do was laugh at him; at the same time, I was thinking like, "He couldn't be serious?" Indeed, he was. He went on and on about us being together. I just silently stood there listening, staring, and trying to see past his looks because his generosity alone wasn't enough for me to overlook it.

During the time Austin was blabbering off at the mouth, his corpulent mother, whose hairstyle resembled Don King's, had walked up on the scene. When her inquisitive ass found out I was there with Charles, she was thrilled to blow up his spot. In her annoying countrified voice, she said, "I didn't know Charles and Sue Ann broke up! I have to call her and see what's up. Where Charles at now… at home?" He was at work actually. Instead of me saying anything, I just avoided her presence. Her anthropoid looking ass was irrelevant to me. In fact, she made matters worse for her brother who I already wasn't attracted to. Her intentions were to make me mad by revealing info about Charles lies and infidelities, but it was actually a lookout for me because I definitely wasn't going to take him seriously. Another thing that made me look down on Charles was when I saw his son running around outside, and his head revealed that he hadn't been to a barber in months. He didn't have on any shoes, but was wearing white, dingy, long socks that should've been in the dirty laundry. I was really blown away when I saw that his sleeves and pants were high waters. The cutest boy in the family was looking like a charity case, and I wouldn't have ever thought Charles was living that way.

Considering I didn't give one flying fuck, nor could I be the judge of his family situations, I continued seeing him. However, I did question him about why he didn't tell me that he had a girlfriend and his own crib. Of course, a liar keeps an excuse, and to some degree, it was convincing. Charles explained, "Sue Ann and I were never together, but we were messing around. Then she accidently got pregnant and had nowhere else to go. So, I had to move her into my house until she have the baby, and get on her feet; believe me, I can't wait. Hell, she's not even my type and not at all attractive. The only thing that was alluring to me was her sex, now that's the truth." The story was excusable, but once again, I didn't care as long as it didn't interfere with us and my money. But what wasn't going to happen again, was me staying at his sister's house, and I made that very clear. In fact, if it wasn't at his house or a hotel, then he could go to hell, and that's exactly how I told him.

Because of my costly ongoing needs, Charles had quit his job, and started selling drugs permanently. He was delivering it hand to hand, so he could make all the profit, which definitely paid off. I was loving his devotion to the drug life. We were together on a daily basis getting that constant dough, navigating through Midway at different crack houses, selling that potent stuff, and getting our names well known for it. I wasn't getting my hands dirty as much, but I was still treated like a drug dealer. That's when I started loving that hustle flow, for I mastered how to chop it up, weigh it, bag it, and then tag it. I got the hang of it quickly, knowing eventually I'd be doing it on my own.

I was too busy counting cash that I no longer had time for school. After two months of missed days, the social service and cops were knocking at Mirah's door, asking questions about my whereabouts, and why I wasn't attending school. At this time, Mirah and I weren't on good terms, which was the primary reason she didn't mind cooperating.

Allegedly, she told the cops that I was an out of control teen, selling drugs, fucking an older man, and I needed to be put away. Okay! It was facts, but what really pushed her to wanna do me like that? It was straight cruelty in my eyes, and I had no choice but to go on the run. The fact that Charles thought I was 16, I told him an old charge caught up with me, I was in trouble, needed to get my shit, and get out of dodge ASAP. I had clothes scattered everywhere, but my first stop was at Aunt Martha's House. She wasn't there, but the kids were, and she left Daishah in charge because she was the oldest. She also told Daishah that she would get a beating if she let me in. "Something smelled fishy, and it wasn't me." But just a minute of that big sister talk, Daishah had opened the door. I was in, gave them my love, and said my goodbyes, then I was out.

My movements were smooth and swiftly, for I wasn't trying to get caught. Every other week I was going to New York; otherwise, I was getting familiarized with Winston. Moving from one hotel to another was annoying, and I needed to be invisibly stable. Therefore, Charles had to make a quick decision on me moving into his place, or getting me my own. Considering Sue Ann was slowing down the process of us permanently living together, he decided to move me into his place, hoping that would run her off. I didn't think he would be that disrespectful, but when he kicked her nine-month pregnant ass out of his bed for me to lay in it, that raised a red flag. What type of man would do that? And, what type of woman would let him? I didn't question him about it at all because I was inconsiderate and selfish about the situation beforehand. Also, he made me feel like I had it like that, so… "BITCH get the fuck out the bed, and go lay on that uncomfortable couch!"

Owing to my ignorance, I thought by me being gone for a few months that everything was forgotten. Foolishly, Charles and I went to Midway, and that one false move got me caught. While they were arresting me, they read me my rights and reasons why, which revealed my real age to Charles. I was then taking to juvenile detention until my court date. The day I appeared in court was the day I found out Mirah and Martha teamed up to get me put away, and it worked. Instead of the judge sending me to training school, I was placed in a foster home. I was heated; my eyes got red, and my voice had gotten evilly deeper when I cursed everybody out. "Fuck all of y'all! Y'all BITCH asses can eat my pussy... I'm not going nowhere!" Then I stood there firmly with my arms folded. In view of my disorderly conduct, the judge had the cops to carry me out to the social worker's car without restraint. Immediately, I spit in her face, and started threatening her. "BITCH I'm going to fuck you up when we leave. It's going to be just you and me... Watch what I do!" The fragile lady was scared, and asked the police to follow us for her protection.

They placed me with this prodigious lady name Big Bertha, and her other foster kids. They lived in the Village East Apartments in Kernersville, which was a little over ten miles from Midway. When I was escorted into the apartment, I mutely stood there with a choleric look while I was being introduced. I didn't want to be bothered or get acquainted with any of them. I just wanted to be alone, so I rudely asked, "Yo where my room at? I'm not feeling dis right now!" That's when I became aware that I was sharing rooms with two other foster kids, and it most certainly wasn't any comfort in that. I was extremely depressed and was crying myself to sleep every night. The only thing that made me feel at ease was writing. For every day was a different story to tell, a different page to read, and every word expressed my feelings, and my daily experiences at that foster home.

When I got enrolled into East Forsyth High School, they placed me in advanced classes with some of the 11th graders. At first, I felt like a complete stranger until I saw Teesah's baby father, who also was Sebastian's brother, Kent. I was thrilled to have someone to bond with and vent to. For my thoughts were always negative, and my tears were always falling. Unequivocally, my sleep was always short as I felt alone and abandoned in a place that was supposed to be my home.

During my isolation and depression stage, Kent was very supportive. When I cried, he always found a way to make me smile. If I was uncommunicative, he found a way to get me to talk. Every time I had doubts, he always gave me hope. I was gratified to have someone genuine by my side, for Kent was there at one of my darkest points in life; from that day on, I realized he was a true friend.

I was mad at the world and everything in it, which had me lashing out all the time. My first victim was one of the foster kids named Sally, who was also my age. She looked at me wrong, so I repeatedly punched her in the face until Big Bertha came and stopped me. I was unaware but was immediately informed that Sally was mentally incompetent; still, I put that on my, "I don't give a fuck list." While Big B tried to calm me down and talk to me, she was smiling like what I did was entertaining. From that moment on, I knew Big B got that foster parent title under false pretenses. Then it dawned on me that I could use her phoniness to my advantage. Slyly, I started shuckin and jivin in order to get some leeway. I did some smooth talking to get what I wanted, and it worked. Being phony was most certainly constructive in that house, for it got me a little bit of freedom, and a chance to spend time with Charles. I couldn't believe she gave Charles the opportunity to come visit me anytime, but under the condition that he paid her. This gargantuan BITCH was getting off with bribery. Moreover, she was defrauding the state because I didn't think she was at all a suitable foster parent. Well, the apple doesn't fall far from the tree, seeing she was exactly like her mother Trudy, who didn't stay too far from us.

When Trudy came over, it was nothing but gossiping, drinking, and scheming on everything and everybody. The two jelly-belly crooks even talked about me like I wasn't there. They plotted on how Big B could get extra money from the government for me, and blabbering off about how my family gave me up for being nothing but trouble. Instead of going off, I peacefully took a walk to keep my cool so that my plans could go accordingly, which was to run away.

Around this time, I met this girl named Trese, who lived up the street from Big B. In fact, she and Bertha didn't get along, which was even better for me. Trese place became an after school hangout spot; plus, my getaway plan, but she didn't even know it. Once Trese started introducing me to all of her peoples, I pretended to be their friends. I knew eventually I would need one of them. Because of Trese, I learned every path and shortcut in Kernersville, which gave me leverage to escape. However, I got a little delayed when Teesah and Charles started coming to see me. Instead of Charles paying fat ass some money to see me, they just came right up the street to Trese's, which made Big Bertha feel some type of way, and then she started acting funny.

One day, I was sitting outside of Trese's house, waiting on Charles and Teesah. When they arrived, we were all outside chilling and having a good time. Due to Big B not getting paid, she wasn't happy. Therefore, she wanted to make me miserable as well. She knew the only thing that could get to me was taking me away from people I enjoyed being around. Instead of her leaving me behind like usual, she expected me to leave my company and go with her to run errands. I immediately got offensive because I knew she was trying to play me. I gave her a hard stare, turned my nose up and rudely responded, "I'm not going anywhere. Don't you see my sister is here?" She got angry and said, "That's not your decision to make, and I said you're going with me!" My blood was on fire, and I started yelling, "BITCH! Who the fuck is you? You're not my mother, fat ass. I don't have to listen to you. I'm staying right here, and you can't do a damn thing about it!" When she told me that she was going to call the cops, I harshly said, "Fuck you! Die of a heart attack you oversized baboon!" Without a response, she quickly drove off while talking on the phone.

Teesah couldn't believe how Big B immaturely handled the situation, but what wasn't shocking was my reaction, knowing how my attitude was. Although Charles and Teesah wanted to help, I insisted on them not getting involved. Then I immediately left, hoping I would eventually see them again. While I was running through the path, my vision was freedom until I got to the end of it and saw the cops waiting. While I was turning around to take another route, the cops ran from different directions, "Damn they got me surrounded!" I knew I was caught, so I quickly started popping off. I was crying and fighting them out of madness as I was discouraged about going back to that place. Thank God they put me in custody with a sympathetic cop. He attentively listened while I explained everything about Big B's integrity, and then he gave me advice on how to rightfully handle things. In fact, he documented everything before we arrived at Big Bertha's house. I had calmed down by then, and the officer had walked me in. Big B and the old grouch Trudy were running off at the mouth, but I tuned them out, and slowly walked to the room like they were invisible, which really made them mad.

Although I thought about what the cop said, I still had plan B flowing through my head because I didn't trust flatfoots. I knew Big B was going to report everything to the social worker. Therefore, I planned not to return after school. I wasn't trying to take any chances of getting shipped off to another foster home or training school.

Before school was over with, I got escorted to the office. All I could think was, "These motherfuckers caught me off guard!" I wanted to make a run for it, but my chances of getting away was slim, especially on foot. Respectively, for the first time, I had followed someone else's orders without putting up a fight. Arriving at the office, I saw a cop and the social worker. Right then, I knew that I was in some deep shit for what I did; yet, I still stayed calm. The car was awfully quiet as we road to Big B's house as I was pertaining to my thoughts, "I'm going to go hard if things continue to look wrong!" But I was shocked when the social worker said, "Are you ready to move back to Midway with your Aunt Martha?" Although that BITCH turned on me, I preferred to live with family and quickly went in Big B's house to get my clothes, which was already packed. Then I stuck up my middle finger and walked out. While the social worker and I were riding, I told her all about Big B's illegal actions, and I agreed to testify against her in court. She eventually lost all privileges, and the other foster kids were placed in another home. My vengeful deed was done, and I felt good about it.

Meanwhile, at Aunt Martha's house there were my two unhappy sisters, Daishah and Caylah, but because I was back in effect, they knew their situation was about to change. Their frowns disappeared since they couldn't stop smiling after they saw me. No more hand me downs when they receive a monthly check, and much more love and affection from me. What Aunt Martha wouldn't do, I was willing if I was able.

I disliked that the social service transferred my Medicaid, food stamps, and checks in Aunt Martha's name, but I wasn't going to let her take control of none of it. I was old enough to know what's right and would reveal her wrongs if I had to, especially when I already had built up animosity against her, for vengeance would always be my intentions. Of course, I was grateful that she agreed to let me stay; still, a grimy person couldn't be trusted, and that's how I felt about Aunt Martha. My experiences with her had convinced me that she was heartless and full of greed. So, who could blame me?

During that time, greed described me as well; I would pick up where I left off eventually, which was getting me. Not to mention, I was bringing hell along. All I knew was evil. Every strain caused me to struggle in different ways, which made it hard for me to see, hear, or think positively. My anger was undefeated, and my bad behavior would come with full force, leaving me unstoppable. Aunt Martha didn't even know what she had gotten herself into; I was worse off than before. Indeed, I was a walking fireball, waiting to strike back. For I was already resenting mommy; primarily because I felt that I wasn't relevant in her life. I had a grudge against Mirah over betrayal. Furthermore, I hated the government system for my setback. In all reality, it was me against the world, which I prepared myself for the good and the bad.

Living with Aunt Martha was a walk in the park considering she wasn't strict with me like she was with Daishah and Caylah. Although I had a curfew, I always came in late or not even at all. For the most part, I stayed pissy drunk, throwing up all over the place and acting a fool, but I never got in trouble. Aunt Martha didn't discipline me; instead, she laughed it off like the shit was funny. I don't know if she just didn't care if I ran reckless, or she didn't have enough energy to put up with a child so disorderly. Whatever the reason was, it didn't matter because I felt like nobody could discipline me anyway.

Getting back to the point about me focusing on doing me was the main reason Charles and I had some unfinished business, which was getting that money. We were like the shadow that followed us walking from street to street, for when you saw him, you saw me. I was the money taker, alongside, the money maker. Step 6: If you are going to get your hands dirty, learn everything, and be unique. Quickly, I became the Einstein of the crack game, and wanted to be more hands on. That's when I learned how to cook the coke. I was complacent with being a dealer; it brought me the fame (recognition), fortune (riches), and factor (influence), which made me feel superior.

We had Midway on lock. We were selling that breakdown with our "more for less" deals. Our good quality and large quantities had generated clientele from every direction, seeing that we weren't ripping them off like other dealers were. As this took place, Charles began facing the facts of real life when the dealers started disrespecting, and plotting on robbing him since they envied his takeover. I wasn't feeling none of that; fucking with him was unquestionably fucking with me and my money. Therefore, I had to ride with my nigga on this one, and I was very helpful in that situation as I made peace instead of prolonging beef.

We decided to change the game up so that everybody could eat. We started offering wholesale prices to the dealers and the heads, that way everyone could get a taste of that bread. Although we made less money, we were moving it quicker, which made our pockets look even thicker.

Charles and I weren't familiar with that fast money shit, but what we were learning together had made us a great team. A team we looked like, but a couple we didn't because he couldn't coincide with my style or personality. He was a nerd without glasses, a bama who had a fashion misfit with no class. He was definitely a lame that needed to be tamed by a city girl, which was me. The one he cherished, who made him happy and feel relevant. Without me, his name would've been a non-factor in any conversation, for he was just a limited edition. Contrastingly, I was immeasurable; I had both street and book smarts, which kept us productive.

Our lucrative wildlife had generated stronger feelings between us two. For a second, I actually thought I was in love. In reality, I was selfish and didn't want any other BITCH having what we started building together since I recognizably had it made at the age of 15. That was the phase when I became overprotective and aggressive over Charles. If I thought for a minute that a female was a threat, then she got confronted, and I put an end to all of that. There were times I ran into a hardheaded BITCH, and I had to prove my dominance.

Rumors! Rumors! Rumors! Indeed, got around in that small town, which was informative for me because it was about Charles cheating. It wasn't proven facts, but most likely it was true. Still, I wasn't leaving him until I got ready to. That is when I went through my crazy episodes. For instance, Charles never could say "No" to me, but when he did, I acted like a spoiled rotten kid and went nuts until I got it. Then there were times, I just took what I wanted. I was in control of all the money.

I recall all the times I counted the money at the end of the night, which he used to tell me beforehand what he thought was an accurate amount, but it never was, and I never told him; I kept it as my backup plan. I continued being shady, and my stash increased over the years of doing it. I wasn't at all remorseful because I just wanted to stay ahead of the game and men. Whatever he thought he was doing to me, I was already doing it to him but just differently.

From the outside looking in, people speculated that I was young, dumb, and whipped. Still, I didn't care as long as I knew my motive, which was surviving by any means necessary. Of course, I had little feelings tangled up in it, but I wasn't going to let it override my destiny. Yes, I did overlook the hearsay about him cheating with a lot of girls including crackheads, but I was more afraid of not having the ability to flourish on my own. Moreover, he was like a father that I never had. He gave me guidance, support, and showed me much love, which made me purposely disregard everything else.

My family wasn't taking my situation lightly. I constantly was hearing, "Your boyfriend is too old for you. He is going to break your heart. We already heard he was fucking around. Oh! Are you selling drugs? Mmm! That's a damn shame if you are. You know if you get caught, you're going to jail." I cared less what they were saying; nobody was supporting me, but Charles. In fact, I rubbed it all in their faces when I left Aunt Martha's house and moved in with him. I knew the cops would be looking for me again, but it didn't matter; I was about to be 16.

Moving in with Charles assisted me with maturity because I was currently the lady in charge. It was a place I could call my own, and I had the freedom to do whatever I wanted. While I observed

Charles 1-bedroom house, I realized that he lived differently from me considering he was very: messy, disorganized, and cheap for a man who was making money. Really? My whole life we lived poorly, but our place was furnished better than that. Immediately, I knew what I had to do to bring the house to life. I wanted vibrant colors, elegant furniture, pictures, silky sheets, curtains, etc. Voila! It looked like a modish place that became a cozy home.

A month after getting settled in, I found out I was pregnant. I cried my heart out, knowing I wasn't ready to be a parent. I was too greedy to share my money. That instant, I knew what would be the best option for me, which was an abortion. When I discussed my pregnancy with Charles, he looked bothered about him not having a say so in my decision. What he should've been worried about was his old ass going to jail for messing with a minor. I believed he knew that wouldn't have happened; my mother was too lenient.

Meanwhile, the news had spread quickly when I called and told Aunt Martha. As a matter of fact, she was the one that talked me out of having an abortion. Well, actually she scared me out of it. She told me about the long, painful tubes that the doctors use to suck the baby out. She also explained that abortions cause infertility. She really had me content and convinced after she stated that she would help me raise the baby. I then realized it was going to be a rough nine months ahead of me, but I actually wanted it to go slow since it wouldn't be just me anymore.

In the meantime, I had to fall back from the streets, and let Charles handle everything only because I stayed sick and tired in my first and second trimester. Moreover, I became very emotional as my hormones were raging, and my mood swings were too. Everything Charles did was wrong in my eyes, and I went crazy every time. For an example, I knew how the hustling game went, which sometimes we pulled an all-nighter or stayed out late. Still and all, I thought things would change, now that I was pregnant, but it didn't. In fact, things got worse when Charles became less affectionate, and more distant, but I wasn't having it. Due to my short-temper, I would break his valuable things, flatten his tires, or crack anything that was harmful over his head. I also let it be known in such an angry tone, "I don't believe shit that comes out your mouth! I wish you were dead… you lame! Nigga I'll take away your freedom if I want to… keep fucking up, and watch me tear your whole life apart!" He knew I was serious, and I wasn't playing any games. For a woman scorn, can be extremely dangerous.

I stayed mad at Charles; primarily over him getting me pregnant. In other words, at a standstill, but not for long because I started back hanging out in Midway. Just because I didn't have to get my hands dirty doesn't mean I didn't like getting messy. I loved the crooked life I was living, and the shady shit I was doing to Charles; he deserved every bit of it. I was the dominant one in our relationship, and that made it easier for me to takeover. At the time, Charles was selling out of a crackhead's house named Sassy. He was paying her a twenty for every hundred he made out of there, which was worth it, seeing all the users were comfortable buying and smoking there.

That was my chance to make my move. So, I smooth talked Sassy into doing side deals with me, and to snitch on Charles. Not to mention, I was paying her with Charles product that I was stealing from him. That's when I found out he was fucking with this crackhead named Freda, who lips stayed twitching. She was also loose, and her mouth-plowed for any opportunity. With confidence, she thought that she was still attractive. I couldn't knock her for that, but I did wonder what mirror she was looking in that didn't show her appearances was quickly fading away. Still, I couldn't forget that Charles saw something in her that I didn't.

The more I saw and heard this loud mouth crackhead, I became irate. Not only about the allegations of her fucking Charles, but also about her trying to be my friend. In my eyes, the BITCH was trying to be slick. Yet, I didn't confront her about shit, but when she came to buy, I sold her crack mixed with embalming fluid, hoping it would put her ass down. Instead, she got extra crunk. She walked in Sassy's house with poom-poom shorts on, her hair was somewhat done, and she kept a pipe in her pocket because she stayed anxious to smoke her one. I was speechless and in disbelief that this BITCH kept coming back for more. She wouldn't go away, but I felt it was necessary for her to leave!

Because of this, I knew I had a little jealousy; it definitely wasn't about her looks or personality. I just knew that it was one thing I didn't want to or couldn't compete with, which was that freaky shit.

Although Charles or Freda never admitted or acted like they were fucking, I had a gut feeling that Sassy was telling me the truth, which elevated my hostility to another level. I took every dime of Charles money, then used some of it to pay off a few young guys to kick his ass whenever he came back to Midway. Kung Fu Charles barely got a hit off because he knew nothing about street fighting. He also was blind to the fact that I initiated the whole thing, that's why he never saw it coming. As I stood over him, shaking my head with a wry face, I had nothing but satisfaction in my eyes.

Hostilely, I handled Freda myself. Every time we had run-ins, my eyes stared cold, but my blood was boiling hot as I was enraged. What really made matters worse is when she tried to get rowdy like she was gangster. Resultantly, I occasionally had to give her a can of whoop-ass. I hated when people interfered; I couldn't do her dirty like I wanted to, such as: knock her and her teeth out, put a knife through her heart, and then burn her alive while I watched her deteriorate into ashes. I guess a murderer wasn't the meaning of my life.

I knew I was losing focus and needed to get back on track. Therefore, I got in touch with my best friend Kassidy, who was my problem solver and soon to be my baby's God mother. She catered to me as though she fathered my unborn child. She cooked, cleaned, and bought everything my baby needed. So, the money Charles gave to me was just an increase to my stash, which Kassidy or Charles didn't know that I had. When it came to money, I was the little girl who cried wolf. I wanted help when I really didn't need it, and sometimes lied to get it. For example, I had caused controversy between Kassidy and Charles when I broke down and lied to her about how Charles didn't contribute like he used to, how he's never around, and that he be putting his hands on me. Because she was an overprotective friend, I knew that would make her lose all respect for him; afterwards, her manners went downhill. When I was ready to attack, she always had my back. If I needed to get away, she helped me; every day I stayed with him, she always tried to convince me to leave, but I couldn't until I felt the time was right.

I was highly upset when I heard Freda and another BITCH named Lizzy was fighting over Charles. "This nigga was really on some hoe shit!" Before I could think of a plot, Karma was already knocking at his door. It was his brother Norton, who was dropping off seven stacks. He wanted Charles to get him that good work for the same wholesale prices he got from his connect. Since Charles wasn't there, Norton handed the money to me, and I put on an intriguing smile, knowing what was about to go down.

Teesah and Vince couldn't had come at a better time, for I was ready to celebrate, spend, and then disappear on them niggas. After I combined Charles 8 stacks with his brother's 7, I thought I was rich. I was smiling from ear to ear while I was splurging foolishly. I took Teesah, my nephews, and Kassidy to Red Lobsters and dropped about $300 really quick. I went to the store and got cases of beers, a carton of cigarettes, liquor, and I didn't consume none of it. Geesh! The time was passing by quickly, and I had to bounce before those clown ass niggas came back around. Sarcastically, I wrote lamo a note with only two words, "FUCK YOU!" With a smiley face and 15 pennies on top of it, which added up to the amount I took. I could imagine their ugly ass faces when they read it.

Afterwards, I paid Vince $100 to take me to the Greensboro train station, which was too much to not be going very far, but it didn't matter; I had many more hundreds to go and was very thirsty to spend it. Taking into consideration that Vince was close friends with Charles and Norton, I paid him an extra $100 to keep his mouth shut. Thereafter, I surprised Kassidy with a ticket to New York since she had never been. I told her, "Don't worry about any clothes… you and I are going shopping! Food… I got it, and you already know you have somewhere to stay." Kassidy smiled and said, "Ok!" Then we blissfully took off on the train.

I was going to be in New York for a while; therefore, I had to go get prenatal care. My first visit, I was diagnosed with Chlamydia. My results had truly answered my question about if that son of a BITCH was cheating. That was the first time I felt hurt by Charles. I couldn't believe he wasn't protecting himself, knowing he was having unprotected sex with me, and I was pregnant. Most definitely, I took it as if he didn't care about his unborn child, which made our relationship even more challenging.

When I made the call to Charles, he denied that he was cheating, but admitted that he could've had that STD beforehand. This is when you make a motherfucker look stupid, "Nigga I've been going to the doctor for almost six months now, and they checked for all of that shit... Who the fuck you think you're fooling? Yes, I did take y'all damn money, and I'm going to spend all of it... you fucking nerd!" He paused for a second, then asked, "Where are you at? You better bring my money back. I told you I wasn't cheating." I laughed loudly, but it was more like an angry scream, and then I hung up on him immediately.

Three months passed, and I went through $15,000 that fast. Without fear or hesitation, I made that call to Charles. When he answered, I suddenly got the giggles as I said, "I'm broke and need some more bread!" In his angry but non-threatening tone, he replied, "You spent all that money? I was looking all over for you until Vince told me that y'all went to New York. Yeah, I paid his ass a twenty, and he told me every detail, word from word including you paying him a $100 to keep his mouth shut. You something else girl, and Norton is pissed the fuck off. You got me in a bind with my bro... He threatened to do something to me and you." I laughed and said, "And! That nerd doesn't pump fear in my heart, and I don't take threats lightly. I will get some niggas to run up on the both of you!" I didn't care if I was in the wrong or not, I reversed that shit real quick.

While I was waiting on Charles to send me some money, I was getting intimate with my ex Micah, who overlooked me being pregnant by someone else. He always was rubbing and kissing my stomach; also, he was fascinated with every kick and movement. He enjoyed feeding me my cravings. Moreover, he was willing and ready to be a part of me and my daughter's life. Apparently, I knew what Micah and I had was only temporarily, but I was enjoying it while it lasted. It was like we picked up where we left off a year ago. Our chemistry was still there, and our love was still strong. In the back of my mind, I knew that I got pregnant by the wrong guy, and wished like hell I could've changed things… But it was too late.

Instead of Charles using the information I gave him to send me the money, his ugly ass decided to hand deliver it. When Charles arrived at mommy's place, Micah had just left, and unaware that I was leaving him again. Although I left with Charles, I knew things would never be the same, but I left due to my needs.

When we arrived at Charles' house, Norton was there waiting, looking, and sounded like Steve Urkel when he said, "Why you do that to me? I want my money." I put on a big smile when I replied, "You should be talking to your brother about that!" Then I walked away, daring for his pussy ass to do something to me. Kassidy was surprised he did absolutely nothing, especially when I responded so boldly. All in all, I was just a disrespectful BITCH like that!

A few weeks after, I was home alone when I began having some intense pain. Even though it was a new experience, I felt like something wasn't right. In fact, my due date was August 1, which was exactly that day. I was lonely, young, and afraid. So, after I called the ambulance, I painfully walked to the next door neighbor's house and waited there until they arrived. Right after I got admitted into the hospital, I called Aunt Martha, knowing she was reliable when it came to stuff like that. Without a doubt, she and Charles arrived shortly after.

Given that I was slowly dilating, the doctor had no prediction on when the baby would come. Therefore, Charles' impatient ass couldn't wait to go back to Midway to make some money. Really! He was thinking about the streets while I'm in labor. Once again, he proved to me what type of man he was, and what kind of father he would be, but me thinking about that was nine months overdue. Regrettably, I had no choice but to care less. However, I was grateful to have Aunt Martha there to help me through it all. I was in labor for a little over seven hours, and at 7:15 PM, my baby girl Aaliyah Hope Daevas was born. Not to mention, Charles didn't make it in time for that special moment.

The minute they put her in my arms, I fell in love. She was a beautiful, brown skin baby, with a head full of curly hair. Although she had features of Charles grotesque ass, my beauty dominated his looks. Unquestionably, his primate resembling family was telling Charles to take a blood test because "good-looking" was barely used towards their family. But their voices were unheard in my ears, and they were certainly far from my thoughts. Furthermore, I still had control of Charles pockets, and it was nothing they could do or say to change that.

Having Aaliyah didn't humble Charles at all. In fact, it made him a little complicated once he built up his confidence after he got me pregnant. What he failed to realize was the only reason he got a beautiful young girl like me was simply because I wanted and was looking for the finer things. If I would've grew up in a better predicament; better yet, had a good father who nourished and guided me in the right direction. Then a man his age wouldn't have ever been able to look my way, but that wasn't the case. Unfortunately, I had a baby by a man that preyed on the needy to feel better about himself.

On the other hand, having Aaliyah had changed my mentality. I was no longer surviving for me; I was striving for us. I hustled harder in the streets while my baby girl was getting nurtured at Aunt Martha's house. I was still young, but Aunt Martha understood why I wanted to continue living my everyday life. She also respected me for not going a day without spending quality time with my baby girl. She never had a moment of needing anything. Moreover, I always paid Aunt Martha for her troubles.

Meanwhile, I came on Charles set to cock block them hoes; also, to take his and make my money. This was another time I really didn't give a fuck, and I was ready to pop off on anybody who pushed my button. I had 40 weeks of anger built up in me that needed to be released. Furthermore, I had some unfinished business to resolve, and it wasn't professional if you know what I mean. Like really, on a daily basis my fight mode was turned all the way up, and I was ready to approach aggressively, especially with the ones who disrespected me indirectly, such as Freda and Lizzy. I harassed them verbally and physical by: downgrading their characters, spitting in their faces, or any other vicious act to prove that I wasn't playing games. I was going to get my respect one way or the other, and I did. Many BITCHES were scared to fuck with me; they knew I had heart, and it was tougher than my man's. What made it so bad was that Charles didn't have the power to control me because I was a loose cannon. Moreover, he was a non-factor in my eyes, and I literally gave him my ass to kiss.

Charles and I relationship was more like a partnership that only I was aware of. He actually thought we were this perfect couple after all of his duplicitous actions. Indubitably, I went along with it, but our clock was quickly ticking, and my plans of moving on was soon to come. Before I could make that move, I needed to take the hustle game to a higher level as well as use a different approach. With those ideas, I reached out to Jacob, who lived in the Bronx, hoping we could get better deals on that coke than we were in the south.

On the strength of me, Jacob was letting them kilos go for $15,000. Let me break it down to you. That was my price; on the other hand, Charles would be paying $18,000, and I would be pocketing the remaining three. That wasn't counting the money I was making, or the money I was taking from Charles. Yet, he still was prosperous considering the prices were tremendously lower than what he was paying. Also, it was the best dope in town. The crackheads were doing all types of crazy shit, just to get that hit. They were pawning their valuables, such as jewelry, electronics, coins and doll collections; selling their food stamps for a little bit of nothing, knowing that they had kids to feed. Furthermore, there were constant burglaries, incarcerations, and then came the snitching. That's what brought the heat to Charles.

Yet, that didn't stop nothing, it just forced us to proceed in a wise and cautious way; also, being brainiacs were very resourceful in this situation. By us knowing Charles was the target, I became the strategy. The cops didn't at all suspect me as being a drug dealer, for my virtuous appearance was disguising my deceptions. Taking this into consideration, I became more hands on doing the dirty work. Plus, I was getting paid additional money to traffic drugs back from New York.

The first couple of times I road dirty, it was tense because there wasn't a prediction of the aftermath. It could go right, or turn totally wrong, which could leave me with a pocket full of money, or a world full of trouble. Yet, I took my chances and continued living on the edge. Then reality kicked in when I had my first experience with a cop while transporting the drugs back.

Kassidy and I were waiting at the Greyhound station in Greensboro. That was the only layover we had coming back from New York, and there he was standing behind the counter, pretending to be a staff. It was a good cover-up. I wouldn't have never thought this street clothes wearing, gorgeous looking man with a Vin Diesel built body was working undercover. Specifically because he seemed very experienced as a Greyhound employee.

He was polite, constructive, and ecstatic when he was doing his job, which made him look even more authentic and attractive. What had caught my attention was when he stared at me with his dreamy, hazel brown eyes and glamorous, bright smile; and I couldn't help but to give him a dainty look back. Thereafter, he invited me into his office, which lead to our private chat. Then about 30 minutes into our conversation, he revealed to me that he was a FED. My face expression showed that I was very shocked. My whole demeanor changed, thinking I was caught, but I had to quickly shift back. I played it off by flattering him with my seductive body, pretty smile, and flirtatious words as though I wasn't worried about what I just heard. Honestly, my heart felt like it was pumping out of my shirt, especially because I was sitting in front of him with a ponytail full of drugs. Not to mention, more drugs in my bag, and in Kassidy's ponytail as well. Even if the cop did think I was one of the criminals he was looking for, he gave me a pass along with his number. I guess he saw my lost soul, and wanted to give me a second chance, hoping I would be able to find myself.

Of course, that fast money was a fog to my vision; actually, that cop episode gave me an excuse for the lie I was going to tell Charles, which was, "I left my bag at the bus station with the other half of the coke in it because we were getting harassed by some cops, and I wasn't taking any chances." His dumb ass fell for it considering my freedom was more important. Also, he was happy that he didn't take a complete lost. "Whaaat? This nigga really fucked up, for every chance I get, I'm going to slowly empty out his pockets and overflow mine."

An incident that occurred during another visit to the city was the time I couldn't get in touch with Jacob, so I decided to go through someone else. That was the first time I stepped out of my comfort zone on my own, which was a huge mistake because I could've lost my life. That's why it's not good to be impatient and greedy, and that described me at that time.

I began shopping around, but it wasn't just for clothes; I was looking for a candy man as well. My drug slanguage that led me in the right direction was, "Where is that killa white girl? Or how can I get my hands in the candy jar?" Most drug pushers knew what I was talking about and would respond with no problem. After talking to and turning down a few potentials, I ran into this guy whose words made me want to continue listening, and his appearance was perceived as though he was a certified dealer. He was a little flashy with his jewels, but was casually dressed, which had me impressed and somewhat comfortable to do business with.

Before we made any transactions, we had our first conversation at a laid-back Jamaican restaurant where we discussed, "When and how much I wanted?" Which I needed it ASAP, and instead of me buying the whole brick, I wanted only half. Then he explained, "Where and what time we would meet." Dealing with big shots in New York, there was no other place to do business, but at their own drug spot. Knowing this, I had to take my chances, which was a part of the drug life anyway. After we shook hands for confirmation, we then went our separate ways. Surely, he would be waiting until I gave him a callback.

After I discussed everything over with Charles, who thought I was getting the whole brick, he agreed to do it. I then called and locked in a time, which was a couple of hours away from my rude awakening. I didn't feel any bad vibes, but due to me being a female, I asked Shaylah to go with me just in case something went wrong. When we arrived at the drug spot, I had Shaylah wait in the cab while I went to go handle business. I was escorted upstairs to the fifth floor where I would view the product, weigh it, and then seal the deal, which took a little over 10 minutes. Then I got a little skeptical after no one escorted me back downstairs, aware of me being an unfamiliar face. In Brooklyn, that's when a lot of bad things take place.

As soon as I got to the bottom of the third floor, I was surrounded by four guys including the one who escorted me upstairs. I already knew what it was, but I ignored them and tried to squeeze through. Subsequently, I got shoved to the floor, kicked, punched, and then guns were pulled out. While I'm lying there petrified, I remember the ugliest, blackest, rough looking guy had moved his gun from my chest to my face asking me, "Where the fuck is it?" I didn't think twice about not giving it up; my life was more important, and I wanted to live and see another day.

When I got outside, the cab was gone, and I was hysterical because I couldn't believe that my sister left me like that. Then I looked up the street and saw the cab slowly driving. I started supersonically running and was breathing extremely hard when I got in the car. After Shaylah saw my bloody face, she hollered out, "What happened? Are you ok?" I serenely said, "I got robbed and could've been killed." I didn't go into details, and I didn't hear a word she said after that; I blanked everything else out, and went deep into my thoughts all the way to her house.

As expected, Charles understood. Also, he felt awful about what I had been through. At first, I felt the same way, but it was just for that moment. I was more thrilled to be alive and was lucky to live and spend some of that money I kept. Still, in the back of my mind, I knew it was another sign that I avoided.

My last days of trafficking for Charles was when I took the Amtrak. From the moment I got on that train, and set in my seat, I had a creepy feeling. As I started observing my surroundings, I noticed three suspicious men sitting in different areas of the train. They all were wearing sort of the same thing, which was a Polo shirt and Khaki's. My first thought was, "Those are undercover cops, and they are about to raid the train." In light of this, I had to get rid of that shit quickly. Before they started searching everybody, I went and hid the coke in the bathroom garbage, and then went back to my seat very calmly. Indeed, they were the police, and that was it for me. In spite of my greedy ass going back to get the coke before I got off, I still told Charles it was another lost. Then I angrily explained, "Next time, do that shit yourself; obviously, you don't care nothing about me… and I'm not risking my life or freedom for you or nobody else!" As I walked away with a frown, I vibrantly smiled when I turned around.

Afterwards, Charles and I started driving up to New York ourselves, hoping that we got back in touch with Jacob. Instead, he got introduced to Miyah's homeboy Snoop, who was a very cool and reliable guy. He was also helpful when he got Charles some work, and that was the factor that fulfilled their connection. Thereafter, they privately discussed and arranged everything, and both of them delivered their end of the bargain. In other words, Charles would send Snoop the money through western union. Snoop would take his cut, make the buy, and then send the drugs through the mail. They did those transactions for months until Snoop stopped being loyal, and he kept Charles $20,000. I was a little surprised but more pissed than anything. He wasn't just taking from Charles, he was taking from me and my kid as well. Besides, I felt like I was the only one who could and should do that to him. What slipped my mind was that there would always be somebody out there grimier than me. What made it so bad was Charles pussy ass just let it ride like he was swimming in money.

Ensuingly, Jacob had got in touch with me the same day he got out of jail. He was very upset about how some young guys were trying to take over his block, and they were making it hot with their reckless activities. He knew eventually it would start a serious dispute, which would elevate into a gun fight because Jacob was that type of guy who didn't play games with nobody. Generally speaking, it was money over beef, and he handled business under any circumstances, and so did Charles. With that being said, Charles thirsty ass paid Jacob a visit a few days after. Unfortunately, Charles arrived in the wrong place at the wrong time as he walked straight into a line of fire. There were bullets flying everywhere, Charles was shitting bricks, and running scared; he never experienced anything like that.

As this took place, Charles panicked, and wasn't thinking straight. Timorously, he passed Jacob his $40,000 to hold and quickly got out of dodge. When Charles arrived in Brooklyn, his heart was still beating fast, and his face looked spooked while he was telling me what happened. "You did what? You are the dumbest motherfucker I know! You gave somebody you barely know $40,000… You were scared like that? I hope you know that you're not getting that money back." Charles was standing there looking stupid, making phone calls back to back to Jacob, but he never did answer. In fact, he never saw Jacob again. That goes to show that the drug life has no loyalty or friends. Due to Charles lack of street mentality was the cause of his decline in money.

A few months later, we found out Jacob got locked up for drugs, kidnapping, and murder. He was facing some serious prison time. Damn! I hated that my nigga got caught up like that. He was like a big brother that did anything he could do to help me stay on my feet. I didn't fault him for that incident with Charles… That was his <u>stupidity</u>. If I was in Jacob shoes, I would've did the same thing. "Money over everything" is a terminology for the streets. <u>Greed</u> is an obsession that makes a person forget about family, friends, love, and happiness.

Another street terminology is, "Snitches are BITCHES who get stitches, and end up red in ditches." Most of the time, it depends on where you're at, seeing only real niggas handle situations like that; otherwise, it's an overstatement. On a daily basis, you run across a snitch, for their undisclosed identity is fear or envy. A snitch might be lying next to you, laughing and crying with you, or maybe even related to you. In Jacob's case, it was mostly everybody he was affiliated with, and that was some deep shit.

To begin with, Jacob was the head of the Caine Gang, which was a drug cartel in over ten states. He was shipping 100's of kilos through the mail until the feds got involved and started locking everybody up. Then all fingers were pointing at Jacob, and conspiracy charges were the outcome. Although Jacob was well respected, there were three things that overpowered him, which was: stupidity, greed, and fear. For those reasons, he would leave his kids without a father, miss their graduations, and miss out on being a grandfather. Me personally, I know he would've been the best in all of those areas, but it's a fucked up situation on both ends.

Assuredly, Jacobs is to blame considering he chose that life to live after having kids, but I don't have room to point fingers. The little time Jacob was around, he was a good father and friend, so thumbs up to him. Even though I lost all connections with Jacob, He will always be a certified gangsta in my eyes. It's a stated fact that most gangsta's are dead or in prison, and Jacob is indeed one of them.

During this interval, Charles and his brother got locked up in Virginia for drug trafficking as he was making desperate moves trying to get his pockets back right. Meanwhile, I was getting my space filled by the love of my life, Micah. We had this passionate connection that was always exposed every time we were in each other's presence, which kept me traveling back and forth to New York, and then I found out I was pregnant. Now here is what corrupt BITCHES do to disloyal men who hit rock bottom. They cheat when needed, and then lie because they can. Moreover, they really don't care if he finds out the truth, for they no longer value their relationship. With that being said, I told Charles and Micah that they both were the father, but I knew Charles wasn't because we were hardly fucking. Anyhow, Charles found out the truth three months later when he got out of jail on bail, which was the same day I miscarried. It was impossible for me to be 12 weeks pregnant by him when he was gone almost five months, but I didn't explain, I just told him to charge it to the game.

Reality kicked in, and Charles didn't want to face the fact that he was losing me. Despite my cheating, he was determined to revive our relationship. Desperately, he tried his best to allure me back in, thinking that all of his wrongdoings were forgiven and forgotten; it most certainly wasn't, but I still accepted his pampering as it rejuvenated my soul, and Charles knew that. He shocked me when I found out from Kassidy that he was trying to do some my age shit, and throw me a surprise birthday party in Midway. Additionally, Kassidy had a different surprise for me when she brought this guy name Brad along with her. He was a street rapper from Philly and had dreams of becoming the greatest of all time. Unfortunately, we met at a mournful moment. He was grieving over his grandparents' deaths, and their funerals were the only reason he came down south. Although I wasn't impressed with Brad's character, I still looked at him as my potential victim.

My so-called surprise party was days away, and Charles still was unaware that I knew about it. The job he delegated to Kassidy, I was doing all of it. I picked out my own cake, food, alcohol, and even passed out flyers. On top of that, I persuaded Brad to come DJ for me without pay. I always got what I wanted, and when I wanted it due to my talk game being tight. My pretty face revealed purity, and my physique was mesmeric and magnetic. That's why I knew my party was going to be live and productive.

The party started on Ruby Lane, which turned out to be an official house party. There was no room to walk; the smoke reduced our visions, the alcohol had us tipsy, and the DJ got us crunk. Undeniably, I was the entertainment of it all. I would provocatively dance a little, flirt with Brad a lot because he deserved it. Then I would go act like Charles was the only man for me, but he wasn't. I was loving every minute of it, until the pigs came and put an end to it over the neighbors complaining about the loud music. Also, we were over capacity. Therefore, we had to move the party to Charles' house, and it didn't end until day break. We continued drinking, dancing, laughing, and having fun. What made it even better was that Charles old ass had slept through it all, which gave me more one on one time with Brad.

From that day forward, I continued having niggas over Charles house. I wanted to explore my options, and believe me it was a different experience every time. It would be around one, two, sometimes three in the morning when Charles came home, and the partying was still going on. There we were, Kassidy and I bonding with a variety of guys. We would be buzzed up loudly laughing, intimately touching, and energetically playing around when Charles walked in, but he wouldn't say nothing in their presence. Instead, he would call me into the room and softly question me about who was my company. I always replied, "Those our homeboys! Why?" Then I would walk out smiling. The most memorable part of those nights was when the guys got drunk, then started clowning and disrespecting Charles, knowing he didn't have heart and was indeed a sucker. That was a proven fact seeing he never tried to defend himself.

In between Charles and I double crossing each other, my little sister Lannah paid me a surprise visit. Primarily because she had some issues with her living arrangements in New York, and needed a helping hand. I had plans on moving out of Charles' house during that time, but it was postponed just so I could support my sister. It was a pleasure to give a little assistance to her, and I knew that I would enjoy her company.

Then three months later, I caught Lannah red-handed with Charles. I couldn't believe my eyes when I stood there, and watched them rub baby oil on each other. It also was crazy seeing Charles massaged her body just like he did mine, and her jacking him off to perfection. Their seductive foreplay had provoked them to move forward. I could've put a stop to it, but why when the betrayal was already accomplished? Instead, I waited to interrupt them in the middle of their sexual actions to rule out all of their justifications. I yelled out, "Y'all some dirty motherfuckers! Damn Lannah, you're my sister, and you fuck over me like this! What have I ever done to you? You know what... don't even answer that. Regardless of what, you were wrong. How does it feel to have my leftovers? I hope it was worth it since you deceived me over a nut. Wow! That's slut tendencies, and your low budget ass didn't even get any money out of it! That's the difference between you and me... I got the power, and you get the disrespect. Well, you have overstayed your welcome... Now it's time for you to leave. Oh and Charles, I expected your dirty dick to do something like this. Anyway, it's been over between us for a long time now, but you just didn't know it. So, continue doing you, and I'll do me... and I'm not moving out until I'm ready! Umm... y'all can wipe those stupid looks off y'all faces, and put some damn clothes on!"

Then Lannah suddenly tried to let out her fake tears and said the dumbest shit, "He made me do it!" I was speechless, but I laughed while shaking my head, and then I walked away. Although this was the utmost betrayal, I couldn't push myself to fight either one of them, even when I had all the rights to snap. Instead, I just lost all respect for the both of them. The question, "What's wrong with this picture?" Always stayed in the back of my mind because the treacherous shit that was going on with some of my sisters were like a plague of envy or lack of morals, for out of all men, they chose mine.

For the time being, Charles and I lived under the same roof, but our daughter and hustling were the only two things we were in accordance with. We no longer did business in the same spots but shared the same product. Charles dealt at his usual crack houses, and I relocated on Midbrook Run where Kassidy, Brad, and his brother Drake were living at. I always had an open-mind for prosperous opportunities, and the Run was where I wanted to establish my own drug dealing foundation. In other words, I was working on building a trustworthy, money making, bold, but cautious team. At that time, I only had Kassidy and Brad to help me build clientele, and generate steady cash flow. We gradually took off, but eventually it started popping.

Suddenly, I got the tenacity to finally move out of Charles' house and proceed to newer things, now that the old was obsolete. Old age, old dick, and an old relationship was finally abaft. Introspectively, I wasn't ready for another relationship, but if I stumbled upon one, then he must be on my level and neighboring my age bracket. Unquestionably, it's not easy to say goodbye when you have time and feelings invested. But sometimes it can be in your best interest to let it go, especially when you have informative signals that are perpetually confronting you, which can be some indications that it's time to depart.

For one, when you constantly give a person too many chances, and they still haven't learned from their mistakes, then maybe they're not trying to, or desire to, and it's your fault if you don't wake up and vamoose. Secondly, is consistently using your kids as an excuse to stay with someone. Stop it! You're just hurting yourself, and eventually it will damage the kids when they start seeing their parents constantly going at it. It's very displeasing for a child to see their parents fighting, cursing each other out, and always seeing their mother cry afterwards. Most of the time, it would eventually end with a breakup, and leaving the child confused and unable to handle it. Taking this into consideration, it's best to explain to your child beforehand in order for them to have a better understanding about how some families are not meant to be together, and why? Instead of giving them breakable promises that you will regret in the long run.

Lastly, but certainly not least, is when the sex or the attraction has vanished. It's unimaginable to have a long-term, healthy relationship without any sexual attraction. Every relationship has different expectations when it comes to their sexual favors. However, both partners should be willing and able to please each other. If a person is inadequate in sexual intimacy, then that can lead a partner to being impatient, bitter, physically and mentally detached from their relationship. In other words, lack of sex means the relationship is going through a problem, or is running into a problem because what one won't do, somebody else will.

Sex is about 50% important in a relationship, and the other half is based upon the kids, love, and stability. Sex can either make or break a relationship. In my case, it was eradicated; I had lost all feelings and interest. Not to mention, his money or what little he had left couldn't keep me around anymore. I didn't want him or like him. Mostly, I wouldn't miss anything about him, for I was completely turned off.

Through and out those three years with Charles, I experienced lust, which had my imagination functioning at an irrational degree. I was going through so many additional things that was illogical, but somewhat helpful in my life. I also experienced ongoing lies that was told to me. Of course, I told my share of untruthful tales that led to reciprocated betrayal. In fact, it worked out for the best because Charles and I weren't meant for each other at all. I assumed he was put into my life as a monetary supporter. He led me along the path of greed since both of us came into our relationship craving for money to earn, and money to burn, which contributed to both of our duplicitous ways. With a little confidence, I would take my wisdom of life and walk the rest of my path without him.

# THE POISONOUS FOOTSTEPS

MALACHI 2:8-9 "But you have turned from the way and by your teaching have caused many to stumble; you have violated the covenant with Levi," says the LORD Almighty. "So I have caused you to be despised and humiliated before all the people, because you have not followed my ways but have shown partiality in matters of the law."

I walked into a new day, every day, taking baby steps towards an unknown destination; but the pleasant thing about it was that I felt tenacious, assertive, and more focused on being a provider for my daughter, and a leader of my drug operation. Although my agenda wasn't really planned out, I still was making things happen accordingly.

The time in between my conversions, my homeboy Brad and I were hanging tightly. Our alliance had been going on for a few months, which led to many late night conversations, and us getting to know each other on a one on one basis. He was an amiable and humorist guy. Still and all, greed overpowered my physical and mental attraction to any man. Therefore, I had no perceptual feelings towards him.

Brad originally came to the south for his grandparents' burials, but after his interactions with me, he had extended his stay, hoping he could defeat his depression and become euphoria. Moreover, he was anticipating on recalibrating himself while adapting to a different environment. His personality was unique and exemplary, but giving up the one thing he loved, which was his flourishing rap career had made me assume that he was running from something more serious, and it would eventually come back to haunt him in the long run. It still wasn't none of my business. He had to walk his own path of his mystified destiny. That's how life goes.

Life is about taking chances, but you never know the outcome until it happens, and that would determine what direction you decide to take, for your purpose comes with maturity. Because Brad was nearly 20, and I was only 18, we both had plenty of mistakes to make, hearts to break, and a lot of growing up to do. However, neither one of us thought about that; at that time, our main introspective was to get money and have fun.

During my pubescent years, I considered fun as teasing men for money, which I had the pleasure of busting a nut while they sucked my tits, or ate my pussy. It was also entertaining when I got wasted. I was boisterous, outspoken, and very energetic while they polished my body with their tongues. Even though I enjoyed feeling woozy, I grasp onto a new habit hanging around Brad, which was smoking weed, and it definitely stimulating my brain.

Cannabis is a thought-provoking drug that had me mentally occupied and observing every little thing, such as seeing the tiniest bump on a talkative person's lip, and it was definitely hard to take my eyes off of it. It also was hilarious seeing a kid struggling to hold up his or her monstrous head, but still managed to play with other kids. Oh! And, those confident females with flabby or shapeless bodies, walking like nobody could tell them nothing… was too funny. Of course, I can't leave out those nerdy ass, bifocal wearing guys that talks like their glasses are putting too much pressure on their nose, which makes them sound very ditsy and extremely annoying.

Then my savvy side would come out when I felt like I knew everything. There were times I felt like I was an astronomer, who observed all the bright stars, which Sirius was the brightest per magnitude. Sometimes I thought I was a math genius doing all sorts of calculations. There were even times I turned into a thesaurus, giving synonyms as the meaning of words. In all reality, I was more astute and vigilant when I was high. Regardless of what, the most contemplative thought that roamed my mind consistently, was how I was going to mastermind the drug game because my reliance was strictly on money. On the contrary, some teenagers would had considered sex as an entertainment, but not me. I thought it was an earned privilege, which very few got that opportunity, or one just might've gotten lucky if I was out for revenge. They were my revenge-based sex partners, who I referred to as a "sexner." Otherwise, they were left with blue balls since teasing became my routine that I was well known for.

Back to the point of revenge, which I suddenly got the urge to payback Charles. Spitefully, I decided I was going to sleep with his younger brother, Bobby. He clearly was ready, seeing he didn't hesitate to get us a hotel room. He did not bring up Charles name or even ask me was I second guessing myself. Instead, he lustfully fondled me. After he daintily started sucking my nipples, I saw a resemblance of Charles, and I was immediately turned off, which prevented me from moving on. So, I stopped him. We didn't end the night with regrets, we just laid there, and cuddled until sunset. The little episode we had was an encouragement to our bond that flourished our friendship, and everything else was left in the past.

Shortly after, I dominantly seduced Sebastian, not just because he was getting teased for four years, but because he was Charles close friend at one point and was definitely a good choice for a "sexner". I gave him a call, put on a theatrical cry, and told him I needed someone to talk to, which he immediately came to my rescue. Then we headed straight to the Holiday Inn where we got drunk and talked about the, "What if's, would've, could've, and should've." But relationship wise wasn't my intention with him, I just wanted to fuck. Thereupon, I entrancingly climbed on top of him, then he slowly started unbuttoning my shirt, and massaging my firm tits with his hands and mouth. A little foreplay got us quickly aroused. Then he gently laid me on my back and gradually stuck it in. After a few pumps, I was done. That nigga had a little ass dick. I pretended my stomach was hurting to save him the embarrassment. I also didn't want to kill his pride, respecting that he was my true friend, and I cared about his feelings. Although we both left without reaching our climax, Sebastian still felt like he accomplished something, which was very little in my eyes.

Through my past experiences, I had learned not to give a man what they really wanted unless he's of value, desiderated, or a means to vengeance; otherwise, he was useless. In light of Brad being a lethal fireball, I knew he would add some spark to my life, which made him valuable to me. That's why I continued hanging around, and made the Run my stepping grounds.

Admiring Brad for absorbing and adjusting to the drug life smoothly, I knew he would eventually become my Clyde because my perception of Bonnie was getting that money the best and easiest way she knew how. Brad and I both lived up to some of their actions and characteristics. For example, Bonnie and I started at a young age associating ourselves with culprit guys. We also were ride or die BITCHES who were fed up with our lifestyles, which motivated us to do felonious things to get money. Looking on the bright side, we both were poetic. On the other hand, Clyde and Brad first interactions with the law was from stealing cars. They both were petty thieves, who spent time in prison and continued going back. Moreover, they both were smooth-talkers. Although our actions weren't horrendous as theirs, we still were notorious lawbreakers. Our illicit ways had caused us to grow closer each day.

Meanwhile, Charles and I still had to communicate, and he also was supporting me during our breakup, that's just how he operated. He actually thought he was going to work his way back into my life, and that's the reason I continued to have possession over his money along with him providing me and Aaliyah clothes, food, and anything else of that matter. In fact, he gave me rides back and forth to Midbrook Run, although he knew it was a possibility that I was fucking one of those nigga, since it was nothing but guys over there entertaining Kassidy and I. Curiosity was killing the cat, and I was delighted to answer all of his questions like, "Who are them niggas?" In a sarcastic tone, I bluntly said, "Nigga's that's nothing like you!" With a stupid look on his face, he told me, "You know you don't have to hangout here to make money; you can just come back to the spot." I angrily looked at him but calmly responded, "I like doing my own thing. I'm not here because I have to be, I'm here because I want to be. I'm free, and that's how I like it." Then the question I was waiting for finally came out, "Are you fucking one of them?" I smiled and said, "Not yet, but Brad and I are approaching intimacy pretty soon!" I felt good after telling Charles that. Contrarily, Charles was sitting over there looking kind of sick, and that had me in high spirits.

Men don't know how to take things when they are the victims, for they feel defeated and weak, knowing they don't have the power to hurt you anymore. That is when desperation occurs, which is your security to humiliate him, and that's exactly what I did to Charles. He was so determined to win me over that he was willing to confess all of his dirty tricks when I told him that's the only way to make things right. It actually was a lie because I really didn't want to be with him anymore, but I felt that it would provide peaceful closure. After he truthfully confessed to fucking Freda and all the other floozies, I told him, "We could never move forward together, but I'm moving forward in life… Goodbye Charles." Then I got out the car and walked away.

Every day Charles was trying to get me back, but all I saw written on his face was incurable disease. That was the first time I felt money wasn't over everything considering my health was more important. With caution, I tried dodging him as much as I could. Until I was walking one day from Midbrook, and Charles pulled beside me, hoping that we could talk. I agreed because I needed a ride, so I got in. At first, Charles was talking cool, calm, and collective. Then suddenly, he became suicidal once we got on the highway. His foot aggressively pushed the gas pedal to the floor, and that's when the car increasingly started floating, doing a little over 100 miles per hour. I immediately panicked, thinking this motherfucker is insane. Then I knew he was crazy when he stated, "If you don't want me, then we will die together!" What? That's how truly in love couples go out... I wasn't in love, nor was I ready to die, but I had to be cautious of every word I said. Strikingly, my words came out smooth and was effective when I softly touched him and said, "Calm down! You letting your anger takeover your train of thought... From my understanding, didn't you want to talk? Well, we can't express our feelings if we're dead. Think about that and our daughter."

His body started looking more relaxed as he calmed down, then he started talking like he had a little bit of sense. He apologized over and over again. As his tears quickly fell down his face, he asked for my forgiveness. Also, he was hoping I would take him back. I was going with the flow; I didn't want to take any chances with endangering myself while we were still in the car. Unsympathetically, I listened while he talked. When he cried, I gave him my innermost sympathy, but not once did I tell him we could work things out. I actually was a little irritated when we arrived at his house because the whole time we were riding, he kept going on with those sob ass stories, and it also was displeasing by just looking at his unappealing face when he cried. To me, it was a pointless conversation; my mind was already made up, and it was nothing he could do or say to change it.

From the looks of it, Charles wasn't trying to take me back to Midway. Therefore, I had to find somebody to rescue me from this nonsense. I eventually got in touch with Kassidy and told her to bring

Brad in case some shit popped off. Kassidy's brother Herbert couldn't bring them that night, but he brought them the next morning. "Boom! Boom! Boom!" Brad was banging loudly at the front door. I knew it was him when I heard his rowdy voice, yelling out, "I know they're here because Charles' car is in the driveway, and we're not going nowhere until Veah comes out!" Charles scary ass was peeping out the window, listening to everything. At the same time, I barely had my shoes on, but was rushing to open the door. Then Charles cut me off and stood in front of it, realizing he had problems standing on the other side, which was Brad, who was very loud, "I'm going to whoop this nigga ass if he come out!" My first instant was to run out the back door, and that's when I bumped into Brad on my way out. First, he hugged me, then he started checking my body for bruises. After that, he asked, "Where is he at? I'm ready to kick some ass."

Before I answered Brad's question, Charles got the guts to walk out his front door. I was absolutely surprised, especially how he approached the situation. Charles fiercely came on his porch, and in his newly masculine tone, he said, "Are you looking for me?" Thereafter, he quickly pounced his ass down the steps, throwing punches at the same damn time. He got a few good hits off, but then the tables turned when Brad knocked Charles down to the ground, and he kept thrashing Charles head to the concrete. On the grounds that Charles was unable to fight back, he just laid there helplessly staring at me. I knew he felt alone that day because Kassidy, Herbert and I was rooting for Brad, which of course he was undefeated. Still, Brad continued to brutalize Charles, and his head was drowning in blood. We tried to stop Brad, but it was difficult to calm him down while he was angry. Instead of me watching a subjugated fight, I just walked away.

When Brad noticed I was gone, he immediately stopped fighting, and then came running after me while yelling out my name. Right after, Charles started staggering behind him and blurted repeatedly in his sluggish voice, "Veah! Can we talk?" I rejected them both, and continued walking as they followed. I didn't see who threw the first punch, but after that, it was round two. Although I watched them fight from a distance, I saw Charles get in his Kokutsu Dachi stance.

Basically, he was setting up for his karate moves. Then he kicked the shit out of Brad stomach. In view of Brad reflex being quick, he caught Charles foot, and laid his ass down again. That time, it was in a gulley. After Brad's fist constantly brought force to Charles head, his eye eventually split opened, leaving him unresponsive. When I ran back towards their direction, Brad was covered in blood. I thought Charles was dead, so I yelled to Brad, "Go before the cops come!" While Kassidy and I stayed back basically to eavesdrop.

Minutes later, Charles woke up dazed after getting punched-drunk. When he finally made it to his house, he immediately called his family for help. Quickly after, Charles mammalian's came with bats, crowbars, and sticks like they were going to demolish some shit. However, they were minutes late, 200 pounds too big, and moved a little too slow to be a part of a man's fight. Negatively, Charles seemed like he had enough. He had a few knots the size of golf balls on his forehead, his eye looked like raw meat; his top and bottom lip were inflated, and his clothes were covered in mud and gravel. In other words, it was over for him.

Charles was discouraged about him losing the fight; he set on top of the kitchen counter with his head down, crying like a coward. We barely understood him when he talked because it was more like a mumble due to the swelling. So, it was hard to commiserate with him since he sounded funny. Even though Charles family tried to encourage him, you could still hear the anger in their voices. Meanwhile, Kassidy and I were in the living room, laughing our asses off.

During the rivalry between Brad and Charles, my mother had moved back down south on Farmstead Road. Surely, I had to move in with her, that was the cheapest route, and also it made it easier for me to stack my dough. The only flawed thing about it was that my poisonous footsteps followed. I was a drug dealer, and wherever I went the crackheads always found me. If I got into any trouble or altercations, it would backtrack to where I rest my head at. Moreover, if I had boy problems, undoubtedly they would come knocking at my mother's door just like Charles did. He wasn't at all intimidated or ashamed of his stitched and beat up face if he was in my presence. Without any remorse, I preyed on his weakness. Relatively, Brad came around as well in hopes that he would be the man I chose. In all honestly, I was greedy, and had a motive for keeping both men in my life regardless of the end results. Since they were on my heels, I definitely started feeling myself. I loved having the ability to control the two. For Brad was basically my runner, Charles was my supplier, and that helped me become prosperous.

On a day-to-day basis, I started my day off with my baby girl Aaliyah, who was a little over one years old. We would take walks, sing lullabies, eat a lot of junk food, and then play until she fell asleep. By the middle of the day, Charles would come over for a little and say a few corny jokes that he only laughed to. Then he'd leave me a package. Afterwards, I would go to the Run, patiently sit, sell, and collected that cash along with supplying Brad and Kassidy with some work, so they could make money as well. Not long after, the spot started getting out of control, and if no adjustments weren't going to be made, then the spot would soon come to an end.

Let me break it down to you. The spot was originally owned by Brad's deceased grandparents who left the house to their ignoble son, Tommy. Shortly after the funeral, Tommy started selling all of their valuables out the house for a little bit of nothing, just so he could feed his habits. Then, when it was time to pay the bills, he had no money for it. Shamefully, they would go weeks without heat and lights. They kept candles burning in order to see, and kerosene heaters to stay warm, which didn't work too well for a big old house. That's when I came about, and helped Brad out.

Brad had everything under control until his packages and money started getting stolen. It also was too much traffic coming in and going out the house all day and night, making the spot hot. What was the most disturbing part for Brad was when he found out his siblings had an unacceptable bad habit as well. In all reality, he was providing for the whole house, and that was his downfall, seeing he was losing more than he was gaining. Something had to give, or I had to go because money reassured my stability and growth. Luckily, after a few days of contemplating, Brad decided to leave the spot, and moved in with Herbert, who stayed with his parents at that time.

Brad really didn't have a stable place to stay, but he thought about putting my happiness in front of his own, and that was a turn for the worst. For one, his physical appearance eventually faded. I don't know if his clothes got stolen or misplaced, but he barely had any. Instead of me feeling sympathy, I was turned off from seeing those same Jordan's he wore day after day. They were so worn-out, it gave him a raging case of funky feet, and I always seemed to get a whiff of it. Everything in his range was a foul mozzarella cheese like smell mixed with malt vinegar and ammonia. That was an odor a nose could never forget.

Brad just couldn't get right. Ridiculously, every dollar he made was just enough to pay for his food, shelter, and some smokes. But becoming a part of the independent world is learning how to distinguish your needs from your wants, which was hard for Brad to assimilate. Any which way, that was a mountain that he had to climb alone in order to become the man he needed to be. Until then, I remained his friend, and tried to be there as much as I could, or when I wanted to be. Of course, life could be hard, and I didn't come or make it easy because the greed wouldn't let me, and for some strange reason, that was appealing to men.

During that lustful triangle phase, my sister Daishah and her boyfriend Lamar walked right into my mix-up. She was unaware of my poisonous footsteps, being that she looked up to me, and never would've thought I was leading such a harmful trail. Although her first priority was to spend time with mommy at her new place, she eventually ended up with me. They got bored doing so much of nothing in Midway and wanted to do something different other than hanging around in the ghost town, especially since it was Lamar's first time in the south. Ultimately, I made that call to sugar daddy Charles, which he didn't mind being subservient to me. Unquestionably, Charles picked us up, and hauled us straight to his place where the fun had begun.

We weren't bound to any restrictions, and we were recklessly ready to do whatever we wanted. While we walked around with opened 40 ounces of Bull getting fucked up, we had stopped at a few hole in the wall bootleggers and danced to the music as we were feeling the country folks beat. Since we were in seventh heaven, everybody was like angels to us, and we didn't meet any strangers, nor were we hesitant to converse. We partied till dawn, had hangovers in the mornings, and hung out every night. Overall, we had a good time. Then Charles had to go out of town for a quick drug run. Everything was "A-Okay" until his one-day business trip was delayed for a whole week, and I was pissed. Primarily because I gave him most of my money to re-up, and the little money I did have was running out. Furthermore, we didn't have a ride back to Midway, which was my comfort zone to make and get the rest of my money. Stranded was like being limited to a little bit of nothing, and that's what we had at the time. Being confined was a pet peeve of mine. Therefore, Charles had sent his brother Norton to come pick us up, and take us back to Midway.

A few days went by, and Norton wasn't seen or heard from. The first thing that came to my thoughts were, "Damn Karma came to visit me for taking Norton and Charles money previously, but I hated that Daishah and Lamar had to suffer for my dirty deeds." It was certainly bad timing after we ran out of food and only had flour and water for nourishment, but it was beneficial for us as we were able to make bread for breakfast, lunch, and dinner.

We also didn't have any cigarettes or beer; basically, we were just ass out on everything, which had me and Daishah reminiscing on our depressing past. Thereafter, survival mode kicked in, and we had to think about our next move. I couldn't call a cab to Midway, knowing they wanted the money up front, and everyone I was calling wasn't answering the phone. The only thing we could do was walk about five miles to Harris Teeter and steal us a meal. Lamar grabbed a pack of ribs and a few beers. I stole a bag of rice and some cigarettes. Daishah took a can of vegetables and packs of Kool-Aid. Then we bravely walked back; also, we were happy that we didn't get caught.

The next morning, something unusual happened; a package was delivered to Charles' house, but mistakenly shipped to the wrong address. Although it was an unfamiliar name, I didn't think twice about signing for it because that was our next meal. After opening the box, I noticed that it was some unknown valuable equipment that could be more useful to a wealthy white person. Happily, Lamar walked around the corner to this hillbilly bar, and sold everything to the owner. Lamar came back with each of us a pack of cigarettes, humongous hamburgers, French fries, fried chicken wings, and an additional $50 in cash. We were happy and relieved, for we knew this would last until Charles got back. Then, out the blue, Norton lame ass came. After five days, he decided to show up with no excuse of why he took so long to come. With anger, I dissed his nerdy ass all the way to Midway while he drove quietly with the poker-face.

After that long week of struggle, Daishah and Lamar still wanted to hang out with me, but this time, it was around a different environment, which was Brad and some of his homeboys. During this particular time, Brad had rented this huge 6-bedroom house from a well-paid crackhead, who went on a trip to Vegas for a week. Without a doubt, we were having the time of our lives. We were rolling up blunts after blunts, which had the house smoggy, and our lungs were inflamed. We threw back shots of Belvedere, guzzled 40 ounces of whatever type of beer that was available, and smoked cigarettes like there was no tomorrow. This is when I realized Newport cigarettes were another addiction. It really wasn't a good thing, but I only live once, so I wanted to enjoy it as much as possible.

One night, I got a little too drunk and passed out. Then Brad had carried me into the bedroom he slept in and began undressing me. Although I was drunk, I still was aware that he was trying to take advantage of me. In a sluggish motion, I automatically started swinging. I was punching him all in his head, face, and struggling to get his big ass off me. At the same time, I was cursing him out saying, "You fucking freak... this is violation!" He couldn't get out a sentence as I was talking loudly over him, then I stormed out. It was about three in the morning. I was enraged, crying, and fast walking to my mother's house.

The next day, Brad paid me a visit, hoping I would listen to his side of the story. I stood there with my arms folded and nose turned up, but I was all ears. He first gave me a sincere apology for the misunderstanding. He went on about how he did make the first move by touching my body in an affectionate way, but then I aroused him more by grinding on his schlong. Afterwards, he took off my shirt, and began sucking my tits. That's when I seductively started moaning and massaging his head. Indecently, he thought I was ready to have sex, seeing I was more desirous instead of unwilling. From this perspective, he felt it was okay to undress me until I started going crazy. "I'm sorry, please forgive me," Brad genuinely said repeatedly.

After a few minutes of contemplating, I decided to accept his apology. Primarily because I was at fault as well. I was irresponsible for not knowing my limit and was too comfortable with my surroundings. However, men know what they are doing when alcohol is involved, for it alters our decisions, which leaves them in control of the situation. Do we blame it on the alcohol or the individuals? In my opinion, it depends on the severity of the circumstances. So, that question should be answered accordingly, but it was a lesson learned for me.

All the bullshit went to the back of my mind after Charles came back into town and brought my package, which was a priority to my thoughts and directions. Of course, I felt some type of way that me and my FAM was stranded in Winston. Then I went to Midway to almost get sexually assaulted, but that was all petty shit if it didn't stop me from proceeding. In fact, my situation could've been worse than what it turned out to be. Yet, I had another opportunity to make a difference whether it was for the good or the bad. I'm not saying I didn't hold grudges forever because I did, especially since I was bitter. My retaliation was always aiming for my enemies to fall flat on their faces, and Charles was certainly one of them on the list. What made it even more goal-oriented is that he was about to serve two years in prison for those trafficking charges. Without sensibility, my main target was to get a hold of everything in his pockets, and any other stash he had before he turned himself in.

Thumbs down and middle finger up to love; I was feeling like relationships weren't nothing but a game, and whoever is the winner takes home the prize. In my case, who and what exactly is a winner? There are many ways I could've looked at the situation. For one, if I based it strictly on money, then I was the conqueror. He was either giving me all of his cash, or I was taking it right from under his nose and didn't think twice about it. Then there is that crazy word called emotions. If I looked at it from that perspective, then we probably would breakeven considering both of our feelings had sort of a passionate connection, but no rules really applied in our relationship because we lived by an eye for an eye.

Once again, it was more like a sponsorship; his finances were the predominant reason I was with him. Therefore, my part of the emotions were all for the wrong reasons. Lastly, is thinking physically, which is the most difficult part, knowing I would have to be a mother and father to my child while he's in prison with no burdens, except trying to keep the men from taken his ass. I would have to step up to the plate. Also, go extra hard on the block to support us the best possible way so that my child wouldn't live an underprivileged life like I did growing up. Overall, I considered myself as a winner; I was a supporter and a survivor. However, I lost my teenage years because I had to focus more on being a single parent.

The day before Charles had to turn himself in, he stopped by my mother's house to say his goodbyes; also, to pick up the only money he had to his name, so he could pay off his lawyer. Geesh, was he that much of a cornball to actually think I was going to give him that $4800, knowing that he was useless to me for the next two years. In all honesty, I don't even think he thought about the struggles that a young teen goes through to take care of a child with no help. It was time to give this nigga a wakeup call.

Instead of me opening the door, I talked to him through the window. "What the fuck do you want?" I yelled out with a smirk on my face. In his BITCH ass, nonthreatening voice, he replied, "Open the door, I don't have time to play games with you... I need that money, and I want to see my daughter!" I laughed my ass off, as I said, "I'm not opening the door... You're not getting shit from me either, and I don't give a fuck about you or your fucking lawyer. Bye... Go do your time!" Then I shut the curtains and listened to him bang on the door while yelling out all types of crazy shit, until he realized it was all irrelevant and left. Of course, I could've gave him his money; I had my own little stash put to the side, but it wasn't enough, especially how I splurged on me and my daughter. Shopping weekly, kept on every new Jordan's, and all other miscellaneous things we needed. Without a doubt, I did the right thing.

Everything was positively going right until things took a negative twist when Lamar got locked up for an open beer container. OMG! Only down south you see something like that; if he was in the city, he would've just been fined, but they gave Lamar a hard time since he didn't have any identification on him because he was only 16. This being the case, his mother had to send certain documents to prove his identity, which took a little over a week for him to get out of jail. Poor Daishah was worried the whole time that she couldn't sleep and barely was eating. Moreover, she was blaming herself, knowing she was the one who introduced him to the south, which she despised ever since she moved out Aunt Martha's disastrous house. More importantly, Daishah's history with Aunt Martha had brought out her atrocious character that was very disturbing. When Daishah left the south for the last time, she never looked back because of her unforgettable experiences, and unforgiving heart.

# SATANICALLY SEVEN

My sister Ladaishah was mommy's seventh gift from God as well as the devil's seventh sin, which is an enraged angel who is filled with hatred and anger. Although seven is indicated as being full or intact, this child was empty and damaged, but Daishah wasn't always like that. In between her unstable life, she transitioned into the devil's wife. She talks to the devil, walks with the devil, sees and touches the devil. Unfortunately, Lucifer not only has her heart, he also has her soul. At times, she enjoys his company, but there are many nights she is extremely afraid of his presence. She hates that he has control of her life, but it's hard for her to let him go, fully aware that she's in too deep. She's walking in the fiery heat with her bare feet, lonely and crippled. The devil causes her to have many sleepless nights as he whispers evil thoughts in her ear, putting evil words in her mouth, leaving evil spirits and feelings in her house. She doesn't pray him off, or out the house, which is an invitation for him to come back, and every time she gets weaker.

Conversely, Daishah was always humbled, reticent, and the blithe one. I hardly ever saw vicious acts, or heard vicious words like the ones she expresses today. At first, I thought it was an act for attention until I witnessed about four different personalities within minutes. She started out with her sweet little sister persona, which was very lovable. In a blink of an eye, she became hostile, in fight mode, and that was weird coming from someone so submissive. Moments after, she started feeling a little guilty, and the cry baby character came out for a split second. Then, hello <u>criticizer</u>. She would belittle herself, and downgrade whomever she pleased. In spite of me being mad and aggressive with her, I still felt sorry for my sister. From my point of view, she seemed so far gone that her path will eventually lead to NOWHERE. It's like she keeps running her head straight into a brick wall without falling, but continues to be at a standstill, hurt, and unable to move because she's stuck in her past. Resultantly, it makes it difficult for her to grasp onto her future as she's presently drowning in her sorrows.

In behalf of Daishah's physical and mental suffering, her drinking exceeds the limit; not just some days, but every day, all day, which diminishes her capabilities to function intellectually. She is in denial about her problem, and when we try to speak honestly, she gets very offensive. I don't think she's blind to the fact, I feel like she doesn't want to accept the fact that her drowning in flammable liquids is what relieves her from all her troubles that is hard for her to face. "Alcoholism is a chronic disorder," which is not only an inheritance in our family; it's also a curse that has been passed down from Grandma to mommy, and now some of her kids, which condemns our characters. The biggest issue is getting the addiction under control before it's too late. Yet, that is up to the individual, and in my opinion, Daishah has a long way to go with little time to waste. Out of concern, I want to know, "Where would she go from here? What steps would she take to make a better life for her, and her kids? If she goes left, will she get left behind? If she goes right, will that lead her to a brighter future?" The answers to these questions are only answered through time. Until then, I will wait and hope things get better.

It all started out when Ladaishah Daevas was born on October 31, 1982. It was nine months after mommy's previous miscarriage, and one year and 25 days following Lannah's birth. I am assuming that could've been the reason why Daishah was a diminutive baby and was underachieving in grade school. Due to her inabilities, she started feeling diffident and more of an outcast, which limited her participation in class activities. Being different was not only happening in the public eye, for at home it was strange and annoying to sleep next to Daishah while she rocked rapidly back and forth, mumbling to herself until she fell asleep. Moreover, she had a speech impediment; she not only substituted letters and omitted sounds, but also her uncontrollable stuttering caused disorganized sentences. It's not anything that a person wants to get teased about. It's a disorder that has no cure, but there are techniques you can use that may or may not help you overcome it, such as talking calmly or learning to control your breathing. Stuttering was inherited from the Daevas side because my father and I were both stutter boxes also. Although I might come across a few stuttered words from time to time, I still have defeated it.

To get back to the point, Daishah subnormal ways gradually change and developed as she got older and went through different life experiences. It all started out when mommy left Daishah and Caylah down south with the one they called the mysteriously wicked Aunt Martha, who pretended like she was going to nurture and love them. Instead, she neglected and mistreated them as soon as mommy left and moved back to the city. To emphasize more, my little sisters were scrubbing floors, toilets, and washing piled up dishes while our cousins Brianna and Trinity were sitting pretty. Therefore, Daishah took on both her and Caylah's responsibilities so that she could keep the burden off her little sister. Ultimately, the tormenting got worse. It wasn't ever fun for Daishah and Caylah to be sitting on the porch, watching their cousins happily ride their nice, girly bikes up and down the street. Of course, Aunt Martha didn't think twice about not buying my sisters their own bikes with their checks she was receiving for them, assuming that her intentions were to keep their money and watched them weep.

It also was devastating when Aunt Martha found reasons why they couldn't go play at the park, so they had to sadly watch their cousins through the window swinging, running around, and sliding on the sliding board having an enjoyable time. Daishah just couldn't understand why everything suddenly changed. What was the reason for their mistreatment? Her unanswered questions were causing her to have the blues. Not only because of that, but for many other reasons, Daishah would stare at the stars every night and cry for mommy, hoping that she would eventually come save them from all the agony.

Due to the fear Aunt Martha put in their hearts, and all the persuading that convinced them that they couldn't move back to New

York, was the reason why Daishah didn't say anything to mommy. She kind of blamed herself for choosing to stay down south considering they were still needy. They had raggedy hand me downs, rarely had their hair done, and still didn't have any toys to play with; it was like they were living in New York all over again. On the other hand, Brianna and Trinity wore new clothes, kept a fresh hairdo, and always had fun things to play with.

After a while, Daishah realized she was better off having bad times with mommy and still get the unconditional love rather than having unacceptable maltreatment and no love at all. That's when Daishah put her thinking cap on, hoping she could find a way out of that unpleasant situation. First, she tried to sneak out the window to run hundreds of miles away, but that didn't work when she realized it was too far, and returned back the same way she left out. Then she remembered my advice about, "Don't take shit from no one; treat them how they treat you. Sometimes bad behavior could be your outlet." With bitterness, she patiently waited for the right time to lash out.

Daishah's hormones were raging, and her uterus was contracting, causing cramps because her "red-letter" day had unexpectedly appeared for the first time. The bad part about it was that she was on the church bus. It also was embarrassing that some of the other kids noticed she had a blood spot on the back of her skirt as she shamefully walked to the front of the bus to inform Aunt Martha. Instead of auntie dearest comforting and advising Daishah about... What a menstruation was? Why it came on? And how they were going to handle it? She just acted like it was irrelevant, and continued talking after she gave Daishah a towel, then told her to sit at the back of the bus like she was contagious.

When they arrived at the house where they were having church service, Aunt Martha still ignored the fact that Daishah needed a pad or something to prevent the bleeding from sinking through her clothes. She just inconsiderately sent her to the basement with the rest of the kids while she was dripping red. As Daishah set in discomfort, she started crying aloud with her head down in disbelief. It was so audible that the kids were whispering to her, "You better be quiet before pastor come down here and beat you." That made Daishah cry even louder, which caused the pastor to stop in the middle of his sermon and ravingly plodded down to the basement with a switch.

When he approached Daishah with the question, "Why are you acting out in church?" Daishah didn't answer. She just evilly stared him in the eyes while breathing hard with her lips poked out. When he aggressively swung the switch at her, she open-handedly caught it, snatched it, and then threw it at him. In her devilish voice, she bluntly said, "You don't have the right to touch me... Don't you ever try to hit me again, or there would be some serious problems... Y'all some fake Christians, and I hate the sight of y'all. None of y'all can no longer have control over me. I am overwhelmed in chaos!" The pastor was shockingly looking at Daishah. He couldn't believe the words that were coming from one of the noblest kids in the church. Ensuingly, he sent one of his boys to go get Aunt Martha.

In the middle of him explaining what was going on, Aunt Martha hauled off and smacked the shit out of Daishah, and Daishah didn't hesitate to smack her ass back. The service was put on hold for a minute as Daishah was lashing out of control. Aunt Martha knew that she could no longer handle the situation. Considering this, she made that emergency call to mommy to come get her kids, and Miyah came to pick them up pronto. They was happy and relieved that the torture was finally over. However, those two years of suffering had her look at family from a different perspective, which wasn't at all a good look. Moreover, her entire character became reprehensible. Although my poisonous footsteps led Daishah out of her misery, it also guided her in the wrong direction.

Shortly after Daishah got to New York, she became sexually active. Both Daishah and her boyfriend Lamar were too young and naïve to put some use to any type of contraceptive. Unluckily, in her tween years, the end result was a positive pregnancy test. That was a huge disappointment to the family. If it was up to mommy, Daishah would've had that baby nine month later because abortions go against her Christianity beliefs. On the other hand, Shaylah felt differently, and made it her responsibility to take Daishah to expulse the fetus. She felt that was the best decision for a child who couldn't take care of herself, let alone a baby.

Daishah continued having unprotected sex, and her fertile ass terminated two more after that. Succeeding those missteps, she eventually gave birth to her first baby. Thereafter, she had three more babies consecutively. It was too much for them to handle without a solid foundation. Therefrom, Daishah thought it was best to give one of her kids up for an adoption. Still, her life continued to be arduous and discouraging, while they were staying at Lamar Aunt's cramped up two-bedroom apartment along with several other people, which really left no space for her or her kids. Besides, it wasn't a suitable place for kids anyway. All the occupants had some type of issue; there were mental disorders, hooch hounds, and drug dependencies all through that apartment, causing a lot of chaos, which left the kids frightened, jumpy, and confined. To make matters worse, it was hard for Lamar to find a steady job, and that caused more tension in their relationship.

As Daishah unpleasant thoughts flowed through her mind, she started to realize that her life was coordinating with our mother's, which wasn't at all helpful to her self-esteem considering none of us wanted to follow mommy's footsteps. But since the apple doesn't fall too far from the tree, there was a possibility that one or some of us were going to be exactly like mommy or even worse, and Daishah was certainly comparable. To emphasize, Daishah dropped out in middle school with no interest or plans of going back. Secondly, after her having many unexpected kids that she couldn't afford, she lost hope and thoughts of future goals to better herself. Not to mention, the kids were so close in age that there wasn't enough attention showed equally amongst them, which caused the kids to feel unloved.

Lastly, it was Daishah's inconsistencies that retained her bold front. She brought out her emotional state where she blamed everybody but herself for her recurring problems. The hurtful part about it was that the kids were more of her victims because they were around her every day. When Daishah got turned up, she would be faltering around the house, slurring at her words, and calling her son all types of feminine names while she shoved, smacked, punched, and kicked her toddler everywhere she possibly could; and she did not once feel sympathy for any tears. Although she showed more favoritism towards her daughters, she still verbally degraded them with her name calling. "BITCHES and dummies" had put doubt in their minds, crushed their hearts, and triggered their insecurities. I actually felt sorry for my nephews and nieces, knowing they were living a very abominable life, and their appearances showed it all. Comparatively, mommy stayed under the influence during her first four kids, but she never mentally or physically abused them, or us younger ones for that matter.

Daishah's dependency had gotten even more serious when they moved into the shelters, which caused her and Lamar to have some intense altercations. Primarily because she wasn't treating the kids to his standards. Yet, beating her didn't stop her actions, it just took her in a different direction from her relationship. That was when the cheating started. She began confiding in other men, hoping it would make her feel better about herself. Moreover, she wanted to get her mind off Lamar, but it didn't. However, having sex with other men became another addiction. Daishah stayed smashed, which made her emotionless and remorseful about spreading her legs; at times, she didn't remember all the details about what happened when she toned down.

It's a fact that dirty little secrets would eventually be revealed. In Daishah's case, she started getting careless with exploring other options, which was the cause of her getting caught in between her illicit activities. For one, if you're going to lie, make sure it's convincing. Daishah would lie, and she didn't have any alibis. Moreover, she couldn't answer his asked questions accurately, which made Lamar leery and distrustful. For two, if you're going to do roguish shit in public, make sure it's around people that's trustworthy. For this reason, Daishah assumed that anyone of her sisters' houses would be a legit spot. Unfortunately, it was the easiest way for her darkness to come to light because a Daevas will be the first to disclose your dirty deeds if y'll in between a rivalry.

Of course, the bad news had Lamar mind-boggled, and he lurked around until he caught Daishah himself. But he did warn her about the aftermath if he ever found out she was cheating. Lastly, if you know that your man is watchful because he's suspicious, then fallback if you love and still desire to be with him; chances are… you're going to eventually get caught and make matters worse. Daishah stayed seeing doubles, and she wasn't quick on her feet, which caused her to get exposed almost every time. She was either hanging with, hugging on, or kissing another guy. In fact, there were times her pussy was still wet from just busting a nut. Most certainly Lamar had no problem disrespecting her by shoving his hands down her pants to inspect. Thereafter, he would call her all types of inappropriate names while dragging her tightly by her hair as if he owned her.

When they made it home, he would make her get undress, and then beat her with his sturdy belt. Given that she was three sheets to the wind, she didn't realize how brutal the attack was until the next day when she couldn't barely move, and her body would be covered in bruises and scrapes. There were times Daishah had to lay there for days until she healed. Still, that didn't stop her as long as she had the energy to keep going. Lamar was heartbroken, which caused him to continuously act out of anger, and the abuse unknowingly went on for ten years straight. Ultimately, they could no longer hold on to each other and went their separate ways.

In between that time, Daishah had 2 more abortions and a miscarriage before she gave birth to her last child with Lamar. Their breach of trust had him a little skeptical about the unborn being his. In fact, he tried to deny all her kids at one point in time, but the DNA test proved he fathered every one of them. From that day forward, he did his best to support and be a father to them.

Meanwhile, Daishah continued to give her son Jamel backhanded compliments. Primarily because she despised him the moment he came out her womb. She felt possessed by his blemished identity and refused to hold him after her delivery. The doctors became worried about Jamel's safety, knowing Daishah was diagnosed with postnatal depression. Thereupon, they advised a social worker to visit her home until she got better. What they didn't see was the times she used to let Jamel cry for hours not caring about what was really wrong with him, or the times she desired to chastise him as though he knew right from wrong; hell, he wasn't even walking yet.

Daishah mistreated that boy from birth... just because she had assumed Jamel was going to value BITCHness over masculinity. She embedded that derogatory language as well as knots and scars in his head for life. Truth be told, I feel like she has something against all her boys. For one, Jamel got the bad end of the stick literally. For two, she gave up her other son, and he barely know her or our side of the family. Lastly, her baby boy gets the same stern treatment like he's a troubled child when he's just as placid as he could be. What was questionable to me was how his tooth fell out before it was time? Although that incident is mysterious, the rumor was his tooth really got knocked out, which was a little more practical to me.

The discrimination towards her boys, I assumed it had a lot to do with daddy who she is delusional and irrational about. If Daishah thought for one second that she was daddy's favorite little princess, then she clearly blocked his absence and neglect out of her mind, and altered it with her fantasy. She was knowledgeable about him denying the last four of us, and not providing for us. The point I'm trying to make is that deep down inside Daishah hated daddy for not being a part of her life, and it did something to her emotionally as a child. That is one of the reasons she resented, belittled, and violated males. Of course, there's no excuse for dispraising any child, but her mental breakdown can still justify some of her behavior, seeing everyone handles their anger differently. Instead of Daishah trying to find a cure for her evil sickness, she'd rather spread the infection to her kids, which they would eventually start to follow the poisonous footsteps.

Because there were many negative things going on in Daishah's house, the social service got many anonymous calls. Presumably, it was some of the family members considering it was too much detailed information that was given. After further investigation, they eventually took the kids out of Daishah's home, and placed them with their Aunt Gayle, until she could prove that she was a suitable parent. As I stated earlier, in my opinion along with a few others, Ms. Gayle's place wasn't appropriate either.

After a few months out the home, Daishah's daughter Arianna lively character began to diminish, and her voice was reticent while she set on the bed for hours as though she was too scared to move. When Daishah came to visit, she overlooked the fact that something was wrong with her daughter since that was normal behavior around her. It didn't cross Daishah's mind that her child feared her. If that was the case, then Daishah would've known her daughter was afraid of something or somebody.

During that time, Miyah was hanging over there as well. She was very observing, and knew that something wasn't right. Concernedly, she took Arianna out in the hallway to have a private conversation with her, and it was very disturbing about what Arianna had told her. "My cousin Ava shoved an object in my private part real hard; it was hurting really bad, and I was bleeding... She... She... did other nasty things to me too, and I don't want her to do it no more. I don't like it," Arianna sadly cried. Miyah had tears in her eyes when she hugged her and said, "Everything is going to be alright." While trying to soak up all of the information she just heard, Miyah became speechless and angry. However, she held her composure and didn't wild out like she normally would. Instead, she informed Daishah about it, hoping she was going to handle the situation like a concerned mother would.

Alternatively, Daishah could've used this as leverage to not only get her kids back, but to put that victimizer away for all the torture she put Arianna through. This is another story that coincides with mommy because Daishah handled it exactly like she did or would've done. After she verified the story with Arianna, she went to Ms. Gale explaining to her like it was Miyah's accusations rather than getting to the bottom of it. In view of Daishah being uninvolved like mommy, it was another tragic story that was unwary, went untold, and unjust. Thanks to all the inconsiderate mothers who doesn't have a voice to defend their child.

A year later, Daishah got her kids back, and they picked up where they left off, which wasn't a good start. Well, at least for Jamel because Daishah's attitude towards him was even more intensified and caused their nonexistence bond to flourish. She made him feel like how she felt amongst her sisters, which was an outcast. For it seemed like she was in her own little world alone with no love and understanding, which caused her to feel lost and depraved. That's exactly how she wanted Jamel to feel, but why? How could a mother prey on her own son weakness like that? Is that at all considered a mother? Whatever the case may have been, Daishah's days of manipulating Jamel had come to an end when he became old enough to fight back.

All her control had vanished when she put Jamel out her house on a wintry school night with no coat. For a week straight, he slept on a bench in the park with his arms tucked in his shirt trying to keep warm. Yet, he still managed to make it to school every morning without a shower, and wore the same clothes only because he needed that breakfast and lunch since that was the only way he was getting his nutrition. Daishah still didn't have no worries, knowing her son was out on the streets with nowhere to go. Every time Jamel knocked on the door, she kept refusing his entry until he gave up trying, and decided to talk to someone at his school for help. They then turned it over to the social service, who placed him in foster care until Lamar came and got him. That was the end of Daishah's and Jamel's tug of war, and he didn't think twice about moving back with her, but he still kept that close bond with his siblings.

After Jamel left, the house was a little more peaceful, but Daishah's soul began to feel a little eviler. At first, she thought it was her guilt eating at her, until one night she woke up to countless dark spirits circled around her bed and whispering creepy words that she couldn't understand. Regardless if their words were soft spoken, it was deafening to her ears. Subsequently, she covered them, but with force, her hands diffused. Immediately, Daishah got scared; before she could fully turn her head to awaken her boyfriend Greg, her whole body was immovable. Thereafter, a heavy mist was either going in or coming out of her mouth; whichever direction it was, it had her breathless. Daishah thought her life was about to end that night. In this state of mind, she relaxed herself without trying to put up a fight. As soon as she gave up, the spirits disappeared, and the room was silent, but felt very cold. Not to mention, Greg was resting peacefully. Daishah thought the spirits would suddenly appear again and couldn't go back to sleep that night.

Daishah kept quiet about her satanical experience. After that night, each encounter got even more vicious. The second time she bumped into an evil spirit, she was watching T.V. in the living room while everyone was asleep. All of a sudden, the lights went out. Then the T.V. started blinking off and on with a loud static sound. When she got up to turn the T.V. down, something bum-rushed her to the floor. She didn't see a spirit, but she felt the vitality while they were tussling. Afterwards, she got lifted up off her feet and thrown to the couch. That's when it started choking her out until she saw darkness. When she woke up, it was the next morning. She nervously jumped up and ran straight to the bathroom to look in the mirror, and the embedded fingerprints around her neck confirmed that it wasn't just a nightmare.

Meanwhile, Miyah had experienced a similar spirit like Daishah's. It happened one morning when the kids went to school, and she was laying on her bed watching T.V. with her door closed. Before she dozed off, the T.V. made a loud sound, and then it went blank. Immediately after, she heard loud footsteps and dishes rattling. She jumped up and fast walked to an empty quiet kitchen; right then and there, she thought one of her kids were playing games. With suspicion, she opened her front door, thinking she was going to catch one of them sneaking off. Instead, she walked straight into a visionless cold spirit, which she felt the evil presence staring her in the face. Her heart started beating fast while she quickly tried to shut the door, but something pushed her with force, and she went tumbling down the stairs. Due to her being frightened by what would happen next, she didn't realize the excruciating pain she was in when she jumped up and ran quickly back up the steps. Miyah, Daishah, and I didn't understand why these evil spirits kept coming to visit. Is it something within us that we inherited? Or is it Satan himself trying to get our attention? Till this day, we don't have any explanations, but every time we get on that conversation, goose bumps appear just knowing and feeling Satan is somewhere waiting to attack.

Daishah, was shaking after her last run-in with evil, so she decided to make it to church on Sunday, hoping God would give her some answers. Before Daishah walked in the church, her whole body felt like it was on fire, and her feet seemed like it had melted to the ground, which prevented her from moving in the right direction. Then she destructively started scratching both of her arms, until her skin was broken and bleeding. She couldn't cry or scream for help because she suddenly became mute. Afterwards, she started hearing those creepy, whispering voices loudly in her ear and automatically knew Satan was there. She began to panic and obliviously ran the opposite direction from the church. Good thing, she got away from Satan, and everything was back to normal when she got down the street. Given this circumstance, Daishah never went back to any church, and every time she passes by one, she gets an eerie feeling.

Satan kept taking shots at Daishah because he wanted complete control over her. Every time she encountered him, Daishah's body was weakened, which made it easier for Satan to intervene in her daily actions and use it against her. For example, Daishah has a short-temper and doesn't think before she reacts. Like when the kids didn't do their chores to her standards or said something slick out the mouth, she didn't hesitate to beat the shit out of them. This one particular day, she couldn't find a decent belt to beat Arianna with. Irately, without any thought, Daishah took the scissors and cut the cord from the lamp while it was still plugged in, and she got electrocuted.

Resulting from the tremendous amount of electric current flowing through her body, she started shaking, her eyes were rolling in the back of her head, and she started foaming at the mouth, then fell dead to the floor. Minutes later, she shockingly woke up with her kids hovering over her crying. As she slowly tried to get up, her body felt tingly, her hair stood straight up in smoke, and her vision was blurry, which had her staggering to her room. Instead of Daishah going to the hospital, she went and laid down for a split second. Then moments after, she was very energetic, but no longer felt like herself. That day, she knew the only reason why she was still alive is because she sold her soul to the devil.

Being possessed have been causing a lot of demonic acts around the house, and the only person that seems to be enjoying it is Daishah. That's why the kids stay confined in their rooms to keep the peace, and Greg tries his best to make her happy. But when Daishah loses her composure, her eyes turn bloodshot red, her demonically deep voice is very intimidating, and when she plods through the house, objects mysteriously move since she has devilish potentials. There are times the genuine Daishah slips out and cries for help, but Lucifer doesn't let her stay for too long after he took control over her life when she became his wife. Immorally, Daishah must please him mentally and physically. Unlike Greg, who is her real man that she wakeup to every morning, but barely have sex with because she gets fucked by the devil every night.

Daishah is caught in between the naughty and the nice, but she still lives her everyday city life as a mother, and a fiancée to Greg, who has been holding her hand through all of her transitions without being judgmental in light of the fact that he has flaws too. However, they are content with each other regardless of the standpoint in their lives.

Daishah is <u>sensitive</u>, but also the <u>reluctant</u> one. Sensitive meaning, she has a susceptible heart, which causes her to be gullible and incompetent in her real-life situations. For those reasons, she stays tense, moody, and could be easily hurt. She wants to do better, but doesn't know how, which justifies her reluctances since she is afraid of more disappointments. Under those circumstances, Daishah continues to live her accursed life for her comfort zone. In my opinion, I think that's selfish considering the kids are our future, and we should want to make it better for them rather than thinking about what's comfortable for us.

Instead of Daishah dwelling on her past, she should use it as leverage to guide her and her kids in the right direction until they're able to follow their own paths, and make their own decisions based on achievements and not just failures. If children have nothing but failures to look upon, then that causes them to be vulnerable towards failing, which makes it hard to stay focus on the right path when they never even saw the right way. At some point in time, somebody has to break the ice. It might be hard, and you probably slip, slide, or may even stumble, but the key word is TRY before you just GIVE UP! Of course, we're not going to know the outcome, that's life, which is like having sex with someone for the first time. You never know what you going to get until you get it. It may be small things, big things, or even in between things, but everything counts; also, it's up to the individual on how well they take heed and continue to find ways to achieve instead of staying complacent.

# BUILDING A CORRUPT FOUNDATION

It has been a little over six months since Brad and I had known each other. Finally, I decided to put all the bullshit aside, and take our friendship to another level. I always thought ahead, and I wanted to snatch him up before anybody else did, especially when all the slurst buckets were trailing him for pleasure, whereas my mind was strictly on business. I needed an ambitious man like Brad to help me build a firm foundation, which comes within a strong relationship. I knew what I had to do in order to open my closed doors. So, I decided to sleep with him to gain the leverage I needed in pursuance of my destiny.

It was one of those nights I knew he was chilling on the Run with his FAM and friends. I surprisingly showed up, and stimulated the environment. That is what an attractive woman does to a room full of men, but my main focus was Brad, and the clock was ticking for the time to make my move. Until then, we were sipping on that crunk juice and smoking on some blunts in a house with no electricity. Still, we continued to have our fun by taking turns telling made-up horror stories, and some of our disastrous life events. Then that "Maryjane" began to alter our brains. Everybody was flying high and was having a field day, basically about Brad. His homeboys were teasing him about how long he's been chasing me and still didn't get the feel of the pussy. They also went on about how Brad didn't have game or enough money to win me over, which was all so true, and Brad's expression showed embarrassment because he knew it too. In my mind, I knew it wouldn't be for long since that was his unknowingly lucky night.

I loved a lot of attention, and I knew I would have those horndogs drooling, so I started off by giving Brad a seductive dance in front of them. Then I fulfilled him with my charming touch from his baldhead down to the middle of his back, and when our eyes engagingly connected, I erotically walked into the room as Brad followed. Although the candles were lit because there was no electricity, it could've been viewed as a romantic setting, which made the room even cozier. Brad was so anxious like a dog be for their bones, and I was the sneaky cat working on getting what I wanted, which caused our bodies to move closer.

Thereafter, some four play went on, which is my favorite part as I quickly busted off. Moments later, he stuck it in my wetness, and seconds after, he ejaculated. In my mind I was like, "Damn that's it!" But in his mind, he was like, "I finally got it!" That's when he quickly put his clothes on, and then ran in the front room to do his happy dance. Moreover, he wanted to rub it in his homies faces. He finally got what they always wanted, but they didn't have the guts or confidence to confront me. To make a long story short, it was their lost, his gain, and my mission was accomplished, seeing I had him wrapped around my fingers instantaneously.

Months into the relationship, Brad and I were building, bonding, and were looking too beautiful. Then BOOM! Kassidy hit me with some bad news. "Girrrl you not going to believe what I'm about to tell you... Brad and Beatrice been sleeping together... And guess what? She said she's pregnant by him! Ain't that some grimy shit? My cousin is really hurt, and he's going crazy right now, but tonight everything is coming out. He's inviting y'all over for an unhappy meal, so he could get both sides of the story!" Pause! Now let me break it down to you. Beatrice is Kassidy's cousin Riley's wife, and he was also close friends with Brad. They all were living with Mrs. Parker at that time. In fact, Beatrice and I were very cool; well, at least I thought we were because I used to confide in her about everything. She even gave me advice on my relationships between Charles and Brad, but the whole time she was just plotting on how to get my man. Wow! I was shocked, but I wasn't hurt about the situation; it was just the principal. I was grateful that

Brad and I were fresh into the relationship, which made it easier for me to walk away. Still, I wanted to hear what both of them had to say.

As we all sat at the table quietly eating, the tensed environment had everybody dumbly looking at each other, especially Brad. He was the only one that wasn't aware of what was about to take place, but he knew something wasn't right. Quickly after we finished eating, Riley stood up with a straight face, and in an angry tone, he said, "I really brought y'all over here to discuss some serious shit... Beatrice you first!" Beatrice had a shameless look on her face, and her big eyes didn't blink not one time as she calmly said, "During the time Brad and Veah didn't really know the status of their relationship... Also, Riley and I were having problems of our own... So, one-night, Brad and I road and parked in a deserted garage, and we had sex in the car. Now I'm pregnant."

Brad quickly jumped up and yelled out, "That BITCH lying. I never fucked her!" By that time, Riley swung on Brad, and they started scuffling until Brad pushed him with full force, then got the hell out of dodge. Riley immediately started disrespecting Beatrice. She was all types of sluts, whores, and BITCHES. He even choked and smacked her a few times until he came to his senses, and realized she might still be carrying his baby, which was the only thing that saved her because we weren't. We felt like she got what she deserved; therefore, we entertainingly watched. Then, after hours of them arguing and crying, my ears were drained, so I left.

This is a prime example of why I don't trust BITCHES! They are poisonous snakes that try to sneakily bite you any chance they get. That describes Beatrice 100%. In other words, she is categorized as a trifling broad in my book, which there are two types. One that's called front door tramps, and the other ones are back door whores. To emphasis more, the floozies that enters the front door are the ones who have nothing to hide. They are openly content with who they are, and what they do, even if it gives them a bad reputation.

In contrast, a back-door whore is a broad that gets what they want in a clandestine way. They are embarrassed of their actions, and they want the public eye to perceived them as being authentic when they are really fake as shit. Moreover, they are the broads that has malice intentions without good reasoning; undoubtedly because they are filled with envy. For many reasons, my circle of female friends doesn't make it anywhere near a complete circle, seeing it's hard to find a strong woman that is truly your best friend in heart, mind, and spirit. Also, someone who would be there for you instead of trying to hurt you; under those circumstances, I only have two best friends till this day.

Meanwhile, Brad was in hiding for about two weeks. I don't know if he was trying to dodge Riley or didn't want to face me. I tried to reach out to him, thinking it wasn't that serious to come in between our business deals. I didn't give a fuck about the relationship, but because he was ashamed of his actions, he couldn't man up to his wrongs. After a while, I gave up trying, knowing my operation had to go on with or without him.

Then one night, I decided to go to bed early. While I'm trying to rest, I kept tossing and turning like something was hindering me from going to sleep. Suddenly, I felt another presence in the room. As I slowly opened my eyes, there it was, a shadow standing at the foot of my bed. I quickly shut my eyes as I thought it was the man of darkness coming to visit me again; but when I felt that my body was still able to move, I took a second look, and indeed it was still there. Out of curiosity, I jumped up and turned on the lights, hoping my eyes were playing tricks on me. They most definitely weren't, seeing that Brad was standing there all dressed in black with a ski mask on like he was about to commit a crime, and that was his intentions if he had to.

He pulled his gun out and said, "I didn't sleep with that BITCH... I've been wanting to come talk to you, but every time I came to the door, I overheard you talking shit about me. Then every day, I started posting up in the woods and watched your every move. Yeah, I saw you and Caylah walk to go meet other niggas and shit. Anyway! I came here wanting to know if you're going to give me another chance. If not, I'm going to shoot you, and then kill myself... I need to know your answer right now!"

Anybody know that an unarmed person doesn't stand a chance with a crazy guy who has a gun. So, of course, I told him I would, and I meant it. Still, the trust would be a big issue in our relationship.

Where there is no trust, there isn't any loyalty. That was something we had to work on building in order for our relationship to survive. honestly, I really couldn't blame Brad too much for being a doggish man considering I was caught in between two guys anyway, and my feelings were all over the place during that time. This being the case, I was somewhat forgiving, well, at least for a little while.

After we obtained a truce, Brad quickly got back on the block like he never even left, which was one thing I loved about him. That ambition, the drive, the energy to hustle masterly and expeditiously is what made him a profitable liability to me as well as I was a valuable asset to him. Either way we looked at it, we both were helpful to one another, and that was the means to our foundation.

With me being the CEO, I called all the shots, such as the amount of work I was going to purchase, how much I was going to supply, and how much I needed to make back to see some profit. Oppositely, Brad was my COO. He did most of the day-to-day transactions like public relations that dealt with communicating and promoting to increase sales by attracting new customers as well as maintaining the old ones, which was easy for a gregarious person like him. Brad's daily duties were somewhat contingent, depending on the conditions of the block. There were times that some areas weren't accumulating money, or he had to dodge the cops, which caused him to maneuver from place to place to be productive. Overall, Brad brought me back the money at the end of the day. Then I'd add my earnings to it, stashed the profit, and re-up with the rest. That was the consistency in our duties. We operated our illegal business 365 days like it was a legal organization, and we loved every minute of it. Although we were considered small timers at that time, we were gradually rising. In fact, each day we lived that risky life, we learned, adjusted, but most of all we progressed in our money, power, and respect.

According to the money that was being made was the level of changes I was making. I knew eventually I had to become self-reliant, and move into my own place, specially seeing that I was contaminating mommy's apartment with the drugs, the users, and the tools to cook the coke up with, which mommy was completely unaware of. It's a true fact that we always brought grief to mommy, and as long as the dragons remained in her wilderness, it would continue. Respectively, I decided to take my dirty work to a hotel called Express Inn. Of course, it wasn't a place I could call home, but it was most definitely a good place to hustle because that's where most of the crackheads went to inhale the poison that they put into their bodies. Since other competing and careless drug dealers were making the area hot, we were maneuvering from Express Inn to the Speedy suites, which was down the street from each other. We were hoping that would keep the heat off of us, but every time I left the room, the consistency of seeing a cop, and them seeing me wasn't a good look. Therefore, I left the risky job to Brad, and took my cautious ass back to mommy's house. In an arrogant way, my money was going to be made regardless.

People always irritated me when they stated, "Scared money don't make money!" How could they speak upon such subject when I was pocketing more than the average nigga that was screaming that? In all reality, they knew my capabilities, seeing how Brad was progressing. That's why they wanted to be a part of my team, but that was very well defined, which accumulated jealousy towards me. Resulting from their negative energy, I had an adverse reaction, which brought plenty of conflicting behavior to my mother's place. There were fights that turned out to riots, break INS just to vandalize shit, and gun involvements that contained shootouts. Even though the rivalries sometimes involved some of the other tenants, my mother was the only one to get evicted. Primarily because the Daevas's was one of the most hated families in Midway.

Mommy had to suffer over our wrongdoings once again, which left her 30 days to get out, and only 4 weeks for us to find her a place. We were definitely lucky because it was exactly a month when she moved on Ridge Road along with us demons. It was me, Lannah, Teesah, Caylah, and Lavinniah, who quickly got settled in the narrow 2-bedroom apartment. Although it was a downgrade from her last place, we felt comfortable with not having strict rules and regulations from the landlord.

Mommy seemed a little bothered by us getting her put out, but she still didn't deny us older troubled kids from moving in with her. I guess it was due to the guilt about never being able to give us a good life. Sadly, she sacrificed her happiness to keep us protected, and gave us shelter, feeling like that was all she had to offer us, which we were no more than grateful just to have a roof over our heads.

Moving in the hood wasn't at all a problem; we lived in areas that was worse than that when we were in the city. However, by us having to purchase our own stove and refrigerator had made things a little complicated for the first few months. Primarily because mommy and Teesah's welfare check wasn't cutting it. Still, mommy didn't mind giving up her tithes and offering to her church, who was knowledgeable about her living situation, but didn't even bother to help her. Me, on the other hand, had a little hustle flow, but didn't feel like I should take full responsibilities when I had other obligations of my own. Of course, a lifetime struggler would know how to survive. Subsequently, I decided to buy some hot plates and a cooler until we could do better.

Meanwhile, mommy continued going to her greedy ass church with peace, goodwill, and devotion, whereas we had hard feelings ever since she joined that so called holy place. For the minister, his wife, and many members of the sanctuary gave off a perception as fake, and we weren't at all fooled, except for mommy. What made matters worse was one of her devious deacons lived 2 apartments down from us, and he had no shame in his game to show his corruptness when mommy wasn't around. Me being the malicious person I was felt no remorse in returning the favor.

It was on a hot summer day when Teesah and I were chilling on the porch drinking and listening to some slow jams. Then Mr. Deacon came out, and angrily shouted, "Cut that damn music off, and ain't y'all too young to be drinking?" Teesah and I looked at each other like, "This man couldn't be talking to us." But his direct eye contact, and the look on his face confirmed it. My heart felt like it was about to explode from the accelerating beats. Then the tingly feeling went through my body as I got extremely mad. That's when I stood up, my integrity walked away, and Mr. Deacon no longer had a title or a face when we started cursing his ass out, throwing tops and empty beer cans at him, and downgraded his title. "You're not a Deacon! That's misstated... You look like one of them crackheads that be walking up and down the streets looking for something. Yo! I got what you need motherfucker." Thereafter, I mooned him. Then turned around and stuck my middle finger up as I walked in the house. We were dying laughing about how Mr. Deacon had no reaction because he wasn't expecting that from us, but I had that "fuck it" attitude! The only person we had to answer to was mommy, which she was disappointed in us when she found out; still, I didn't regret anything. In fact, I was hoping mommy would've been too ashamed to go back to that church, but that didn't work, seeing she was already indoctrinated by the minister; once again, it left her vulnerable and blind.

Even though we were accustomed to mommy being the victim of churches, we still supported her belief in God. In fact, we all were supportive of each other at the time, for one struggle was all of our struggles, which brought strength that held our bond close. Until Teesah got off track considering she couldn't cope with the fact of losing custody of her daughter, which caused her to become bitter and negligent towards little girls. It didn't matter who child, what age, or which little sister it was; she was ready to attack as she felt defeated and sabotaged by her own family. Yet, she was gunning in the wrong direction, and that caused some raging behavior, which emerged to a venomous matter through and out the Daevas family.

During this time, I had an emotional outburst of my own because at the age of 19, I found out I was pregnant with my second child. Oh! No, I wasn't ready at all. I cried like a baby when my doctor told me the results, and I was indecisive about keeping it or not. In my opinion, an unplanned child is a distraction from success, and a hindrance in the future, especially when a person is young, striving, and living a risky life like I was. Under those circumstances, I had to think hard but not long about both decisions, although either choice I made has an outcome that could either ruin my life, or determine my destiny.

Brad and I weren't prepared, but we made the decision to take on the responsibilities as a family. Instead of me just thinking like a drug dealer, I started thinking like an independent parent as well. First things first, I knew I had to get us a place of our own where we could manage bills and stack money too. My best option was taking advantage of public housing since I was starting from ground up. Hereupon, I thought about Mirah and gave her a call. Although she was very well disliked at that time, she still was an informative and reliable person when it came to getting the job done. She immediately made me an appointment for section 8 and public housing in Greensboro. Understandably, I wouldn't be able to be in Midway as much due to me handling some constructive business, and Brad had to take full responsibility in conducting the risky operation on his own. To make things less complicated, with a little stability, and for the sake of me, mommy gave Brad a place to lay his head while I was gone.

A few days after I left, Brad called me and said in an annoyed tone, "When are you coming back? I don't think I'm going to stay here for long… Your sister Lannah is tripping. She's walking around the house naked and shit. She's not even caring or respecting that I'm here… And when I told her to put some fucking clothes on… she going to tell me, hell no! If you don't like it… then leave, this is my mother's place! What type of shit she's trying to pull? She is fucking grimy and crazy for real!" Indeed, she was, and I was pissed, but couldn't do or say anything until I got back to Midway.

Once again, my petty sister tried to seduce a man of mine. That time, she wasn't successful. Brad was the type of guy unused through dalliance. He had so much to lose with very little to gain from sleeping with my sister. By Lannah getting rejected, she felt bitter and had animosity towards Brad, which was irrelevant to me. Anyhow, when I got back, it was no smiles and very little talking as Lannah and I were standing face to face, body to body, and both of us were in defense mode. It wasn't about any feelings at that point, it was a matter of principle and respect, which she did not have. With much anger, I punched her in the face. Then the brawling began.

Since we both were firecrackers, we exploded. The best part about it was that no one was there to stop us. We lit up the place with a lot of banging up against the walls, throwing everything we could get our hands on at each other, pulling hair, scratching, and swinging wild and aggressive punches until we were unable to continue. Then Lannah started crying and denied everything Brad said. Actually, she reversed everything on him. "Brad is lying to you... I don't want him, he tried to come on to me, and I told him I was going to tell you... that's why he called you first to cover his ass. Oh! And keep an eye on Brad and Caylah; I think they have something going on. They have been hanging around each other the whole time you were gone. He only smoke blunts and talk to her. Now what do he have to talk to a 15-year-old about. You can't trust him, Veah." I was puzzled and dismayed by these accusations, knowing it's always three sides to the story, which was Lannah's, Brad's, and the truth. Honestly, I didn't know what to believe because men are manipulators and cheaters. In like manner, Lannah was a liar and a betrayer, but both stories were convincing. Instead of me taking sides, I just was wise and used my eyes to be watchful of my surroundings.

When I confronted Caylah on having any dealings with Brad, she was displeased with my implications. She also got extremely bothered after I told her Lannah was the reason I asked her that. Taking into consideration that Caylah was a little offended, her voice sounded somewhat irritated when she explained, "Brad treat me like a little sister. If he didn't or acted any differently, I would've been came and told you that. When Brad and I smoke, we be talking about you... He be telling me how much he misses and love you. I don't know why you would believe anything that comes out of Lannah's mouth. Everybody knows that she is a compulsive liar. For anything, she wants Brad herself and mad that he doesn't want her. She is the one you should be worried about... it ain't me."

Caylah was right, and I felt terrible for even asking her that. Truthfully, I believed Lannah was jealous that Brad bonded with Caylah instead of her. Once again, she was in her sister's shadow, and she was determined to be in the spotlight. With this idea, she went over and beyond to get the attention she wanted, but she didn't, and that's why she tried to stir things up between Brad, Caylah, and I because she was mad and humiliated over getting exposed for her trashy ways.

In spite of all the confusion, I still wasn't beat. My days of living under one roof with my sisters were only temporary. It took a little less than a month of waiting before public housing gave me an apartment in Laurel Oaks. It was rent free without exceeding $25 a month for my light bill. WOW! That was indeed in my favor. It gave me an opportunity to save, live independently, and get all the furniture I needed, which I truly took advantage of.

My Oakwood bedroom set was the first set of furniture I ever owned. Then a month later, I paid off my 3-piece burgundy and white modern living room set that I had on layaway. Every other week, I was buying some piece of furniture. 2 months after living in the Oaks, I got accepted by section 8. I was proud of myself; every room was furnished, and everything was paid in full. That was the first time in my life that I lived in a place with all new furniture instead of hand-me-downs. It was jazzy and all so comfortable for me and my family. At that moment, I was prepared to move into a house, but because I didn't have no driver's license and limited transportation, it was more convenient for me to transfer my vouchers to Midway. Thinking outside the box, I decided to move in a remote area to keep my kids out of the hood but close enough to have easy access to get to it.

Despite my imagination being all over the place, I always kept focus on achieving by trying to find different outlets to better my life; not just for me, but for my kids as well. However, at that time, the fast money was what I needed to move on, even when I knew it would eventually have a negative impact in my life. In all honesty, I didn't care, knowing I was already corrupted and couldn't turn from my wicked ways. When the day that evil no longer exist in me, will be the day the curse will cease, and I would feel complacent in life. Meanwhile, the demonic things will continue to intervene until I'm cured, that's if I could be.

Prime example was after 3 months of staying in a newly built 2-bedroom house, I was served with an eviction noticed stating that it was too much traffic coming in and out my house, and they believed I was dealing drugs. Bullshit! Anything I sold was far away from my home, which was the whole purpose of moving in a secluded area. But let me take you back, the moment I met with the private owner and his wife Mr. and Mrs. Villain, he was very flirtatious and bold, whereas his wife was nosy and arrogant. The moment she saw me, it was written all over her face that she disliked me, seeing her husband loved me.

Her unprofessional ass started bringing up rumors and other negative things about the Daevas's. Yet, her husband disregarded that, and he still rented me the house. He was coming by damn near everyday checking on me, mowing the lawn when needed, or would find some reason to stop by for a small talk. Suddenly, I'm getting evicted for having too much traffic. If anything, it was her husband that was running in and out of my house; and one of those snooping neighbors informed the wife about it, which led to the false accusations on those papers that was served to me. I explained all of that to the judge, but he still gave judgment in favor of the plaintiff, and I had 30 days to get out. It was unbelievable that as soon as I was blessed with something virtuous, then something abominable was looking directly in my eyes in hopes to see me cry and give up trying. I was discouraged because I was 7 months pregnant and had a three-year-old child. I still couldn't let that keep me down. I had to be open-minded to any alternatives.

During my debacle, Brad had a tragic death in his family and had to go up to Philly for the funeral. By us getting ambushed at the same time, it exhausted our state of mind. Yet, it invigorated and strengthen our hearts because we knew we had to make power moves efficiently and effectively, which it was best for us to do it together, knowing it would open doors to a different connection between us.

After Brad sadly left, I happily threw my baby girl Aaliyah a huge 4-year-old Barbie birthday party. I had the Barbie theme through the whole house inside and out. As a tribute to being my little Barbie, I got her a full sheet cake with her face on it. Then I had the outside setup with a kiddie pool, a slip-n-slide, a bucket full of water balloons, and plenty of other water activities for the kids. What really topped it off was when I surprised Aaliyah with a power wheel Barbie jeep, and a crown to go with it. I was elated to see when her eyes lit up, and her smile shined so brightly. For that was a day she would always remember, and a day I always dreamed of having when I was a kid.

A week after that happy moment, it was time to move out. Due to me being mad about how that shit went down, I trashed the house the day I left. I wrote, "BITCH DIE! FUCK YOU, and GO TO HELL" on every last wall with a knife to carve through the paint. I pissed on the floors, stained the carpets with nail polish and markers, broke some windows, and I left all the trash including food, paper, and other junk I didn't need all through the house. My reactions were devious, but that BITCH was deceptive, which had a negative impact on me and my kids because I had lost my section 8.

It turned out that Brad's trip to Philly would be longer than expected; he got caught up behind some old pending charges. Discouragingly, I was left homeless, lonely, and pregnant. That made me feel like I was at my lowest considering I had to start all over again. Moreover, on my own with not just one, but soon to be, two kids, which was foreseen as a burden. However, Aunt Martha understood my situation. She offered me and my daughter a room with an agreement that I help her buy food for the house. That wasn't a problem at all; I was receiving food stamps. Also, she stayed in a known drug area, which made it easier for me to make and save money along with having a reliable babysitter. Once again, I was grateful for Aunt Martha's assistance. She always been there for me at the right times, but mommy hardly ever was; yet, I always hoped that one day she would lend a helping hand, for that's what I needed and wanted from her.

As soon as I moved into Aunt Martha's place, my name started ringing bells in the area impulsively about the potent pharmaceuticals I was putting on the streets. It had traffic coming through wee hours of the nights; they wouldn't never knock on the door, but they'll keep tapping on my room window just so they could get a hit with the little bit of money they scraped up. It started to get out of control. Fiends don't understand English when you tell them, "You can't come here... this isn't a trap house!" All they are worried about is their next numbed, geeked up moment. Out of respect, I had the crackheads to start meeting me at Kassidy's house, who lived a few blocks from Aunt Martha at the time.

Kassidy was the one who insisted. She always wanted to help me out considering I was her best friend, and she was my daughter's God mother. Not to mention, she couldn't do as much for or with Aaliyah like she used to since her leg was amputated. That is when she changed and dissociated herself from everybody, except her husband Darnell, who was up to no good. I didn't bother to tell her that, seeing she was happy and even more insecure about losing her leg. Sympathetically, my tight-lips were sealed, not wanting to hurt my best friend.

Speaking of hurt, this word was always associated with my family. It seemed like each breath I took, every word I spoke, and each step I walked, evil had struck at me from all angles. For many reasons, I continued walking the devil's path, even when I knew anger and vengeance was the only existence that had me unbalanced. What kept me slightly sane was my daughter, and me generating money; the money created enemies, and some of the enemies were containing a few of my family members. Mirah was one of them; she didn't like that I was staying with Aunt Martha instead of her. Primarily because she wanted to charge me out the ass for rent, and it didn't happen. I was looking at what was more beneficial for me, whereas Mirah was looking at what was profitable for her.

Staring in Mirah's eyes, all I could see was cruelty, deception, and greed. It kind of describes majority of the Daevas's sisters as we staggered in the shadow of darkness, but Mirah's devilish ways were the reflection of Lucifer himself. Her extraneous reasons and acts of destruction were beyond the bounds of retaliation. Mirah didn't do simple things that made it easier for us to forgive her, seeing she had no boundaries. She didn't care who she hurt, to what degree she hurt them, and was unsympathetic about the aftermath; all she wanted was to see someone hurt.

Mirah's reaction towards me moving in with Aunt Martha was very childish. I would never forget the day I was leaving out and saw an envelope laying in front of Aunt Martha's door addressed to me in sloppy handwriting. When I opened it, I was shocked to see Aaliyah's picture cut into pieces with BITCH written on the back of it. "Whaaat," we all strikingly said. It was wack for a grown woman, in fact, an aunt that would go as far as putting a child in the middle of what really was nothing. Truth be told, she never had any family standards, which made her an extremely dangerous person. Still, I was fearless but vigilant of her. Mirah definitely violated, but I wasn't going to give her the satisfaction of knowing she got to me because she feeds off that. Besides, that picture was just a meaningless memory to her, but I had a portrait of my daughter in the flesh, and that's all that mattered.

Instead of giving Mirah a negative feedback, I gave her a call without even bringing up her youthful behavior. In my unbothered tone, I said, "Whattup Mirah? I was calling to see when you can bring over that money you are holding for me?" In her deep angry voice, she replied, "I used that money to get my car painted when Brad hit it with a rock!" I was quiet for a second, but I was pissed about that shit. For one, she should've took that up with Brad, knowing that didn't have anything to do with me. Then by her not informing me about the overall situation was pretty bogus, especially when she called herself being mad at me. That's when I cursed her grimy ass out. Also, I disclosed some violent threats, such as beating her, her husband, and the car up with a bat as the gates from hell had intensively opened, and we were at war.

The battles I was already facing, and the conflict I was going through with my sister were taking a toll on my pregnancy. Resultantly, I began having contraction pains at 36 weeks, which was four weeks too early. I eventually had to go to the hospital. I looked extremely miserable as I wobbled into the emergency room to only find out that I had a false alarm. The doctor did recommend that I be on bed rest. Then he sent me home with some sedatives that had me drooling and slurring my words, but it didn't ease my pain at all.

While I'm taking it easy, Brad's mother, Ms. Rose had come down from Philly to stay until I had the baby. In my opinion, I felt she really came down south to do a "gene check" opposed to filling in for Brad. Whatever her intentions were, it still gave us a chance to bond considering neither one of us was familiar with each other. She also gave me a letter from Brad, stating, "I miss you like crazy! I hate that this happened because I wanted to be there through all those special moments. Can you find it in your heart to forgive me? You know I dream about rubbing your belly every night and imagining how big it then got. Even though I'm not going to be there to see my first born come into this world, I promise I'll make it up to the both of you. Oh! I know you mad at me, but can you name our baby Leah Rose Eve Please? Yada... Yada... Yada!" For the letter started getting a bit bored after I read that part; I really had to think hard about that. Although I was loving the name Leah, Rose Eve had to go, but out of respect of it being his mother's name, I eventually agreed; she was getting my last name anyway.

A few days after, Brad's sister Shydae came down south along with some big time dope dealers from PA. They had a large garbage bag filled with kilos of crack that they were trying to get rid of. Due to Shydae being oblivious to the grimy, hungry, so-called hustlers in Midway, she started spreading the business all over town. That rung bells in a few people ears, and they immediately started plotting.

In the interest of me always trying to keep my hands in the cookie jar, I agreed to help them, but on the terms that they had to comply with certain rules of mine. I wasn't trying to get caught up with the police. First, they had to put majority of the drugs in a safe place where they could easily get a hold of it, but without having bulks of it in their possession, especially if it wasn't going to get sold right then and there. I advised them to keep under an ounce on them. It would be easier to flush it if they had to, knowing Midway was a hot town. All the other rules were common sense if you were living the drug life. If not, then it was time to get out the game.

After they dropped the felonious bag off, we all went to Express Inn Hotel, which was less than five minutes away. As we huddled in the double bed room, we enjoyably got acquainted with one another. Everybody was laid-back, unworried, and anticipating on some phone calls to get the ball rolling. It was a little over an hour when Lannah jumped her hot ass in the bathtub. For what reason? I don't know. Then moments later, there was some police sounding knocks at the door. Everybody completely got quiet. Afterwards, Shad and Jah immediately jumped up and headed straight for the door. With all their might, they held it shut until Shydae got rid of all the work. On the other hand, I was startled but relieved when Shydae confirmed that it was all gone. The whole time we thought that it was the cops trying to kick down the door. Come to find out, they were some stickup boys. It was four guys with their own made-up ski masks that covered majority of their faces with big guns pointing at us.

Their biggest mistake was that they had on the same clothes from earlier that day. Resultantly, I knew who every last one of them were. So, when one of the gunman who name was Ryder tried to humiliate my sister by bringing her out the bathroom naked, we both just started cursing him out, and evil looked him directly in the eyes. By us teaming up on him had gave him the impression that we weren't scared, which made him nervous. When he reached for the trigger, the clip fell out. OMG! That nigga didn't have any bullets. As he quickly tried to reach down for the clip, his ski mask fell off verifying his identity, and showed that stupid look on his face.

Across the room was the second gunman whose name was Liam. He embarrassed Brad's cousin Sean by having him strip from head-to-toe. Then told him to lay face down on that dirty ass floor. After that, he demanded Shydae to do the same until she hollered out, "I'm a girl!" He shockingly looked at her when he said, "Sho yoself!" After she quickly threw up her shirt, he responded in a funny tone, "Those some little ass tits!" But it saved her from getting humiliated tho. Right across from them was the third gunman named Jordan, who was also my sister Miyah's ex-boyfriend. Jordan was the worst out of them all. In fact, he was the only one that was somewhat convincing.

He was hollering from the top of his lungs, spit splattering everywhere, but the utmost disrespect was when he had the barrel of the gun at the tip of Jah's mouth, demanding him to open it. Jah gave him that gangster look when he calmly said, "I'm not opening my mouth, and if you're going to kill me, then do it because you're still not going to get shit." He was truly an authentic HNIC, and I respected him for that. When Jordan realized Jah wasn't going to break, he started ram shacking the room. After he turned over the mattress, everybody including us were surprised to see Shad under there. If by any chance

Shad would've had a gun, he could've popped those niggas off one by one, but that wasn't the case. Still and all, it sent them petty ravagers out the door with $750, a chain, and ring to split between four people.

As they all jumped in the slowly moving car, the driver who was the fourth gunman named "Rasta Boe" had pulled off quickly. Overall, nobody was hurt, and we all laughed about the situation afterwards. Of course, it left Jah a little skeptical about me since I knew all of the niggas, but I had to reality check his ass when I said, "Yo! I think big because small things don't go a long way with me. If I would've set something up, it would've been for all of that shit... Trust and believe." He then gave me this sexy look and smiled, knowing I was so right. Thereafter, he started rubbing my huge stomach. To put it briefly, they brought down more niggas from Philly; and the beef had led to fights and real gunfire, which left people wounded, but not dead.

All of the daily drama had drove me back into the hospital where I got admitted, but not at all ready to push my baby out. After a few hours of the nurse sticking her fingers in me, checking my pulse, and constantly filling my IV up with drugs and fluids, she finally decided to induce my labor with this long hook that looked like a needlepoint. I don't know if it was that or the contractions, but that shit hurt like hell. Hysterically, I squeezed Lavinniah's hand tightly, and we both started moaning in pain. Despite the discomfort I was putting her through, she still stood by my side during my whole labor process, which was courageous for a young teen. The reason why I allowed my 14-year-old sister in the delivery room with me was so she could see the horror and misery females go through when having a baby, and hopefully she would think twice about having sex, for there's more to life than fucking and getting pregnant. Simply because I was misguided, I had to learn everything through my own experiences. Therefore, me being an older sister and a mentor, I wanted Lavinniah to do her best in order to receive the best.

Getting back to the subject, that was the longest and very painful child birthing process. I mean, what baby doesn't want to come out after all that torture they put their mother through? I was miserable for over 12 hours, and then her stubborn ass wanted to come out at 1:15

a.m. on October 23, 2000. I was relieved, revived, and also happy that Leah Jazelle Rose Eve Daevas was finally born. Leah wasn't nowhere in my plans, but I was delighted to hold her in my arms, and I was grateful that she was a part of my life. There wasn't any words that could express how I felt, but being a mother was definitely in my heart. It's crazy how having a baby can be the creation of aspirations, imaginations, and full of astonishments.

As I cherished that special occasion without Brad, I thought to myself that this was my second time around that I didn't have the child's father standing by my side during those precious but "can't leave out" painful moments. It supposed to be a prodigious change, and a memorable opportunity for both parents to share when they conceive and deliver. Somehow, parturition was left solely to me, which made me feel deserted and bleak. Is it that I'm choosing the wrong guys, or the right guys just went wrong? Whatever the case maybe, I still can't change what's already done. There were times I wanted to back down. Instead, I gained ground, and I tried to be the best mother I could be, regardless of who was around.

I had everything I needed for Leah three months before she was born. The only thing I was lacking was a home, but I had managed to save almost $8000. Of course, I was prepared to get one, but I decided I would leave all the house searching to Brad since he was getting released in two months. In addition, I wanted to add more cash to my savings. Before I could make or do anything, there was a ditsy, blonde headed, white lady with a file in her hand, knocking at Aunt Martha's door. I was surprised when she walked in and said, "I'm with the department of social service, and I'm here to speak with, Na 'Veah Daevas." I immediately put on my screw face when I said, "For what?" Thereafter, she pulled out some papers and responded, "We got an anonymous call stating that you're selling drugs, and you hide them in your daughter's pamper. Also, it was a concern that you have your kids around men that are potential sex offenders, and that is an unsafe environment."

While she continued to talk, I turned into a flame of fire when I started hollering out, "BITCH! Do I look stupid to you? My baby is not even two weeks old yet, and you're telling me I'm stuffing drugs in her fucking pamper. Then there's accusations that my kids are getting molested... Come on now lady, get the fuck out my face. This isn't nobody anonymous, it's that demon sister of mine. Who y'all need to be fucking investigating is her, and her kids' pussies. They are the ones who's being touched while she's three shades to the wind. Thanks for your concern lady, but go somewhere else with that shit. I'm done talking!" Then I paced my angry ass in Aunt Martha's room and got straight on the phone to report to the section 8 about Mirah having Joseph living with her without him being on her lease. I also told them about their marital status, and their unreported income. I was trying to do everything in my power to ruin that BITCH's life. Meanwhile, Aunt Martha and mommy was talking to the lady about me and Mirah's rivalry. Resultantly, that case got closed expeditiously. After that episode, I lost all respect for Mirah and phased that BITCH out of my life.

Of course, I had shed a few tears because I was fed up with a lot of shit. My family always informed against me, my hormones was still unbalanced, and I felt incomplete; hell, the list goes on. I was overwhelmed and feeling empty; I needed to go back to the city to clear my head, get some comfort, and feel that firmness and security from a man. That special guy was Micah. He was the only one that came to my attention when I visited the city.

Due to the lack of trust from NC to NY, I decided to have some faith in mommy to secure my $5000 until I got back. Then I anxiously packed me and my baby girls' bags, and I headed straight for the Amtrak. When I arrived in NY, I made my way to Miyah's house. She was the one who always took the initiative to reunite Micah and me every time I visited. Indeed, he was going to be astonished about me having not one, but two kids, for I broke my promise again about not having any more babies unless it was by him. Under any circumstance, he always found it in his heart to forgive me considering we were soulmates, even with us walking different paths.

Because Micah was no longer my objective, I realized that we could never be together, although there were beats that remained in our hearts for each other. There were thoughts of our special moments that lingered in our minds, and we continued to fill up each other's souls when we were together. With that being said, when I came around, everything was shutdown. People might've thought it was just a booty call, but most of the time, he was just caressing my body and holding me tightly all through the night. If I decided to fuck him, it was that "I miss you like crazy" sex because we truly did. Plus, the whole two months I was in the city, we got back into our "forever together" relationship. As always, that was our favorite routine, which made him obligated to do everything. Therefore, he wasn't just catering to me; he always had time for and adored my kids as well.

It was such a turn on to see him waking up in the middle of the night to nurture Leah, and then laying her on his chest to rock her back to sleep. It also was so adorable to see him entertain Aaliyah with kiddie talks and goofing off. Seeing them bond was the moment I wished that he was the father of my kids, but I had to come to reality that he was only temporary. Of course, he made my mental phase blossom; he had my sexual stage drizzling and slippery, but I didn't want my emotions to get too involved, knowing Brad was coming home soon. Most Certainly, I was cherishing those memorable moments in light of our relationship having a deadline. Nevertheless, we would always have that love, bond, and companionship that would follow us.

Thereafter, I met up with Charles while he was in the halfway house. I definitely didn't have any intentions on sleeping with him, I just was bribed by his paycheck he was willing to give me to come visit. Because Brad was getting out the same day, I didn't think it was a waste of time or money, especially when I was getting reimbursed for my expenses. Taking this into account, I agreed, and Charles had got a hotel on the outskirts of NJ, which he was only expecting me and Aaliyah; also, he was unaware that I just had a baby. As a matter of fact, I brought along Daishah and her newborn as well. That's why Charles horny ass paid hourly for two separate rooms just so we could have a private talk, and I was disgusted, but delighted to see that money. The upshot of it all was that I felt nauseated and turned off, and he noticed that through my facial expressions. Instead of me playing mind games with him, I let Charles know that I'd completely moved on, and Aaliyah was the only ties we had together.

I was at another level in my life where I actually felt womanly. I was ready to settle down and become a family that had love and solidarity. I was tired of playing games; in fact, it was time to banish the lies, and say adios to the cheating as my centerpieces were strictly the kids. That immature shit was out the window, down the street, around the corner, and in someone else's face. I no longer had time for that! Moreover, I was hoping Brad was on the same page.

After my visit with Charles, we went to Ms. Rose's house and sat tight until Brad got released. While his family and I began to interact, I was ecstatic to hear them brag about my exquisite, pure features, which was somewhat different than the last time they saw me. My fresh blowout left my hair full, bouncy, and swaying down my back. By my weight increasing from 100 to 110 pounds, it added a little thickness to my body. Moreover, my skin was still glowing, and my smile was forever glistening. I was totally ready to show and give Brad the new me.

Before Brad walked through the door, Daishah and I decided to challenge him to see if he would pick the right baby since Leah and Arianna were only nine days apart. Deliberately, we laid both of them side by side on the bed, and after taking one look at Leah, Brad knew she was his. The proud expression on his face, and his firm "I never want to let her go" hold had given him more reasons to try and make wiser decisions, so he could continue to be in Leah's life. From then on, he knew he had to transition himself into a man, devise his strategies and movements to build up instead of down. Remarkably, we were on the same page. For that reason, we only stayed a week in Philly, so we could quickly find our home.

When we arrived back to NC, the first place I went was Aunt Martha's house. As I walked in with the most bigly and vivacious smile on my face, I got hit with a room full of negative energy and dispirited looks because they knew I was going to be upset about the bad news I was about to hear. My heart started beating fast when mommy said, "Veah, I need to talk to you in private." After we went in the back room, I was in silence and tensely stood there with my arms folded, waiting to hear what she had to tell me.

At first, I didn't think it was too bad, seeing she was smiling like the shit was cool. Until those awful words came out, "I know you're going to be mad at me, but I took $4000 out your money, and gave it to Pastor Filch to help towards building his church. I would eventually pay you back when I get some money." Blah! Blah! Blah! Was all I heard after she told me how much money she'd took. My soul was crushed; I couldn't believe the one person I put my trust in had stabbed me in the back, which caused me to be irate and disrespectful for the first time ever to mommy. Hell, I forgot she was my mother, and a Christian because I barked so many profane words as I cried, "What? How the fuck is you going to take most of my damn money, and give it to that fake ass church? What type of mother are you? You know that was the only money I had saved up to get a place for me and my kids, and I specifically told you that before I left. You truly betrayed me BITCH, and I could never forgive you for that. You and that con of a pastor is going to rot in hell. I hate you… Fuck you! No real mother would've done that to their daughter."

When I snatched my $1000 out of her hand, she saw the hurt in my eyes as they looked weak. She heard the pain in my voice, for I was dismayed and scorned about her inexcusable actions. She was wrong, hypocritical and foolish. I couldn't believe she had the audacity to give all that money to that narcissistic church when she was staying with her sister, and didn't have her own pot to piss in, but in that backwards mind of hers, she still thought she did the right thing. In reality, it was a slap in my face, and I had lost all respect for her because she had no loyalty. Instead, her devotion was within any deceptive church that she always put before her kids, which made us feel abandoned and umbrageous; we never really had terms of endearment, or guidance from mommy. Under those circumstances, I walked away from her, and I left our relationship standing right there. Her words or the name "Mommy" didn't mean anything to me at that point. I knew it would take some time to dismiss this from my mind; therefore, her presence wasn't at all needed.

In the meantime, I had to put my feelings to the side, and humble my thoughts, which was awfully hard as my mind fed off evil. That's what strengthened my abilities to where I couldn't see my wrongs or feel any wrong. In all honesty, I became heartless, more treacherous, and my middle finger stayed up. I was tired of getting double-crossed by my loved ones, so it was time to focus on the new creation, which was my kids, Brad and me.

Quickly after, Brad and I were working different parts of the town, pulling all-nighters to get that money back. At the same time, we were still looking for us a place. Within a few weeks, we were back on track, rented a house, and then bought a car in as little as a month. We moved into a big, old, dark brown house on Hartman Road. It was very spacious, beautiful, and contemporary inside. Then we had that 1979 intact, bright yellow Cadillac sitting in our driveway like we were a "work in progress" family.

This was our maturity stage, which was a remarkable development in our relationship. We were proud of our accomplishments, devoted to each other, and were bonding as a family. This was something I always wanted growing up, but because it was never fulfilled, I was delighted to accomplish it with my kids. I wanted them to have both father and mother figures in the home to: provide, guide, and love them unconditionally. Indeed, Brad and I were doing it all. After having Leah, something within me felt even more different. My affection was more sentimental, I finally felt at peace, and I yearned for Brad's presence as well as he did mine. We were at a point in our lives when we fell deeply in love with each other, and I was determined not to let anything or anyone come in between that.

During this point in time, Brad and I weren't at the level of splurging, but we were at the level of comfort. We were budgeting a little over $5000 a month minus our total bills for the house, which left us roughly around $4000 that we could utilize anyway we wanted to. Looking back, we clearly weren't making a lot of money, but it was beneficial for us considering we weren't struggling at all. Yet, my demands were expanding, and I was aiming for the top. I always had the urge of living like a ghetto superstar. In order to get in that spotlight, I knew that I had to network, and find a new approach. Indeed, with my mentality, I was going to make it happen.

By us gradually climbing the ladder, I became aware of the burdens and troubles I was going to encounter. The phrase, "More money more problems" is a true expression, which I began to learn through my personal experiences. The anxiety started when I became complacent with being at home with the kids, while Brad became more content with being on the streets, which was a signal to all the money hungry BITCHES. Moreover, he unintentionally tipped off the cops about his illegal activities as well. Yet, Brad was blindsided by the cash and the popularity, so he didn't realize he was being watched and followed by the police, which led them directly to our house.

Lavinniah and I were playing in the yard with the kids when I noticed an unmarked black Crown Vic car continuously circling the block. The four dress down detectives kept their focus in our direction like they were looking for someone in particular. I didn't think for a second that they had a probable cause to search or arrest anyone because we weren't selling out our place, but I still had a gut feeling that something bad was about to go down. As soon as Brad got home, I said in a nervous tone, "You need to go hide all of the work outside somewhere. The DT's have been riding in this area, and our house look like the target… No I'm not paranoid, I'm just being cautious." Brad followed my instincts and immediately left out to put it away.

Moments after Brad walked back through the front door, the DT's busted in behind him. At the same time, the other half of them had kicked down the back door, which fell on top of my four-year-old daughter Aaliyah, who was unharmed. However, she cried her little heart out. Primarily because she was scared; also, too young to understand what was really going on. I held her tightly until one of the cops took her out my arms, so they could search me. While one of the DT's tried to butter Aaliyah up, I was cursing them all out while struggling to swallow the eight ball that was in my mouth. My eyes watered up as it got stuck in the middle of my throat. Yet, I played it off very well, although it was hurting like hell. Still, I continued running off at my mouth. "Y'all fucking pigs always messing with the wrong motherfuckers… Don't y'all have some real crimes to fucking solve? When this shit is all over, Imma sue y'all BITCH asses for child endangerment and harassment!" Then a voice in my head had told me to look over at Brad, and boy was his face expression showing that he was scared. Right then, I knew he didn't do what I told him.

As I gave him a mean stare, his eyes responded back like, "Yeah, I fucked up!" Then my eyes replied, "Where the fuck you put that shit stupid ass?" Instead of him continuing to give me the eye, he told one of the DT's that he had to use the bathroom. From that point on, I didn't know what Brad was up to. All I knew was that it scared the shit out of him, literally. In fact, it was so much shit in the toilet that the DT's didn't bother to check it, which was their intentions until they saw how disgusting it was.

After hours of searching the same areas of the house repeatedly, they weren't successful in finding anything. As a matter of fact, our room window seal where they kept flashing their lights in was exactly where the three ounces were hidden at. It was just our luck that what could've been visibly seen went unnoticed, but it was a lesson learned for Brad to never go against my instincts, seeing it was definitely a close call. In the meantime, I had my head over the toilet, and my finger down my throat struggling to get that eight ball back up. After regurgitating and searching through that slimy waste, I was relieved and grateful to find the package unopened, and none of the drugs leaked in my system.

Relative to that disturbing visit, I didn't feel comfortable at the house anymore; it was known as a "drug spot". I wasn't worried about having four months left on our yearly lease because my mind was set that I was moving out ASAP anyway. During our search for a new place, a negative effect had hit our home again… and then again! At any rate, I wasn't too surprised. All through my life, the bad repeatedly came in three's. So, that wasn't really what got to me, it was the motive behind it.

The negative energy started when Brad allegedly tried to fuck Herbert's girlfriend Dasleeza, who was a well-known whore in Midway, and the surrounding boroughs as well. Regardless, Herbert was always a sucker for any BITCH that gave him a chance, so of course he believed her hard-featured looking ass. As a matter of fact, what made Dasleeza accusations a little more convincing was the similar story about Brad supposedly sleeping with his cousin's Riley's wife. Specifically for that reason, Herbert felt like Brad was a sneaky, two-timing bastard pretending to be his friend. From that day forward, they became enemies, then the conflicts began.

Herbert and the whore took shit a little too far when they brought the beef to my home by throwing a wine bottle with a note attached through our window while we were gone, stating, "Imma get you motherfucker!" At that point, they put me involved, which had me pissed, and I was indeed ready for retaliation. Resultantly, Lavinniah and I grabbed some beer bottles and other solid objects while Brad loaded his gun. Then we headed straight to Herbert and Dasleeza's house ready to pop off.

When we arrived, we parked down the street and walked to their dark house. As I banged on their front door for a few seconds, I realized they weren't at home. Knowing this, we went to the back and busted their window to invite ourselves in. While we quickly searched the house, we destroyed a lot of their valuable things. Thereafter, we went in each room, and busted out every last window. Then we ran like hell to the car, and laughed our asses off all the way home. It wasn't shocking to Herbert about my comeback; he knew me. So, when they crossed the line, he knew I was going to be on the other side waiting on them. Considering this, their response was NOTHING!

A week later, Brad came home awfully late, smelling like weed and cigarettes. As I laid there pretending I was sleep, I saw his husky ass trying to tip toe in, and eased his way next to me in bed. I still didn't say anything, I just waited until I heard him snoring. Then I started going through his pants, and there I found in his back pocket a damn near naked picture of this unattractive ass slut bucket name Hedrika. Surely, I knew who bobble head was; her pleasuring mouth was well-known in Midway. Yeah, I was pissed, and I knew eventually I had to confront that BITCH! Moreover, I wanted to hear what this clown had to say, knowing how men are. They would still lie even when the truth is staring directly in their faces. Regardless of what, I was going to get to the bottom of it.

When I stood eyeball-to eyeball with Brad, He convincingly explained, "Sean left that picture in the car, and I put it in my pocket because I knew you would be mad as hell if you found it." I gave him a look like Oh! Ok, and I left it like that until I saw Sean, and asked him about it. When he had no acknowledgement about the picture, I knew Brad was lying... He left me no choice, but to go pay a visit to the source.

A few days later, I saw Hedrika at her friend's house. Without hesitation, I insistently said, "Come outside for a second!" She had a leery and fearful look on her face when she daintily responded, "I'm not feeling well... Can we just talk right here?" In all reality, she thought she was safer inside; actually, I was going to do her dirty inside or out if she didn't answer my questions correctly. Of course, she denied all accusations, but it wasn't at all excused. However, we would meet again in the future if I found out the truth.

Through all of this commotion, Hartman Road had come to an end. We had found some newly built apartments on Crescent Circle, which we were anxious to move into. It was in a cul-de-sac, barely known, and we were the first tenants. It was definitely a kid's friendly area, which was exactly what we were looking for. What made it even more comfortable was that the pigs didn't know where we lived at, and that was an advantage. There is no pleasure in setbacks, especially living our independent lifestyle. Therefore, I felt it was best to stay invisible; if we're out of sight, then we're out of mind, which makes it easier to become prosperous in the drug life.

In spite of me and Brad relationship being a little tense, I decided to let the shit ride. We were learning, growing, and could accomplish more together than apart. Anyhow, I wasn't going to stay closed-minded about his wrongful ways, nor would I continue to accept them. I just became aware that living in the spotlight brings forth temptation, haters, and more problems, but you cannot let it defeat you. Yet, men seem to become weaker, whereas women grow stronger during those phases. The only thing that's left to do is take our lives one step at a time, and work our wisdom along with it.

# SNAKE PIT

---

## *The complexity of life*

MALACHI 3:7 "Ever since the time of your forefathers you
have turned away from my decrees and have not kept them.
Return to me, and I will return to you," says the LORD
Almighty. But you ask, "How are we to return?"

Moving in a different environment wasn't the only thing that changed. I do agree that both Brad and my confidence level shot through the roof as we worked our way up, but Brad had completely lost sight of himself. He started having an "I don't give a fuck" attitude about a reasonable time to come home as well as spending quality time with the family. It had provoked many arguments, which initiated plenty of fights in front of the kids, and around his "so called" friends. Speaking of his associates, who all were in their juvenile years, and amateurs in the drug life had a huge impact on the way Brad acted, thought, and progressed, which imperceptibly started to tarnish our relationship. I was working towards completeness, whereas Brad couldn't or didn't want to find a way to escape from his emptiness.

During our madhouse phase, my monthly didn't come see me because I was pregnant again. Oh my, that really caught me by surprise; it was my second abortion after having Leah. Moreover, she wasn't even one yet, so having another baby was definitely out the question. When I went to my scheduled appointment for a sonogram to determine how far along I was, I found out I was further along than I thought, which had increased the cost. As I broke down in the clinic, I sighed, "What? Four months... How? And it's $1500, I don't have that right now!" The Dr. Response was, "Well, Na 'Veah, you don't have a lot of time to waste, and every week you wait, the price goes up $150. Whenever you're ready, just give us a call."

As I wistfully walked out, I was thinking about all the money we just put down on our apartment, the new living room set that we bought but really didn't need, and my Maxima that I had paid in full for. Due to my excessive spending, I didn't have enough to pay for what really was important. I was left with only $500 and two ounces of work, which was meaningless until I converted it into cash. Before I could inform Brad about the information, I got a call from him telling me that he had got locked up. That shit was ridiculous; it was like all types of bills started coming all at once, which was delaying the process. Because of our stumbling blocks, it took us nearly two months to get my abortion. I was 24 weeks pregnant, and the price had gone up to $2700. Regardless of how thrilled I was to finally proceed with the termination, I was also a little disturbed over feeling lots of movements and had some time to bond with the baby. Still and all, I stood by my decision considering it would've been more of a hindrance than a blessing.

By me being so far along, I had to go through a Dilation & evacuation procedure, which was a two-day process. Day one, I had to go to Chapel Hill where they took a sonogram, sedated me, and then put dilators in my cervix to soften it. Thereafter, the contractions increasingly started coming, and the medication they sent me home with wasn't working at all. All I did was hovered over Brad, popped pill after pill, and whined like a baby due to the unbearable pain. The first time I got up to use the bathroom, it was a trail of blood clots the size of plums coming out of me. Brad and I panicked, so he quickly called 911. When we mention that I was going through an abortion procedure, they told me they couldn't do anything unless I was unresponsive.

I thought I would die that night, but I made it through day 2. That procedure would take place in Raleigh… I barely could prepare myself that morning. With care, Brad had washed me up, got me dressed, and carried me to the car since I barely could walk. I was so much in distress that I couldn't think clearly. After every slurring word, I had to pause because it was so much going on in my head. I felt ashamed, groggy, and grouchy. Moreover, I had to ride almost two hours away leaning on my side as the baby was hanging out of my vagina.

As soon as I arrived at the clinic, they placed me in a cold room that had all bright white walls. After the nurse asked me a few personal questions, she sedated me, which had an instant effect. The medication was so powerful that I was spaced out. Still, I could see what was going on, but everything was moving in slow motion. I couldn't interpret what they were saying because their voices seemed out of earshot, regardless of them standing right in front of me. After the doctor started performing the procedure, I sluggishly swung my arms trying to stop him. While the nurses restrained me, I mumbled out, "No! I… Don't wan… St…" but they ignored my incoherent words, and continued doing their job.

After everything was done, they put me in a huge empty room for an hour. I was sitting in the wheelchair, head slumped over, and drooling at the mouth. As the drugs began wearing off, I started having some emotional reactions. I was feeling sad, empty, and guilty. My conscious really started eating at me when we had to leave out the back door due to protesters being at the front. That was most certainly a traumatic experience that did some physical and mental damage, which would be difficult to escape from my memory.

I was reticent as I cried on the way back home, for I was angry at myself and Brad as well. Even though Brad was there through and out the whole process trying to uplift me with gifts and catered to my needs, I still didn't want to be bothered with him or anyone else. Therefore, I shut everybody out and laid in bed for a few weeks, so my mind and body could heal. But the baby smells, baby cries, and baby dreams kept haunting me. Proceeding on this track, I never fully recovered.

I became extremely hateful towards Brad because I despised him at the time. Inconsiderately, I decided to go to Teesah's house for a couple of weeks; I needed some space. While I was there, Teesah commiserated with me, then gave me words of advice and encouragement. All at once, I started thinking about Brad, and the good memories we had. Suddenly, I realized that the only way we could move forward in our relationship was to wash away the past, and be cleansed for the future. Undoubtedly, I was willing to make that sacrifice. For that cause, I headed home with clear thoughts, a loving heart, and an open mind.

When I pulled up in the parking lot, a hurtful pain had gone through my stomach like something wasn't right. Then my kitchen light immediately cut off, which had me really skeptical. My heart started beating fast as I quickly got out the car because I was unaware of what was about to pop off. Yet, I was willing to face it. As I opened the door, everything was very dark and quiet, but I knew someone was in there and had to be hiding. That's when I grabbed a sharp butcher knife and slowly walked in the living room where I spotted two champagne glasses, and two pair of shoes on the floor. From eye view, a pair of them looked like a big feet BITCH shoes, and that had me a little baffled as I walked through the hallway to get to my room.

Then there was Brad standing right in front of it like he was blocking me from going in. The look on his face was unforgettable, and his eyes was filled with guilt and tears, which enlightened me on what was going on. Before I saw any BITCH, I swung the knife straight at his face, but I missed as he ducked and grabbed my arms. While he was struggling to hold me, I repeatedly screamed out, "You got a BITCH in my house!" Instead of him responding to me, he fearfully hollered out to her, "Trixie! You better come out and leave!"

As she rushed out barefooted, she said in a contrite tone, "I'm sorry, I didn't know he had a girlfriend." Then she quickly got the hell out of dodge. When I saw the cute BITCH with my own eyes, my body had weakened. My heart was so heavy that I got numbed, and my ears became congested. For a quick second, I blanked out. Suddenly, I felt overheated and became incredible hulk to get Brad up off me. Thereafter, I ran straight outside to catch up with that BITCH, which she was parked in someone else's driveway. As I was approaching her with my knife, she was struggling to unlock her car door. Still, I didn't make it in time to assault her ass, but I got a chance to vandalize her car with some nice size rocks as she was driving off. Hearing her windows shatter didn't give me too much satisfaction; indisputably, I wanted to reach out and touch that BITCH.

That was one of the longest, dangerous, and emotional nights. Luckily, the kids weren't there, for I was out of control. I was swinging the knife at Brad nicking him, but not puncturing a wound like I wanted to. It was just his luck that the walls got more knife marks than he did. I then repetitiously started smacking him and pounding on his chest, while he stood there defenseless and reticent listening to me cry out, "How could you do this to me? I thought you loved me. Why?" His dumbass excuse was, "I'm so sorry, I… I thought you left me… and didn't love me anymore!" I gave him the crazy look while I paced back and forth. Afterwards, I went in the refrigerator and grabbed a beer. Every time I drunk one of them, I threw the empty bottle at Brad as I asked in the most derange voice, "What gave you the audacity to bring a BITCH to our house, you fucking bastard? I hate you, and I think it's best for you to leave, or you might not live to see the next day!"

As I held my aching heart, I cried all night and barely got any sleep as I was trying to gather my thoughts together. Obviously, I was thinking out of anger. This was the utmost disrespect a woman could experience, and it happened to me, a fool for love. How do I make this awful pain go away? If I leave him, what type of effect would it have on the kids as well as myself? Do I love him enough to accept what he did? These were the type of questions that was lingering in my head along with a vision of that BITCH running out my house, which had got me emotionally enraged all over again. I started grabbing every pair of Brad shoes, clothes, and electronics; basically, everything he owned. Then I began cutting, smashing and bleaching them all. As I Psychotically stood there, I imagined him lying dead next to his shit. From that moment on, I knew I couldn't forgive him or forget; I just wanted to make him suffer for what he did to me.

I accepted him back; primarily for the wrong reasons. What the hell, that relationship was erroneous from the beginning anyway, and we still got ahead. Not forgetting that, I wasn't expecting things to be peaches and cream. As a matter of fact, my bad news always triplicated. Therefore, I was expecting another disappointment sooner or later. It actually came earlier than I thought because a few weeks after, I found some pictures of Brad hugged up with Bambi. It was meant for me to find it, being that I wasn't looking for anything at all. I was just stashing my money in an unthinkable spot, which was in a hard to reach cabinet above the refrigerator, and there the pics were, just lying there. That motherfucker couldn't be serious, pictures with that baboon! OMG! It suddenly dawned on me that she worked at the hair supply store, and that was also the number that was calling my house, then hung up every time I answered. What the fuck! Her too? That nigga was definitely a fool.

For the reason that I knew Brad wouldn't be truthful about what really was going on, I wanted to dig up more dirt on his grungy ass. Like always, Brad sleep time was the best time to uncover information. Instead of me using the house phone to call the number back, I used Brad's cell, knowing Bambi wouldn't hesitate to answer. When she heard my voice, she was dismayed, but she willingly clarified her dealings with Brad. "No, it's not nothing going on between Brad and me. We are just friends." My bitter ass responded, "Brad can't have BITCHES as friends… I don't trust him, you, or any other harlot! By the way, I know you've been calling my house… Please lose my number unless you want bigger problems!" Then I hung up; I didn't want to hear nothing else she had to say.

Facts: When your girlfriend ask you a bizarre question out the blue, don't lie about it; she already knows the truth. With that being said, Brad flat out lied while looking me straight in my eyes, "I would never disrespect you, and take pictures with a BITCH!" Until two weeks later when I smacked him in the eyes with them. Afterwards, I cut the pics up, and then hogged spit in his face. His reckless ass was looking dumbstruck as I madly walked away.

I was an irate woman, and I constantly fucked with Bambi every chance I got. Primarily because I didn't believe or like her manly looking ass anyway. One day, while she was around her home girls, the BITCH suddenly grew balls, and started popping off at the mouth. Then drove off in her raggedy punch buggy. Since negative energy always seemed to encourage me, I felt it was a need to attack. With my vengeful mentality, I got in my car, followed her, and realized she was headed to work. I had to think! Think! Think about how I was going to approach the situation. Caylah and my home girl Cadence were telling me to wait until she got off, but I impulsively wanted to handle it at that moment. Immediately, Kent came to my mind as my getaway driver. When I picked him up, I told him what I was going to do. I needed him to stay alert, and be quick on his feet when it was time to make moves. Unquestionably, Kent was down, and he drove me back to the hair store.

When I walked in the store, I stood straight in line and mean mugged Bambi the whole time. With that uptight look on her face, she knew something was about to go down as she continued holding a conversation with a buying customer that was standing in front of me. I got impatient and had to raise the temperature in that motherfucker, seeing that she was procrastinating her beat down. Resultantly, I took the lady's bottle of whatever she was purchasing, and threw it across the counter at that BITCH. I was really aiming for her head, but since she was the size of Andre the giant, it hit her in the neck hard as hell. When her doofy ass came from around the counter, I was already approaching her with punches. Instead of her trying to fight back, her gigantic ass was trying to lockup with me, hoping she could get me on the floor, but it didn't work at all. Then all of a sudden, I felt blows to the back of my head. As I swiftly ducked and looked up, it was Caylah trying to jump in. I got her out that fight really quick considering it was my battle, and I didn't want her apart of my troubles. The few people that were in the store didn't hesitate to put Caylah out, and they locked the doors, so we could continue our tug-of-war.

We brawled about another ten minutes until we deadlocked, and then we both fell on our knees. While I tried to uproot her eye, that BITCH caught one of my fingers and started biting it. That shit hurt like hell! With anger, I spit out my blade, and then sliced her a couple of times in the face, which got her teeth up off me. Quickly after, blood started squirting everywhere, and that's when the referees decided to stop the fight. I continued to attack until I realized how serious it had gotten. In a lickety-split, I ran straight to my car because I knew the cops were on their way.

I was covered in that BITCH's blood and had to immediately find somewhere safe. Without hesitation, Kent sped up to like 80 miles per hour all the way to Kassidy's place. As I quickly ran inside to clean myself up, Kassidy had informed me that Bambi's brother stayed up the street from her. Damn! I stopped what I was doing and immediately left. When we were pulling out, Bambi's cousin Sophia, and her brother Ash had followed behind us while talking to the cops on the phone. Suddenly, cowardliness started catching up with Kent. He got totally forgetful and jumped on the wrong highway when I just had told that nigga to take me to Winston. Instead, we were headed towards Sanford.

I was highly upset and started yelling, "What the fuck are you doing? Turn the fuck around!" But it was too late to do anything, seeing there were dozens of cop cars with their bright, blue lights and loud sirens hastily chasing behind us. "Don't pull over," I repeatedly said. Then out of nowhere, Sophia got in front of us and came to a complete stop. I hollered out, "Keep going and run straight through that BITCH!" But Kent desperately put both feet down on the brakes. We were surrounded with cops and guns in our faces, "Put your hands up and slowly step out the car!" One of the cops vociferously said.

When one of the cops placed me in handcuffs to question me, I heard all types of threats coming from the family. As I eyeballed them all, I had a smirk on my face, showing no remorse as I said, "Do what y'll do... Does it look like I'm scared? If anybody fuck with me, they better come correct, or get the same treatment just like Bambi did. Fuck all of y'll, and your big for nothing sister, daughter, cousin, or whoever she is. By the way... How she's doing?" Then I smiled while the cop read me my rights.

Meantime, the other policeman had surrounded my car, harassing everybody in it. Cadence scary ass began to cry; Kent put in his vampire fangs, making the situation as a joke, and Caylah got arrested because they saw her on camera, which placed her at the scene as well as accessory to the crime. Eventually, Caylah charges were dropped, but she had to pay a bogus fine for vandalizing store property. $750 a-piece for some bullshit they said was damaged, but to keep the owner from coming to court, we paid him. The end results were settled in front of a judge, and I pleaded "No contest" to an assault with a deadly weapon. I was also ordered not to go within 100ft from Bambi. Of course, that was attainable; I did what I wanted to do to that BITCH. But I have to be honest, I never walked away when I saw her in public.

Between all of this court shit, the beast had unleashed, and I wanted people to fear me. I began to make plenty of enemies as my anger had completely taken control of my mind, communication, and my behavior, especially around Brad, and his "so called" friends. I hated them in my presence. The thoughts of them made me puke, seeing that they were leeches without value. Then I kept hearing this little voice in my head, "They are against y'll... You need to get rid of every last one of them!" I knew it was time to use the best repellent to keep those critters away. From that day forward, they never had a peaceful moment at my place. I didn't hesitate to belittle, fight, and of course my favorite was throwing things at them while I was putting them out my house. I was happy that they hated me; it was a reason to not come around. Brad was opposing my speculations about those intruders, and I felt like he was against me, which brought even more tension, and daily fighting amongst us. I felt overwhelmed, burning for reprisal, and my love was diminishing every second I looked at his deceitful ass. Therefore, it was time to separate.

I moved back with Teesah, and Brad became roommates with his cousin Buster, who was also Hedrika's cousin-in-law. I wasn't born yesterday, so I was certainly on the lookout. I made unexpected pop ups at Buster's house, and I surely got a thrill out of seeing the dumbass looks on their faces, for they didn't know how or when I was going to destructively react. There were times I came with peace, but most of the times, I lashed out, breaking windows and shit, especially if I saw Hedrika there. We would argue about that BITCH like she wasn't even present. "Now you fucking with this butterface?" As I pointed in her directions. Brad, on the other end, angrily yelling, "I'm not dealing with no hood hopper! Come on now... play me better than that!" I wasn't convinced, but I let it ride considering I had other possibilities on my mind.

I had got a new job as a security officer at the Winston Salem journal, which gave me the opportunity to meet this guy name... Well, actually I forgot his name because he was more like a project to me, but I think toy-boy suited his character profoundly. He was a dark, handsome, well dressed guy with that deep New York accent and swag. He also was energetic, genuine, and a great companion. Although I was a couple of years older than him, he still was up to speed and had many effective ways and means of getting money; at times, he got grimy with it. But living in not only the drug life...Just life period, you will come across some trifling people. So, what the hell, I got down with some of his schemes.

For example, he was the middle man that introduced me to some of his big time weed dealers. Supposedly, I was going to buy many pounds of their green. Instead, I used toy boy gun, robbed him, and his connect. Then drove off in my rental. I could've left with everything. Toy boy didn't know nothing about me, not even my real name. But because I felt the adrenaline, I knew I would need him again, that's why I stuck with the plan and waited a few hours for him at the Holiday Inn Express in Kernersville.

When he finally arrived, I could see it in his eyes that he was surprised I really went through with it. After we split everything, he started dandling my body, and that was the day I found out he was a tongue master, which I most certainly enjoyed. Still, he left with a hard on. That's how I usually did it. Then a few months after, we had our one-night engagement. Yes, I was satisfied, but I couldn't make it to that second night, in light of him catching feelings too fast. I wasn't looking for love; I was looking for victims, and I had to make it clear that we couldn't be nothing more than friends. However, that came to a halt when he got caught up, arrested, and killed shortly after he was released from prison.

Although one of my outlaws was gone, I still had Brad to fall on. We never let nothing come in between our flow of money. Despite the love I had for Brad, I was no longer loyal to him, but always found myself trying to make our relationship work, knowing it was a possibility I would get hurt again. But in the midst of our infidelities, I had learned how to put my feelings aside and not have a guilty conscious about my wrongdoings. I stopped worrying about, "Is he?" And started doing me, living life, and having fun with and without him. Yet, I continued to fuck up BITCHES over Brad, thinking he was my property. I know that I was acting immature and unsophisticated, but deep within, I knew Brad really loved me; and eventually he would get his act together, then give me his all.

Until then, I got a kick out of hassling and embarrassing Brad out in the public eye, giving everybody a performance to remember. My constant violence had transpired to something a little more diabolical as I suddenly got the urge to use my car as a weapon against Brad. One occurrence was the time he refused to keep Leah, but I never took "no" for an answer. Therefore, I made it my business to take her heavy ass car seat out, set it on the edge of the sidewalk beside him, and then carelessly drove off. When I looked through the rear view mirror, I saw Brad walking away from Leah. Out of anger, I made a quick

U-turn in the middle of the road and headed full speed towards him. Damn! He jumped out the way in a nick of time. Quickly after, I put my car in reverse to try and hit him again, but he already had Leah in his hands. As I slowed down beside them, I gave Brad a crooked smile and hollered out, "You better had BITCH!" But what I really wanted to do was joyride his ass over.

Another episode was the day Brad was playing basketball, and I pulled up expecting him to stop what he was doing, and come see what I wanted. But because he didn't come fast enough, I got riled up. Then one argument led to another leaving all the attention on us. I guess he tried to prove a point to his boys when he was standing extra close to my car like he was going to swing off on me; at the same time, he was popping some tough guy shit. That's why I intentionally ran over his feet. Then I backed up leaving one foot immovable under the back tire and watched him painfully scream for a minute while I unsympathetically laughed. His homey's was staring in disbelief, whispering to each other, and shaking their heads like, "Damn, this BITCH is crazy!" Thereafter, I crudely drove off, sticking up my middle finger out the window as I hollered out, "Fuck you pussy!" When I looked back at Brad, he was hopping his fat ass back to the basketball court. I knew he was hurt, and I felt my mission was accomplished.

I didn't care if my troubled appearance wasn't necessary because my objective was to turn my adversaries' smiles into frowns. Moreover, destroy their images as much as possible since I was truly a cold individual. Living a chaotic life had made me that way, which was the reason some people didn't understand me, some may have hated me, but they still <u>respected</u> my gangster, which was one of the recognitions that kept me sane. However, Brad and a few others had to learn the hard way.

I was a gangster on the streets, but I still was scared to be alone, thinking I didn't have the confidence to do everything on my own. I felt feeble without Brad, and thought if I didn't have him, then my life would be incomplete. Respectively, after all of the torture and controversy, Brad and I decided to try and make our relationship work again. We didn't know where we went wrong, or which direction we were going to take, but we knew that a relationship was a process and was willing to hold hands and walk together.

During the process of us moving on Payne Road, I continued to stash my drugs at Teesah's apartment. She lived in the projects that I had on smash, which made it more convenient for me and my customers. But then an unexpected delay occurred at the wrong time. I had just bought 4 ½ ounces of work and hid it in Teesah's ornament box that was in the pantry. Afterwards, I had a big sale to make. I was happy go lucky as I walked to my stash spot and noticed that my whole package was gone. I started panicking and looking in places where I knew I didn't put it. My heart started pounding as my thoughts were boiling over considering the hand few of people that came to Teesah's house were mostly FAM, and their boyfriends. With my frame of mind, I didn't exclude nobody. Whoever stepped foot in Teesah's place that day were all suspects. When I called my nephew Kian downstairs, I had asked him, "Who been here today?" He flat out said, "Carlton was the only one… He was looking for something in the kitchen." I automatically assumed it was him and angrily called Brad. I was hollering from the top of my lungs, "Bring the car and the gun; Carlton came here and stole all of my shit while I was gone! Hurry up so that we can get this nigga before he get ghost!"

While I was waiting on Brad, I kept calling Carlton's phone but didn't get an answer, which had me furious, knowing it wasn't like him to not answer his calls. When Brad finally arrived, I was already waiting outside for him. I didn't want to waste any more time. The whole ride to Carlton's house, I couldn't keep my legs still, or my mouth shut about what we were going to do to that nigga when we saw him. After we reached our destination, my adrenaline started rushing as I banged on his door. Thank God Carlton opened it. I didn't have time to argue with his evil controlling ass mother. "Come with us to Teesah's house… it's an emergency!" I fiercely said, and he willingly came in spite of him not being fully aware of what was going on.

Riding in the silent car was so awkward that you could feel the tension amongst us, which gave Carlton an indication that it wasn't a real emergency. I saw it in his twitching eyes that he was getting a little worried, especially when I kept giving him the evil look as though I was ready to slaughter him that instant. As soon as we walked into Teesah's house, Brad immediately started choking Carlton out as he forced him to the chair. Then we tied him up with duct tape. Afterwards, Brad pointed his chrome plated 38 revolver to Carlton's head and said, "Where the fuck is Veah's shit? We know you got it!" Carlton had raised his eyebrows like he was shocked about our accusations when he fearfully said, "What? I would not do nothing like that to her... I don't have anything! When this happened?" I aggressively snatched the gun out of Brad's hand and started tapping Carlton's head with it while I screamed in his ear, "Nigga, why you trying to fucking play me? You the only person that came here today. Imma ask you again, where the fuck is my shit?" He started shaking his head as he dispiritedly said, "Please don't hurt me, I've been nothing but good to y'all. I swear I never came over here today... Who told you that because they're lying?" I wasn't trying to hear that bullshit. I just pulled the trigger of the unloaded 38, attempting to give him a little scare in hopes that he would breakdown and tell me. Instead, he closed his eyes, and held his breathe like it was his last one.

When Carlton realized he was still alive, he started to cry out, "I don't want to die, if I knew anything about it, I would tell you... Please!" Brad demandingly said while he put one bullet in the gun, "Shut the fuck up before somebody hear you! Now we going to tell you why we don't believe you. Kian! Kian! Come down here." Little did we know, Kian was on the steps listening to everything.

As Kian approached us, he had a straight face with unconcerned eyes as he sincerely said, "Carlton was the only person who came here today. He went and got something out of the pantry, and then left." I could see the bleakness in Carlton eyes while he pleaded for his life, "Please don't shoot me! He is lying. Why would you tell them that Kian? You know you haven't seen me none today. Tell them the truth... My life depends on it!" Kian stuck with his story, which had Brad and I really fed up with that punk and his lies.

Seeing that Carlton wasn't trying to admit anything, it was time for him to die. While Brad languidly said, "Why would a ten-year-old make up this shit? Do we look like booboo tha fools to you? I'm done playing around!" After that, Brad pulled the trigger a couple of times until I stopped him. I had a gut feeling that something wasn't right, especially when I saw the continuous tears falling down from Carlton's eyes, the deep breathes he took after every clicking of the gun, and the words he said to God, "Help me Lord! I didn't do this, but if I must go, I shall go in peace."

My sixth sense had instantly kicked in, and I began to think that we were torturing the wrong person. For Carlton wasn't built for that type of life and would've been threw in the towel. With much sincerity, I decided to let Carlton go with an apology, along with him promising to keep his mouth shut and not to pursue any charges against us. He agreed, but I knew our close relationship would never be the same after we dropped him off, which was the last time we spoke to each other.

In the meantime, I had to figure out how to get the truth out of Kian, knowing he was trying to cover-up for somebody. At first, I thought it was his mother until I saw her angry reaction when she found out I was hiding stuff in her house; right then, I knew it wasn't her. Then it dawned on me about what Kian said. If Carlton was the only person who came by, and there were no signs of a break-in, then that leaves only Kian sneaky little ass. I couldn't believe that a 10-year-old just tried to outsmart me. Moreover, jeopardized our freedom and someone's life. Given this circumstance, I knew Kian was troubled, and it was time to give him a rude awakening.

I didn't want to approach him at that moment, seeing that I had to come from a different angle considering he was a prevaricator. Therefrom, I observed Kian's every movement in and outside the house with his friends up until he went to bed. Then I dropped a bomb on him. "By the way, your homeboys told me that you showed them a large amount of drugs... You're the one who stole my shit... What the fuck is you doing touching drugs in the first place? Where is it at?" Of course, I was lying, I just tried to run reverse psychology on him, which seemed to work because I saw nothing but guilt on his face as he told another lie. "That's not true... I don't even know how drugs look! Whoever told you that is lying," Kian swiftly said. While I was looking right through him, I calmly said, "Well, we'll see tomorrow when all of y'll face-to-face!" I left out with nothing else to say; I wanted him to sleep on just that.

The next afternoon when Kian came home from school, he was all of a sudden keen to helping me find my package. I wasn't looking anywhere else; I knew where I put it, I was just waiting on Kian to return it back to me. In less than three minutes, he brought a clear plastic container with all of the coke in it. "I found it in the top cabinet in the kitchen." He mendaciously said. Wow! That little nigga was a terrible liar like his mother, and he could no longer be trusted. I was mad, but I was also relieved that I got my work back.

Kian wasn't prepared for any consequences after his actions because Teesah hardly ever disciplined him for his bad behavior. Shortly after I gave him a pep talk about how lies, drugs, and thieves can get someone hurt or killed, Brad and I took turns giving him excessive tough guy body blows. Then made him stand in the squat position for over 20 minutes. Still, I saw in his watery eyes that he was a damaged child.

None of this came in between me and my sister. Therefore, I continued my establishment there with precaution and vigilance; but for some reason, Teesah's place had continued to rub me the wrong way, which caused me to blackout, and I let my alter ego take over with satanical outbursts. For an example, it was me, Teesah, and a couple of guys genuinely enjoying ourselves playing cards, talking, and drinking at the kitchen table. Then Vince arrived with a lot of negative energy. Given that none of us acknowledged his presence, it crushed his spirit, and caused him to become violent. "Teesah... Can you come upstairs for a minute? I need to talk to you," Vince politely said. Then moments after, Teesah came fearfully running and screaming down the steps. When I saw her lip split open with blood gushing out, and a knot on her head, I got extremely mad.

"What da hell... This nigga put his hands on you again! Yo, Rusty and Sticky let's go fuck this nigga up!" Then we all plodded upstairs, and there was Vince coward ass standing in the corner, holding my nephew tightly in his arms, thinking that was going to save him. Not that night; Rusty and I damn near broke his fingers by twisting and bending them, which forced Vince to let go. Immediately after, all hell broke loose. I hated that my four-year-old nephew had to watch his father get brutalized, but seeing his mother get beaten by his father was even worse. So, fuck it! When Rusty and Sticky boxed Vince down to his knees, I busted a lamp and beer bottle over his head, which left broken glass all over Teesah's room floor. Then I used full force when I consistently kicked him in: the ass, dick and balls, and in his swollen face with my Timbs. I had no pity for that man. I also wanted him to feel weak and hopeless like Teesah felt when he was terrorizing her, which he indeed proved he was a wuss that night.

After we thrashed that punk, he was laying on the floor unresponsive and leaking blood. My first reaction was getting this nigga out the house. While Rusty and I grabbed Vince legs, dragged him down the steps, and laid him on the porch, Sticky was searching his car for valuables. Of course, his necessitous ass didn't have any prize possessions, but his car was definitely his only transportation. For this reason, we flattened all four tires. Then Sticky put the car in drive, jumped out, and let the car slowly roll down the street until it hit a pole. Then, Rusty and Sticky got out of dodge before the cops came. When Vince got up, he staggered down the street to his car. Moments later, the pigs came. Without any info giving on Rusty and Sticky, Vince could not take out charges. Instead, he took a warrant out on me.

I was trying to stay low-key, so the cops couldn't serve me that warrant. Then I got a troubling call from Brad whispering, "I just got chased by the police, and I'm hiding in somebody's back yard. This rat face BITCH Freda called the cops on me because I wouldn't front her nothing. I had to leave the Caddy in her driveway… And you need to get the car before they tow it. Then come pick me up by Wal-Mart." I had a tigerish flame in my eyes as I speedily drove to the other side of town. Instead of me rushing to go pick up Brad, I went and banged on Freda's door. "BITCH come out… Imma fuck you up! That's one thing you don't do is mess with my money or my man!" Minutes later, a police pulled up. Then all of a sudden, the geeked star wanted to show her face. "Officer she came to my house harassing me! Could you please make her leave?" Before he gave me any orders, I was already driving off shouting out the window, "I'll see you soon BITCH!"

A few weeks after, I felt the energy of jealous rage coming from Teesah, seeing I was hanging less around her and more with her old rivalry Livia. Teesah didn't care about it being strictly business, she felt like it was betrayal, and told me to get everything I had out of her house. That didn't bother me none, knowing I had little petty shit over there; besides, I had my own place anyway. What bothered me was how she kept starting trouble while I was getting my belongings out. "BITCH this... and BITCH that!" She repeatedly yelled out while pacing back and forth to her room, which had me somewhat irritated. I was about to smack her ass, but she was already calling the cops on me. I'll never forget her exact words, "Are y'all looking for Na 'Veah Daevas? Well, she's here at 222 Lori Lane!" They had to already be in the Gardens because as soon as I tried to run out the door, there were pigs everywhere.

I felt like I was purposely setup, and I couldn't believe it was from the sister who I was trying to protect. What really had me mad was she used the phone I gave her to turn me in for a nigga that was manhandling her ass... now that is considered betrayal. Before they arrested me, I tried to run straight through that BITCH. Then two of the cops carried me out and aggressively forced me into the police car, which didn't stop me from barking on Teesah and the cops. "BITCH when I see you, Imma fuck you up like Vince did, and fuck y'll cock sucking pigs, etc...." Resultantly, I got released after signing my own bond, and also agreed to appear in court.

There were too many people calling the housing authority office complaining about me, and I got banned from all the projects in Midway. They thought that was the only way to keep the peace, but that didn't stop me from trespassing, I just was less invisible to the public eye, and I still managed to keep my money flowing. That was the time I searched for a user who wasn't fiend out and lived in the pj's with certain standards, such as having a comfortable place where I could eat and sleep at if I wanted to. I also couldn't be at a spot that had a lot of traffic coming in and out their apartment. That would've made it easier for me to get exposed. Moreover, they had to have runner capabilities, and my trust to handle all of my transactions that came within the project vicinity.

I managed to find two spots that I was maneuvering back and forth to, but it wouldn't last for long because once a user got a taste of my medicine, they started making crackhead moves. For instance, my runners started pinching off the work that they were delivering to my other customers who started complaining about the size, which was becoming bad for my business. Then they started coming up with excuses like, "They drove off without paying!" Which could've been true at times, but I always instructed, "Money before serving!" So, that shouldn't have been an issue. I could go on about how the crackheads lied when they fucked up, but the bottom line was, it caused me to lose money, and I couldn't settle for that. Therefore, I had to go to plan B, which was getting acquainted with the upcoming hustlers that needed a little lift from the bottom and was willing to work with a BITCH like me to get to the top.

That Avenue was definitely the road I needed to take; I had more personal time with the kids and limited headaches. This was the stage my popularity began to sprout. For once, I wasn't selfish and showed loved to the underdogs that started off just like I once did. I left all of the small plays to them niggas, and they brought all of the large sales to me, which made us all productive and led to many potential buyers. By me being skeptical about new customers, they went through a middle man, but got the same treatment as though they were dealing with me hand-to-hand. Regardless if I was greedy, I still moved very cautiously, for one slip up can be a fuck up for my freedom and money.

Of course, I loved the spotlight but couldn't stand the heat. That was the difference between Brad and me, which was the primary reason we always clashed. Due to us moving back in together, we were willing to make some adjustments, move on, and put the past behind us. Of course, it was going to be hard for me, knowing it wasn't easy to let go of things, especially when my wounds were still healing. Yet, I was content with giving us another try.

Hooray! Our house was finally ready to move into, and we were completely at peace with unity. My kids no longer had to be cramped up in one room with me, or bound by someone else's strict rules. They had their own room and could freely play with their toys whenever they wanted to. Moreover, I no longer had to dig in garbage bags to look for our clothes. For that is the love of having your own home.

Knowing that I was doing nothing but illegal activities, I tried to do something slightly legitimate as a cover-up. Indifferently, I started taking trips to New York and invested in some bootleg clothes, pocketbooks, shoes, and cosmetic jewelry. Due to me being well-known at many shopping areas throughout the triads, very popular in the hoods, and marketed my product on my appealing body extremely well, it helped my black-market business jump off immediately. I then had to start making trips to NY more frequently.

In between me traveling back and forth to the Big Apple, I met a guy name Taheem that was a God body who was speaking that black empowerment shit. In all honesty, that is what got my attention, for I always had time to learn something new. Moreover, I got the impression that he was not only knowledgeable about his NOGE, which means Nations of Gods and Earths, but he was also very wise about the streets. After many civilized conversations, Taheem had enlightened me about the secret to the hustle game that would take my profit over the top. "Cocaine is the leading drug on the streets right now because the main buyers would be the drug dealers. You manage it just like you do crack... cut it up, bag it, and tag it; the only difference is you're doubling it up... for $20, you give them .4's... $40 is .8's, and so forth," Taheem constructively said. I was absolutely impressed. In fact, I couldn't wait to put that coke on the market.

First, I had to find me a reliable connect, and the best place to search was Winston. I went to see Charles, but because he wasn't there, his nephew Austin helped me. He introduced me to one of Charles' connects. His name was Jabari, but everyone called him Barz for short. Mmm! The moment I got in the backseat of his suited up Beamer, I felt the chemistry amongst us. It might have had something to do with his butter soft leather seats, but what the hell, a BITCH gotta eat. Barz definitely confirmed that the feelings were mutual as he was flirtatious throughout the transaction. He kept looking in his rearview mirror smiling at me, winking and giving me the googly eyes. He also openly expressed, "I hope this won't be the last time I see you again!" He had me modestly smiling and feeling a little bit of butterflies as I charmingly responded, "If I have a good reason to... Why would it be?" Barz decided to give me a wholesale price for his good quality coke along with his cell number, which automatically eliminated the middle man if I needed to deal with Barz again. This is when Austin had something smart to say, "Damn man! You're sprung already. You don't give me or my uncle that price, and we've been dealing with you for a minute!" While Barz looked back at me, he said, "Well, y'all not her." I was smiling from ear to ear, then shook Barz hand and said, "I'll call you soon."

Outside of business, Barz and I enjoyed our daily conversations on the phone. We were getting familiarized with one another's character, knowledge, and goals. Then we started going on dates, and Buffalo Wild Wings was our favorite hangout spot since I loved their chicken, and they kept a nice little crowd. A few months after remaining friends, Barz started giving me his input on how to take the drug life up another notch. He taught me how to use inositol to blow up the coke, and give it extra weight, which would accumulate more profit and re-up quicker.

I kept that in mind, but I had to build my clientele up first. Sagaciously, I decided to give out testers. I went to every hood and stereotyped every person I thought was a potential coke head. I listened to the way they talked, looked at how they moved, and stared at their nose for clues. If anything looked or sounded suspicious, I would slip in my favorite line while we were talking, "I got some good coke I was trying to get rid of... Do you know anybody? I have a few testers if they want to try it out before they buy." Their shocked reactions were, "You got that tissue? Or you got that nose candy? Let me try it, I know plenty of people I could put the word out to!" I then would give them a line to snort, and my cell number, knowing they would be calling. It was unbelievable how the word traveled fast around Midway about me having that ether. I was content with my phone ringing off the hook, but I was unaware that it was a 24-hour job considering those motherfuckers wanted to stay geeked up all night. However, I was loving that extremely fast money.

Even though I continued to sell crack, the coke was more of a full-time job for me, which had Brad and I money on different levels. Surely, it was time for us to separate our stash, but because I was the dominant one, I continued to have control over his. Despite us splitting all of our bills in half, if we had any emergencies, or did any splurging, his money was the first to be spent.

I was at a happy place in my life, and I thought it was best to share it with my kids. Therefore, I had to learn how to separate business from family since they were mostly with me through it all. Resultantly, I set a time of the day when I put my customers on hold, and sent them to Brad, for I didn't want any intrusions during my motherly hours. There were times the kids and I shopped till we dropped. There were days when we just went to the movies and out to eat for a little kiddie chat. Oh! They really enjoyed the celebration station, putt-putt, and the water park filled with slides and pools. Then there were occasions when we only visited family and friends.

Visiting family was an up and down situation; at times, our presence was idolize, and there were days we saw the jealous eyes. Still and all, I continued to drop by as I enjoyed confronting envious people with my kindness. There were plenty of times the treat was on me. I kept weed for us to smoke, liquor to drink, food to eat, and paid for people to get in the clubs. I wasn't expecting anything in return, but respect, and that's what I got.

We also enjoyed visiting my two best friends who were Kassidy and Melody. Although I shared a separated friendship with the two, our bonds were unbroken, for I understood them, and they understood me. We comforted, confided, and believed in each other as though we were sisters from another mother. And the best part about it was that my kids recognized them as family instead of my friends. We had many memories of traveling and lots of fun parties. Most importantly, we were enjoying life.

# TOO LATE CAN SOMETIMES COME TOO EARLY

One day, Kassidy and I had an unexpected quarrel over a house party she invited me to, but her husband invited some of the Reagan's family. That was very strange, knowing our beef was still fresh and provoking. But being that I had an "I don't give a fuck attitude," Me, Lannah, and Cadence had stayed anyway. However, I couldn't seem to enjoy myself because the whole time I had bad vibes. While Lannah and Cadence was mingling around getting drunk, I had a small talk with Kassidy, and I was a little bothered about how she gave me the cold shoulder. But I tried to be somewhat understanding; losing a leg can bring forth mood swings, especially when you see everyone else doing what you used to be able to do.

When I went to use the bathroom, seconds later, I heard a lot of commotion. My first thought was Lannah. I instantly jumped up and quickly wiped myself while still dripping piss. I couldn't believe how fast the house got empty and jammed-packed outside. As I forced my way through the crowd, I had pulled out my pocket knife, preparing to jig whoever I felt was any harm. Then Kassidy's cousin Riley grabbed me from behind with both of his arms wrapped around mine. For some strange reason it seemed like he was trying to prevent me from helping my sister.

With rage, I spazzed out, wildly kicking and head butting him until he let me go. Then I saw Cadence helping my sister through the crowd. Lannah was holding the side of her head, which was bleeding as she sluggishly said, "That BITCH Herbert fucking with had hit me with a bottle!" I angrily responded, "What... Where that BITCH at?

Yo, Cadence put her in the car, I'll be back!" As I ran back through the crowd with my knife swinging wildly, everybody was quickly moving out the way. Then I saw a car speedily passing by, which was Herbert and his BITCH Dusty. As I energetically ran back to my car, there was Darnell and Riley, defensively standing there. Then Riley hollered out, "Yaw need to leave, and take that trouble somewhere else... Yaw Daevas's always starting something!" Before I drove off, I rolled down the window and wickedly said, "Fuck the both of y'all, and if y'all didn't mean shit to Kassidy, I would've did one of you lames in!" Then I slowly drove off with a stare from hell.

While we were riding, Lannah blurted out, "I'm good! I don't need to go to the hospital for this little ass gash... I'm bleeding heavy like this because I've been drinking... Look!" Instead of me going all the way to my house, we stopped in the Pj's, and I parked in front of Teesah's place. Looking at the little scratch in her head, we all began laughing as I said, "This crackheadish BITCH probably think she did some damage... What she hit you with a baby bottle... Hahahaha! Hold up... Where the fuck was Kassidy? I didn't see her while all of this was going on." Cadence responded, "Darnell took her next door. Veah, I was trying to help Lannah, but everybody was holding me back like they had all of that shit planned out. That BITCH kept bumping Lannah without saying excuse me. So, Lannah swung off on her ass. Then everybody surrounded Lannah like she started it... Afterwards, I heard glass splatter."

Hearing that information had me skeptical about Kassidy's loyalty since Dusty was Bambi Reagan's cousin; she also was Kassidy's brother's girlfriend, which had me wondering why she still invited me and didn't at all warn me that my enemies were going to be there. That didn't sound like the Kassidy that I thought I knew because she wouldn't ever let any of that happened. What had really taken the cake was that she didn't call to check up on us or anything. For Certain, the whole family was suspects in my eyes, which caused a feud and a separation between the Parker's and the Daevas's family.

I stopped talking to and hanging around Kassidy. My feelings were hurt, and I was waiting on an apology call because she knew that was dead wrong. Apparently, her pride wouldn't let her speak. I never heard the word sorry, or received any type of phone conversation. Resultantly, our bond went downhill. I still had much love for Kassidy, but being stubborn had made matters worse, especially when I had another best friend. Basically, I said, "Fuck the friendship!" But I couldn't let our feud interfere with her and Aaliyah, they had a close bond; also, she was a great God mother. For that cause, I dropped Aaliyah off from time-to-time.

Six months later, Miyah came down from NY to visit for a week. She was surprised that Kassidy and I didn't rekindle our friendship yet and was hoping that she could help us bury the hatchet. I was still holding a grudge, so I didn't think the time was right since I would've came off as being phony. Instead of considering it then, I continued taking a rain check.

The night before Miyah left, she consistently said, "I need to see Kassidy before I go back to NY. Can you take me there now? It's right around the corner." Oppositely, I wanted to stay at Uncle Brodey's house and continue drinking. In my slurring words, I said, "I'll take you tomorrow because alcohol and enemies don't mix... In order to stay calm and collected, I have to be sober for that."

The next morning, I was slumped over the bed hung-over when I got that unexpected call from Aunt Martha, sadly saying, "Did you hear about Kassidy dying last night? Her sugar level went above 600 milligrams, causing her to go into a diabetic coma. I can't believe she's gone, I'm so hurt. Veah... Veah... Are you there?" I dimly responded, "Yeah!" I had tuned out for a second as I was lost for words. So much guilt was eating at my thoughts like, "Damn! I should've made things right, and now it's too late to invalidate the wrongs. I was supposed to be there by her side, holding her hand, and telling her she would defeat her sickness because she is strong, but now she's gone."

My words no longer had meaning and will only remain in my thoughts. Moreover, leaving our friendship as memories. "Wait a minute... am I dreaming? This can't be true." I couldn't even get emotional; primarily because everything happened so suddenly, which had me somewhat in disbelief. Therefore, I ended that call with Aunt

Martha; plus, I needed to sleep off my bad headache and hopefully wakeup to reality. Meanwhile, Miyah cried the whole time, which had her eyes puffy and bloodshot red. She was hurt, and angry about her not being able to make it to Kassidy's funeral since she couldn't change the date on her ticket, and it was also nonrefundable. Under the circumstances, Miyah had to leave that night, and Shaylah was on the next train down south. Although Kassidy wasn't related, she was still family in our hearts. Most definitely, we felt like it hit us all close to home.

Breaking the news to Aaliyah had her looking confused, but she slightly understood why she wasn't going to be able to see Kassidy again. I had honestly explained to her, "Kassidy is happier in heaven, and she would always be with you in your heart… Okay? In a few days we have to go say goodbye, so God could give Kassidy her wings. Do you understand me?" Aaliyah softly responded, "Yes." Then she held her head down as she walked in her room. When Aaliyah returned, she had her own written poem that she wanted to read aloud at Kassidy's funeral. Since I wasn't talking to any of Kassidy's family, but her youngest brother Gabe, I gave it to him, so they could put it in the obituary.

The day of the funeral, Shaylah and I had walked in the funeral home all dressed in white resembling Kassidy, who looked angelical laying in her gray and pink casket. As I viewed her body for the last time, reality hit me that she was really dead, and I wasn't going to ever see her again. My whole body got numbed into absolute quiescence as I stared at her lifeless body. When I touched her cold hands, and gave her that one last kiss, my heart started racing as tears began to uncontrollably fall. While I walked back to my seat, Aaliyah was tightly holding my hand, and sadly looking up at me as I cried, but she didn't know how to console me during that time.

I cried so much during the ceremony that one of the ushers stood there and kept passing me Kleenex's the whole time. Then I heard Kassidy's peaceful voice in my ear, "I'm sorry best friend, and I hate that I didn't say it sooner. It was me that changed; I was hating my life, and my family that was taking advantage of me… Sadly, I gave up in order to be free. It's not your fault… Stop thinking about what you could've done and continue taking care of the little ones. I hope you find happiness because Brad isn't your soul-mate. Oh! Tell Aaliyah I said hi, I love her, and she was the best thing that happened to me. I also want to say thank you for giving me a child I could never have, and you gave me that opportunity to feel like a parent. I was truly grateful! Well, I have to go… Until I see you again… I'll be watching over y'all."

It felt like Kassidy was hugging me through her whole conversation because after she said her goodbyes, I no longer felt that clinch, but I did get some closure and was relieved. When I tuned back into the ceremony, they were on the eulogy, and I was very disappointed in Herbert's arrangements. Instead of him putting Aaliyah's poem in the obituary, or let her say what she wrote from the heart for Kassidy, he let Dusty, who barely knew her make an untouchable speech. Moreover, he didn't even acknowledge Aaliyah as Kassidy's God child in the obituary when he knew that was one of her dying wishes.

After that disheartening moment, Amazing Grace was beautifully sung by a young man as they carried Kassidy out. We were headed to the burial to finally let her soul rest. For Kassidy was fighting her diabetic disorder from the age of nine up until she lost the battle at the age of 23 on April 2, 2003. That was only three months and 13 days away from her birthday, but God had much better plans for my friend, and she would be truly missed. RIP Kassidy Y. Parker.

Eight months later, I found out I was pregnant again, and the first thought that came to my mind was, "How many months I was?" Primarily because I was doing the hanky-panky with Barz, and we had some mishaps a few times. That one particular night at his studio, we were so much into our sexual congressing that neither one of us knew that the condom busted until he ejaculated. That was three months prior, then out the blue, a positive pregnancy test.

When I went to my doctor, I found out that I was 12 weeks pregnant. Shit definitely got interesting, knowing it wasn't Brad's according to my marked down calendar, which started on the day of me and Barz incident. "Now my game shall begin!" And neither guy would know that they're a part of it. Barz wouldn't know it's his baby, and I would continue letting Brad think he's the father until I give birth. Then BOOM! I was going to give him the bad news, and laugh when I see the hurtful look on his face while he's holding the next man's baby. I felt like that was my opportunity to crush Brad's soul, just like he did mine, and I didn't think twice about it.

Time was passing by so quickly; in a blink of an eye, I was five months sitting in my doctor's office, waiting to find out if it was a boy or a girl. During the sonogram process, the doctor not only verified that it was a girl, he also told me that I was six months instead of five. "Fuck! Fuck! Fuck! This changes everything!" I cried out. My game was not only over, but I was having another child, a girl at that, and it was by that clown ass nigga. I wanted the pregnancy to end, but it was too late to have an abortion. Without a doubt, I had to take matters into my own hands because I hated that baby, and it was time for her to go.

The whole night I was unable to sleep, thinking about what I could do to miscarry. Then the next day after getting out the shower, I saw a hanger dangling on the doorknob, which was a sign that it could be my only option. I started unraveling the metal clothes hanger until it was straight, hoping it was long enough to reach the sac. As I slowly inserted it in my vagina, I kept poking at God knows what for a few minutes, but nothing happened. I didn't feel any pain, nor did I see any blood. After trying it a few more times, I said to myself, "This shit not going to work!" Unfortunately, I had no choice but to accept that I was having a baby.

Later on that day, Brad had got a discouraging call that his grandmother died. It left him mournful, depressed, and heartbroken. Under those circumstances, he wasn't thinking clearly, which caused him to slipup. It was out of the ordinary for Brad to make a sell down the street from our house, knowing that could jeopardize everything, but he was thoughtless about the outcome. Conflictingly, I had a keen intuition that something was shady about that deal and was highly upset that he was reckless like that. At that time, I didn't give a fuck if he was grieving, I cursed his stupid ass out.

Exactly 48 hours after Brad left for Philly, I got a visit from the pigs. I kind of expected them, and that's why Melody and I dropped off my kids in the pj's. I wanted us to stay far away as possible from our house until I felt like the coast was clear. Recklessly, I rushed out with all the drugs on me, but eventually I realized that I forgot my money. I ran inside when we arrived back, wanting to get in and out promptly.

While Melody waited in the car, within seconds, the cops had surrounded it with guns aiming at her yelling, "Put your hands up and step out the car... Get down! Get down!" When I nervously looked out my glass door, there were a few cops pinning Melody to the ground. That's when my big belly ass started running, so I could get rid of the drugs I had on me. I really didn't have much time to do anything. Therefore, I threw the 3 ounces of coke, then one of those pitiless pigs tackled my pregnant ass to the floor with my stomach hitting first. "Calm down! You are not who we're looking for," the pig hollered in my ear while he was handcuffing me. Afterwards, he aggressively set me on the couch as they began searching the house.

Within 10 minutes they found the coke behind the couch. Thereafter, they seized my money, which was about $4500 along with some valuable coins, jewelry, and my $5 bill that was autographed by one of my favorite R&B groups called Jagged Edge. Then they read me my rights and hauled my ass downtown. As soon as I got my one call, it was to Melody calmly explaining to her where my emergency cash was stashed at, so she could bail me out. Within an hour, I was free again.

Possession of cocaine was my first drug charge. It was truly a setback for me, and Brad was the blame for everything. After he paid for my lawyer, the charges got dismissed since my name wasn't on the lease, which created confusion on proof of possession, especially because they didn't find the drugs on me. I got lucky that time around, but of course I was ready to pack up and move again. However, we wouldn't make that mistake in moving out until we had another place to move in.

Meanwhile, I stayed cautious, and I always was observing our neighborhood as we continued doing illegal activities. Then on June 25, 2004, I was paranoid, pacing back and forth to my door while talking on the phone to Miyah. Suddenly, I started feeling pressure at the bottom of my abdomen. After that, it felt like a water balloon popped between my legs. It was a tremendous amount of fluid showering my living room floor. I didn't move, I just stood there in shock while telling Miyah what happened. Given that she had a similar experience, she immediately knew what I was talking about, and concernedly said, "Veah, that's serious, and you need to go to the hospital right now." I took her advice and went to the emergency room, but I was thinking and hoping that a miscarriage was the outcome.

Although I explained to the nurse that more than a bucket full of water came out of me, she did nothing but the basic procedures, such as temperature check, blood pressure, and a urine test. Then she sent me home after telling me it was leftover pea. I took it as that because I wasn't feeling any type of pain. I went home and continued doing my everyday routine. Then five days later, while I was lazing on the couch, watching TV, a sharp contraction had instantly balled me up. At first, I didn't think anything of it until they started coming back-to-back. Out of 24 years, that was the first time mommy came to my rescue when I really needed her, especially when Brad and I weren't on speaking terms due to the charge I caught for his reckless ass. I couldn't stand the sight of him, or wanted him around me. That's why I called the ambulance instead of him.

When I arrived at the hospital, they rushed me straight to the back where the doctor performed a sonogram. He looked very bothered after he observed that I was breached and had no amniotic fluid in my sac. With a stern look on his face, he called in and anxiously briefed some of the medics, telling them, "She need to be transferred to Cone Health Hospital ASAP! I already sent over her information to them; therefore, they will be prepared when she arrives there. I also want to know the name of the nurse who sent this young lady home last week because she didn't follow the proper procedures, which could've prevented this from happening." My whole body started trembling out of control like I was freezing, but it was just a nervous reaction by me not entirely being aware of what was going on. Still, I knew it was something severe if they were transferring me to a specialized hospital.

Before they put me in the ambulance, the nurse wrapped me up with a few freshly heated covers, which was soothing to my body, but didn't calm my nerves at all. Taking off with the loud sirens, and bright lights flashing on the congested highway, it took the ambulance exactly 7 minutes to get to Greensboro, which is at least a 20-minute drive; instead of me praying to God, I had talked to the devil, hoping it was the miscarriage I was longing for without it being life threatening to me.

Then one of the doctors clearly explained my situation, "Your baby is in critical condition right now. Your sac has been broken for almost a week, and you both have been exposed to bacterial infections. Also, your sac has no fluid, and the baby's feet is hanging at the edge of your vagina. Unfortunately, she is ready to come out, and you have to make a quick decision on the way you want to give birth. If you choose to have a breech birth, then your baby is at risk of the umbilical cord getting wrapped around her neck, which slows down the oxygen and blood supply. You also need to be aware that her head is going to be the last body part to emerge, which will make it harder to ease it through the birth canal, and it can cause abnormalities or disabilities. That is why I'm recommending an emergency C-section because premature babies are small and more fragile."

I sedately stared at the doctor for a second before I asked, "If I choose to push her out, and she's born with any kind of birth defects, can you just put her soul to rest?... Because having a cesarean is not an option since it would leave a visible scar on my body... And I just be damn if I be awake while y'll cut me open, especially for a baby I don't want anyway." All of the specialist were speechless as they shockingly looked at me, and then looked at each other in disbelief.

Thereafter, one of the doctors had explained to me in a calm tone, "That's definitely not an option since that would be considered murder. We are doctors that will do everything in our power to save your baby, and we're hoping that you'll make the best decision for your child instead of yourself. What I can do is give you a bikini cut, which will be a less noticeable incision that causes less pain after surgery, and you'll have a faster recovery. Also, I can give you something that'll put you to sleep through the whole operation. But you have to make a decision pronto." After a few minutes of contemplating, I decided to get the C-section.

When I woke up, my throat was dry and sore from the tracheal tube they put in it. My lower abdomen had a stabbing and burning sensation that made me hesitant to make any sudden movement. Moreover, my eyes were still cloudy from the medicine, but I was very happy to see mommy finally by my side.

I was in the hospital for two days and ignored going downstairs to the NICU to see my daughter. I don't know if it was the guilt, or the anger of her being alive, but I didn't feel like I gave birth to my own child, which had me thinking I was less obligated to love, nurture, or even give her a name. Then after a few encouraging conversations with mommy, and some of the nurses, I decided to pay the baby a visit. As mommy pushed me closer to the incubator, my heart dropped when I saw a hand sized, 1½ pound, frangible baby with tubes everywhere. They also had bright blue bililights placed over the incubator to treat her jaundice. I was breathless as I held my head down and busted out in tears, feeling ashamed.

Taking into consideration that I put her in that predicament, I started to feel obligated to make things right. Thereupon, I went to one of the doctors for a solution. He told me, "Due to your baby being born very early, she has a 50% chance of surviving. The main and healthiest medicine for her right now is your breast milk providing that it offers protection in fighting off certain complications in preemies. Your baby isn't ready to be fed at your breast, but she will get her nourishment through a catheter that's inserted into her veins until she gets bigger and stronger. Another remedy is bonding with your baby while she is in the NICU. Becoming actively engaged with her can build an emotional connection. Of course, she is too small for you to hold her right now, but for her to hear your voice and feel your touch can help her recovery as well."

I had no further questions, all I needed was the equipment to get those tits pumping, even though my milk was adulterated with marijuana. But she immediately showed progression, which was earlier than the doctors expected. My baby was gaining about a quarter of an ounce a day. I was pumping like crazy as her feedings were gradually increasing. Every time I visited, the nurses would be amazed how she opened her eyes when she heard my voice. It was also unbelievable to me how she clinched onto my finger like she never wanted to let go. Although the love wasn't there, at that moment, it started to grow on me. I stared at this determined little baby, and decided that I was going to name her Miracle because it was her destiny to serve a purpose on this earth. Besides, it was time for me to stop procrastinating and finalize the paperwork for her birth certificate, which was a little over a week after she was born.

Brad, the kids and I were visiting Miracle daily. With the way she was progressing, we were expecting her to be coming home soon. Then I got a call from the doctor with some devastating news, explaining to me about Miracle's condition and my options, "Your baby is suffering from fecal vomiting, and she needs to undergo surgery on her intestines. If she doesn't get the operation, and her situation doesn't reverse back to normal, then she could die. On the other hand, if you decide to let us do the surgery, she has a 50% chance of survival. It also would leave her with a visible and permanent scar on her stomach." I was skeptical, and I didn't authorize it until Brad explained to me that, "It's better to do something that could help her, or we'll regret doing nothing at all."

Hours of waiting, and I had already accepted that she was at peace. I felt it in my bones, and then seconds later, the phone had rung. The words came out slowly, and his tone of voice sounded disappointed as he said, "Unfortunately, she didn't make it through surgery, we have her on life support, which is a ventilator that is breathing for her until you come and decide to remove it. I'm very sorry for your lost." I hung up on him, and we rushed to the hospital. When I got there, the chaotic waiting room was filled with my supportive family members who were upset and wanted some answers for my baby's sudden death. However, the doctors wouldn't talk to anybody until I got there. At that moment, I didn't feel like having any conversations; my only concern was saying my goodbyes, and also ask Miracle for my forgiveness.

The last moments I spent with Miracle was in a secluded area alone. That was the very first time I held her, which was tightly. The only time I got to smell her, and she had that baby scent I would never forget. Then I kissed her smooth delicate skin. I played with her tiny little toes, and I held her puny little hands as I rocked her in the chair. While I rubbed her soft curly hair, she started glowing. Afterwards, her beautiful features of me had blossomed all over her caramel colored face. That's when more guilt started pumping through my blood. Thereupon, it dawned on me that Miracle purpose for life and death was my punishment. My cursed words of miscarriage just came in a different form in order to reveal to me my wrongs. After Miracle showed me the beauty and the blessing in having a baby, she left me with nothing but memories and humiliation. It had me feeling empty and full of pain. Damn! Too late came a little too early, and I can no longer right my wrongs with my baby girl.

June 25-July 19, 2004, Miracle survived on this earth, but she became a peaceful angel on Abrianna and Jayden's birthday. Therefore, our grievance was also a celebration of their lives and her afterlife because she was no longer suffering. Instead of having a funeral, three days later, I cremated her, so she could be with us forever.

In a little over one year and three months, I lost two people that I never properly got a chance to say goodbye to, which seemed to me as part of my curse. For every tragedy I suffered, and every pain I felt had broken me instead of molding me as I kept the evil going.

# MOMENTS OF ADVERSITIES;
## STILL STRIVING FOR PEACE

MALACHI 3:13-14 "You have said harsh things against me, says the LORD. Yet you ask, 'What have we said against you? You have said, it is futile to serve God. What did we gain by carrying out his requirements and going about like mourners before the LORD Almighty?

# YOU PROVOKED THE BAD WITCH

Self-pity had taken me into a deep depression, and I was at war with my life, hoping I could defeat it. Moreover, Brad and I concept of life was totally opposite. His exertive dick kept slipping out his pants, his pockets kept taking losses, and he didn't know the true meaning of a boss man, seeing he was too comfortable being my employee. Therefore, I treated him just like a worker and less of a man.

During that time, we were getting settled in on Fieldstone Drive, but I wouldn't completely unpack because after we moved in, I realized it was roach infested. They were like all of the hidden secrets Brad had that eventually got exposed through the light, and I couldn't bare the sight of them. Desperately, I continued to look for another place.

Meanwhile, Brad younger brother Jacian had come to live with us. He was hot, young, a new face from Philly with a family inheritance, and let's not leave out horny, which had all the southern girls chasing after him. Moreover, it gave Brad extra leeway to run wild. Then blamed his fuckups on his brother until I caught him red-handed through his phone messages stating, "My sister and I enjoyed you and your brother lastnite... I hope it wasn't just a one-night stand."

After I had a mature phone conversation with the female and got all of the facts, of course, Brad and I had a physical fight, which left him with deep scratches all over his face like always. Then I went looking for Jacian. When I found him, he was looking dumb as fuck while I was cursing his ass out. Afterwards, I shouted, "Get yo shit out my house!"

Later on that night, I walked down the street from my house to Chase's, who was always flirtatious, but very respectful to me. When he opened his door and saw me full of tears, he held me while I confided in him. For hours I set and talked his head off, and he continued pouring me drink after drink. I kept guzzling them down like it was a cold glass of water, until I got drunk. Then I gave him a couple of lap dances, grinding and rubbing on his short but chunky dick. After kissing on his neck, and making him aroused, I wanted to go to a hotel and fuck the shit out of him for the hell of it. So, I went home and told Lavinniah to relay my message to Brad, "I'm out with Chase, and I'm going to fuck him tonight. I threw out the old, and now I'm horny for some new dick... Oh! By the way, he sure nuff got some competition in his pants. Mmmhmm! It felt soooo juicy. Don't expect me to come home tonight... Fuck you and your life!" I was slurring my words and staggering, but I was aware of everything I was doing and saying.

Chase and I rode around for a little, talked, laughed, but in between I cried. From a friend to a friend, Chase gave me some advice, "You're a pretty independent woman that don't need to take any shit from a man. With that being said, if he's fucking around like that, then leave his ass. There are plenty mo other men waiting in line! Don't be out here fucking niggas for payback... Do it because you want to." Chase was right! So, when we arrived at the Marriot, I decided not to go through with it. Not because he wasn't an attractive man, but because I wasn't sexually attracted to him, which would've been less pleasure for me, and more pleasure for him. Either way it went, I would've still lost that battle.

On our way back to Midway, Brad was calling and texting both Chase and my phone back-to-back, but we kept ignoring it and laughing at the dumbass shit he was sending, "That nigga only using you for some pussy. He be fucking everybody... Why y'all not answering? Y'all scared? I'm riding around looking for y'all now!" Blah! Blah! Blah! He sounded so wack. If he would've ran up on us, knowing he had no wins with Chase, it would've been even more embarrassing getting his ass kicked. Without any worries, Chase dropped me off at Melody's house.

The next evening after researching and talking to an old witch that lived on the outskirts of Rowan County, I had made me an appointment to go see her. When I got dropped off to my car, I ran in the house, and grabbed a pair of Brad's socks to use for the hex I was about to put on him. I wanted every step he took for him to walk directly into trouble. I didn't want the curse to end until his life was completely ruined. Oh! Now you know I didn't forget Jacian, but I only wanted his spell to be a few days of hell in order to give that immature motherfucker a rude awakening. They didn't know that the devil had my soul, and I was the wrong witch to fuck with.

When I drove damn near through the woods to get to the witch's old looking house, I felt at home. It was a dark and wicked place, and surrounded by many trees; it had a decaying roof overlaid with shingles and some outdated black drapes hanging down the windows. Her porch was cluttered with thorn like plants, and fluffy black cats with glowing eyes, which were a bit creepy. When I opened the squeaky screen door, a straw broom fell right in front of me, and I jumped as it caught me off guard.

Then the wrinkled old lady with long white hair and a black robe welcomed me in. On the inside was quiet, warm, and lit up with black candles. When I walked through the beaded curtains, I was in this secluded room with more lit candles, and a round table with a cauldron in the middle of it. We set across from each other with no expressions as I explained to her why and what I wanted. After we meditated to bring evil force, we cut and burned Brad's socks with both papers that had Brad Malik Hogan & Jacian Shurwood Parker on it. Following some lines that we kept repeating, "You are going to pay for what you did to me... There is no escaping it... evil will stand before you." After our session, the lady didn't want me to pay her. She predicted that I was one of them, and expressed how I did it all on my own. When I left, I was bewildered as I thought about what she said all the way home.

From that day on, things were drastic. Brad continuously got chased, caught, and locked up by the police. His criminal charges started adding up, bonds were getting higher, profit was getting spent, and I didn't bail him out until I felt like it. Then there was baby bro, who just paid a little over $6000 cash for a BMW, and he totaled it a day later. From the looks of the damages to the car, the guys should've been dead or badly hurt, but all four of them walked away with minor injuries. OMG! The spells were really working, and I was silently sitting back laughing at their asses while they were looking like lost puppies.

Thereafter, I found me a beautiful house located in a quiet area on Country Lane. I could've handled all the bills on my own, but I still needed Brad because he was an asset as well as my fall guy. Since he was unaware of my evil capabilities, we moved in as a phony happy family. Lavinniah also came along with us. After that, she told me that she was pregnant and was hoping for a little girl, so she could name her after Miracle if I didn't mind. Of course not; it actually uplifted me, and also touched my heart, knowing at that time, I was still grieving over her lost. Lavinniah didn't realize how much that meant to me... How much she meant to me. She wasn't just my little sister, she was also helping me nurture my kids while I ran the streets.

I trusted her with everything, knowing she had my back. I kept her under my wings, so she could get the feel of success; better yet, survival of the fittest meaning, "Do what you have to do to take care of home." And I did that. I remodeled the castle for the princesses with their canopies beds and royalty theme. I got them a wooden swing set, a pool, bikes, and the newest power wheel Barbie cars that kept them occupied in the backyard. Every top quality clothing, shoes, coats, and every new toy that came out, I blessed them with it. What was really priceless was the love and quality time I spent with them.

Moving all over Midway was definitely an unstable situation for us, but Country Lane was the best move by far. I was content with getting settled in my upscale home, driving my snazzy dark green Q45 Infiniti, and dressed in my classy Baby Phat clothing. I was progressively on another level where I no longer had to chase money; money increasingly followed me, which was indeed a come up from a street hustler to a distributor.

I had to give partial thanks to Barz for helping me get above average. Because our friendship was beyond business, I had a special way to express my appreciation to him. As soon as the house got established, I invited him over to bless my new red silky sheets. After we conducted business, I gradually started caressing his little aroused dick. Then the foreplay began on my black leather couch. As we passionately made it to my bedroom, which was defined by black glass, I watched his muscle bound ass make love to me with my legs highly flexible in the air. My loud groaning was from his pleasant movements slowly sliding through my waterfall. After we both reached our peak, we laid there with a brilliant smile, and a big relief. I also was hoping that Brad walked through the door and see this fine man pleasing his supposed to be woman, but Barz left before that could ever happened.

After sundown, Brad came home, and laid in all of my infidelities. Moreover, he was in the mood to give me some head, and I didn't think twice about spreading my legs. Although his tongue wasn't too experienced, he still pleasingly got the job done. Blithely, I laid there relaxed on my silky sheets, thinking about what happened earlier that day. I didn't at all feel any remorse because paybacks a BITCH, and Brad tasted it all that night without even knowing it. I know it's a saying that, "Two wrongs don't make a right," but that's absurd, especially when a motherfucker consistently doing you wrong. In my opinion, the only way to make it right is to make some mistakes as well.

Brad and I both made plenty of snafus, but the difference between me and him was he constantly got caught. Even if it wasn't exactly with his pants down, he still left pieces to the puzzle, which opened all gates from hell. That was the primary reason our relationship was based on more negative than positive behavior.

Speaking of behavior, I was a bad BITCH all the way around. My temper exploded easily, which was one of my biggest downfalls. It was about three months after our move when I unintentionally drove right into some trouble. I was on my way to Winston that day to re-up, but before I hit the highway, I had to stop and make a sell. As I was cruising through the hood in my rented black Chevrolet Camaro, I drove past one of my enemies name Beetle, who suddenly got the courage to throw her hands up in the air like she was ready to go a few rounds with me.

In a New York minute, I made a U-turn and pulled directly in front of her house. I rolled down the window and asked in a relaxed tone, "You have something you want to say to me BITCH?" She and her friend Birdee were looking like two pussies standing on her porch, popping off at the mouth. That's when I impulsively stepped out in the middle of the street and angrily hollered out, "I'll take both of you BITCHES down one-by-one if anyone of you have the heart to step to me!" Beetle slowly started walking down the steps, but instead of her meeting me in the street, she quickly grabbed my pocketbook and skedaddled her way in the house. Then locked the door behind her. I damn near banged it down as I was enraged, not about her taking my $60 in ones, which was chump change to me. It was the principle of how she did it.

Minutes later, the NARCS ambushed the block, and the first thing that came to my mind was, "These BITCHES just set me up!" Before I could walk back to the car, one of the police approached me. After the cops heard both sides of the story, they decided to search my car because Beetle had falsely stated that I pulled out a knife on them. I honestly told them, "I always carry a pocketknife, which is less than three inches long and is considered legal, but I never pulled it out on neither one of them pussy BITCHES." After I told the officers where it was exactly at, they then arrested me for disturbing the peace.

I couldn't figure out how the cops knew that my name was the only one on the rental car contract without me providing none of that information. While I waited in the police car, they explained to Brad, "Since you're not listed as a secondary person on the contract, you're not able to drive the car. Therefore, it will remain in our possession, but before we repo the car, we must follow proper procedures and search it." That was definitely some bullshit, and the whole ride to the jailhouse, I kept thinking like, "Damn! I got over $8000 in the glove department, and a few grams of work in there… That's going to be a huge lost, and also a drug charge all resulting from me not being able to control my anger towards BITCHES that were beneath me… BITCHES that envied me… BITCHES that wanted to be me but couldn't get close to my prosperity. But I give it to that BITCH… she hit me where it hurt, which was my pockets and my freedom, and I couldn't do anything about it, but blame myself, for I knew how the invidious streets worked."

After I got booked with a $7500 bond, another cop came and charged me with possession of crack cocaine and a drug paraphernalia, which raised my bond up to $15,000. I was expecting that, but I took it like a boss lady, kept quiet, and waited to be bailed out. Sitting in that holding cell had me disappointed in myself when that bigger picture had come to reality. - 3 ½ grams of crack + -$8000 + -$1500 + lawyer fees and fines, equals a huge set back. All of that for nothing. I didn't get a chance to demolish that BITCH, nor did I prove anything but my weakness to harm her by any means necessary. The bad part about it was I still didn't learn my lesson, and that incident didn't solve her problems at all. Actually, it made her matters worse because every time I saw Beetle, it was a different scenario.

There were times I'd chased her ass back to safety, tried to run that bug looking BITCH over if I saw her walking, mace her and a few of her family members in their mouths and eyes while passing her house, which caused her to go to the hospital as she damn near suffocated. In fact, I staked her house out plenty of nights, hoping I would catch her off guard. Then the BITCH took out a restraining order on me, knowing I wasn't going to stop until she felt the weight of all them 1000's I had lost.

Just because I couldn't reach out and touch that BITCH without violating the 50C order doesn't mean I couldn't stealthily use other sources. Eventually, I phoned one of my ruthless exterminators, who didn't mind getting his hands dirty for a reasonable price. After I explained to him the whole situation, he surprised me when he didn't take the job. Genuinely, he was looking out for my best interest instead of money in his pockets. He advisedly said, "Sexy, I would love to do the job for you. Yes, of course, that BITCH deserves it, but it's too soon. If something happens to her now... the fingers will point to you. In this sense, you need to stop thinking out of anger, fall back for a minute, and let nature take its course.... You dig?" No, I really didn't understand, especially when I despised a person and wanted them to suffer, but I listened since he had more experience than I did.

Although I was still walking the path of vengeance, I couldn't let that Beetle incident make me lose focus on what really mattered, which was getting that money. However, days of adversities kept coming my way. I don't know if the spell I put on Brad had an impact on my life since we lived together, or the jinx had reversed on me because a month later our house got burglarized, and they took over $10,000 in cash and product, which majority of it was mine. Seeing that our house was untouched, and our other valuables weren't taken, I knew it was an inside job. In fact, my primary suspect was Rusty, who was Lavinniah's soon to be baby father, and also Brad's pushover who he trusted a little too much. Conflictingly, I trusted no one. So, when Rusty came over my house, I didn't hesitate to beat him down with my wooden bat. Of course, Brad tried to stop it, but I was uncontrollable; and that's when the both of them quickly ran down the hill to Brad's car and peeled out. That was the last day Rusty came to my house.

Now let's fast forward; the truth eventually came out that Rusty was the mastermind of the break-in. He clandestinely had a grudge against Brad ever since he felt that he ripped him off a few years prior, but he didn't have the courage to confront him about it. Instead, he kept his enemy close, gained his trust, and waited on the right time to retaliate, which was quite clever. Conclusively, he hooked up with a couple of stickup kids fresh from LA that was broke as hell and needed a quick come up. Rusty then filled them in with the details, "I know this guy and his girl who got Midway on lockdown right now. They keep good work, and I know they're making money 'cause I be with the nigga every day. I know his every move; hell... I know exactly where he keeps his shit at, but there is only one problem, and that's not knowing if his crazy ass BITCH is going to be home. I think it's best to do it on the weekend 'cause no one hardly ever be there. In fact, we are going to a club Friday, so as soon as we hit the Ville, I'll send a text as a signal to go. I showed y'all where the house was at... You just have to go to the back, and it's the third window, which is the only one that doesn't have a curtain. There you would find everything inside the tank of the broken toilet."

After breaking the bathroom window, one of the guys went in, and he came out less than two minutes with a quick come up in their pockets, but not Rusty because they didn't give his pussy ass nothing. Did his dumbass actually think that was an even score by giving someone else the money when he really needed it? After I found out that information, I had already charged it to the game; besides, I knew it was that nigga, and that's why I disrespected every time and anywhere I saw him.

After the break-in, I felt an immediate sense of unease, which had me thinking that Midway was too small for me. Surely, it was time to relocate to another city. Before I could discuss any of this with Brad, our neighbor's door was getting knocked down by the cops. Actually, it was supposed to be ours, but the unknown informant had given the cops the wrong address. Obviously, the rat didn't get that reward money. That was a close call considering Brad was harboring a fugitive, which could've cost us everything if the snitch wouldn't have had that one number on our address wrong. I was done with that house! Within two days, I moved most of my stuff in storage. Whatever furniture, appliances, and outside equipment that couldn't fit, I left it. Then I moved in with my little sister Caylah until I found a place, and Brad moved in with his brother Jacian.

# CRAZY EIGHT

During my stay with Caylah, we decided to move to Kernersville together, then find a drug spot in Midway and build the Daevas Empire. Because of my continuance run-in with the law, I wanted to handle business a little differently. Therefore, I decided to pass the baton to Lacaylah, and stay out the spotlight. I knew Caylah would be the best candidate; I trusted her, she had no criminal background, she was a reflection of me, and was determined to get that money.

Lacaylah is Daevas number eight; she also is the last child mommy and daddy conceived together. Eight can be evenly divided, but in this case, "Crazy Eight" has more of a destructive than a constructive side after her innocence started deteriorating around the age of eight. Yet, no one knew about her anger or dishearten soul since her words were unspoken. Her silent cries were unheard, which gradually caused her faith in God to fade. Then her evil ways appeared unexpectedly. She no longer looked at mommy as an inspiration. She didn't even go to her for any affection or support. As she got older and wiser, she realized that mommy gave her all false hope. Therefrom, she looked up to some of us older sisters for motivation, which still led her to negative situations, but she also became fit to survive and well-polished so that she could shine. Still, she had such an anguish of supplication within her character, and her tone of voice.

Lacaylah Daevas was born February 18, 1984 with a resemblance of daddy's swarthy brown skin, svelte figure, and his egotistical personality along with a few other traits, but she wouldn't define her pretentiously twisted character until she started experimenting the streets in her early teens. Running down the block TRIAL Avenue, and making that left turn on <u>ERROR</u> Drive, is mistakes most teens tend to make. I could take partial blame for some of it because I was one of Caylah's role models. In actuality, she thought that following my poisonous footsteps was the right direction, and I didn't convince her otherwise.

Caylah was at the age that made her susceptible to develop one or some kind of dependency issue. Because of her impaired judgment, and no self-restraints, a virgin was no longer in her mind. The purity that was once between her legs had vanished. At that time, she started dating a guy name Clive, who was damn near 10 years older than her. Why? Just like a lot of adolescence, she needed security. Then there was an unexpected shift after Caylah became emotionally and physically attached to him. He spoiled her with many expensive gifts, and gave her plenty of money, which was his booby trap to lock her down. In fact, his manipulative actions really worked on my young and needy sister.

Thereafter, his bossy and jealous ways came wandering out of nowhere. Instead of him acting like her boyfriend, his old ass was trying to play the daddy role by telling her when, where, what, and how she was going to do something. That was unappealing to Caylah, and seconds away from having his baby didn't make things any better. As a controlling older sister, I had to intervene in her relationship, which gradually persuaded Caylah to break up with him a little after Abrianna Daevas was born.

Afterwards, Clive began pursuing Caylah aggressively. He consistently appeared or always knew her whereabouts. He constantly called and communicated threats, which instilled fear into her heart. He knew where and what she ate. When she used the bathroom, and how long she was asleep. He gave us the impression that he was obsessed over Caylah's every day actions. Hereinafter, the extreme dislike came amongst Clive and me because my intimidated sister felt defenseless, and I had to protect her. Of course, when the angry witch is provoked, she reacts in an evil way. Thereupon, I convinced Brad to rob Clive at gunpoint, rough his ass up, and make him feel defenseless like Caylah felt.

With ease, Brad did exactly that. He took a little over $5000, a few valuable weapons, and 5 ounces of cocaine while taking pleasure in punching and pimp smacking him up a little bit. That wasn't the only time I set Clive up to get robbed. In fact, just about every break-in he had after that incident was something I arranged because I wanted him to get the message through his thick ass skull that he couldn't fuck with us. From here, our actions elevated to another state of hostility. He envied Caylah and me so much that he cogitated and discussed with others about how thrilled he would be if we were six feet deep. Personally, he was a joke to me.

When his pussy ass drove past us, and shot his gun in the air, he was hoping that put fear in our hearts, but we laughed at him instead. Conflictingly, when we saw him on our terms, he was dodging bullets. It was always some confrontation when we were in each other's presence. Nothing ever got resolved, and we remained enemies.

Meanwhile, Caylah was learning how to adjust to the independent life, which was difficult considering the streets and parenthood was fresh to her. It was even harder without her fully completing secondary school, but she was just a reflection of us older sisters; and at that time, she wasn't worried about the consequences, feeling that there were many ways and means to survival. Therefore, Caylah was willing to find that niche.

Before I got her into deep with the hustle game, mommy moved to Greensboro NC, and Caylah thought it was best to move with her. That was a moment of transition for Caylah because she had the opportunity to become a model, which would put her in a different and positive spotlight than I was. That was something to be proud of.

After taking her modeling and acting classes, she was ready for lights, camera, and action! Her oval pretty face, long dark hair, and slim waist was progressing in the modeling industry until she came across another stumbling stone. She met a guy name Cain, who was searching for Mrs. Right, and Caylah unexpectedly walked through his path. After a few dates, and that one night of sexual congressing had led to Caylah's unwanted pregnancy. "How did this happen when he put on a condom?" Facts: Using condoms properly on a regular basis is

98% helpful in preventing pregnancies. With that being said, somebody made an error purposely or by accident.

Caylah felt overwhelmed and stressed because she knew her only choice was an abortion. For one, she barely knew Cain, and she was a little suspicious about his character and sneaky ways. Secondly, it was an obstruction to her modeling career that just started taking off. It became even more devastating when the process was prolonged a little too long until it was too late for her to get the abortion.

After baby Jordan was born, all hell broke loose when Caylah had broken up with Cain. Given that he was raised in an unduly protective family, they thought Caylah would not mirror their lifestyles without Cain around, and then the tug-of-war began. Caylah was young, underprivileged, and oblivious to the means of real life situations, such as someone wanting personal control over a life other than theirs. She didn't know that having a supportive family through the midst of her trials and tribulation would've been more beneficial for her. She couldn't understand why her past became relevant? Why all the lies and the false accusations were convincing? And why she was labeled as an unsuitable parent when Cain was nowhere near a saint? Under those circumstances, Caylah had lost that battle, then she became an entirely different person in mind, body, and soul.

Thereafter, she cried damn near every day, every holiday, and every birthday. Those were precious moments she had to share with a family who she despised and vice versa. She knew that getting back full control would be a long process, and not a guaranteed win; therefore, Caylah delayed her course of action until she feels the timing is right. Even though Caylah and Jordan share a special bond, there were plenty of other opportunities that was taken away from them, and that is the missing pieces in their hearts. As maturity sets, Jordan began to ask more questions, "WHY? How come mom...? Etc." Whatever Cain explanation is or was couldn't be close to the truth because he would never tell his child that he was the cause of their disjunction. Eventually, the lies would come back to haunt him and his family along with my curse for Jordan to bring them nothing but burdens and agony.

After all of that distress, Caylah and I started back collaborating on moving to Kernersville together. When I talked to my new friend, lover, and business connect Savion, less than a week, I was signing the lease for a huge house on Pondarosa Drive. Although Brad was helping me pay the bills, only Caylah and Savion had their own key to the house. At that point, I felt in my heart it was over between Brad and me, but it still wasn't the right time for us to completely breakup. Primarily because I still had mixed feelings, we shared a child together, and he was my main source of making my money. Truly, I thought by letting him go was giving up everything. Anyhow, things began to fall in place for me and Caylah after we found our drug spot in Midway.

We were surrounded by Mexicans, it was in the hood vicinity, and it had cheap rent, which was absolutely perfect for me. For one, the Mexicans were doing illegal shit just like we were, and that left no room for complaints. We all minded our own business, and we respected each other boundaries. Secondly, it was a good view of all traffic that was coming in or out. Lastly, it was quiet and somewhat in the woods, that's why we called it the "Honeycomb hideout".

I was feeling real lucky around that time, and I decided to surprise Caylah with her first car, which was a bluish red Chevrolet. It wasn't anything spectacular, but she was just as happy as she could be, especially since it made it easier for her to make her distant deliveries, and she no longer had to pay for rides to get from point A to B. When I was unavailable, Caylah was the chief that handled the coke, crack, and weed sales. On the other hand, Brad was mainly the crack dealer, but anytime I had a large varieties of products, he voluntarily helped me get rid of it for little to no pay. Then there was my little sister Lavinniah, who just couldn't get right, seeing she was more focused on boys that didn't care anything about her financial state as long as the pussy continued to chase the mouse.

As a concerned and avaricious sister, I felt we both could benefit from something, even when I knew her mentality was a little different from the rest of us. Since Lavinniah lacked the hustling and street capabilities, I started her off with some weed. Then gradually gave her a limited amount of crack and coke that was already bagged and priced tagged to make an even exchange with the customers. Overall, I was supplying them, while Lavinniah was keeping me maintained.

Aware that I was affluent, supportive and dependable, Shaylah had reached out to me and concernedly explained, "Ciara kept getting in trouble for fighting at school, so they kicked her out. I was hoping that she could come down south and stay with you until she graduates." Without no hesitation, I said, "Of course she can! I'll do anything for anyone of my nieces and nephews as long as they're willing to better themselves, and have respect for me, then they're good. It also would give me an opportunity to do a good deed as an aunt. At the same time, bond with my niece." It was nothing else to discuss after that.

Since I had my younger sisters out there selling, some of the family members thought I would turn Ciara into a drug dealer as well. What they failed to understand was that my sisters and I were already off track when we dropped out of school, had kids, and had to find a way to survive. On the other hand, Ciara was a 16-year-old virgin that was determined to finish school, but had minor obstacles that she couldn't avoid. Given this circumstance, she had to adapt to a different environment to focus on completing her education. Why would I want to ruin that? Everybody that spoke negative about me had the shut mouth after I got her enrolled in school, and when they saw that I treated her as if she was my own. I gave her guidance, words of wisdom, and I interacted with her through love, gave her hope and stability, which strengthened our bond.

When my other nieces came around, there was a passion of jealous rage towards Ciara over our bond we shared, which they thought was a distraction to their relationship with me. In fact, Mirah played a key role in convincing them that I was showing favoritism towards Ciara, which definitely wasn't the case; I loved my nieces equally. The main factor that stood before us was that southern kids live life at a slower pace than northern kids, especially if they had parents who were strict or marked by opposite extremes like Mirah. One minute it's right, and the next minute it's wrong. In this respect, it was limited things that I did with my other nieces because I didn't want them to pick up any bad habits on my watch. Plus, I didn't have time for drama.

Distinctively, Shaylah was more of a down to earth mom who was lenient in the disciplinary actions as long as her kids were respectful, and nothing wasn't interfering with school. Therefore, she didn't see a problem with clubbing and drinking with Ciara. Actually, I picked up where Shaylah left off, and Ciara loved every minute of it.

Seeing the fights and hearing my nieces argue had me reflecting back on how we used to be with our ongoing controversies, which made me aware that the curse duplicated itself. The children of evil had our vengeful ways, gave no impression of being remorseful, and didn't at all care about having unity as they were walking the trail of our poisonous footsteps. Those reasons stood in between them resolving their issues, but the number one rule when hanging out at the Honeycomb hideout was keeping the peace or staying away; we didn't need for the spot to get hot over bullshit. I also had a few other rules for the Honeycomb hideout: There was no stealing tolerated; whoever failed to comply would suffer consequences. Don't touch any of my product unless you were authorized to. Lastly, there was no outsiders allowed without my consent. If the rules were followed, it left no room for problems, simple as that. The Honeycomb hideout was supposed to be strictly a crack house, but I let little to no traffic come there. Primarily because Ciara had to stay there to attend this particular school for troubled kids, and I didn't want to put her too much in harm's way.

Subsequently, Ciara introduced me and Caylah to her friend Wyatt. He was damaged, unstable, and unloved by his family. I didn't give a fuck about his issues as my eyes immediately saw dollar signs. I figured I'd give Wyatt a place to stay, feed and clothed him, put fear in his heart, then mold him into a good runner/hustler. Moreover, have Ciara as my eyes and ears since they were together every day. However, Caylah felt differently. She thought because he was convertible that he could easily switch and bring us nothing but trouble. Advisedly, she suggested that I shouldn't add him to the team, but I followed my gut instincts, and everything was going smoothly until a few months later, I got that call from Ciara telling me it was a break in.

After a few minutes of inspecting, I knew it was an inside job. For one, there wasn't any force entry; therefore, it had to be someone who had access to get into the spot. Secondly, they only took nine ounces instead of the whole 18. A ½ pound of weed instead of the whole two pounds, and my daughter's mini, red, motor bike that I bought for her to ride on those dirt roads. I immediately suspected Wyatt; I really didn't know or trusted him to the fullest. With much anger, I brutally started smacking Wyatt's face, kneed him in the balls, and gave him a few body blows while he stood there and cried out, "Na 'Veah, I didn't do it… Ciara was with me the whole time! Why would I do something like that when you're taking good care of me?" I had to think on that because Ciara did vouch for him. Until then, he was restricted from eating, and he had to work without pay until I said otherwise. I warned him that if he tried to leave, then things would get much bloodier if I had to come find him. He had to understand that nothing is fair in the game.

A few weeks after, my purse with a couple of $100's and Caylah's gun got taken right from under our nose while we were drinking, laughing, and reminiscing at the Honeycomb hideout. It was really a difficult situation because I had to check everybody that was there, which was Ciara, Shyann, Wyatt, and wait a minute… where is Kian? He was nowhere to be found for hours. When he did suddenly appear, Caylah's gun was back in her trunk. Although my purse never got recovered, we saw thief written all over Kian's face. What really put his signature on it was when his simple ass placed the gun neatly on top of everything that we just had taken out the trunk numerous of times. Even with him being close family, we felt he definitely couldn't be trusted. Thereon, he was banned from the spot after we had Brad to come rough him up once again.

I saw that same look in his eyes that gave me conformation that Kian enjoyed living dangerously. Of course, some kids have to learn the hard way, but for some, they never do until it's too late. In my opinion, Kian was headed in that direction, but I didn't want him to keep walking towards that dead end. Still, it was nothing I could do when I did all I could to try and turn him in the opposite direction. At the end of the day, I'm not the one who has that final say so.

Taking that lost a few weeks earlier wasn't too much of a setback, especially when my boo thang Savion helped me bounce back. Then I shopped around at a few car auctions and eventually bought a cashmere beige metallic 1999 ES 300 Lexus for a little over $6000 cash, which suited my style perfectly. Then a week later, an elderly lady ran straight into me with her old Cadillac Eldorado. My whole driver side was smashed in. However, me, and Aaliyah, who was sitting in the passenger seat were okay. I could've look at it in a negative or positive way, but $5000 worth of car damage gave me the opportunity to get a special paint job, which was pretty beneficial to me.

I always wanted a lavender car because it's my favorite color. It was unique, and I knew it would stand out, which finalized my decision. So, I called my special friend up considering I needed a special deal. Then he introduced me to Drew out in Burlington, who promised that he would remodel my car exactly the way I wanted it. The finished job would be an acrylic lavender color, which would make it glossy. A car system that would send a vibration through your whole body. A lift kit so my 20 inch rims with the lavender inserts could properly fit, and my lightly tinted windows, so you can slightly see who I am. All of that for $5000 was indeed a special deal for me.

Bad luck struck at me again when I was on my way to Myrtle Beach to meet Savion and got lost. I was riding through some country dark roads with the speed limit going up and down like every minute. Surprisingly, I was headed in the right direction. I was still a little frustrated as I lit up my blunt to stimulate my mind. After one puff, I was looking at blue lights through my rearview mirror. "Damn! This shit is impossible!" As the cowboy hat wearing, hillbilly cop approached my car, the weed smoke blew directly in his face when I rolled my window down, which was a probable cause to search.

After finding the $5000 and an open container of Hard Mike, they hauled my ass downtown to Darlington, South Carolina's jailhouse where they found the $20 bag of weed that I stuffed in the back seat of their car. Resultantly, they kept all of my money, and charged me another $5000 for bail. Wow! A major lost and rip off all resulting from me going five miles over the speed limit. In all honesty, I felt like they were some prejudice motherfuckers that wanted to make an example out of another brown skinned color, and my cellmate confirmed that racism operated hard in that town. When the pigs gave me my one phone call, I got in touched with Melody, who went to get the money from Brad to post my bail. Thereafter, I was whining to Savion about the run-in I had with the law. Sure enough, he got me back on my feet once again.

That was the bond me and my two boss friends Savion and Barz had when it came to helping me financially. They loved the determination of my destiny, the courage I had for the hustle game, and of course my good, wet pussy. As long as I had them two men on my side along with my true hustler Brad, I was going to continue to prosper. While I was engaging in the trio luxury, my personification felt like a male because I was somewhat like a player. I was a liar, a cheater, sneaky, reckless, and charming while I was doing it. Veraciously, I was enjoying it.

Meanwhile, Caylah was picking up and using a little of my expertise on her new guy friend Josiah, who eventually became her boyfriend, soul mate, and partner in crime. A few years later, they had Jaden, then began building their own foundation. Caylah was quite happy, but she still seemed a little off track as she was uncertain about her obscure lifestyle. Every quandary she faced had pushed her further into the corrupted streets, which she thought was the answer to all of her questions, and I couldn't blame her.

I describe Caylah as conducive, but self-centered and erratic. Caylah was inseparable, dedicated, and effective when it came down to making that money to any extent, if it was convenient and beneficial to her. That part was quite understandable. On the other hand, Caylah had transitioned into the narcissistic phase of her life, and she was totally inconsistent with the reality of the social connection. For those reasons, Caylah thought the world revolved around her, and everything or everyone besides her kids were irrelevant. The bad part about it was she mostly expressed how unimportant we were when she was either mad, stressed out, or drowning in her sorrows.

Caylah also was unreliable and insincere when it came to one of us needing her during difficult times. For an example, my car had broken down about an hour away from home one night. It was pouring down raining, the thunder was roaring, and the lightning was frightening on that dark narrow road. I was very worried about my battery being low, and nobody wasn't answering their phones. Then, I finally got in touch with Caylah, who lied for hours about coming to pick me up, but she never did. Instead, one of my acquaintances from Midway came out her way to come get me. Getting upset was beside the point; I was more bothered that Caylah wasn't apologetic, nor thought that she was in the wrong. I know it wasn't her obligation, but from a sister's perspective, it should've been.

Another situation I thought Caylah took lightly was how she told fibs to the kids and put off that quality time with them as well. I believe every hustler does that through and out their hustling game; they are either too busy on the streets, or they're out partying. Still, there comes a time when you must learn how to separate the two, and Caylah didn't really know how to do that. I'm not saying she wasn't a good mother because she had good intentions. She supported her kids financially with all the expensive clothes, toys, etc.; she always expressed her love and devotion to them, but to me, she had a crazy way of showing it. For example, she would be busy all through the week doing whatever, but somehow found an excuse to postpone those special moments with the FAM or came home during witching hours, which canceled out all plans. Out of guilt, Caylah would give out many wishful promises. Although the kids were disappointed and hardly ever believed anything that came out of her mouth, she eventually made it happened. Yet, Caylah seemed blind to the fact that it had a negative impact on her kids regardless of the rebounds.

Caylah was also oblivious about her heading towards the path of destruction because she was illiberal, and on her high horse. That was around the time she picked up certain bad habits that brought out her devilish ways. She was recklessly putting other peoples' lives in jeopardy just to get her meaningless point across. Moreover, she felt like she was untouchable. Caylah was another feisty one that used obsessive force. She always wanted to be in control, and there was other personalities that played a huge role in her behavior as well. Her mouth was opinionated, especially when she disliked or wanted to hurt someone's feelings. She stayed in an argumentative tone, which most of the time it elevated to a fist, bottle, or gun fight. Furthermore, she hardly ever recalled why or how the riot started. She was very bossy towards and always belittled her man Josiah as well as other acquaintances, which caused a lot of undisclosed animosity against Caylah.

Being a replicate of me was the main excuse for her constant outbursts. To a certain extent, I do agree; I was extremely wild, I spazzed out, and I still do from time-to-time. But most of my controversies were to gain my respect from motherfuckers who were disrespectful, whereas Caylah's altercations resulted from her uncontrolled temper and anger that made her lash out on people for the hell of it. Ultimately, there comes a time when it's best to be mellow. You MUST learn how to separate yourself from immature situations, especially when you have a lot to lose, and plenty to gain. In a not so cocky way, you also should surround yourself around people on your level or above. Caylah's childish ways were difficult to overcome, and it became more challenging for her to grasp on to maturity, which comes with class, and class comes with status. Taking into account that Caylah and I had different statuses, distinctive mentalities, and dissimilar goals, it had left me no choice but to separate the business me from my big sister character until she got her shit back together.

Point to remember: Bad may seem good and make you feel powerful for a moment. In a course of time, bad can also cause you to be down for a lifetime because it's sinful. To overcome your sins, you must acknowledge, accept, and have willpower to defeat your wrongful ways. It might be challenging, and can be a persistent process, but anything's possible. Life is always what you make it. Moreover, you live and learn, but you can't really manage one without the other adequately.

With that being said, Caylah was stuck in her comprehension process, and reality had not yet hit her, but when it does, it's going to be an instant knockout. The only real that Caylah knew was herself. Well, I'm guessing everybody might feel that way about themselves, but what is the actual meaning of <u>real</u>? Real is the original person whose appearance looks and feels authentic rather than façade. A person who has credibility because they stay true to themselves as well as others. Adding to this, a person can't be real today and fake tomorrow. That shows inconsistency in their physical state of mind, which means that you're not 100% real. But you can't tell Caylah's arrogant ass that because "fake" to her is everybody else and their clothes.

Caylah's lack of respect, unsympathetic wrongdoings, and ignorant attitude, which reflected her selfishness would leave her oppressive and lonely. Caylah's priorities were off track, and her presence was no longer wanted, for we couldn't benefit from drama. She repeatedly made the atmosphere gloomy just because she was having a bad day, and didn't care about ruining everyone else's, which had severely damaged our relationship. In fact, Caylah and my BITCHY attitude, also, our pride wouldn't let us visit or express how much we loved and missed each other for a little over a year. It was tormenting during the times I needed her and vice versa, but being supportive and having empathy was no longer a part of our relationship or feelings. Honestly, our fallout was surprising since we bonded more than any of the sisters.

Life is too short, and there should be no excuse for sisters to be so distant, and bickering with each other for petty ass reasons. However, being in the Daevas family you must adapt to the: negativity, violence, greed, disconnection, and most of all vengeance. Surely, I had more peace without some of my sisters when I surrounded myself around love. Did I want it to be that way? Hell no! But sometimes you must face reality, and look at YOU as the bigger picture. Acknowledge what YOU did or didn't do wrong, then move on regardless of who's moving with YOU.

# FORCE MAJEURE

Besides not having a father, the separation between us sisters had made it harder for me to distance myself from Brad, seeing we were the opposite from my family. We had kept the <u>unity</u> regardless of what obstacles we faced, what anger we felt, or what bitterness we tasted; unification was our obligation to each other. It also made it easier for us to <u>revive</u> our relationship we once had. We spent weeks together without arguing, had many fulfilling conversations, and some moments of pleasure. Then the condom unknowingly bust out all of that contaminated sperm in me, and I was furious because I wasn't ready for the consequences.

A little over a week, I was lying in bed when I started feeling some intense pain in my lower abdomen. At first, I ignored it, but when I had to slowly get out the bed slumped over and barely could walk, I knew something was wrong. The pain was even different and unbearable. For those reasons, I went to the hospital.

A pregnancy test ruled out a miscarriage. The lab results eliminated some of the STD's, but the doctor still prescribed me some antibiotics as a precaution until the final results came back. 3 days later, I found out I had "The clap! It's an STI caused by the bacteria Neisseria gonorrhoeae, which is easily transmitted because most individuals are usually symptomless."

In spite of me occasionally sleeping with Savion safely without any mishaps, he was still a suspect after reading the facts. Sure as hell, I confronted both of them, and of course they denied all allegations. Coincidentally, I found a card from the health department with a scheduled appointment that happened a couple of weeks prior to my incident, and it had Brad's name written all over it. Out of all those years we had been together, he never got a checkup, but all of a sudden his fiery insides needed one. That truly didn't add up, and the dumbest motherfucker could've put two-and-two together. That's why I followed my intuition, and it led me to Brad where I lashed out on him, then exposed all of our dirty business to the public. Like a typical nigga, I expected him to try and reverse everything on me, but his deceitful eyes were not in disguise. I don't know who in the hell he was trying to convince, me or himself. The key point was it didn't matter, but my hatred block that I was building did.

After the flaming cooch experience, I definitely started looking at sex from a different perspective, especially when motherfuckers were melting through condoms. There was nothing or no one worth being easily exposed to life threatening situations. Therefore, my pussy was off limits, and I focused strictly on getting money, which is still a disease, but a fulfilling one minus antibiotics.

Around this time, Savion and my feelings were somewhat in too deep. So, he didn't take my celibacy very lightly. He started getting a little aggressive, demanding, and for his own arrogant reasons, he was putting a claim on my pussy. Thereon, the raping started. I had to put up a fight every time we dealt business, seeing he was always trying to get some pleasure. As a result of me resisting, he would get his goons to chase me down before I got in my car. They would tie me up with duct tape, ropes, or anything that prevented me from running, talking, or fighting back. Then they'll carry me into the master bedroom where he would damn near tear off all of my clothes.

After tangling and tussling, I realized I wasn't strong enough to get his muscular ass off of me; with anger, I would scream out, "Please! Could you at least put on a condom?" That was the only thing he respected me on, but my body felt totally disrespected afterwards. Yes, It was an illegal matter, but I didn't do anything about it because he was the best connect I had. Also, he was a very powerful man on the streets, which protected me from those shysters around the triad, but not from him. More importantly, he was a huge opportunity to continue progressing. By me disregarding the overall situation, I gave him the authority to continue to take advantage of me.

Getting raped by the man that was part of my retaliation towards Brad in the first place was definitely not in my plans, but I had to accept that bad endings come along with doing evil things. Still, I continued to do them. In fact, I had something else up my sleeve, which would unfold the truth about one of Brad's closest homey's, and I would reach the ultimate level of betrayal to prove it.

Sex wasn't going to be involved in the plot because I was using a different strategy that time around. In all honesty, I felt like Karriem was an undercover brother anyway seeing that he was very meticulous with his grooming. He had an annoying feminine laugh, was very homophobic, and fucked any and every BITCH that threw their pussy at him; to me, that was just a cover-up. Although it may be offensive to some, I always was straight up when I questioned a guy about their manhood. However, something was always telling me that Karriem never honestly answered.

Despite Karriem effeminate tendencies, I still buttered him up with my captivating words. Conversely, he responded with his deceitful but sexy eyes that revealed chemistry towards me, but griminess towards his friend. Without saying a word, Karriem had proven to me that he had a love-hate friendship with Brad, just like the rest of them. Yet, Brad was oblivious to the truth as it was hiding behind all of the idolizing they were giving.

Karriem <u>loved</u> that he hung around the popular Brad, so he could get a little attention himself. He also needed to be schooled on the crack game because he was the new kid on the block trying to hustle. Oh! We can't leave out the homey discount on the drug prices, or any other form of help when it came down to doing business with Brad. Those were the positive things about them being friends. Negatively, Karriem <u>hated</u> that he wasn't as productive or had as much potential as Brad with females or street wise. He despised that he wasn't able to gain popularity like him, and just knowing that he couldn't never be with Brad intimately had caused a lot of mixed feelings. That's where the jealous part of the friendship came in at, which made it easier for

Karriem to betray Brad. After a few days of communicating, without any hesitation, I convinced Karriem to break-in Jacian and Brad's apartment.

The day of the incident, Brad, Jacian, and Karriem were playing the Madden NFL game on the X-box. I was in Brad's room hiding my work inside one of his construction Timbs, and $2500 cash inside one of his black uptowns, then I unlocked the side window. In view of them being distracted by the game, I decided to buy an ounce of weed off of Jacian, knowing he would tell me to go get it myself, and he did. There it was, four pounds of weed, inside two separate shoe boxes, in the left corner of his closet covered up in some clothes. My plan was definitely intact as my slick ass walked out texting Karriem all the information.

Later on that night when Brad and Jacian returned home, the house was untouched, but all of the drugs and money were gone. When I got the call from Brad, I already knew what was going on as I rushed over there pretending to be mad about all the crack and coke that got taken, which was everything I fronted him. The stolen money was Brad's partial payment to me; therefore, his dumb ass was currently in debt and broke, which means worthless. I was getting a kick out of the overall situation. I had all of the stolen goods in the trunk of my car besides Jacian's weed, which was Karriem's compensation. The bad part about it was I didn't show any mercy, and Brad had to still pay off his debt he had with me, for that was strictly business. In actuality, I was getting paid twice, and I didn't give a fuck about him or Jacian struggle to get back on their feet, and neither did Karriem.

Then I tried to cause more problems by putting a little twist in my plot. I wanted to convince Brad and Jacian that Karriem sneaky ass had robbed them since he was the last person at their place that day. Plus, the apartment was untouched, which means the thief had to see where their stash was. But they believed that Karriem didn't have the courage and was too much of a good friend to do such a thing. I sort of expected that response from them clowns and left it alone; basically because I didn't like their asses anyway, and it was their lost instead of mine. In fact, Brad and Jacian never found their thief since Karriem continued coming around like he didn't do shit. He was smoking and selling Jacian weed back to him, and he continued buying work off of Brad after I fronted him the same work that supposedly got stolen. The after-effect from the break-in was they had to move out their apartment as their bills piled up.

Although I was destructive and mean, Jacian and Brad didn't have a clue that I was that vicious. But the image in the mirror was showing my new identity. As I stared at my reflection, I no longer saw the beautiful Na 'Veah. My flaming eyes were burning with evil, which left me visionless to good. My heart was no longer beating for love but kept experiencing the meaning of hate, and my brain was thoughtless as I no longer thought for others; I was thinking for myself. I learned to manipulate frenemies, destroy the unwanted, and still lived a somewhat happy life.

Like I stated earlier, evil actions eventually have an evil comeback because Karma slowly creeps up on the corrupted. Of course, she had to pay me another visit, which was at my place on Pondarosa Drive about a month after my dirty deed. I was surprised that night I was home alone sleeping comfortably in my bed when I woke up to three tall guys with ski-masks on, and some machine looking guns pointed at me. After they tied me up with some of my t-shirts, power punched me a few times because I wouldn't tell them where my stash was at, they got impatient and started searching every room themselves. Ultimately, I managed to get a loose, and I fearfully ran straight for the front door. Then I heard but didn't see one of the gun's cock back. In a deep demanding tone, one of the robbers said, "BITCH stop right there... Don't run! Don't run!" I was expecting to get shot in the back since I wasn't stopping for shit. I fleetly fled up the street with just my t-shirt and panties on. The bottom of my bare feet was aching from the force of impact to the ground. Yet, I didn't stop until one of my neighbors opened the door.

I ran three blocks up, banged on many doors before an older sympathetic man had slowly opened up his for me after he was on the phone with the police. That was bad business; I didn't want the cops involved with all that crack and coke I had stored in my house. I only wanted to get somewhere safe to call Savion or Brad for help. I guess having blood dripping from my face, a swollen left eye, and holding my side like I had a bruised rib was definitely means for some legal assistants. Instead of me communicating with the cops, I immediately headed back to my house, hoping I'd get there before the pigs arrived on the block since they didn't have my address.

As soon as I made it in my front yard, there were cops quickly coming from each direction of the block. By me being the only half-naked lady walking that night, I was easily spotted. When they jumped out, a few of the cops blurted, "Ma'am step back and let us go in first." Before I told one of the pigs that it was an attempted robbery, they were already searching my house like they had a search warrant. But I nipped that in the bud when I asked, "If y'all looking for intruders, why the hell are y'all searching through my draws, shoes, pocketbooks, etc.? You're not going to find nobody in there! Are y'all here to protect me or trying to get a raise? I'm good, their gone, so I no longer need y'all." After falsely answering a few of their bogus questions, they left.

That time, I didn't take a lost, but it was mind-boggling that I was under surveillance by the crooks and cops. I took heed to my exposure, but I stood up to the challenges. I wanted to be prosperous until my time expired. Brad knew he couldn't always protect me; for that cause, he bought me a 25-pearl pink and chrome pistol. Savion, on the other hand, had parked one of his cars in my driveway to let it be known that I was a part of his alliance, which meant I was off limits, and whoever violated would suffer serious consequences.

Meanwhile, I found me a sucker to chauffeur me around in Midway considering I didn't feel safe driving anything in my name while I was consistently getting harassed by the pigs. In other words, I was HOT, and Jelly-belly took a load off me. He called himself Big Romeo because he did anything for females. He was the type of guy that kept just enough money to buy off those hood rats in the projects, but he never got the satisfaction to intimately be with me. However, I was the treasure that he dreamed about, and fulfilled his obsession by being in his presence when he took me to make my drug runs.

I was a dominant woman, which had fatboy always trying to prove his masculinity, and it caused him to be reluctant at the wrong damn time. He was so naïve that he didn't know the difference between me being bossy, and me telling him to do something for his own good, which led us straight into a road block. Suddenly, the BITCHness came out of him as he cried out, "What am I supposed to do? I don't have license, and we... we both got work on us!" As I rolled my eyes in the back of my head in disbelief, I angrily said, "Nigga ain't nothing else to do but run through them motherfuckers. I told your dumbass not to come this way, but nah... You didn't want to listen, now look!" He got quiet and had the permanent shit face when he slowly pulled up to the Narcs, but didn't make a complete stop as he nervously tried to speed past them.

We didn't get very far. I guess his scared ass forgot how to put the pedal to the medal, or he mistaken the brakes for the gas as we came to a whiplash stop. I was pissed as I hollered out, "Nigga drive this motherfucker... At least so I can get rid of my shit! How da fuck you gonna stop right here?" His hands were shaking, and he wasn't acknowledging shit I said because we were still at a standstill. Therefore, I had no choice but to throw my coke out the window before the cops surrounded the car with guns.

Of course, they found the drugs, but at least it wasn't in my possession. Then they found drugs under the driver seat, and that's when they began harassing fatboy. I quietly stood there like the innocent passenger and listened to them put fear into his heart, "You're facing 15 to 20 years for this. You're throwing your life away for who... Noah? Roscoe? Liam? They're not going to worry about you when you go to prison. If you want us to help you, then you have to help us by telling me who you're working for!"

While eight to ten cops were over there traumatizing fatboy, one of the unfamiliar detectives came over to ask me my name. I softly said, "Na 'Veah Daevas." I didn't want the other cops to hear me since they knew a little about my background, but the detective couldn't understand me and wanted me to speak louder. Once the NARCS heard my last name, they quickly turned their heads, and shift their focus on me. "Daevas! Not again... How many 1000's you have in the glove department this time? Well, it looks like you would be headed downtown as well; the dope did come from your side," one of the detectives said with a big smile on his face! I responded cleverly, "Y'all weren't thinking about me at all until y'all heard my name... Now it's mine, right? Y'all being real subjective right now! I have nothing else to say, and I'll let my lawyer handle everything."

After they booked us, we set in separate interrogation rooms for hours. Then fatboy eventually signed a statement with my name written all over it. Still, I was innocent until proven guilty. It was a good thing that I had a well-paid lawyer because he got both of my drug charges consolidated. Subsequently, I had to take a plea bargain in order for the judge to drop one of them. I was very disappointed when I walked out of the superior courtroom as a convicted felon two years after. I got supervised probation, monthly drug tests, 72 hours of community service, and had to pay a few $1000's in fines. The luckiest part about it was that I could've went to prison; instead, I walked out a free woman, and I thank my lawyer Brice for that, especially when he didn't get paid in full. I guess my indecent exposure balanced out my payment, which still wasn't the price his other clients were paying that was facing lesser drug charges than I was. Now that's what I call VIP status (Very Important Person).

During this interval, I barely had any encouragement from my family. Some of them enjoyed seeing me discouraged. They couldn't wait to see the day I got trapped, thinking that was going to make me hit rock bottom. I know that sounds backwards, but that's how the Daevas's train of thoughts works. We bring our past to the future, which causes our life to be incomplete (6). We deceive each other, which make us imperfect (66). Also, we're egotistical, which brings out the power in the beast (666). That's why we are damaged, and our painful hearts will never heal because it's hard for us to change with the continuous flow of evil through our veins and souls.

Getting back on the subject of me, I couldn't let my troubles interfere with my progression. In fact, it became clear to me about why I shouldn't depend on just the drug life, which had got me in a receptive mindset. Unusually, I decided to focus more on a positive lifestyle, hoping for better outcomes. Primarily, I needed to further my education to strengthen my career opportunities, so I enrolled myself into Guildford Technical Community College, majoring in Business Administration. I chose that field because it was a reflection of my entrepreneurial personality.

Some people including a few in my family was puzzled and jealous that I continued to stand on my own two feet during and after my court case. But I had learned to overlook haters and continue to let my life be a riddle to them. That was a humble myself phase. It was a point in my life where I really felt like it was time for a change. Although I was taking baby steps, it still was a working process. Of course, I couldn't stop hustling at that time. It was my means of survival, but I tried to be conservative and tamed in every illegal move. I dreaded losing my freedom and my kids.

I couldn't expect everybody I dealt with on a business and family level to be in a transition phase like I was due to the different battles we faced, which brought about different approaches. You either grow from it, or slowly lose everything. With this in mind, the Honeycomb Hideout had shut down the day I walked into a demolished apartment. It was blood smeared on the walls, the kitchen and bathroom floors, and on the couch. There was broken glass through the entire place, kitchen chairs looked like they were thrown around, and nobody was there to explain to me what happened.

I rushed out of there quickly dialing numbers because my first thought was my niece had gotten hurt. Then I heard my name called, and when I looked up it was Wyatt sitting on the neighbor's steps terribly beaten. I almost didn't recognize him; both of his eyes were swollen and shut closed. His nose appeared to be broken, and his top and bottom lip looked like they were filled with helium. He seemed to be awfully weak, and he kept gasping for air while trying to tell me what happened. I barely understood him, being that he was talking like his mouth was wired.

After I interpret him saying Caylah and Melody had something to do with it, I was extremely shocked. But once the Mexican lady informed me that the police were on their way, I had to take my remorseful feelings with me, and get the hell up out of there. Before

I left, I quickly ran back in the apartment to make sure the spot was cleared from drugs and paraphernalia. As I casually drove out, the police were quickly driving in.

When I finally got in touched with Caylah, I blurted out in anger, "How the fuck y'all going to do that at the spot? Why y'all motherfuckers didn't take that shit somewhere else? The cops are down there right now, and from the looks of Wyatt, I know he's going to expose y'all... And I don't want my name nowhere in that shit. I'm shutting the spot down!" Caylah responded in her hyper voice, "Na 'Veah, you know I really didn't like that faggot motherfucker anyway. Then money kept getting stolen from the spot... Shiiit, after Melody's money got taken, I said fuck that! We have to teach that motherfucker a lesson... So, we got Melody's brother Dameer and Faybian to help us beat his ass down. His faggot ass put up a fight, but he couldn't for long after we were bashing him in the head with all types of bottles and shit... when he stopped moving, we all left. I hope that motherfucker don't give the police my name tho!"

Although I felt disrespected, I couldn't change the fact about what happened. Then I got the breaking news from Ciara that Wyatt was hospitalized. He had broken ribs that caused him to bleed internally, and Wyatt could've died if he wouldn't had seen a doctor in time. The cops wanted Wyatt to give up everyone who was responsible for his injuries. The charges were no longer assault and battery; it had changed to attempted murder to a minor. Hearing about this had them really scared because they'd thought he was 19. Turns out, Wyatt was only 16 years old, which would make the judge less lenient on their jail time. Moreover, the prosecutor can add-on a hate crime since Wyatt knew that they disliked him over his sexual preference.

Wyatt had their freedom in his hand, and In light of him being indecisive about whether he was going to turn them in or not, I had to pay him a one-on-one visit to clarify and hope to settle this whole situation. I didn't have any level of concern about what could've happened to Dameer and fat ass Faybian. I actually thought jumping a faggot was a pussy move anyway; plus, I disliked them. If Caylah and

Melody weren't involved, I would've told Wyatt to lock them up and throw away the key, but that wasn't the case.

First, I told Wyatt that Caylah and Melody apologized. They really didn't, but I thought it was a great way to start off the conversation. From his gestures, I could tell that he was still angry and unforgiven. Truth be told, I understood why, but I wasn't there to empathize with him. I just wanted him to know that if he pursued those charges, it would no longer be peace, and every day would be war; it was entirely up to him. I couldn't see the fear in his eyes because they were still swollen, but Wyatt never exposed their names, and no charges were ever filed.

Caylah and Melody dodged that bullet, but the heat got hotter on us when the cops found Caylah, Melody, and my pictures at the spot. They also found a scale, razors, and torn baggies in the outside trashcan with residue on it, which gave them a pretty good idea of what was going on at the Honeycomb Hideout. Still, they couldn't charge us; the apartment wasn't in any of our names, and we were gone during their search. However, we were put under investigation, particularly me since my name was already ringing bells with the cops. I was very pissed off at Melody, but mostly Caylah; I left her in charge, and she jeopardized my operation without thinking about the repercussions. That was the time Caylah and I separated as partners, but she continued to do and bring business to me. I had no hard feelings when it pertained money. Although I didn't have a plan B at that moment, I knew that Brad was somebody I could fall back on anytime, and I was good with that.

After that incident, I received more disturbing news. The owner owed back taxes on the house I was living in on Pondarosa Drive. Despite me paying my monthly rent, I still was forced to move out. Since I had signed a year lease, I could've took her to court for a breach of contract to receive some of my money back, but I didn't considering I couldn't stand the sight of a courtroom at that time. The BITCH was lucky that I left with no problems. Actually, I wanted to move because I needed to feel safe, but somehow I always got exposed to danger. I wanted to feel peace, but continued to be at war. My mentality, circumstances, and decisions revealed the reason for my repetitive outcome. Indeed, it was all due to me living wrong.

Before I completely moved off of Pondarosa Drive, Caylah and I had a night out in Raleigh. We walked in club Dynasty like we owned it; anticipated on splurging at the bar, but got all of our drinks for free, and of course, on the dance floor it was all about us. Then I spotted the envious Clive in a corner, watching our every move with an evil look. I wasn't feeling that, so I went over to confront the lame. We started arguing, using all sorts of hateful words towards each other. Thereafter, I punched him in the face. When his slow ass tried to swing back, Caylah and I started jumping him. Soon after, the security guards rushed over there, and they began forcing everybody out the club. At the same time, Caylah and I were popping shit and laughing about the overall situation as we walked to my car. Within seconds, Clive approached us, and we started fighting again. While we were fighting, Caylah took off one of her stilettos, then banged Clive in the head with it, leaving him leaking blood. Unhesitatingly, one of the security guards came and pepper sprayed his ass all in the eyes. It backfired on me and the security guard a little, which left our eyes burning and blurry. With caution, Caylah held my hand, and directed me out of harm's way.

Prior to us getting to my car, this oversized BITCH name Bridgette, who we knew for quite a while had got herself involved in the altercation when she tried to protect Clive. I was glad my eyes cleared up by then because as soon as I saw that grizzly bear swing on Caylah, I blanked. I got straight in front of Caylah, then me and the grizzly started going at it. Since Caylah could never sit back and watch any of her sisters' fight, she had to jump in to get a piece of it. With much pleasure, we kept taking turns pouncing on that BITCH until the cops came, and they attempted to pepper spray anybody that made one false move.

After the cops advised everybody to leave or suffer the consequences, Bridgette tried to be "Billy bad ass" and come for round two. We weren't fighting no longer than 30 seconds when one of the cops came and Taser that 9-milliliter barb through her big ass after he saw her come and approach me first. It was hilarious how she got an instant full-body muscle spasm, and I definitely didn't want none of that body trauma; therefore, I held my hands up, and got my ass in the car.

I was content with my win, so there was no need for retaliation. Conflictingly, Bridgette felt some type of way. I guess because Caylah and I made her realize that she was big for nothing. That had her anxious to prove to us that she was hard body. Besides, she didn't want her two cheerleaders that set in the car and watched her get her ass kicked have something to gossip about. Audaciously, the BITCH came to my house trying to get her face back, but she left that at the Dynasty Club parking lot. At the same time, Brad and his brother Gabe had pulled up in light of what happened, which he immediately dropped everything to come to my rescue.

While Brad and his Bro were standing between Bridgette and me, trying to calm us down, Bridgette tried to blurt out my intimate relationship I had with Savion. Yet, nobody but I understood her because at the same time, she was trying to keep the razor from falling out her mouth. You could tell that BITCH had no clue about what she was doing as the razor flew right in the grass. Then the subject switched on that fat BITCH trying to cut me. I had nothing more to say, but I did have something to do.

I quickly walked in the house and put a pan of grease on, then waited till it started popping. Afterwards, I went outside to cook those fat BITCHES. When I tossed it at them, they started screaming and running quickly to the car. I know that I was in my transition stage, but I get in beast mode when I feel threatened.

The next day, Bridgette car went up in flames, for the beast wanted her to burn in hell. It was just her lucky day that she wasn't in it, but I'm pretty sure she understood the message. The day after the combustion, a detective came to my house, asking a bunch of questions about me and Bridgette's altercation. I put on my innocent act as I explained in a sweet tone, "Sir, I have no problem with Bridgette to the extent where I would blow up her car; if the beef was that serious, I would've made sure she was in it. What happened the other night was a complete misunderstanding, and I have no quarrels with Bridgette. Y'all need to be investigating her... it sounds more like an insurance scam to me."

The detective response was, "Ms. Daevas, I'm just here doing my job. I actually believe that you're not responsible for this, but the only way to clear your name is to take a lie detector test." I agreed; I knew ways around passing that as well, which I did, and no charges were filed against me. Moreover, I had no more problems out of Bridgette.

Meantime, the kids had moved with Brad, and I continued to live on Pondarosa Drive for the last two months' rent free. After that, Savion and my alliance had completely formed. Our trust was equally earned, and then he welcomed me into his world. OMG! That nigga was like a drug lord. He had uncountable kilos of coke that took an entire day to cook up for his crack dealers. It had a very strong chemicals smell in my house that I had to cover up my face with a mask, or I would get high and dizzy off of it. He also had a few large hefty garbage bags filled with weed that was so strong even after he vacuum sealed it in some food saver bags. He kept singles, doubles, and triple stacks of Ecstasy in many different colors and designs for the pill poppers. Even If he didn't have or sold a certain drug, he definitely had a connect that did.

My house was like a pharmacy, if you needed a prescription filled or refilled, I had the medicine. Although I was an underling, Savion gave me the opportunity to get on that big boy status by letting me take the business trips with him to DC to get the same wholesale prices he was getting. He showed me how to turn 4 ½ ounces of coke to 9 ounces of crack, and if I ever fell short, he was always there to pick up the pieces. I was so glad to be a part of his team.

Resulting from Savion giving me open opportunity, profit motive, and wisdom to get ahead of the game, I was even more dominate. I used my power to clandestinely take over Midway and a few other cities if I wanted to. I was disliked by many of my competitors after I began supplying their customers, which was less money for them. That's when the guys actually became jealous of me, seeing I hustled better and smoother than they did. Ensuingly, my name was informed to the cops, hoping that would get me off the streets, but it didn't because I moved like a shadow. Then I heard from a reliable source that a few dudes were plotting on robbing me. Those BITCH ass niggas knew to come correct; I always stayed strapped with something. Furthermore, I had much respect on the streets, and many gangsters on my team that protected me.

It was easy and pleasurable in making the money, but it was tough living the drug life. Some people think that drug dealers are incompetent and too lazy to work. For some dealers that maybe true, but that wasn't my case. Many fortunate people don't know how it feels to not have anything, which gave me the urge to get something the best way I could. I thought about being a prostitute, but I had too much respect for myself. I could've robbed people blind, but that was more of a death trap. Therefore, I chose to hustle since I was a part of the streets; and once you're in, it's hard to get out, especially when you pick up other habits, or you face uncontrollable situations (Force majeure) that hinders you from getting out. Drug dealing was just like if not more than a 9 to 5 because we work just as hard. The difference is it's not taxed, which makes it illegal. Furthermore, it requires more time and effort to protect yourself from enemies, friends, and most of all family, which can be very difficult. Why judge me for trying to survive?

# WHAT IS MY ALTERNATIVES?
## TURNING POINT

# UNDERSTANDING CHOICES

At this point, I was triplicating my money, doing well in school, and temporarily moved in with Brad and the kids on Country Lane. It was a suburban area, so I was comfortable there. Because I was the devil's child, he always hovered over me, which kept me in a heated situation. That fiery moment was the night my niece Lilah and I were trying to bar hop in the Boro, even when we knew that we were pushing for time. After we arrived, I thought it was best to hang out at the Citgo gas station until the bars shut down since that was one of the after spots that stayed popping. While we were parked in front of the gas pump, smoking weed and getting drunk, people started to arrive. Within five minutes the parking lot got packed.

We had posted up on the hood of the car, chitchatting with mad niggas. Then an old rusty hoopty pulled up with about seven rowdy and really intoxicated BITCHES in it. They were hanging sloppy out the car windows and rapping along to the music, "Knuck if you buck" as they pulled up to pump some gas. When they realized that the pump couldn't reach the tank, they started popping off at the mouth instead of asking me politely to move my car back. Rudely, I ignored them and continued having my conversation. Then the driver came over to me and aggressively said, "BITCH you need to move your car back!" All I saw was her head rolling, and her mouth moving, but I didn't hear nothing she said as I blacked out. Then I punched her chunky ass straight in the face. She was dazed as she tried to grab me, but my jabs were too quick.

Then one of her friends tried to sneak up on me, so I shift the focus on bashing her face in. Hereinafter, the others started jumping me. I felt hits coming from every direction, my hair was getting pulled, and my shirt was getting torn. Still, I held on to and kept pounding on that one BITCH. They tried to force me to the ground, but my satanic legs wouldn't allow me to fall, and I was definitely in my violent mode.

It took a little over five minutes before Lilah got the courage to come help. "Get off my aunt!" She repeatedly said. Thereon, they started jumping her. Full of rage, I walked to the car, got the gun out of the trunk, and cocked it back while I was walking towards the enemies. That little voice in my head whispered to me, "Kill or they will destroy you!" My eyes saw nothing but blood as I aimed the gun at the crowd with my finger on the trigger. Before I got trigger happy, a young guy walked behind me and softly said in my ear, "You stood your ground... It's not worth it sexy!" He was right, I did have an alternative. Immediately, I came to my senses and put the safety back on. Then I went straight to the BITCH that was on top of Lilah, and I started pistol whipping her ass. The BITCH that was standing next to me, I pistol whipped her ass too. I didn't care if she didn't have anything to do with it, she was too close. "Everybody get the fuck back!" I said repeatedly while pointing the gun in every direction, which had people running scared.

After I cleared everybody from the parking lot, we were unable to leave because Lilah had lost my keys. Immediately, I called Brad to come get us. Before Brad arrived, a couple of cops pulled up to talk to the store owner. I just knew he was going to rat me out, but he didn't, and I was off the hook. I didn't care if I had to pay $100 to get the car towed; I walked away with my dignity and freedom. Moreover, I was that gangster BITCH that everybody in the Boro was talking about.

A few days later, my big surprise was parked in Brad's driveway when I pulled up. There it was, my lavender Lex, looking exquisite and jazzy. I was extremely satisfied with the feminine look, seeing it suited me and my girls. When I took my Princesses for a joy ride through town, they were all smiles. My reggae, and Remy Ma music had my car vibrating, rims were glistening, and the car was flashy. All heads were turning, jaws were dropping, and all the youngsters were pointing and screaming out, "Wow, that car is unique!" In fact, I was the first person in NC with a lavender Lex and the rims to match, which had all the surrounding boroughs vocalizing about me. They were wondering who I was, and what nigga I was rolling with. Savion definitely let it be known it was him. However, I was branding myself into a new me, a different style, and headed in another direction. Although I was unclear of where it was going to take me, I just had this clairvoyance that something was about to change.

Meanwhile, Brad and I were on good terms as partners in crime and as parents; relationship wise was a little iffy. I just couldn't find it in my heart to trust him, but I was too selfish to let anyone else have my cash cow, and that's why I continued to act like his girlfriend, even though Savion was more of my paramour.

Because Brad and I wasn't on that intimate level, I was curious about who was fulfilling his needs, and thought it was only right to look through his phone. First, I looked through his pics and saw some wore out looking pussy that a dirty butt had sent him (smdh). Then I went through his incoming, outgoing, and phonebook where I saw a few unknown names, and a couple of numbers that weren't stored. Lastly, I went through his text messages. In the middle of me doing that, a message popped up from an unknown number, saying, "You dirty dog, did you not think I would find out that you tried to holla at my sister? Fuck you Brad, and I hope Na 'Veah finds out everything!" I knew that deceptive prick couldn't keep his dick in his pants.

Of course, I was mad, so I started banging his face with the phone until he jumped up in defense mode. "Who the fuck is this BITCH? And what the fuck is she talking about?" He tried to look puzzled while he read the message, then he stupidly said, "Somebody playing a prank, but I don't know who number it is." That was too easy to find out, so I called Loco. Less than three minutes, he found out it was that BITCH Hedrika, who I confronted a few years prior, and she denied all accusations about her and Brad. She was definitely on the top of my hit list. I told that BITCH if I ever found out otherwise, she would most certainly see me again. Therefore, I continued calling her; her phone continued going to voicemail, and every message I left was a threatening one.

The next day, my cousin Brianna and I were chilling over Melody's house getting high as fuck. Then I got that devils call through Karmin saying, "Girrrl... Hedrika in front of my apartment popping mad shit! She said she was looking for you." I anxiously responded, "Oh really! Well, why the hell that BITCH didn't call me... She definitely got my number from last night! Stay there, I'm on my way!" I already knew my alternative when I had Melody's pregnant ass take me straight to Karmin's place.

As soon as Hedrika saw me pulling up, she started taking off her jewelry like she was getting ready to shoot the one. Before Melody put the car in park, I jumped out and fast walked straight to Hedrika in fight mode. Then that scarecrow quickly reached in her passenger side window and pulled out a big bat. I was thinking to myself, "Damn this BITCH got me!" But I saw the fear in her eyes as she sluggishly started swinging the bat, and I was dodging that shit with ease. 1, 2, 3 strikes you're out! Without delay, I started moving in on her, knowing I could take the bat. Her last swing, I blocked it with my left arm, then grabbed the bat with my right while she was falling to the ground, holding onto it for dear life. After that, Brianna came behind me and strong-armed the bat from both of us.

Then the tables had turned when Brianna started beating Hedrika ass with her own bat, and every swing had contact. I guess it was too brutal for her brother to watch as he struggled to take the bat from Brianna, and passed it to their cousin Stella. Without much hassle, I took it from Stella's pussy ass while Brianna and Hedrika were fighting. The mini riot had come to a halt when Hedrika's brother picked her up from the ground, and shield her retarded looking ass to the car. As she quickly drove off, I angrily swung the bat, hitting the trunk of her car. My intentions were to break the window, hoping the glass would splatter in her eyes, and cause her to go blind, so she could've drove straight into oncoming traffic, and had a fatal head-on-collision. Of course, that's evil thinking, but that was just the devil in me.

As soon as my adrenaline stopped rushing, I watched my left wrist instantly swell up. I automatically knew it came from that block considering it was the only hit that came in contact. I thought it was only a temporary bruise, so I went to the pharmacy to get an elastic bandage, and an ice pack that I used for a few days. Then a week had passed, and the condition was still the same. I dreaded going, but I eventually went to the hospital. I was informed that I had a Greenstick fractured wrist, and I had to wear a cast on my arm for six weeks. His words had deafened my ears, my heart started skipping beats, and my eyes had darkened as I had vicious thoughts about that BITCH Hedrika.

As I'm tuning in and out, I heard the doctor having a conversation about me outside my room door. Come to find out, it was a cop that wanted to question me about my incident. I grew up in the hood where we handled our own beef, and we didn't get the pigs involved. Therefore, I gave him no information about Hedrika. That was my battle to confront. Due to the cops knowing about the Daevas's warlike history, he tried to convince me that retaliation would lead to more trouble, and it was in my best interest to let the police handle it. That shit went into one ear and out the other because I had already let the witch back out the gate.

The first thing I did when I walked out the hospital was call Hedrika. "BITCH you would never be at peace until I torture your ass," I said with an evil pitch. She kept giving me the dial tone, but that flying animal knew that I was coming for her. Then I called Brad and yelled, "You joker looking motherfucker, you will get what's coming to you, and it will be a life full of grief." Before he could respond, I hung up.

I was a ball of fire, and my thoughts were all over the place. I couldn't sleep as I was impatiently waiting to retaliate. I consistently had ferocious dreams of brutalizing Hedrika with her own bat, and everyday Hedrika was in my conversations. Seeing that my cast was an impediment, Brianna decided to stick around until I got that BITCH.

While I was giving my wrist some time to heal, I decided to attack the easy target, and that was Brad because I saw him on a daily basis. I thought, "Why not poisoning his food." After a little research, I decided to try a poison that was used on dogs. First, I had to find a few wild mushrooms that I got out of the woods. Secondly, I soaked it in fingernail polish remover, and let it dry out for a few days before I crumbled it up. Then I mixed it in his grape soda, and passed it to Leah to take to him. I tried that for a little over a week; I also mixed the same ingredients with his food and alcohol, but I increased the dosages each time. When he started breaking out in cold sweats, vomiting, dehydrated, and had diarrhea, I thought it was working. Brad, on the other hand, thought he had the flu, and tried some home remedies like drinking the hot tea and soup that I had hog spit in; plus, he stayed on bed rest for about a week. I was a little angry that it didn't kill him, or at least gave him a serious health problem. Damn! He was a lucky dog.

There were many nights I woke up frustrated and enraged that I couldn't get even with Hedrika or Brad. On one of those angry nights, I stood at the edge of Brad's bed with his gun, and sized him up with it. Even though his loud annoying snore gave me even more of a reason to shoot him between the eyes, I couldn't pull the trigger. I don't know if it was relative to me not wanting Leah to grow up without a father like I did, or God was truly protecting this nigga as death kept passing him by. Brad had no clue how much I hated him; primarily because I stayed around. But if he only knew the destructive thoughts that kept wondering in my head, he would've been preparing for the worst.

Although my kids brought out the best in me, my nieces had some effect as well, but I had been neglecting them for a couple of weeks because I was angrily plotting. Thinking of which, I decided to take my kids, nieces, and Wyatt out to Hibachi Grill. Everybody was exuberant as they went back-n-forth to the buffet. While having desert, Hedrika had pulled up to get her nephew Bug, who worked there. Yeah, I knew all of that, but what I didn't know was the time Hedrika comes to pick him up. Without any hesitation, I jumped up, ran out the door, and Wyatt was right behind me.

Out of fear, Hedrika had desperately drove off, and Wyatt ran like a track runner as he chased the car down. The fact that she was at a stop sign on a busy street, her reaction was to back up and pretend she was going to run him over, then she quickly turned out on the main road.

What a smart BITCH! When we went back into the restaurant to finish eating, all eyes were on us, and the kids were in a state of shock. I still had that slow burn, but I played my anger off at the table in order to make my kids feel comfortable.

When we left Hibachi Grill, I saw Hedrika car parked at Circle K's gas station. Impetuously, I pulled behind it to block her in. I went to my trunk, got the bat, and leaned against my car until she came out. Bug was the first person to walk out the store, and he was on the phone talking to the police, "She has our car blocked in, children in her car, and she has a bat... Blah! Blah! Blah!" I didn't care about that shit, I had a little time to get Hedrika before the cops came. Then Bug tried to play captain save a Hoe when he picked up a big stick and stood in front of Hedrika. Thereafter, Hedrika's aunt Jezebel had got out the backseat of the car trying to pop off. I laughed and said, "I don't give a fuck about your mouth, I'll leave that to all the dicks you suck... All I want is Hedrika!"

The kids were terrified, crying, and yelling out, "Come on mommy/ Auntie please!" By then the cops arrived, and that's when Hedrika finally opened her mouth, which only was to give her statement to one of the pigs. Then the same police that was at the hospital questioning me a couple of weeks prior had come over to me awfully mad. He confiscated the bat, and then told me to leave before he lock me up. A few days after, the cops came to Lateesah's place trying to serve me a 50b that Hedrika took out on me. I didn't live there, so I never got served, meaning I could still get that BITCH.

The whole town knew I wanted revenge, and people were eager to see what was going to happen. I started receiving all types of calls from random people that I didn't even communicate with. In fact, I was wondering how the hell they got my number. Anyway, they were only informing me about Hedrika's whereabouts. By all means, I wanted her badly, but I had to do it attentively if I wanted to fuck her up to where I had a peace of mind. Therefore, I was focus on getting her on my time. When I finally got my temper under control, I incidentally ran into Hedrika, and right then I knew that was my opportunity to attack.

There was no other <u>alternative</u>, no second-guessing, and I felt no pity… that BITCH had to get it!

Owing to the darkness, Hedrika was unaware that I followed her all the way to club Ziggy's in Winston. Since the parking lot was packed, I had to park three cars down from her, and then I noticed she had three other slut bags with her. I was at ease because La-La was in the car with me. Graciously, I gave her some money to enjoy herself at the club, and also keep Hedrika occupied while I went to pick up Caylah and Brianna.

I wasn't gone no longer than 30 minutes, and the BITCH had left; on the bright side, La-La had convinced Hedrika to come to the liquor house in Kernersville, thinking she was going to meet-up with this baller name Tristian. He was just a decoy to make that BITCH feel comfortable. Anyhow, we all anxiously headed to the Ville to get this settled once and for all. Knowing that La-La lived two houses down from Tristan, I parked my car four blocks up the street in someone else's driveway in order for it to remain unseen.

La-La had three athletic boys with a collection of bats, and I chose the smedium wooden one, seeing that it was manageable using only one arm. My adrenaline started rushing, and I was ready to give that BITCH the concussion I've been dreaming about for a little over a month. As we walked to Tristian's place, everybody was happy go lucky, but I had a straight face because that reprisal was serious to me. Although that was Tristian's place of business, he didn't care if I was armed since he was digging me. While Caylah, Brianna, and La-La were chilling in the back, sipping and talking loudly about their plans on jumping in, I fiercely waited in the front dimmed room for that BITCH as I was content with what I had planned to do.

The guys that were sitting on the porch knew I was waiting on a Red Ford Escort, so they informed me when the car had passed. My blood was sizzling, and my heart was racing, for that time had come. Immediately after Hedrika and Stella came sashaying their thirst bucket asses through the door, I jumped off that couch and bashed Hedrika head in with the bat. Her eyes rolled in the back of her head as she fell down in slow motion. I didn't care if the BITCH was unconscious or not, my one arm repetitiously swung destructive and viciously. In fact, I didn't want to stop beating her until the BITCH stopped moving.

After five to seven minutes of whoop ass, the four men managed to stop me. Then Hedrika staggered out the door, looking dazed and walking lopsided because her shoulder blade was out of place. Damn! Where her cousin Stella go? That wilderbeast needed to get it too, but she ran out as soon as she saw Hedrika get molly whopped in the head. Now, what type of cousin was that? Oh! I forget, she did call the police, which is what scary BITCHES do.

When the cops did arrive, Tristian told them, "A fight had broken out with her and another female who is no longer here." Off the rip, Hedrika started snitching, "You protecting that BITCH... Sir, this is a liquor house, and they sale drugs out of there... Oh! Tell that BITCH I was fucking her man!" Tristian immediately walked off and left that injured BITCH talking to the cops. After Hedrika and the pigs left, we had a vengeance celebration, and we partied until daybreak. The liquor house got shutdown after the BITCH revealed its identity.

Through and out my life, trouble consistently followed me, but my evil response was always fulfilling to my body because I would not let my obstacles defeat me. I felt like a conqueror, and that's why I needed to stay on the right path regardless of what flaws I had. Meanwhile, I was in the middle of everybody's gossip in Midway. Some people gave me much respect for my comeback, while others were jealous that I got the opportunity to retaliate. Whatever the case was, I didn't care as long as nobody fucked with me. I kept my head up high and had those watchful eyes. I smiled with the haters who thought I was unaware that they disliked me. I had conversations with the jealous group purposely sounding cocky. So, when I did walk away, they could have more bad things to say about me, and I liked it, seeing that they couldn't get where I was going.

My life was like an elevator, always going up and down because a few days later, I moved into a spacious three-bedroom house on the West end of Winston Salem, which was a breakthrough for me. I settled in ASAP, but continued to drive back-n-forth to Midway every morning to see the kids off to school since I didn't want to transfer them until the semester was over. The more I hung out at Brad's place, I started observing him break a few of the ten crack commandments, which was a big mistake.

Rule #3, "Never trust no-bo-dy!" But Brad had a different outlook; he didn't understand that every street boy wasn't his homeboy. He was getting comfortable, and revealed too much information, business and personal wise, without thinking about the consequences behind his stupidity. He also broke rule #5, "Never sell crack where you rest at!" Now Brad and I had been in the drug game too long for him to keep making dumbass mistakes like bringing his street life home. I was highly upset when I walked in his place and saw one of his fiends standing in his kitchen, waiting on him to finish cooking up the coke. After he served her a quarter of crack, I saw the guilt in her eyes as she walked out. Right then, I felt something was wrong, but considering we were dealing with her for over five years, I thought I was just paranoid.

On the third morning, I had arrived a little early at Brad's place to take the kids to school. While they were getting ready, I dozed off on the couch. Minutes later, the police kicked the door in with a search warrant. When they placed me and Brad in handcuffs, they told the kids to come sit next to us on the living room couch while they ransacked the house. Once the police found a few ounces of coke, crack, weed, a scale with residue, and drug paraphernalia in the kitchen cabinet, Brad expression on his face showed that he got hit with reality.

My heart started skipping beats, and my under arms were tingling as I was nervous about them finding the kilo of coke that I had stashed up in the kids closet. It was just my luck that they discontinued the search because they were content with the large amount of drugs that they already confiscated. Before they hauled us downtown, Brad had to call Karriem to come pick up Aaliyah and Leah. While they were taking me and Brad to separate unmarked police cars, the kids started crying and screaming out, "Mommy! Mommy! Please don't leave me." My heart was aching; I wanted to hold and console my kids, and tell them that everything was going to be alright, but my mouth couldn't find the right words to say, not knowing what the outcome was going to be. Wistfully, I just told them, "I love y'all" as Karriem drove them away.

I couldn't hold my tears back. I was feeling like I failed as a mother and could no longer keep them safe being in jail, which could expose them to all types of troublesome situations. Then I had a flashback of how mommy wasn't there to protect me when I was going through my afflictions. Sadly, I thought about my kids the whole time we were riding to the police station. When we arrived, the pigs took us into separate interrogation rooms instead of the magistrate office for our bond.

They sent the more aggressive cop in the room with me, thinking he would scare me up by threatening to take my kids away. My response was, "I don't care what y'all think Brad do as long as he's taking care of home… Besides, I don't live there, so how can y'all take my kids from me?" I didn't fold, or show any signs of fear. In fact, I already knew that Brad was going to own up to the charges anyway.

Afterwards, the other pig came and told us that Brad had already confessed to everything. I smiled with a big relief on my face, knowing they had no choice but to release me. Then they laid a written statement in front of me, stating it was Brad's drugs, and they wanted my signature. I knew I didn't have to sign shit, but it was hard evidence to send Brad away for a few years, which gave me the pleasure in signing it. Right after, I felt I had evened the score with that dog of a baby father.

While I'm walking out the jailhouse, Brad surprisingly come strutting his ass right behind me. That was untypical, so I wanted to know what type of agreement he made with the pigs. As he deviously explained, "They want me to snitch, or imma be doing ten years or better in prison. I'm not trying to be gone that long, so I agreed. Here's the thing, I have to bust somebody with more dope than they charged me with, which had me thinking… I'm going to buy 4 ½ ounces of crack, and plant it underneath Pablo's car the night before I attempt to buy some work off him… What you think?" I told him to do what he had to do. In all honesty, I was thinking that prison sounded just fine to me. Therefore, I interfered in his scheme by removing the drugs he planted. Brad was devastated when his plot wasn't accomplished, and that's when he became desperate. Under those circumstance, he had to choose between his freedom and busting his friends. Of course, a few of his street buddies were the decision, but their bum asses weren't holding enough weight to get Brad off the hook. Quickly, he had to take another route as his time was winding up.

He then started collaborating with a few of his adversaries in rap battles, hoping that would open the doors to make a few drug bust. After Brad and Ryder got on a track with each other, everybody was feeling the Northern and Southern combination. Subsequently, Brad and Ryder decided to throw a release party at club Candlelights, which would include other rappers from Midway, freestyling competitions, and other performances. I felt this was a great opportunity to inflame the party.

The jam-packed party definitely was a success, but I decided to let the dirtballs enjoy themselves before I let my devilish ways take action. During the freestyle battles, I decided to pass the word around that Brad was working with the pigs, and he was going to snitch on some of them niggas. Right after, Brad and his peeps went on stage to perform. Of course, my grimy ass, and Caylah were up there representing, while other niggas were screw facing them.

Immediately after we stepped off the stage, the lights shut off, and I headed straight towards that lit up exit sign to get the hell out of harm's way. I barely could see, but I heard screaming and a lot of bottles breaking. While I'm standing against the wall, having pleasure in hearing the pain in people's voices, I rubbed against the light switch and immediately turned it on. There was Caylah, on top of the bar, busting bottles over the niggas heads that was jumping Brad. I was pissed that I had to get involved after I saw some guy aggressively give Caylah a few body shots. I then picked up a chair and bashed him over his back, which caused him to fall to his knees. Suddenly, we heard different types of gunshots outside the club like we were in the Vietnam War. With full Force, I grabbed Caylah, and we ran into the loud crowded bathroom where BITCHES were bloody from falling on broken bottles or from the impact of the chairs that were wildly thrown.

I was feeling a little claustrophobic, so Caylah and I left out. As soon as we walked outside, there were countless cops in bullet proof vests with M16 assault rifles, some had shields and ballistic helmets for protection. Any civilian that was on foot had to slowly walk to their cars with their hands up, or get shot; those cops weren't taking any chances at all. Then we saw Brad's Cadillac speed pass, and out of nowhere, some guy with all black on started running towards Brad's car shooting at it. Of course, shots were fired back from the passenger side window, but the outcome wasn't a good sight when the cops opened fire on Brad's car as it slowly came to a halt. Also, they shot the unknown guy numerous times until he fell to the ground unresponsive.

At the time we arrived at the hospital, I thought I had to go view Brad's body, but the bullet had just grazed his head, leaving him unconscious. "That's it?" I said disappointingly, but nothing was more discouraging than his right hand man losing his life and seeing his family mourn. They say that gangster living leads to gangster endings, which majority of the time its death; still, no one wants to see a loved one leave too soon. Come to find out, the unknown shooter was someone who had beef with Brad from the past.

After a few x-rays, implants, and a few stitches on the side of Brad's head, he was released from the hospital. Then I had to play the supportive girlfriend role until I took his ass home and started back treating him like shit. Thereafter, all the nosy people came to visit Brad, claiming they were concerned. I would listen to what they had to say, but still refused their visitation, and rudely slammed the door in their faces. Of course, they were mad; did I care? Hell no! The Bottom line was the controversy amongst a group of guys in a little ass town had made it unclear if a person was advocating for the North or South. For that reason, the phonies were not welcome.

After the beef calmed down, Brad's second year of continuing his court date had come to an end. Because Brad couldn't give the cops a big bust, he had to pay his lawyer a little over $30,000 to get his time cut in half. However, Brad had to turn himself in within 24 hours, or the three to five-year deal was off.

Before Brad left, he set the kids down to explain that he was going to be gone for a few years. The instant sad looks in their eyes were disheartening, especially when Leah said in tears, "You not going to be here for our birthdays, X-mas, or eat with us for Thanksgiving?"

Brad responded with tears rolling down his face, "Not for a few years... Daddy sorry, but I'll make it up to y'all, I promise." During their long group hug, they all were crying, and holding each other tightly like they didn't want to let go.

At first, I thought if Brad was out of my life, it would give me a piece of mind, but it was no longer about me when I saw my kids hurting. I felt a little guilty in behalf of it being partially my fault that they were caught in the middle of the crossfire. Unfortunately, I still lost, for my kids' happiness was more important than mine. I went to court with Brad the next morning to send him off. It was somewhat depressing, knowing that my partner in crime was gone, but I felt at ease. I no longer had to wonder about Brad anymore. My aching heart was healed, and I was able to breathe again. Yes, I shed a few goodbye tears because I knew it was over between us.

As I was leaving the courthouse, I received a call from a guy named Uziah, who I had met four months prior to his basic training for the Army. He determinedly said before he left, "I'm coming back for you when I get home." I wasn't impressed with his pickup line, but he was a man of his word. Uziah wasn't the typical guy I dated since he had a legitimate career, family oriented, conservative, but was a little thuggish. So, I figured I would give him a try; after all, different is good. Actually, it could be a turning point in my life.

The little time I hung around him, his character came off a little lamish, but his conversations and charisma had an effect on my connection with him. I wasn't looking for a relationship, but he was still a good candidate for a party buddy, and a homeboy that could keep me company when I'm bored or lonely. On the contrary, Uziah was hoping for a commitment, which had me scared and a little confused. I didn't know whether to run as fast as I could, or face my fears like a woman.

In behalf of me being a woman scorned, I kept my guards up to avoid getting hurt again. With this in mind, I decided to take me and Uziah friendship slowly. I didn't want to rush into something too serious at that time, especially when I knew it would take a strong man to handle a complicated woman like me. From this perspective, leaving my options open was a smart thing to do. I took advantage of living the single life and enjoyed every minute of it. Moreover, enjoyed every moment of me, for I wasn't deep in my feelings, I didn't let any of my men friends be a distraction, and I was living my life fully to my satisfaction.

Each guy served me a different purpose, gave me a golden smile, and an electrifying feeling every time I was in their presence, especially my friend Lateef, who was the best at performing cunnilingus- meaning the art of orally making sweet love to the vagina, which he did after he freakishly tore off my clothes. Ensuingly, he'd began with his gentle kisses slowly going down my body until he reached my pussy with his soft wet lips. Then delicately played with my clitoris with his tongue ring, which had me stimulated and sloppy wet. As he went back and forth sucking and playing with my labia minora and my clitoris, I erotically rubbed his balled head. After he started grazing his teeth on my butt cheeks and made sweet love to my asshole, I began to loudly moan, and tears gradually fell from my eyes as I reached my peak. Thereon, he'll hold me all through the night while we listened to Jamie Foxx.

Then there was my boy Logan, who was my nipple sucker, pussy eater from time-to-time, but most of all he was a true friend. He was compassionate, kind, comforting, and always gave me a helping hand. Still, I didn't have an intimate connection, but I led him on like it was a chance between us when I knew it could never be. Surely, that was wrong, but at that time, I was too narcissistic to let him go in the interest of him having something to offer me. We never got on that relationship level, but our buddy-buddy bond was always there.

Thirdly, was small dick Barz, who gave me some superb loving every time. With him, it wasn't about the size of the boat, it was about the motion in the ocean, and I rode that wave every time. Barz was also a homey who I connected with on that Rap tip, he was always encouraging, and someone who was supportive through my comfort and my displeasures. Being that BITCH who most men got along with, helped us build a bond that not even his girlfriend could break. Moreover, the attraction in his eyes were hard for him to hide because we had that phenomenal love.

Then there was big dick Savion, who was gifted with his penis size, but not with the sex. However, his money, power, and respect had made him too arrogant to understand that it wasn't about the length he had in his pants, for it was more about what he had in his pockets that allured the women, and I was one of them. I would never have looked at Savion if I didn't know his lucrative background, but I was delighted that we crossed paths. Despite the motive for my actions, Savion and I had a sincere friendship, comparable characteristics, and developed deep feelings for each other. I also was digging Savion black mafia life as it gave me assurance and security. Moreover, people feared him or got dealt with, and that dominant shit was exactly what I needed.

My fourth guy was Brad the jailbird that was stressing me about our relationship every time he got that ten-minute phone call, but I would send him back to his cell with a broken heart along with crazy thoughts about the next guy laying in my bed; a man that treated me better than he did, and the worst of it all, a man that was spending quality time with his kids. I didn't care about his BITCH ass cries, his played out "Forgive ME's," and his desire to continue our relationship. I always asked him, "What do you have to offer me in jail?" I answered it for him, "Nothing! Exactly my point." But it wasn't seeking through Brad's thick skull that I no longer wanted him, and that our ten years were nothing but history to me because I was ready to move on.

Facts: "A SHIP is arranged to take me places if I get on board. So, if my relationship isn't going anywhere, then it's time to abandon SHIP!"

In and out of prison I knew Brad would never forget me after realizing I was the best he ever had, and the only thing I wanted in return was to feel appreciated instead of neglected, which he couldn't do. That was his fuckup when the next man did, which was Uziah, who was gradually winning me over. I loved how he held my hand while we walked through the mall unhurried with vibrant smiles on our faces. How he took me to his family events, and most of all, he gave me his undivided attention. Actually, he was too good to be true, which had me nervous about where our friendship was headed. I didn't know if it was God's plan, or the devil's plot for another disaster. Since I was 80% evil and 20% spiritual, I was convinced that evil would be the outcome.

Being around Uziah was something unique, but my eyes were useless if my mind kept negative thoughts. Therefore, it was hard to see that I wasn't completely tarnished. Sometimes it takes another person to bring the good out of you, guide you through your darkest path, and open your eyes to reality to show that it's never too late to change. Uziah did that, which had a different effect on my life because I was getting more positive feedback and was learning how to become a better person.

I didn't do a complete 360 considering I was still in the drug business. Despite Uziah wanting me to stop hustling completely since he was supporting me financially, I couldn't for the sake of my independency. I had to keep my own income flowing, but my thug life was gradually fading away as I was constantly in a positive environment dealing with Uziah.

On the days I was away from Uziah, I was back to the norm. I needed to re-up to recover from the days I took off. I didn't want to deal with Savion; I was fed up with his consistent violations, but what was the utmost disrespect and final straw of any sexual activities was the day he raped me in my ass. I would never forget that painful night when he came to my house, and I honestly told him, "Uziah and I are getting a little serious, and I can't deal with you on an intimate level like that anymore!" Savion had that bizarre look while he pushed me roughly on my bed, and said in his Mike Tyson voice, "You really going to give that lame nigga a chance, and I knew you way before him, I got something for that ass!"

Then we tussled until he got me face down on my hardwood cold floor. When he put his body weight on me, he aggressively started taking my pants down. That instant, I started screaming, hoping Shaylah would come into my room, but she didn't until she heard my tone of voice change. While Shaylah fighting Savion off, I was laying there damn near paralyzed and badly bleeding from the rectum, which never healed correctly. I was hurt physically and mentally, angry, traumatized, and lost all respect for someone I looked up to. Every thought of him disgusted me. Any type of feelings or attraction were gone. I ignored his calls, and I didn't want to see his black ass face from that day forward.

Getting back to the point of needing to re-up, which was difficult that winter to find coke, crack, weed, or any type of drug because it was a drought. Then Drew, who Brad and I were dealing with for a few years prior was the only person who came across some coke at that time. Of course, his prices were extremely high, but I expected that during a dry spell. Therefore, I didn't mind buying a kilo for $30,000, knowing I was going to triplicate my money anyway. After Drew left, I went straight in the kitchen to cook up the work. Before I whipped up a large quantity, I started off with an ounce first. Everything but an eight ball evaporated in the Pyrex pot. The texture of the crack was gooey and wouldn't harden. I immediately started calling Drew, and it kept going straight to his voicemail.

After I had a crackhead to test and confirmed it was fake, I automatically lost my train of thought. I understood that in the drug game NO rules apply, especially around drought time. That's always the season that everybody has their reasons to be despiteful. But I spent too much money through and out the years with this nigga, so it never crossed my mind that he would do me dirty like that.

I was ready to kill or be killed because I wasn't letting that shit go down like that. The one thing I dreaded but had to do was call my ravisher Savion. He had the connections, which gave him the power, and he had the goons that handled unlawful acts expeditiously. After Savion got Drew's information on his drug spots he was running in Winston and the Ville, there was shoot outs, a couple of people got wounded, some got beaten, robbed, and a few of them disappeared. But Drew was nowhere to be found. I'm pretty sure he got the message because he secretly relocated, changed his phone numbers, and was driving unfamiliar cars since he didn't want to be recognized. Little did Drew know, Karma would unexpectedly be knocking at his front door eventually.

I was an angry woman all over again. 30,000 had put a big dent in my savings, especially when I had to take care of two kids, monthly bills, and buying my expensive necessities. It was tough trying to adapt to bargaining when I was already prone to the "I get what I want lifestyle!" But I guess the shit happened for a reason because it had me looking at life from a different perspective. After careful consideration and much thought, I decided to move from the West End after my year lease was up.

For the last six month living at my house, I had to connive each of my men friends into paying my bills without them actually knowing the facts. All I had to do was put on my crybaby act, and they would show me sympathy by giving me money, which relieved some stress. My mission was to reserve my cash as much as possible and spend everybody else's. I didn't care about them niggas well beings; I was more concerned about my baby girls' happiness and security. My kids were unaware of my struggles since I never stepped outside the mommy role regardless of what I was going through.

Then one day, my baby girls and I were riding when we heard a commercial on 102 Jams about auditioning to become an actor/model at the coliseum in Greensboro. Out of the blue, Aaliyah said, "Mommy! Mommy! Leah and I always talked about acting... Can we go, please? I promise you we're going to make it! We're going to be on TV, become famous and rich, then all of your worries would go away." I was shocked that my eight and twelve-year-old were not only planning their future, but was thinking about me in the process. I was wondering how they knew about my worries when I never even spoke of it. However, kids are very intelligent these days. What I thought was a disguise to them might have unintentionally revealed others cues that something was wrong.

The following Friday, we went and stood in line for a little over two hours. After finally making it in the room that was filled with judges, us parents had to sit aside because we were unable to be a part of our kids' interviews. Then the judges announced their picks, and it was one of Aaliyah's happiest moments when she was chosen to go to Atlanta and show off her talent in front of 100's of agents, such as Disney, Nickelodeon, ICM, UTA, and so forth. On the other hand, Leah and Abrianna were recommended to come back next year to give it another try, seeing they were too shy at that time. Regardless of the overall outcome, it was still one foot in the door, so we were going to use that as an advantage. Although I temporarily stopped hustling until the drought was over with, I decided to dig in my stash and utilize it for a good cause, which was fulfilling my baby girl's dreams.

During that uplifting moment, I got a call from Uziah saying, "Veah, I have to leave in a few days to go to Petersburg, Virginia. I'm going to be stationed out there for six months. I hope this doesn't interfere with what we are pursuing, and I will love you to come see me as much as possible." Of course, nothing was going to interfere with our friendship, or my visits; I actually started liking him. In all honesty, I thought it was a good thing that he was leaving due to me being in my transitional phase where I had no trust, no respect, and was trying not to accumulate feelings for any man. With this mentality, the less connected I was with Uziah would leave me with less feelings I had to fight off. Also, I didn't want a good man like him to get caught up in the middle of my vindictive ways towards men, which was using and abusing them until they were humiliated like I was. My heart had been broken many different ways. It started off with my father and ending with Brad, so I needed that space in order to heal.

The day Uziah left, I decided to introduce him to Aaliyah and Leah since we were close friends for a little over five months. My kids instantly felt Uziah and I connection when they saw the radiant smiles on our faces, and our jaunty eyes as we communicated with each other, which made Aaliyah and Leah comfortable enough to open up to him instead of interrogating him like I thought they were. Although Uziah and I were saying our goodbyes, it was more like we'll see you soon because we knew that we would stay in contact with each other. I didn't keep all eggs in one basket, but I knew Uziah was a man I should hold on to.

Days had gone by... A few months had passed, still Uziah and I friendship were on the right track. All my life I wanted someone to fulfill my insatiable cravings for love. I needed that proper guidance towards rectitude, and most of all, I desired some understanding, which Uziah accomplished it through every visit, every conversation, and every compatible thought about adding life to years and not years to life. Uziah was a different breed, somewhat identical to me, and that was the essence of our friendship.

I started thinking about Uziah more because his concrete words were embedded in my head. His appearance was impressive to my eyes, and that's why I anticipated on seeing his chestnut brown complexion, short height with his muscular body any day of the week. I also had a pleasure in talking to him as he continued to uplift my spirit all the time. He knew I was doing wrong, but instead of him judging me, he continued to motivate me in doing right.

I progressively started listening, and as my footsteps walked in a different path, I got caught in between a tug of war that was pulling me backwards, which was staying as the devil's advocate, or pushing forward in becoming a disciple of God. Which way do I go? Although I was a little hesitant, I had to think about what was best for me permanently rather than temporarily. Given that the fog was no longer cloudy to my vision, I had a sense of direction towards my futurity. If I was to fall again, I understood that's what makes me human. I didn't feel alone anymore and didn't have anyone holding me back. This was definitely my turning point.

At the same time, I had moved into Asterpark in Winston with Lateesah. That was the last thing I wanted to do, but something I needed to do in order to save money. The peaceful part about it was Lateesah was never there; she stayed with her significant other in Midway, so it kind of felt like my own. My kids felt differently due to them not growing up in the projects; therefore, the hood was too ratchet for them. Immediately, I had to give them the "When I was growing up" speech about going in-and-out of shelters, living in rat and roach infested apartments, sleeping on other people's hard floors when we got put out, and so forth. I explained to them that hardship comes in many different forms, so they should be grateful that it wasn't worse than mine. After that, it was clear to them that they still had it made, and they kept their heads up high with their beautiful smiles like they were appreciative. What they didn't know was they inspired me to do better, and I was truly thankful they didn't love me any less through my darkest moments.

Aaliyah was my first born. She was compassionate, intelligent, and friendly. Yet, she had that mean streak in her only when she was provoked, which was very much like me before I became completely corrupted. Aaliyah also disassociated herself from negative surroundings because she knew that her education would result in a positive outcome. She put her books before hanging out, which edified her with words of wisdom, and gave her the power to sagaciously speak with sophistication. She was persistent in achieving, outspoken when needed, talented, and full of beauty inside and out. Aaliyah didn't want to follow my footsteps, she wanted to walk her own path. Still and all, my cursed blood was traveling through hers, and I'm hoping it won't corrupt her future.

Then my baby girl Leah Rose, who was humorous, wild, and outspoken. Yet, she was benevolent and helpful to the people she loved, which was exactly how I acted after I was transitioning from the good to the bad. Unquestionably, Leah was smart, but she was easily distracted by anything that interest her. Leah was also content with her negative surroundings, even when she knew it would confront trouble. Out of concern, I started keeping a close eye on Leah because I didn't want her to get lost in corruption.

I encouraged her to continue to be herself, achieve her goals, but walk the right path. I knew she needed some guidance, understanding that the absence of her father had a negative impact on her life, which I connected with her on that situation in so many ways, but under totally different circumstances. Everyone has dissimilar reactions to dilemmas regardless of the severities. For that cause, I did what no one had done for me when I really needed it, which was consoled and held Leah while saying, "It's going to be alright. I'm here for you every step of the way. You're never alone as long as you have me, okay?"

I was startled and my heart melted when Leah replied, "Mommy, we should call ourselves the "Three Musketeers...," all we have is each other." She was right; their fathers weren't in their lives to help them through their journeys. The Daevas family values were no longer solid, which left little support. Therefore, my kids' fair opportunities and strengths were based fully around my capabilities. Most definitely, I had to keep my head on straight, and we firmly held each other hands regardless of how heavy the burdens were.

Although I was going through my own little difficulties at that time, I still was caring enough to help Caylah by letting Abrianna stay with me, despite me living in Lateesah's apartment. Then I started feeling unappreciated when Caylah discredited me for not handling her responsibilities to a certain standard. The initial plan was Caylah would come to Winston at least once a week to pick up and bring Abrianna school clothes; basically, that was her mommy time. But because Caylah had her head in the clouds, there were times we didn't see her for two to three weeks straight, leaving Abrianna with barely anything to wear. Sometimes I went out my way to pick up her clothes, but Caylah took advantage of that. So, there were times Abrianna had to wear Leah's clothes, which didn't quite fit but was decent enough for her to wear to school. Negatively, Caylah didn't like it, and she had the audacity to complain like I owed her something. Immediately, I relieved myself from her responsibilities and sent Abrianna back with her.

I always tried to help some of my family members the best way possible, but they always expected more out of me when they wouldn't have done nearly the same if the shoe was on the other foot. Sometimes its best just to let things go, and let people fight their own battles. Let them learn through their own experiences just like I did. I was tired of being the family support person. I needed them to back me up for once, but that didn't happen. Luckily, that pushed me to the point of no return where I started taking control of my inner self to build up my vitality, and used a different approach towards certain situations, which gave the impression to others like I was arrogant and selfish. "Arrogant" I might've been a little, but selfishness was caused by my unappreciative family. From that moment on, I didn't give a fuck anymore. What my FAM didn't realize is that their actions would never change how I cherished myself, but would change how I treated them.

# NEVER NINE

Regardless of the changes I was making, Lavinniah always had a soft spot in my heart. She was my baby sister that had that unconditional love, positive thoughts, and a strong belief that we could overcome any trials, seeing we were still standing strong after defeating many. In behalf of Lavinniah's surviving struggles, she was grateful for even the insignificant things since she grew up with only the minimum.

Lavinniah was always at a point in need, and most of us sisters were there to help her through it, except Lateesah. When we were growing up, we all knew that Lateesah had a grudge against Lavinniah. She didn't like that Lavinniah had a different father, but as Lateesah matured, we thought she would get over it. Instead, it got worse, and she had vicious ways of showing it.

I would never forget the day Lateesah found out about Lavinniah staying at her place with me because she had an unexpected breakup, and she was forced to leave her toddler behind until she found a stable place. Lateesah wasn't haven't it, so she immediately came to Winston just to cause trouble. I was out making a few runs that night when I got that call from Aaliyah. She was frantically crying and had a shortness of breath as she tried to tell me, "Aunt Teesah tried to fight me and Lavinniah. Then she told us to get out, so now we're sitting outside in the cold rain!" I angrily responded, "What da fu… I'm coming right now!" I impulsively headed straight to Lateesah's house.

I peacefully walked in and started packing up all of our belongings. When I loaded everything in the car, I violently went to attack Lateesah. I put my small hands around her neck, then rammed her destructively into the wall and continued to choke her. Although her eyes were rolling in the back of her head, and her mouth was wide opened gasping for air as she tried to dig deep in my arms with her sharp nails, I still wouldn't let go. For a second, I wanted her to stop breathing. I knew that I couldn't revive her, so deep down, a part of me wanted her dead, but her strength gave her another chance at life. And my weakness, which was my kids voices, "Mommy! Please stop..." had gave me another chance at freedom. Then I peacefully walked away like nothing ever happened. We went straight to a hotel and stayed a few nights until I found the Ambercrest apartments on Split Rail Circle, which was absolutely perfect for the "Three Musketeers". Most certainly I couldn't leave out Lavinniah and my niece, so they moved in with me for as long as they needed to.

Never nine was mommy's last special blessing. Lavinniah was born on May 04, 1987, which was the day her and mommy almost lost their lives due to delivery complications, but God had his own special reasons for them to survive. Even though Lavinniah was born out of wedlock, that was mommy's only sin she didn't regret. In all honesty, that was mommy's only child that she gave her undivided attention to, cherished every moment with, and placed her on a pedestal. In other words, she showed Lavinniah favoritism, and we all noticed it.

Lavinniah grew up to be a lot like mommy. For one, Lavinniah struggled keeping a man, and a long-term relationship as she was seeking love for all the right reasons, but in the wrong places. She was naive to the fact that all men weren't cut out for relationships, but they would convince her otherwise, just to get what they wanted, and she fell for it every time. In all honesty, I felt like Lavinniah was a little promiscuous, and that could've been one of the reasons why the good men undervalued her potentials of being girlfriend material. It also could've been from the lack of education, financial stability, standards, or because she seemed to not have any sense of direction, which had her mind all over the place, making it difficult to attract a suitable guy. Perceiving that her self-esteem was low and feeling a little underrated had left her vulnerable to even more mistakes.

Lavinniah's main stumbling block was continuing to make unwise decisions. Despite her physical obstacles, she chose mind over matter and dealt with the consequences when that time came. For instance, if you know that feeding your habits might alter your train of thoughts, sway you to choose desires over needs, spend unnecessary money that you don't have, or slow down the process of you handling important business, then it's time to get your priorities straight. That's where Lavinniah struggled at, but she just needed a little push towards getting her life together. I always told her, "It's okay to have fun! Enjoy life to the fullest... It's not what you do, it's how you do it. Just remember... It's a time and place for everything."

In between her missteps, she had three kids by three different deceitful men. Rusty was the first father that I felt didn't deserve the title. He stayed in and out of jail, and he didn't give her any financial or physical support. Lavinniah, on the other hand, was highly in love with him, but he crushed her heart when he slept with our niece Shyann. Lavinniah was definitely a victim of betrayal. Even though she knew about him cheating beforehand, a family member was unexpected and more hurtful.

Jacob was her son's father that was doing his daddy duties since day one. Unfortunately, Lavinniah didn't get an equal opportunity to fully get to show her good mother figure since Jacob thought that she wasn't stable or mature enough to raise their son without him. Therefore, he took Demarcus after breaking up with Lavinniah, and then he moved in with his new pregnant girlfriend. Although she gets to see Demarcus from time-to-time, it's still not enough. However, Lavinniah somehow was persuaded that if she couldn't provide for her son, it's best for him to stay with his father, even when Jacob is always at work and barely give him that quality time. I don't agree with Lavinniah's decision; indubitably, she can make some type of child support and visiting arrangements with Jacob without going through the legal system if Demarcus was to stay with her. Besides, her other two kids are living a fair and stable life without their fathers at all, but to each its own.

Then there's Logan; it took us all by surprise including Lavinniah when she found out she was pregnant by him. Primarily because Logan recently got released from doing over 15 years in prison for drugs, first degree kidnapping along with a couple of other serious charges. At first, we thought she was enjoying the preserved prison body and youthful look. Until a month later, she missed her period, and Logan had got arrested for robbery. Lavinniah had this ridiculous look on her face and was lost for words, especially when she found out he was facing up to 18 years. Then came the rumor, "I heard he was gay and wanted to reunite with his boyfriend in prison!" I wasn't shocked at all about the accusation; in my opinion, if a person does over 10 years in prison, it's a possibility he could change his preference. It could be by force, out of curiosity, or absence of the opposite sex. There's no supportive evidence of why, it just happens.

Meanwhile, I was very disappointed in Lavinniah as she continued to make the same damn mistakes by having babies by men she hardly knew. Men who didn't care about her, or her well beings. I know she can't erase her past, and it's much love for her kids, but she can make a difference in her life by readjusting her immature thoughts and behavior.

I describe Lavinniah as very helpful and loyal but unprosperous. Helpful meaning assisting others the best way possible immaterially and subjectively without seeking anything in return regardless of what financial state she was in, she'll be there for you. She always had a loyal heart, which was in a different place from us Daevas's. The bond with her family was more important than money or anything of that matter. I believe that's where she was messing up at. Instead of her encouraging and being concerned about others, she should've put that energy towards advancing herself. That's one area she struggled in, which caused her to be in indigent circumstances. I can't say she was completely impoverished, but she and the kids were stricken from certain necessities because she didn't push herself.

Lavinniah must learn how to stay focused and let her mindset get accustom to taking chances in order to move to the next level. She should stop using her kids as an excuse to why she can't go back to school or find a job. There is assistance out there that she can take advantage of, which could help her to achieve. Until she takes that initiative, every night she lays down, she will continue to hope for a better day.

In a way, Lavinniah felt like an outcast in the Daevas family. She was the only one that had a different father, different features, and a different personality, which had an impact on her personal life due to her feeling like she wasn't accepted as our whole sister. Therefrom, she consistently tried to prove her love and passion she had for being a part of the Daevas's. Another issue was she hated us picking on her dissimilarities, which made her cry while we were laughing with tears. We basically were trying to make her strong and become vicious like us, but it didn't work. Although the obsessions in her thoughts were negative, she continued to stay positive, for never nine didn't have an evil spirit. Being heartless and barbaric just because… was never nine. Always chaotic and very disobedient because we were reckless doesn't at all describes never nine. To get to the point, Lavinniah wasn't a wild child, she was humble, but could become enraged if she was pushed to that level. We always thought Lavinniah was weak, in some cases, it may have been true, but psychologically she was stronger than us.

It doesn't matter how far Lavinniah and I lived away from each other, we kept that bond, continued to communicate, and confided in one another; we have that trust, we needed that sisterly love, and we both hoped for success. Although Lavinniah hasn't completely gotten her life on track, she is independently stable in her own apartment and raising her two intelligent kids, which is a start. She no longer tries to prove anything to us, now that she's comfortable with herself, making her own decisions, and following her own path. Lavinniah has created her own identity, and doesn't need approval from the Daevas's. This self-appreciation will lead her to success if her actions are executed properly.

# THE TESTIMONY FROM
# THE CHOSEN ONE

# THE TESTIMONY

Getting back on the subject of moving on Split Rail Circle, I had handled my business quickly and effectively. The best part about it was I did everything without seeking benefits from any of my men friends when I knew I could've took advantage of that; yet, I didn't. I wanted my fulfillment to come through my own independence. I no longer wanted men to think that they had access to my personal life just because they were giving me money. Therefore, I paid my deposit and two months rent, got my lights turned on, rented a U-Haul, and paid some movers to professionally transfer and set up my lavishing furniture. We had everything in my apartment within 24 hours, and I was completely setup within three days; thanks to my family for working hard together to get the job done.

I was proud that I finally gave up my Machiavellian approach. I felt like I no longer had to expose myself to danger due to greed. I wanted to take that risk in proceeding as an individual, finding myself, and using my intelligence instead of my attraction to get ahead. That was something I was always afraid of doing, thinking I would fail, but I was ready to take that huge step and face my fears. I had no reason to be hesitant about doing the right things when I always did wrong. The chances I was taking couldn't hurt me any more than I already hurt myself. Accordingly, I was moving forward with no prediction of my future, but I had a content feeling that everything was going to be okay in due time.

For me to focus on my future, I needed to leave the past behind me. Ensuingly, I began to isolate myself from unfavorable situations, knowing temptation wasn't easy to resist. That's when Uziah and my bond became unbreakable. We really started cherishing our auspicious moments because every minute we looked into each other's eyes... we saw nothing but passion. Every stimulating kiss was with affection, and every word we expressed was full of hope for us and our future.

Uziah and I knew we were soul-mates, seeing that our flaws within ourselves were a reflection of each other's. We understood our differences, and we weren't at all judgmental towards one another. Negatively, some people on both sides of our families had doubts in our relationship. His side thought he was too good for me because I was from the streets; contrarily, my family thought I was too much for him, since I was addicted to the fast life, fast money, and big time drug dealers. All of those negative assumptions didn't have an effect on our relationship, for we knew what we wanted. What our families didn't realize was our uniqueness had brought out the beauty of our love, and the energy in our happiness. Therefore, we continued to take our chances with each other.

We were a little over a year in our relationship when Uziah got deployed to Iraq. At first, I was terror-stricken because it was a possibility that he might not come back the same, or at all. After he left, I was sad more than anything. The only man that kept me on track was gone for 12 to 18 months. In a way, this was a prodigious step towards strengthening our relationship and trust. Moreover, gave us time and space to see what we really wanted.

Certainly, without a doubt, I knew Uziah was coming back to me, but my stereotyping sisters were leery about military men. They were so inclined on the bad things he was capable of doing, such as being abusive, having babies or other relationships overseas, and bringing me back some foreign disease. Not near one time did they mention the good things like how Uziah changed me for the better, or how jubilant he made me feel. In all reality, they didn't care, or understood what complete happiness was since discouragement was always a blemish in our lives.

We as sisters are a hindrance to one another, especially when one exceeds their expectations. Why is that when we all grew up under the same circumstances? Why is that when we all had different opportunities to prosper? We all need to realize that we are our own roadblock, and we should stop trying to find others to blame instead of pointing the fingers at ourselves for being at a standstill. We need to understand that we are our own enemies fighting for the wrong cause, and I'm not content with being the victim of duplicity anymore. For us to live a peaceful life, the curse must stop somewhere, and I'm going to do my best in taking that initiative. In fact, I hope we all do.

With Uziah being so far away, and with very little positive support, I had a setback when I suddenly got the urge to hit the streets again. Hustling in the old neighborhoods had led me back to that son of a BITCH Drew. Well, not him exactly, but his wife Kara, which was close enough for me. Kara had no idea who I was, and I definitely was going to use that to my advantage. Yeah, I know that I gave into evil easily, but the fact is, an eye for an eye probably would always be a part of me as it triggers every violent bone, and it fires up the corrupt blood that flows through my body when I am betrayed.

Although I was content with being the good Veah, I felt incapable without the control, but very powerful having the authority over making things happen. So, a conscious I didn't have when I was in my vengeful ways. Spitefully, I lured Kara in by correlating with her through the conversation she was having with one of my groupies. By us having that little small chat, I had quickly distinguished her strengths and weaknesses.

Kara strengths were her being an attractive white woman that looked and smelled like money. Therefore, she wouldn't have a problem getting a black man. She also was talking wisely like she had some sort of education, which could come in handy as well. Dissimilarly, Kara weaknesses were her sluttish dressing that gave the perception of being "easy". She had on some poom-poom shorts that was showing off her goods including her cellulites, a braless tank top that revealed her hard nipples, and her red high heel pumps that made her walk like she wanted some attention her husband wasn't giving. Her attitude was perceived as an imitation black girl, which showed insecurity within herself. Her bad choice of words had expressed infidelity, so I knew she was up to no good. It was just a matter of time that I would see all of her flaws that was hidden under her excessive makeup.

I befriended her with ease as she was captivated by my natural black beauty, my urban style, and my mind-boggling black woman knowledge, which was something she wasn't good at portraying. Still, she tried her hardest. She wanted understanding and acceptance from her black husband who always reminded her that she could never be a woman of color. I saw it in her eyes that she was tired of living a lie, she was drained from being used as a cover-up for his illegal actions. Moreover, she was bored with the everyday routine when Drew came home 3 or 4 in the morning smelling like pussy. With desperation, she wanted tips on being magnetic and spontaneous. OMG! That works out perfectly for me. Her vulnerabilities would let me lead her in the right direction, but for all the wrong reasons.

I planned my work, and now it's time to work my plan, for those hard feelings I no longer wanted to feel. Whatever happened prior to my transition should be put to past, so I wouldn't need to look back. For that reason, I had to continue to collaborate with Savion. I felt like he owed me for all the times he defiled me and didn't suffer the consequences behind it. Respectively, we set down and discussed a well-organized plan for that sneaky little bastard. Because I knew Kara had a coke addiction that she'd been hiding from Drew for years, I wanted to turn that BITCH into a fiend. Then smut her ass out with any man who was willing to pay me the right price.

At first, I knew she would be a little nervous, so I was going to introduce her to other whore addicts who she could relate to without getting criticized. At that point, she should feel comfortable enough to open up and bring out her privily freakish ways. Once that's accomplished, she would feel seductive, spontaneous, and adventurous, which was what Kara desired for many years of her boring married life.

By that time, Kara guards should be down, and I'll be the one who would catch her slipping. Hereinafter, my plan would fall into play. My idea was to follow Kara home one night after she finished tricking. Then stakeout their house for a few days. Thereafter, I would wait until black mass hours to make that force entry. Here's where Savion comes in at. He would send the soldiers with the guns to delegate the job Mafioso style, which means shit can get bloody or deadly if Drew didn't cooperate.

Before the plan got executed, Karma got to Drew first, and his life quickly came crashing down on him. It was very disheartening when Drew found out about Kara's addiction to not only cocaine, but had transitioned to a crackhead as well. Moreover, she was sleeping with every drug dealer in the hood. It was also damaging to his bank accounts when she emptied it. On top of that, one of Drew's partners got caught coming back from Texas in Drew's transporting truck, which was loaded with over 15 kilos of coke. He lost his drugs, truck, money, wife, and the FEDS were on his ass. Under those circumstances, I had to step back from the whole situation, knowing it was pointless and risky when the Sherlock Holmes were involved. I hated that I couldn't get my money plus a bonus back, but I was happy that Drew got the feel of taking a tremendous lost, and I had a little something to do with it.

It seemed like every time I was in a negative state of mind, Uziah always called me. Then I had to play the role like I was a saint, knowing I was just about to torture a nigga, or just came from buying some coke, cooking it, and meeting a few of my customers. The only thing I was a saint in was not giving up my pussy for a whole year. Those months went by slowly, but I was very happy when I saw him walking out of the Greensboro Airport Terminal with his Army fatigues on, clean cut, and stern but sexy walk. We hugged each other tightly like we never wanted to let go. We both were smiling from ear-to-ear like we just hit the jackpot, and of course, we were anxious to pick up where we left off.

That was the point where we were ready to take our relationship to another level, and unify us and our girls as a family. Therefore, we decided that we were going to move to Fayetteville together due to Uziah being stationed there. That was a huge step for the both of us, but was probably the best decision we made. Most definitely for me because I was giving up everything and starting all over in order to better myself without any interference from my past. There would be no more hustling for me; I would be two hours away. No more lashing out at my enemies; they wouldn't be in my presence to tempt me, and lastly was being away from my family and their negativity.

When I announced the good news to my sisters, it was more like evil words coming out my mouth as they went from 0 to 100 really quick. They all thought I was moving too fast and felt like I barely knew him. I didn't care; it was my life, and I was following my gut feeling. The one sister who truly took it to heart the most was Caylah. Although we were having our ups and downs, we always remained close. However, that time was a bit different, for the distance between our residences became the distance between our relationship since Caylah considered me abandoning her for a man. Ultimately, the bitterness and anger she felt had developed to hatred towards Uziah because she blamed him for our separation.

Separation to me was the transition that I needed in 2010. I was tired of making U-turns, so I felt it was best to depart from the old, and arrive to a new beginning. That didn't mean I was leaving my sisters behind. It meant that I was growing up, seeking and pursuing opportunities, hoping for a better outcome than before. After all, change was my purpose, and progression was my main goal. Even if failure became an obstacle, I must still keep my eyes on the road and proceed like I'm not afraid in order to become a conqueror.

Life is full of sacrifices, which is up to the individual to make. It's up to that person to either live full of regrets, or build off experiences, and I did both through and out my life. Proceeding on this track, I left for Fayetteville with an open-mind. Then a few months after moving into our condo, I began to see a tremendous change in Uziah's behavior. For example, before we moved in with each other, he had some jealous tendencies about how provocative I dressed, and he didn't like certain men I associated myself with, but nothing to the extreme where I thought it was a problem. Actually, it was cute because it showed that he cared, and I understood where he was coming from. But that cute turned to ugly when he became completely controlling. If I didn't do what I was told, then I didn't get what I wanted. Wait a minute! That was not part of the plan.

OMG! I was entirely surprised that this new guy stood before my eyes. Therefore, my reactions came off defensive as I felt insulted. I didn't like that I couldn't go anywhere without him, and if I did, it was a big argument. I hated that he was too strict on the kids to where they wanted to stay bound up in their rooms. They could only go a certain amount of feet from the house, which was boring to my kids since they had a little more freedom than that. Then Uziah started complaining about simple shit like the kids' bathroom had a piece of hair in the sink, a tiny crumb was on the table, or Aaliyah having her door shut. It started getting overwhelming, and our arguments became physical at times. It wasn't nothing too drastic, but there were mornings I woke up with bruises on my body, and one time, I had a bruised rib and certain movements brought out the intense pain. Because I wasn't a scary BITCH, I fought back, leaving him with a bunch of deep scratches all over his face that he had to wear to work (Ha-ha).

Our ups and downs became a complete burden on the entire household. There were many silent moments through and out the day, for nobody wanted the wrong words to come out their mouths. When something was out of place or broken in the house, my kids were always the blame as though his daughter could never do anything wrong. It got to a point where it became a separation between us two families. There were times Uziah would take his daughter and just up and leave. Then when they came home, Mikayla would brag to Leah and Aaliyah about how much fun they had, played with all the entertaining toys he bought, adored all the clothes and shoes he got her, which was hurtful to my kids, knowing Uziah only did that when he was mad at me. That's where he crossed the line, and it was time for us to go. I couldn't take anymore of his childish and spiteful ways.

I was disappointed and embarrassed when I was right back where I left off 10 months prior, and what made matters worse was I had to start all over again. On top of that, I had to face my "I told you so's!" I got prepared for those downgrading conversations, and anyone who was exhilarated by what they thought was a downfall. It was more like a minor setback to me, and a learning experience. It taught me that a man can sell you dreams, but don't buy them, until it has been received.

Actions speak louder than words, and words have no meaning without any truth behind it. In behalf of that experience, I feel that jealous, controlling, manipulative, and arrogant men has other dysfunctional things going on in their heads that makes them feel or act that way. I was glad to be in control of the situation instead of the situation controlling me.

As I left my problems along with my relationship behind me, the kids and I went straight to New York for the summer. I needed to clear my thoughts from all the agony, and the Big Apple always did it for me. I continued to smile, pretending like everything was alright, but the overall situation was really affecting me deep inside because I truly had feelings for Uziah. By me being a strong individual, I stayed busy to keep my mind off of him, and I focused more on moving on.

Then Uziah began to call me, which was a distraction when he sounded like the man I once knew. The Uziah that was humble, considerate, and spoke words of love. There were also some calls when he was a little obnoxious, drunk, rude, and threatening because he couldn't have his way, or he just didn't know how to take constructive criticism. Then I'll get his apologetic calls, which would be emotional and sincerely crying out for help. I quickly caught on to Uziah's multiple personalities considering I had a few of them myself, so I could relate to him in many ways. However, his hostile behavior towards me was very unpleasant, especially when I was used to myself giving the displeasing situations, but the shoe was on the other foot, and I was getting a taste of my own medicine. At that instant, I realized that I finally met my match. We both were dominant and too stubborn to let go of that power, which is where we clashed at. For me, I was a boss lady for so long that I had no means of being controlled. Then realism hit me! My whole life I had been controlled by evil, love, money, family, and enemies. I always gave into their needs whether it was negative or positive, but I didn't look at it like that until then.

I was gradually finding myself, becoming stronger through every obstacle I faced, and getting wiser as a woman, mother, and an individual. I was no longer grasping for my physical needs; I was more focused on my mental demands. I would continue being a leader, and at times, become a good follower in all hopes that one day, I could be a success.

In the meantime, our vacation had come to an end a little earlier than expected; I had to get stable before the kids started school. Not to mention, Brad had got out of prison a few months prior, so Aaliyah and Leah were anxious to see him. I wasn't at all on the other hand, but it was time for me to come face-to-face with Brad, and give him some closure. He needed to understand why we would no longer be together. It wasn't only because I hated his guts, or no longer was sexually attracted. It was more like I moved on, and I got a taste of something that was better than him. In light of this, why bother going back to someone when it's really not worth it. Besides, Uziah and I were in love, and we were working on reestablishing our relationship, but we remained living in our separate places, thinking that was best for us at the time.

I moved back in Ambercrest apartments next to the one I stayed in prior to leaving. I didn't have to go through the same waiting process like before because the young, sexy, white owner knew me, and he adored me. Brad adored me as well, and that's why he gave me the $1600 to move in. He also helped me get my work off, and he built my clientele back up when I started back hustling. Brad was full of guilt for all of those years he mistreated me, and he wanted to prove his love by showing me how he transitioned from a boy to a man with effective communication in hopes to develop a connection with means of us getting back together. That was a perfect time to manipulate him, and get what I wanted. I know that was a contradiction to being the new and improved me, but sometimes a BITCH has to do what she has to do, and I had that nigga eating out the palm of my hands.

Brad put his heart all the way into it, while I put mine against it. I knew that I couldn't never give him anymore of my time. In all honesty, I was disgusted by his appearance, but I loved that I could continue to be vindictive and vengeful towards him; I just couldn't find it in my heart to forgive him at all.

Because I pretended to be so welcoming and warm-hearted to Brad, it backfired. He started showing up unexpectedly; there were times he came in the middle of the night, banging on my door. Then he started questioning me about my whereabouts? Who was at my house? And who was I seeing? Like he was my man. The beautiful picture he envisioned was definitely not the one I had painted. Therefore, it was time for him to take a walk, and get over me.

As I looked Brad in the eyes without even blinking, my dilating pupils gave a perception of disappointment and hate when I told him, "I don't want you... You're a distaste to my mouth, I was just using your dumbass... the only thing I need you to do is be a father to Leah. Now get the fuck out my house." Brad looked weak as his tears quickly fell down his face. His heart was painfully pounding as he cried out for forgiveness, which my scorned heart couldn't accept. As he sluggishly walked out, overloaded with all types of crazy thoughts, and feeling abandoned all over again, that was the day I began my healing process.

In the middle of all that bullshit, Uziah and I found our focal point for the soul of our relationship, which was communication. We needed to open our hearts, and share our deepest thoughts. Moreover, not hold back on nothing that was bothersome or intrusive to our behavior. That would give both of us a better understanding about our discrepancy, so we could try and work through them together. When Uziah and I took that step, we broke the ice. We found out that we were bearing the burdens of guilt, acceptance, insecurity, anger, responsibilities, and so on. After everything was out in the opening, we began to relieve our pain by holding each other firmly as we emotionally cried, wiped each other tears afterwards, then we laughed with joy. That night, our bond was closer than ever before. Also, it brought out the best in us.

While Uziah and I had made peace, Brad was at war as he was jealous and enraged. He started aggressively pursuing, and the threats never ended. He wanted to physical hurt Uziah or me since he couldn't do it mentally. Due to the fact that Caylah was team Brad, and she hated Uziah, it gave Brad easier access to get to me.

One weekend, I went to visit Caylah at her house, not knowing Brad was there. Brad wanted to talk, and I gave him the same reasons why we couldn't be together conversation. It wasn't getting through his thick skull. I then felt it was no point in talking or being in his presence, especially when we all were under the influence, so I called Uziah to come get me.

When Uziah knocked with aggression, and acknowledged who he was, Brad became filled with raged as he immediately headed straight for the door. I jumped in front of his big ass and pushed him back, hoping I could fast talk some sense into him. "What the fuck you're doing or trying to prove? Do you want to go back to jail and leave Leah again?" I said in my hoarse voice. He bitterly responded, "If you leave, I'm going to shoot him!" At the same time, Uziah continued banging on the door. Then Caylah said, "Imma go talk to Uziah while you calm Brad down." Instead of Caylah trying to keep the peace, she goes outside and make matters worse. "Listen here, don't be coming banging on my door; I shoot motherfuckers that's disrespectful. Na 'Veah is not leaving with you... she's talking to Brad about their relationship, so you can get the fuck on!" What Caylah didn't know was that Uziah had his registered 380 pistol on him, he was extremely mad as well, and without hesitation, he would've protected himself if he had to. However, his daughter and career were more important. With that in mind, he maturely, but angrily walked away.

Caylah came back in the room with a crooked smile, telling me, "Uziah left... I told him you were coming, but I guess he got mad over Brad being in here." I rushed outside, hoping I could catch him, but he was already gone. When I called Uziah, he was pissed at me, saying, "If you were getting back with your baby father, why would you call me to come pick you up? Then your sister threatening me with a gun and cursing me out... Boy was I ready to step back into my old character. Hell, my cuzzo was ready to reach out and touch your sister or whoever wanted it. That was some fuck shit, but you know what... do you with your baby daddy!" Then he hung up, and he kept hanging up every time I called.

I was in disbelief, disappointed, hurt, and angry by Caylah's actions. She was very spiteful and didn't at all think about my feelings. When I confronted Caylah in tears, she tried to deny everything, but I knew she was lying. After I explained to Brad and her for the last time, "Brad hurt me to the core, and it's no coming back together after that. I don't love, want, or need him. If you love him as your brother-in-law, then that's between y'll; I have moved on, so all that Brad and Na 'Veah mess is in the past. Get over it! I'm happy now... Thanks to you Caylah, you might've messed up the one thing that was right for me!" Caylah started feeling guilty, admitting she was in the wrong. She constantly kept apologizing, and she promised to never include Brad in anything me and her had going on. I listened to what she had to say, but didn't believe a word that was coming out her mouth.

Uziah was astonished by Caylah's behavior, but that didn't keep him away from me. However, he became aware of the Daevas's vicious ways, which caused him to be vigilant when he was around them. On the subject of the Daevas's, who all of a sudden was team Brad, didn't seem to care about Caylah's spiteful doing. They were more concerned about Brad's feelings, and thought it was a good thing that he was fighting to get me back. They forgot all about the deceiving shit Brad did to me for those ten years, and they thoughtlessly believed he was a changed man.

Caylah had spread all types of harsh rumors about Uziah being abusive, bossy, and a lame who thought he was better than everybody else, he was trying to change me and keep me away from my family. The list went on if Caylah was telling it. Moreover, she convinced majority that it was true. Some of my family members didn't take the time to really get to know Uziah because they were already judging him by unsubstantiated information. No, Uziah wasn't perfect, but everyone has their flaws including their relationships. Yet, they all were focused on mine.

Despite that we all were distant, we still were a phone call away. In all honesty, a phone call from a Daevas could either make or break you, for it really depends on the strength of the individual. As the calls came in, I was prepared and confident towards any insults. If they were talking positively, then I was all ears, whereas negative talk I always cut it short. I didn't have time to hear that bullshit.

Hearing how my sisters consistently spoke the cursed words for Uziah and me to separate, it eventually came true, but not in the form of breaking up. Uziah had to leave for another deployment to Afghanistan for nine months, and that gave my sisters something else to throw up in my face. "He's going to always be gone like this… A military life will never be normal. You better leave him while you got a chance!" I kept hearing from the meddlers.

The differences that separated me from most of my sisters were my determination, agility, and my courage to take chances. I had a receptive frame of mind, whereas most of them are uncertain about anything that's going on in their lives, a few of them are a little slow witted, and some are very closed-minded to life changes. Our different personalities and beliefs were the cause of our division, and it accumulated a lot of hostility amongst one another. It can't be all nine of us in the same room without an argument, a fight, somebody's nose turned up, or a couple of eyes rolling and so forth. It's a very sad and a disturbing situation. For many reasons, I taught my kids how not to be towards one another. Sisters should always love each other and have that special connection. In addition, being supportive under any circumstances, now that's the meaning of family. Although my kids listened attentively, I was still concerned, but hoped that one day they didn't lose sight of themselves and forget who really is important to them.

It was the year of 2012; Aaliyah just turned 16, and Leah was soon to be 13. Because of them, I had to stop making excuses of why I was still a drug dealer. Moreover, I needed to set good examples, so they wouldn't follow my poisonous footsteps, and lead their own way to prosperity with my support. As a corollary, I took my position as being Aaliyah's manager, sponsor, and mother in her actress/modeling career she had been pursuing a little over four years. I dedicated my time and money. We did a lot of traveling to ATL, New York, and a few cities in NC for auditions and trainings where she gained competitive advantage and received recognition for her talent. It wasn't just a new experience for Aaliyah; it was an amiable adventure for Leah and me as well.

Meanwhile, I had to figure out how we were going to make the extra cash to take Aaliyah to the next level without me hitting the streets. I immediately thought about fundraising; it was a positive income, and my kids could be involved as well. In the middle of me thinking about selling raffle tickets, plates, and washing cars, party promoting had overflowed my mind with big dollar signs. As a result, I was able to keep my bills up and pay for Aaliyah expenses, which made her vibrant eyes glow, and her brightened teeth shine. The shut doors had eventually opened, given her the opportunity to prove herself, and find her identity. Ultimately, I would give myself all the credit, but surprisingly, some of my family members gave much support. In all honesty, I don't think that all of them did it out the kindness of their hearts. They did it in hopes that when Aaliyah made it to the top, then she'd return the favor. Whatever the case may have been, we still appreciated their help.

Although Brad and I were always at war, he still stayed obligated to the kids. Until his reaping season had come back to haunt him for his wrongdoings. Brad had got caught slipping with his so-called friend, who I think had purposely set him up with an undercover cop. Thereupon, Brad went on the run with the intentions that he could hideout at my place, which was definitely a no go. First of all, it was too risky. Secondly, I didn't fuck with him like that. Lastly, I didn't care if his dumbass got caught; he was once again meaningless to me and the kids.

Brad was disappointed that I refused to let him crash at my house, so he started lashing out. For the first time, I saw hatred in his eyes with much aggression coming from his body. He was ravaged, and he felt betrayed that I no longer was there for him when he really needed me the most. He had the nerve to say, "I'm not going no fucking where!" Until I threaten to call the police, and his ass ran up out of there really quick.

Brad had nowhere else to go, so he went to Caylah's house, assuming it would be safe, for very few people knew where she resided. However, a few weeks later, the NARCS kicked down Caylah's door and arrested Brad. Hmmm! That was very suspicious, for it had to be an inside job, which I had brought to Caylah and Josiah's attention. They were dealing a high volume of drugs, and I was explaining to them that they had to be more careful about who was in their inner circle because whoever sent the pigs to their house was out to get them as well.

Given that I already been where they were trying to get to, I wanted to express my concerns and provide my knowledge. Also, I wanted them to be prepared and beware of harm's way. They took heed to what I had said, but it was the least of their worries at that time; clearly, making money was the only thing relevant. The fame created arrogance, and it had them thinking that they were untouchable. The overburden of certain habits and behaviors had made them careless about their surroundings, and failed to notice their undercover enemies. For those reasons, they continued living their dangerous life like everything was harmless.

Meanwhile, I was continuing to work hard on bettering myself. My kids and I started attending Uziah's family church, hoping I could find peace within God. Before I got too involved in the church, it was time for me to get sentenced for the fraud charge I caught while I was on probation a couple of years back. I wasn't expecting the judge to be too lenient on me violating probation. But the fact that I had a well-paid lawyer, and my probation officer lied for me, the strict judge gave me 30 days in jail; however, I only had to do weekends because I was attending college.

It was 15 weekends of torture, so my weekdays were nothing but pleasant times with my kids, my nieces, and Lavinniah, who moved in with me until I got over that impediment. Every Thursday, the day before I had to report to the County Jail at six in the evening, we would cook a feast, have lots of alcohol beverages, and danced to reggae music till dawn. So, when I got to my cell, I was hung-over and still feeling drunk, which helped me go straight to sleep.

Then the butch looking guards will wake us up at five in the morning to serve us that disgusting breakfast that I never ate. I didn't eat the whole time I was there and couldn't wait for Sundays to come, given that I was weak from drinking just water for two days straight. It was crazy how the clock was ticking very slowly; I guess because I was anticipating on going home, which made it difficult to keep my eyes off of it. But being lockdown in that cell 23 hours a day for 30 days had gave me plenty of time to think about the important things in life. It also came to my attention that I did a lot of illegal and grimy shit through and out my life, but never did any prison time. It was a blessing, another opportunity for a change, and a sign that God was trying to tell me something.

I started going to church just about every Sunday to hear the words of encouragement and to get some type of guidance. Every time the Reverend preached, it seemed like he was talking about me. It always gave me a warm feeling like someone was hovering over my body. I kept ignoring it; I was too nervous to accept that God was dealing with me. Then one Sunday, I was sitting on the last bench in the church, and my heart started feeling like it was bearing too much weight. I tried to hold back my tears, but my eyes had overflowed, leaving me unable to stop crying. While the Pastor called up people for prayer or to get saved, it was like someone lifted my body from the seat and walked me up to the altar where I hugged the pastor tightly and cried out. That day, I amended my soul and asked God for forgiveness, which had my body feeling weightless as I left all of my burdens with him. I was proud that I became a Godly woman. Of course, I wasn't a 100% Christian, but I was working on getting closer to God, which was something that took me a long time to do.

The first person I told about my God-fearing experience was mommy who cried tears of joy. Then she went on telling me about how I was her spiritual baby, and that she been waiting years for me to get saved, so I could be a prophet for God. I really couldn't picture that happening, but I didn't see me being a religious person either. Anything was bound to take place, but everything comes with steps. What was really important to me was getting through to my sisters, hoping they would give God a chance as well. Some of them had postponed going to church; they felt that the timing wasn't right, which was understandable. A few was skeptical because of every unforgettable episode that happened with mommy was undesirable and not Godlike, which is how I felt prior to getting save, but I was learning how not to be bitter anymore. I wanted them to realize that mommy faults doesn't have to be a perpetual hindrance to us. Until we let go and let God take control, we will continue to be cursed by the devil. What was a little discouraging was out of eight sisters, only one, which was Lavinniah decided to take that step and come to church with me a few times.

In the middle of my transition, Uziah came home. After seeing and having a long conversation with him, I saw a huge change in his character. It seemed like he matured and became conservative those nine months he was gone. There wasn't a day that went by that we didn't spend time drinking, fucking, and partying. Also, found time to pay God respect on Sundays.

Uziah and I felt like the weekends weren't enough time together, so we decided to move back in with each other. I was willing to take that step, hoping it would make us instead of breaking us. Before we moved back to Fayetteville, Aaliyah, who I put on a pedestal had started feeling herself. I was shocked! I never really had a problem out of her until she met this manipulating older guy that I was totally unaware of. Due to Aaliyah getting up in age, I gave her a reasonable one o'clock curfew on the weekends, thinking she would continue to be that trustworthy teenager who made the right decisions. But one Friday, she disobeyed me by staying out all night. I didn't know where she was at, her phone kept going to voicemail, and I was worried that something seriously happened to her.

The next day when I didn't get a call from Aaliyah or anybody else, I decided to get the cops involved. It would've been much easier just to hop in my car and search the whole city, but I had given Aaliyah my Lavender Lex for her 16th birthday. Also, Uziah wasn't in town at that time. After giving the pigs the description of the car and her donor's address, they found Aaliyah in no time and told her, "Your mother is very concerned and she want you to come home now!" Aaliyah left acting like she was coming straight home, but it took her another two hours to get there when her donor lived only ten minutes away. I felt disrespected, I was angry, so I lost it; I persistently beat Aaliyah with my fist, took away her car, and then I put her on punishment.

The next morning, I heard my front door constantly opening and closing. When I looked out my room window, I saw Aaliyah taking out her bags. I hurriedly put on my clothes, and then I ran straight outside in an aggressive manner. While I was grabbing her bags out the back of her donor's car, I belligerently said, "BITCH if you want to leave with this motherfucker who never did shit for you, then you won't be leaving with nothing I bought you. Let that BITCH ass nigga buy you what you need!" Then I turned to Charles with the most despicable look and said, "Nigga what type of man are you? A father would try to lead his daughter in the right direction, teach her that disobeying her mother is wrong, and explain to her about how boys is after one thing only. Yet, you're encouraging her to do the opposite, and you think that is the role of being a daddy. You are a disgrace to the real fathers out here!" Charles had the dumbest look on his ugly face while he was on the phone talking to the cops.

After the two policemen arrived, one went over to talk to Charles and told him straight up, "Sir, she is not breaking any type of law... We can't make her return any items that she has purchased." At the same time, the other one was telling me, "Ma'am, you can't make her stay with you; she turned 16 already. When she does find out that she made the wrong decision, it's up to you to welcome her back in." I couldn't believe how the law had changed. From my understanding, a child had to be 18 to legally leave the nest. Now the authority is all in the minors hands, which was absurd.

I suddenly got hit with a sense of Déjà vu. I saw my mother experience the same situation nine times. What made her circumstances even worse was we all were a few years younger than Aaliyah. Surely, that had to hurt her because the pain I felt was like a stab in the back. My heart started knotting up, which made my heart rate pump over a 100 beats per minute. I was drowning in my tears, and hyperventilating for air as I had the "broken heart syndrome," which caused me to have many sleepless nights. Then my guilt started eating at me, thinking that I failed as a parent just like mommy did. How could that be when I nurtured, protected, guided and encouraged my kids like a mother should? Where did I go wrong? Is it all my fault?

Normally, my family would've found some type of reason to blame me for that incident. Instead, they were castigating Aaliyah about her sudden transformation and disobedience. Everybody knew that I was an outstanding parent, spoiled my kids rotten, and was blind by their best, not wanting to see the worst in them. That's why we all were surprised and disappointed how Aaliyah just left like that. Moreover, gave up what she truly loved the most, which was her acting and modeling career. She was days away from signing a contract in LA, which was one step closer to the Lights! Camera! Action! But that never happened because she was easily sidetracked, just like I got from time-to-time. After all, history does repeats itself in any way, shape, or form. That's just life, which is mixed with complexity and simplicity without any compromising. Keeping this in mind, I couldn't dwell on something that has already been done. Although it was an obstruction, I had to move on and continue raising Leah.

Meanwhile, I moved back to Fayetteville with Uziah in a spacious 2 level, 4 bedrooms, and 2-bathroom brick house on Lynette Circle, which was a perfect family home in a peaceful neighborhood. At first, I felt a little tensed; I didn't know if Uziah was going to do another 360 on me, but we hit it off properly. However, some of our family members still had their doubts about our relationship, they assumed we weren't going to make it, and us moving back in together was a huge mistake in their eyes. It was disturbing to me that they felt that way. Also, how a few people in Uziah's family believed I was using him for his money, which was definitely not the case; I was doing perfectly fine before him.

On the other hand, some of my judgmental family members thought Uziah was a distraction towards my independency, assuming it would be a slow progression with me finding a job, which would leave me depending on Uziah once again. Moreover, they felt if he was to ever have another setback, then I'll be right back where I left off. It was possible, but the love I had for him was telling me something different, and the love he had for me was showing me a whole lot more. I needed to find the missing pieces to my puzzle, and Uziah was filling in the empty spaces. Even if he didn't make me complete, my actions always had a meaningful purpose, and I would continue searching... and searching... until I feel it's sufficient.

A year had passed, and our household was holding up pretty well. We all were bonding through good communication, family days out, or movie nights in. Furthermore, we had our religious times when we attended different churches, hoping to find our spiritual home. It was the life I always dreamed of, it was filled with love, encouragement, stability, and hope, which was something I never thought I could experience all at one time; and I was definitely cherishing those special moments.

Then Uziah had gotten the news that September 2014 he was getting stationed in Germany for three years. He wanted us to come along, and I was ecstatic about moving to another country. I thought it would be an unusual and enjoyable experience for all of us. On the other hand, Leah and Mikayla weren't very happy, thinking it would be hard to adjust without their families and friends. We listened while they voiced their opinions. Then we explained to them, hoping they would get a better understanding about the military verses the civilian life, which most kids don't get the opportunity to see different parts of the world, and that they should be grateful for those experiences. Even if they didn't take heed to what we were saying, it still wasn't their decision to make.

Around that time, Uziah and I were doing a lot of clubbing together. We were two lovebirds that played pool, got drunk as hell, and danced to reggae as long as they played it. We were living up every moment of the nightlife until we changed up our routine that one time, which was a jinx that violently followed us. To clarify, normally we entertained each other the whole time in the club. That particular night, Uziah decided to play pool with one of his co-workers, and then sent me to the bar with his wallet. That was a mistake; by me being a sexy and attractive woman, I never had a problem with men offering to pay for my drinks. Truthfully, I didn't see nothing wrong with accepting it. That night, the men were excessively jocking me, and anything I wanted was put on their tabs. Unusually, I stayed at the bar throwing shots back and having friendly conversation until I realized that I was gone a little longer than expected. When I finally brought Uziah his drink that some other nigga paid for, I got pissed when I saw a couple of BITCHES lurking around his pool table. I immediately cleared the area with my foul mouth, and I was definitely in the mood to fight if I had to.

After Uziah finish playing his last game, he wanted to have one last drink. When he realized that I didn't spend any of his money, the questions began, but the answers I gave was nothing he wanted to hear, and we both left out the club heated. On our way to his truck that was parked way in the back of the dark parking lot, we started terribly fighting. Afterwards, he tried to force me in the truck while he repeatedly punched me in the face. I was dazed for a minute, but when I got balanced, I jumped out of his truck while he was driving at least 50 miles/hour. I hit the ground hard, and then started rolling in the middle of a busy intersection. Luckily, it was late night because it wasn't traffic out; otherwise, I would've had a lot more than some scrapes and bruises.

Uziah put on brakes, made a U-turn, and speedily drove off in fear that he was seriously in trouble. Me, on the other hand, was hysterically crying, limping, and walking barefooted down the main street three something in the morning. I was headed towards home, then realized that I left my house keys and phone in Uziah's truck. "Damn! I'm shit out of luck." Of course, a lot of cars stopped and asked, "Are you ok? Do you need a ride?" But I couldn't find the guts to say "yeah" because I didn't want to be the next person on the ABC 11 news.

When I finally made it to the 24-hour store that was a few blocks from home, I felt comfortable enough to ask a guy, "Can I please use your phone?" And he kindly did; Besides Uziah, Caylah's number was the only one I remembered, so she was the one I called. I drunkenly cried my heart out when she answered, then I told her that I was having a little bit of relationship problems. I didn't want her to know that Uziah put his hands on me because Caylah would've irately brought all types of niggas to Fayetteville causing even more trouble; therefore, I left it exactly like that.

I wasn't aware that Caylah called back the unknown person's phone, who described me as the beat up woman. OMG! Caylah was highly upset and unease, especially when she couldn't get back in touch with me. She didn't know where I lived, nor did anybody else in my family, for they didn't care to come visit me. The only thing Caylah could do was wait till I called. Until then, she broadcast the violent news to the family.

The next morning, I woke up next to Uziah in our guest bedroom. I was hung-over and intense; I felt like Uziah took shit totally to a different level. While I'm lying in my vicious thoughts, I started breathing fire, my body was slow burning, and my ears were blowing out steam as the voices in my head told me, "Go look in the mirror, I'm sure you're not going to like what you see!" I jumped up and ran straight to the bathroom. Looking at my reflection, I suddenly saw the vision of my two personalities I symbolized for all of those years, which was the good and the bad. The imperfect side of my face was totally disfigured. My eye was shut closed, cheek was purplish green, and my bottom lip was busted and swollen. Tears began to quickly fall down my face as I stared in the mirror in disbelief. Also, I was very disappointed in myself and Uziah. For one, no matter how hard I tried, it seemed like I could never get right. For two, Uziah showed me a person I never thought he could ever be, and his actions were unacceptable.

Uziah woke up unaware of the results from his violent actions. When he eventually saw my face, he broke down and cried, asking me for forgiveness. I saw the remorse in his eyes, and I didn't want to give up on him like people did with me when I did wrong. Without hesitation, I accepted his apology. I was prepared to fight for our relationship until it wasn't nothing left to fight for; frankly, everyone who has true love should be willing and able to go to war.

The most humiliating thing was me lying to the kids, telling them, "It was a riot at the club, and I got hit in the face with a few bottles… Don't mention this to nobody… people talk too much." For the reason that they never saw my face in that type of predicament, they believed me and were very sympathetic and supportive in keeping everything on a hush-hush.

As soon as I turned my phone on after it got fully charged, all types of text messages and voicemails were consecutively coming through. Some of the messages from my sisters were stating, "Leah, what's going on? I've been trying to get in touch with you all day… Call me." Others were saying, "I heard what happened… Are you ok?" Then there was mommy on the other hand, who was genuinely expressing her concerns. "Leah, I hope it's not true what I'm hearing about Uziah putting his hands on you... you don't deserve that. I'm praying for y'all... I love you, and I hope that I hear from you soon." I was just shaking my head, knowing that most of my FAM was calling to be nosy since I hardly ever got a call from some of them. When I finally decided to answer my phone, I denied all allegations. It wasn't like I was seriously in an abusive relationship; moreover, I felt like it was none of their business. Despite them not believing a word that was coming out my mouth, they still couldn't prove anything because I stayed in hiding for a month.

During my concealment, Uziah started partying more with his military buddies, and his attitude came off even more arrogant than before, which was a complete turn off to me, but it seemed like it didn't bother Uziah. His reactions started showing that he was unsure about what he really wanted relationship wise, and I began feeling some sort of detachment between us.

Denial hit me like a physical blow; it was hard to accept that things weren't working out. I wanted to think that it was a little phase he was going through. Still, a BITCH can only take so much, especially when his belligerent words tried to deprive my self-esteem because he felt that I needed him, but I wanted him, which was a big difference. Gradually, his downgrading words started to have an effect on my self-worth considering I was no longer in the spotlight and was living in his shadow. Besides, I never had a man to belittle me like that, for I was always self-contained. That's what gave me the strength to not give up on myself. With devotion, I continued filling out 10-15 job applications a day, month after month, but my felony charge hindered me from getting callbacks. I was overwhelmed and desperate enough to think about hustling again.

During this drastic moment, Brad had got released from prison, and he still had love and opened arms. At that time, it had cross my mind to give him another chance; it would've been easier than starting all over again. However, easy had always been my weakness, and the outcome never was completely fulfilling. Also, Brad wasn't who I desired because my heartbeats were for Uziah, until months after I got fed up with his ongoing verbal abuse, which made me less content in our relationship.

To make the situation less stressful for me, I gave Leah what she was desiring for months, which was moving in with her father. During this time, Brad was living with his brother and felt like he was unprepared. Conflictingly, I thought it was time for him to man up; being a parent, there will be situations that come unexpectedly. Besides, I had to woman up when neither father was in Leah and Aaliyah's life, leaving me no breaks in between. Therefore, I needed some me time, and I was hoping to sprout, explore, and find myself in the midst. I really didn't care that Brad was bad mouthing my name. He was just mad about me dropping Leah off. In all honesty, I was and still am a better parent than he could ever be.

In the meantime, I separated my feelings from my priorities in order to stay focus on my goal, which was graduating. By applying my passive aggressive behavior, I was able to cope with Uziah for five more months. Then on May 2014, I would have my associate's degree in Business Administration. That was something nobody could take from me, unlike my dignity that almost got stripped away. We all are human and hoping for the same thing, which is a favorable outcome. Just because Uziah was in the Military doesn't make his life more meaningful than mine. I knew I had a lot to offer in any relationship; in fact, life itself. If only I got that one chance to prove myself without being judged by my incriminating background, and be valued for the treasure I am, I would be unstoppable and prosperous.

To change the subject, the holidays had arrived, and I was looking forward to reconvene with my family. Out of nine sisters, only five of us, which was Lateesah, Lamiyah, Lacaylah, Lavinniah, and I along with many other family members, friends, and secret enemies had brought in Christmas and a Happy New Year's in together. Oppositely, the other four sisters would bring in 2014 still holding grudges. That goes to show that some things just don't ever change.

We partied until the break of dawn that whole week like it was our last time together. We were full of laughter and reminiscing about everything while getting extremely lit and full off that delicious food my brother-n-law cooked. For many reasons, it felt so special, and Josiah was the man who made it all happen as he catered to all of us. That gave us more sister time while the kids were running around freely and recording our memorable moments.

A few days after New Year's, Uziah decided to come pay me a visit at Lateesah's house. I wouldn't say I was happy, but I did miss him a little bit. Instead of me resenting him bitterly for not coming around, I indulgently acted like it didn't bother me, and we began exchanging stories about our entertaining holidays. In the middle of our conversation, Caylah gave me a call, sounding totally irrigated, loud, and upset that her affaire de coeur was no longer a secret or entertaining, and she wanted to get away from the burning triangle before it blew up in flames. That's why she decided to come to Lateesah's house. When she arrived and saw Uziah there, her attitude shifted towards him. With Uziah being a self-composed type of person, he tried to talk nicely to Caylah. Still, she continued to be disrespectful and violent, but when she smacked Uziah, I had to step in.

We were standing face to face as we spoke criticizing words back and forth to each other. Our eyes were sparked with fire as we were ready to fight. Although I wanted to attack temptation, I fought with my words of wisdom instead, which hurt her worse than a punch. "You're lost in the drug peddling life, but I been there and done that... Now I'm a part of the real world, which is something you don't know about! It's more than just having fancy clothes, cars, and getting that fast money... that's short-term; I'm striving for long-term prosperity. With all due respect, if you're not speaking logically, then you're not on my level, but eventually you'll run into your wakeup call!" I said passionately. On the other hand, she continued to speak words of ignorance because she was bamboozled by the streets, which led her to believe that we all were jealous of her.

Lateesah, Lamiyah, and I looked quizzical, "Jealous what? Jealous of who?" But her defense wasn't admissible. We started laughing like she was a joke to us, which made Caylah even more furious. That's when she cursed us with words of death, and proclaimed that she cared less about us. Of course, we weren't in disbelief; every time Caylah gets in her feelings, she says vicious shit like that. Knowing this, we ignored her barbaric talking. Our ears were already overloaded from every despicable word she said prior to that. Also, that day, her behavior confirmed that she was out of her mind because the nonsense didn't stop. The bad part about it was that nobody in that house was the cause of her misery, but she still kept going... and going... and going.

She was angrily energetic, intensely crying, and calling her so-called goons to come to Lateesah's house to fight Uziah; allegedly, he busted her lip while he was trying to stop her from swinging on him. For the record, Uziah never hit her. She also told them that we turned against her and were taking Uziah side. That was definitely not the case. We all felt and clearly saw that Caylah was in the wrong, and her temper tantrum was uncalled for.

For the reason that Caylah was talking and acting so uppity like she was better than all of us, I wanted to bring something to her attention. Kindly, I asked her, "If Josiah was out of your life, what you would do?" Her answer was, "I get money... You not da only balla! Oh! I forgot, used to be balla; but you gave it all up for a wack ass army guy who don't have as near as much money as your ex-men. You didn't have to want for nothing. You always stayed in designer clothes... and you would've been had a new car, but you're still driving that Lexus. Girl... You fell off, so don't ask me shit!" Regardless of her uneducated answer, I knew that she would be lost without Josiah.

After that destructive day, Caylah and my relationship had gone to hell. Our perception on life had separated our hearts and cluttered our minds with betrayal, which kept our animosity blazing. Due to the fact that Caylah and I were the closest out the nine of us, everybody was in disbelief of our vendetta. In all honesty, I was as well, knowing our bond was tied to tight to let something so simple unravel it. However, being a Daevas, you have to expect the unexpected. For separation convey our message of anger.

Anger also brings forth tragedies, and most of the time disasters are unforeseen. To start with, it was around 3:20 a.m. on a Sunday morning when they found Josiah lying dead on the family room floor. He didn't live to see the age of 35 because his cousin thought he was proving his dominancy by pulling that trigger. The day I met Glock, I felt like he was a conniving snake. On the contrary, Josiah and Caylah mistakenly thought he was an asset. Unfortunately, he was a liability that developed envy over the years, for he could never get right. Through and out those years, he played the role like he was their true "ride-or-die" nigga. He did any and everything to prove to Caylah and Josiah that he was an outlaw who needed a top level position in their illicit actions, which made them feel like they could trust Glock; and that was the biggest mistake they made.

In retrospect, I remember when Josiah first started bringing uptop nigga's down south. He provided their food, clothes, and shelter in exchange for them to hustle his work. At first, it seemed like a great idea, seeing that he progressed really fast, but in the drug life there will be unanticipated controversy that can promote more problems, and can also leave a person unaware of the aftermath. For example, Glock continuously kept getting arrested for his careless acts. Eventually, Josiah stopped bailing him out, hoping Glock would face reality. Instead, he gained animosity towards Josiah, which brought about problem #1.

During Glock incarceration, his brother was killed in a gun fight over tough guy challenges and intrusion of territory, which happened during his visit and drug dealing with Josiah. Indeed, Glock was sad and angry; moreover, he blamed Josiah for his lost. Then the bitterness switched to hate, and his deep vicious thoughts were all about vengeance. Glock heartless plot was problem #2. Thereafter, he was released from jail and went straight to Josiah for help without giving any signs of his enmity. Josiah still showed sincerity and put him back on his feet regardless of the bad rumors that was spread through and out the jailhouse that Glock was going to rob him because he didn't bail him out. Due to Josiah avoiding the capabilities of a deadly snake had definitely made that problem #3.

Glock played it smart when he kept his enemies close. He was involved in Josiah's everyday life. He knew their routine, knew when and how much work they were buying, had their undisclosed address that held the key to their lives, which he was welcome to come anytime.

Moreover, he knew where they hid their gun at, and that made them easily exposed to troublesome situations.

What made matters worse was Glock had a weakness for those worldly goods and well-known whores he was trying to sustain, which was the cause of his extensive debt with Josiah. Therefore, Josiah had no choice but to cut him off completely because there was no means of paying them back. That is what started the beef and the loss of respect. With Caylah's hot-blooded mentality, every time she saw Glock on the streets, they consistently argued. She always communicated threats and belittled him in front of whoever, which had Glock deep in his feelings, and that was the trigger to proceed with his plan.

After a short period of being completely insolvent, Glock felt like that was the perfect time to make an example out of Josiah and Caylah. Allegedly, he got another one of Josiah workers involved, who thought it was going to be just a simple, sneaky robbery if it went as planned. Yet, Glock had other brutal intentions in his walking on air thoughts.

It started out on the night prior to Josiah's death when his homeboy Spade had deceitfully invited him and Caylah to a formal event. It appeared that he was trying to give Glock enough time to break into Josiah and Caylah's house to take their money and drug stash, but it didn't go as plan. Glock only found their fully loaded gun, which made him furious, armed, and even more dangerous.

While Caylah and Josiah were enjoying the moment, they were totally unaware that their every move was being observed, and someone was updating Glock on everything. Before the event ended, Josiah and Caylah decided to leave a little early. Right after, Josiah got an unexpected phone call from Glock. Taking into account that Josiah was a benevolent guy, he listened to what Glock had to say, and the conversation continued after they arrived home, which was almost 30 minutes away.

The whole time they were on the phone, Glock was theoretically waiting on the side of their house, watching and anticipating on them getting comfortable, which was the best time to make his move. Supposedly, while he awaits, he stimulates his mind, which made him feel dominant and invincible when he knocked on their door. Caylah and Josiah had a confused look on their faces as Josiah blurted out, "Who the hell is it?" A surprising voice responded, "Glock!" Josiah unconsciously opened the door without asking him the purpose of his visit considering he was FAM to him, even though Josiah was mad about the money situation. Afterwards, he incautiously turned around to continue rolling his cigar, not noticing that Glock was standing there with his hands behind his back and had a suspicious look on his face.

Then Glock hollered out, "Caylah, where is your gun?" Since Caylah thought he was being sarcastic, but mostly because there was still a grudge, she immediately went straight to where her gun was stashed at while popping shit, "Nigga, I always have my gun, and I will pop off on a motherf…!" That's when she noticed it was gone, by then, Glock was holding up two guns with his pure white gloves on, and he was aiming them at Josiah's back. Caylah was speechless, her eyes got extremely big, and the horrifying look on her face was a signal to Josiah that something serious was about to go down. When Josiah shockingly turned around, he asked, "Why you going to do me like this man?" Glock sternly replied while looking Josiah directly in his eyes, "You turned your back on me, so I have no loyalty!" Resultantly, Josiah charged at him, trying to put up a fight. Immediately after, three gunshots went off, then Josiah fell to the floor and started quickly bleeding out.

During that commotion, Caylah ran in the room with her son who was still asleep. Glock came behind her, forced her out the door, and into her room to torment her about the money. Caylah fearfully searched, but when she couldn't find it, Glock hit her in the head a few times with the gun. Her body instantly got warm, she was dizzy and bewildered while blood leaked down her face. Her cries became intensely loud as she pleaded for her life, "Glock please… please don't kill me. You can take whatever you want!" He violently responded while pointing the gun back-n-forth to her and Josiah, "I want the money, and if I don't get it, I'm going to kill Josiah!" Caylah heart was racing while she paced around the house, looking in every possible spot it could be hidden at. Then she started crying out, "Josiah! Josiah! Where is the money? He's going to kill me!" Yet, Josiah laid there unresponsive and lifeless in a pool of blood. When Glock started getting impatient and angrily walked back to the front where Josiah was at, it gave Caylah an opportunity to escape. Fearfully and quickly, she ran out the side door.

Afterwards, she heard a few more gunshots that she thought was meant for her. In a lickety-split, she dropped to the ground and cautiously crawled to her neighbor's house. While she timidly knocked on the door for help, it was a relief when the older man opened it. She stood there crying, half naked, and covered in blood, "Can you help me? Somebody's trying to kill me, and they shot my boyfriend. Please! Can you call the cops?" A few minutes after the cops were called, Caylah realized that she had to go back home and make sure everything was clear of any illegal substances before the cops arrived. While she awaits, she phoned her other man, hysterically crying, "Glock killed Josiah… He beat me with a gun! Oh, God… My son!"

Caylah ran in his room, and it was nothing but God that he was still asleep. She held him and cried until the cops came. When they arrived, they accompanied both of them out, and that's when they saw Josiah laying in blood on the floor. "Is my daddy hurt?" There wasn't a response at that time, knowing it wasn't an easy way to explain to a child that his father was dead. Mournfully, Caylah just continued crying the entire way to the hospital. Her heart was weakened and felt empty; all she could think about was Josiah. She was hurt that she lost her fiancé, best friend, and more importantly, her favorite man. The bad part about it was neither one of them saw it coming.

All of us were saddened about what happened to Josiah, and we were also concerned about Caylah and her kids' present condition. Thereon, everyone tried to reach out and sympathize with her, hoping she could overcome that tragic nightmare. We knew that was going to be hard and take some time, but Caylah took no time in taking her anger out on the wrong people. She was rude, argumentative, and ungrateful because the favors that were given wasn't up to her standards. She acted like everyone owed her something when we were only trying to be supportive. It got to the point where some of us got sick and tired of feeling unappreciated, so we stepped back until Caylah stepped forward with a little sensibility.

As a matter of fact, we thought that disastrous experience would've been a wakeup call for Caylah, but it wasn't. Instead, her negative behavior elevated. She'd excessively washed down her heavy heart, which altered her eating, influenced her cries, and grievously had her reliving that catastrophe in just about every conversation she had; also, it triggered her multiple personalities, and one of them came gunning for me over our prior altercation when I had stated, "If Josiah was out of your life, what you would do?" Foolishly, she felt my spoken tongue was the curse of death, and she blamed me for what happened to Josiah, whereas her cursed words just had backfired when she wished death upon me, Lateesah, and Lamiyah that day.

In all honesty, that wasn't the time to be pointing fingers at each other, for the trigger man was the only one to blame. Glock's actions and my words were nowhere near the same because "Death" wasn't what I meant, or a word I used in my vocabulary. In fact, Josiah and I were very close. He was the best little brother I never had, a man with much potential, morals, and goals besides just being a drug dealer. Moreover, he was a terrific father, fiancé, and friend. That being said, the shortening of his days were shocking, hurtful, and upsetting to me.

While Josiah was in the morgue waiting for the funeral, Glock was still an erratic fugitive, and he continued to call from blocked numbers, communicating threats to Caylah, "BITCH when I find you... You're going to end up just like your man. If I don't get to you before the cops get to me, then my only defense is you put me up to it... Oh! And I'm the one who took your gun, which is the only evidence they need!" Now that Caylah no longer underestimated Glock, and she knew he was capable of killing again, she was paranoid. She constantly was jumping out her sleep, peeking out of windows, and couldn't stay at one place no longer than a few days because she felt unsafe. Furthermore, she changed her phone number like damn near every week or two.

What really was some crazy cold-blooded shit was that Glock had the audacity to call Josiah's family a few days after the murder. He was trying to convince them about Caylah and her affairs, and how she allegedly set it all up. He didn't give his condolences, nor admitted that he had any involvement. As a lifetime so called family member,

Glock's dispassionate and blunt conversation was bizarre, more like a confirmation as being the number one suspect. Although it was false accusations, Josiah family still disclosed it to the detectives, which had Caylah irate, feeling she was already being treated like a suspect, until they ruled out the love triangle implication.

That wrongful disaster had taken a horrendous toll on Caylah, and it was hard for her to adjust during that vulnerable moment. Surely, I wanted to be there for her, but Caylah grudges, and my pride were in the way. With much regret, our miles of separation was the main reason I couldn't make it to Josiah's funeral because I was unaware of the official date.

Since Glock was still on the run, and there were many other allegations floating in the air, the family really didn't know who to trust. Under the circumstances, the funeral had some armed security, and also was restricted to only his and our family members. They wanted Josiah to rest in peace instead of disharmony. While his soul laid peacefully in his casket, fully dressed in all white polo, his family mourns over a special one leaving them too soon. The demoralizing part was they had no understanding or complete closure of why it happened.

Meantime, Caylah incoherently walked up the aisle screaming, "Josiah! Josiah! We weren't done yet!" As she laid on his cold body, her uncontrollable tears had drenched his clothes, then she emptily asked, "Why you? Do you know all the pain I'm going through?" Thereafter, she gently touched his face and softly spoken, "I love and need you so much... our son need you too. I can't believe he done this to us!" Then she started back screaming, "Josiah! Josiah!" Her voice was filled with so much hurt, and her heart was pumping pain as her temperature rose. Suddenly, she got weak in the knees and fainted. Lamiyah, who was standing behind her, picked Caylah up and walked her outside to catch some air where she gave her an encouraging talk that calmed her down for a little while. Until they arrived at the burial, then she started all over again.

Caylah was at her lowest point, and the shameful part about it was only one sister out of five that lived in New York came to the funeral.

Primarily because the others were more concerned about which sister they didn't want to be around due to their quarrels and differences instead of putting their bitter feelings to the side for a few hours, just to give Caylah the comfort she needed. Due to the narcissistic truancies, Caylah was feeling alone and defenseless. She started to isolate herself from the family and began showing more attention to men, mostly her lover boy Imperial, who took her to a totally different place that no one would've ever expected her to go.

To emphasize that incident, Caylah had moved from High point to Raleigh, which is about a 1½ hour difference. She was running away from her past. Still, she couldn't get that tragic moment or Josiah out her memories, and Imperial was there to try and fill in that empty space. Although money was the cause of her lost, Imperial knew that was something she desperately needed, and that was the beginning of their partnership.

Caylah didn't think for a second that Imperial might've been feeding off her vulnerability. The way I saw it, she didn't care as long as he met or exceeded her demands. So, getting on board gave her access to the money train. With two up north mentalities, trying to get that down south money, had to develop and implement a strategy. With the impression that nothing overrides money, it will be made in any possible way, to any extent.

That was around the time Caylah started hanging at Lateesah's house, which was very unusual since she was an infrequent visitor. Yet, Lateesah didn't mind; she knew Caylah was still going through her battle. While Lateesah was at work, Caylah was allegedly receiving packages at her house, which was the reason why the NARCS had Teesah under an investigating for a few months.

Then one morning, Lateesah and her colleague were on their way to work when a UPS truck delivered a package. With Lateesah automatically thinking it was Caylah's, she told them to leave it at the door. The same man that made the delivery was the NARC who raided her house moments later. Lateesah had no idea that she just accepted a box full of different types of drugs. It had over ten pounds of marijuana, two ounces of crystal meth, 4 ½ ounces of coke, and a little over 100 ecstasy pills. Lateesah was hysterical while the detective was showing her pictures of Imperial and Caylah. Also, asking her questions that she was unable to answer because she didn't know anything. Then she remembered a month prior when Caylah met the UPS man outside, but she claimed it was her daughter's school supplies that was sent from her father. On the grounds that Lateesah really didn't have any street mentality, she believed her. In spite of the cops knowing Lateesah wasn't involved, they still used her as bait due to the fact that she accepted the package. Unfortunately, if no one else was there to claim that package, then Lateesah was going to wear those charges.

When Lateesah called Lamirah, she was already on her way but unaware that the cops were there. Out of anger, Lateesah said, "You got another package here, I told you not to have people sending stuff to my house… You got your own place, so why not send it there?" Caylah skipped the subject and said, "Tell Mae Lee I said hi… I'll talk to you when I get there, Teesah." Upon arrival, the NARCS were hiding in and outside of Lateesah's house. Caylah sensed something wasn't right when she pulled up, but she got out anyway. Thereafter, she heard, "Get down! Get down!" As the cops approached her with guns. After they placed her in handcuffs, they arrested her driver, assuming that he was Imperial, but they eventually released him after interrogating him a little. In the meantime, things didn't look so great for Caylah and Lateesah after they got charged with trafficking and conspiracy, which left them both with a $100,000 secured bond. Instead of Caylah telling the cops that Lateesah didn't have anything to do with it, or give them the information they were looking for, she kept quiet but continued to claim her innocence.

While they set in Forsyth County Jailhouse for weeks, Lateesah lost her house and job. That was a fucked up situation for her to be in, especially when she wasn't down with the drug dealing life. Therefore, she shouldn't have been held accountable for someone else's devious actions. What was also damaging was during that time, her son Kian was on trial for a murder he didn't commit but got sentenced to 18 years in prison for it.

After Lateesah got out of jail, she couldn't find her way out of her deep depression. All she could do was cry, drown in her sorrows and sleep. Moreover, she had that fiery passion of hatred in her heart for Caylah as she kept thinking about how she ruined her life, which was unforgivable. In all honesty, majority of our family felt some type of way towards Caylah, even though she's innocent until proven guilty; still and all, we believed that she played a major role in that crime.

That situation really caused miles of separation between the sisters because we were at a point where we had to choose sides. Whoever chose Caylah, they were not trusted, and damn near not even liked. Shit was really crazy! This one didn't want that one to have their number. That one didn't want this one to know where she lived or worked. You couldn't say certain things around Lateesah, and you had to watch what you say in front of Caylah. At one point, I felt like we weren't even sister when we were acting like those fake ass friends that sat around and talked shit about the one who wasn't there, which was very annoying. I know what happened to Lateesah was cruel, but the Daevas's was detached way before that. In all honesty, it's going to take God, a lot of forgiving, and all of us sisters to grow up in order to stabilize our relationship. As long as there is still ignorance, we are going to continue to traveling our distance. We will remain blind by the darkness of evil that causes us to be complacent in our ways. Under those circumstances, our minds would no longer imagine the good, and our hearts would never feel the fullness of the Daevas family again.

As I stated in the beginning that nine sisters were cursed since birth, it's sad to say, but unbelievably it's true. For each of us has our own dealings with the devil. It's just on different levels, at different times, and for many different reasons, which basically defines us as demons. We are damn near burning in flaming fire as our lives are controlled by Satan's commands. We don't want to let go of the anger, bitterness, and cruelty to take pleasure in the bond we once had when we were striving as a family together. Instead, we are content with discouraging, humiliating, and being deceitful to one another; sad to say, we no longer know the value of life, of love, and of family.

By me revealing the evil powers that transpired amongst us should somehow bring us back to reality, help us visualize the bigger picture, and eventually come together to put out our erupted flames so that we can better not only ourselves, but one another. Just imagine how far we could've been if we were for and not against each other. Teamwork is a productive way to achieve more; most importantly, it helps in overcoming anything. Regardless of how stubborn we are, at some point in our lives, we're going to need some type of support from someone else. Unfortunately, you never know who that person might be. With that being said, we need to put our differences to the side as well as our pride. Completing together is more powerful than competing with one another. I know it's not going to be easy because the Daevas sisters have done some unforgettable shit to each other through and out the years. Regardless, anything can be forgivable if you're acceptive to the fact that mistakes happen, and they can't be changed. After all, we as people could work on the changes that can be made within ourselves, our lives, and our hearts.

I'm speaking my words of encouragement, for I am a work in progress of change. I was a victim and the culprit of hurt, betrayal, rivalries, crimes, and many other situations that involves Satan. Still and all, I survived, which brings forth my testimony. To start with, I am the middle child of an uneven number. Therefore, I bear the weight from both angles, and that made me a dominant person. Primarily because I did not only obtain the nine curses, which was: deviousness, bitterness, viciousness; demonic, conniving, rebellious; selfishness, privation, and cultivated ignorance. However, I substituted them with my faith in God who encouraged my every move through my five senses that helped me take full control of Satan's curses.

For one, I was gifted with the sight of evil. To clarify, my bad visions that came to me in my dreams were a warning of what would or could transpire if I continued to take the route that is surrounded by destructive adversities. Resultantly, I turned and walked away from the wrong and headed towards the right direction. Secondly, my ears only heard distinctive voices that expressed different types of anger according to my level of madness, which made me approach any bad situation in a violent or vicious type of way. Gradually, I domesticated my quick-temper; I replaced my frowns with smiles, and most importantly, those raging voices were finally at peace when I became humbled. Thirdly, I loved the taste of flames. My mouth blew out words of fire that criticized, intimidated, manipulated, and intended to hurt whoever stood before me as an adversary. I didn't care about people's feelings; I was too busy worried about mine, but when I got a taste of my own medicine, I felt the belittlement and fear that brought me unpleasant pain and tears, which made me mindful of others. Nowadays, before I spit my nasty words out, I taste them first. In fact, I'm trying to stay more focused on motivational and influential words.

Then there was me keeping my nose turned up. I always smelled trouble, given that I was the trouble. For that reason, I stayed in a conflict; it was the easiest solution for me personally. I kept negative thoughts, felt powerful and undefeated when I acted out in rage. To tell the truth, by me feeding off negativity, it was comforting to my built-up anger, but after losing loved ones through different types of controversies, I knew that my disputative habits would eventually lead me to prison or into an early grave.

I questioned myself, "If I'm gone, where would that leave my kids?" The answer was simple… they would be lost just like I once was. Unloved like I once felt, which would make them vulnerable. I definitely didn't want that, so I decided to get my act together. It wasn't easy, but I managed to walk away from trouble. At that point, I understood that my troubles could only go as far as I took it, and that it could actually be resolved through other positive approaches. I didn't have to physical fight anymore, seeing that I could get better results if I killed people with kindness. With that knowledge in mind, my nose no longer has the scent for trouble. I'm smelling nothing but the goodness of life.

Lastly, it was my sense of touch, which is one of my most powerful senses. It took me forever to realize my gift because I was too busy getting the feel of money, power, and respect. After five years of being out the drug life, reserving was the wisest choice. I no longer had that big-time money and couldn't splurge like I wanted to anymore. It was depressing, but that helped me define my true identity. I realized that money wasn't over everything, and it didn't make me, God did. As of today, I'm using my powers to influence people's decisions, and listen to their problems or desires. Then give them honesty, words of encouragement, and guidance. In fact, I have that potential touch that can turn an individual's life around, for I'm the chosen one.

I wasn't only chosen by God, but Satan as well. However, the devil no longer lives inside me, or fights my battles. The moment I made that decision, I've been receiving positive results in my life. To explain, I'm happily married to Uziah, we're living in Germany and traveling all over Europe; also, if it's God's will, we want to extend our family. I have nobody but the man upstairs to thank for that. Uziah and I crossed that same path for a specific purpose, and that was to change each other's lives. Now I want to share my blessing in hopes of doing the same for others, especially the D–A–E–V–A–S family since the curse still remains. Actually, it's getting worse. I put the lines in between the letters, now that our name represents individuality rather than unity. I know we all consider ourselves as strong individuals; truth be told, by us being divided is a true sign of weakness. One person can be quickly broken, but not all nine of us if we were consolidated.

One of our biggest obstacles is that everyone wants to be the President, but lacking leadership, morals, and have unjustified actions. A point to remember: How we carry oneself rely upon the destiny of all. With that being said, if we learned to set good examples, then our entity would follow. STOP pointing your finger in the opposite direction, and take a long look in the mirror… you're the one to blame. Everyone is responsible for their own actions regardless of who did what first.

If we had a little more acceptance, then it would be less problems we had to worry about. If we let go of grudges and forgive, then we'll have more love in our hearts. If we did more giving than taking, then there would be a lot of sharing. Most importantly, if we get vengeance out of our thoughts, we would no longer be at war. It's well worth it because when our time stops, it's going to be too late to do anything of that matter. Therefore, I'm opening up my heart and shedding many tears while I ask all of my sisters for forgiveness. Even if I didn't do anything wrong, I still want to clear my conscience. Also, I want to open the door for beatitude and lock out the madness.

With love and affection, can my big and little sisters come together? It's a start. Hopefully, somewhere down the line we can hold hands, which would be a progress. When we start walking side by side, that would be a success, and we will no longer be unbalanced. Until that time comes, we as Daevas's would no longer reflect our originality. The curse will continue to have us burning in flesh, and corrupting our bloodline causing us to drown in our deadly sins that can keep us forever doomed.

# CURSED

Blessings passed us by like the clouds dancing through the light blue sky.
Ever saw so much darkness, or felt so much pain?
Things hurt so much, it makes you use the word love in vain.
It makes your whole body tremble and go insane.
Were the two people that intertwined are the ones to blame?
Or does it go deeper?
Does this curse on our souls' curve and get steeper?
Are we the devil's keepers?
Then I wonder…
Is it just me?
My cursed soul?
My cursed mind?
My cursed feet?
That walks me into these dark places, crying out, while my heart races.
Sometimes I feel like I can't take it.
I've cried out all my tears, I dropped to my knees every time,
Asking God for just one little sign.
In a blink of an eye, I've committed one little crime.
Trying to pick the hours, minutes, and seconds
Wondering when it will be my time.
My time to be blessed.
The time for less stress.
The time my buttons are no longer pressed.
I'm no longer drained or depressed.
We were cursed since birth,
Hell raged when we stepped foot on this earth.
Can we wake up one day?
And our curses are blessings?
Our pain is our lesson?
What's your suggestion?

Walking in darkness, somewhere there is a light,
But our curse won't leave, unless we put up a fight.
Because we are 9 sisters cursed since birth.
Listen and take Heed!

# CLOSURE

**W**hat is love? From my perspective, majority of us don't know the meaning of love. Anytime this question is asked, it's generally because a person is skeptical about whether someone truly love them or not. But if you're firmly committed to providing and obtaining love, you don't contemplate on this thought. It's particularly when something feels incomplete. Therefore, we start comparing and deliberating what true love is.

**Love-** Is the most dominate sensation a person can encounter. It's a diversity of mental and physical states that varies from interpersonal endearment to easy pleasure. Love is more prodigious than you and I. It has no boundaries, stipulations, or demands.

Love identifies the results of hurting someone or oneself because it's congenitally humanitarian and empathetic. Love accepts that a person is his or her own individual; also, cares and respects what that person becomes, for it understands that we are interdependent.

Love recognize the supremacy of every living soul. It does not discriminate, intimidate, abuse, log off, or abstain for disciplinary acts or stubbornness. That's why it gives opportunities for grievance, pain, and misery to be revealed and set free.

Love isn't used for allurement, entrapment, persecuting; substitution, impersonating or insinuating because genuine love can't be conveyed if it's not deliberately coming from the heart. That's the sincerity of love, which can't be negotiated or controlled.

**If** there is no love... Do you at least care? If not, it's nothing but dislike or hate, which is a form of evil. To whomever this addresses, it's time to set things straight. Give love, receive love, but most importantly, love yourself because true love starts from within...

# ABOUT THE AUTHOR

*Na 'Veah Rose* is a freelance writer that likes to inspire people with the senses and images of reality. She invigorates people's mind with her soulful poetry and powerful lyrics. Na 'Veah always had the heart for writing, and she will continue to write non-fictional, poetry, and children's books. Her upcoming book for the young generation is *"Jealous who? Jealous for what?"* And, her poetry book *"Heart pumps 1000's of words"* will be very motivational, full of love, and a little touch of seduction. Her informative writing transpired through her life experiences, and it became more efficient and effective during the course of her education in Associates of Applied Science (AAS) Business Administration, and she is currently pursuing her BS. She also will commence her journey with a Masters in Creative Writing (MA) to become more proficient in creativity and film production. Na 'Veah will continue to strive for accomplishments, and her daughters along with her husband is the foundation to her success.

Printed in the United States
By Bookmasters